RASAGAṄGĀDHARA

RASAGAṄGĀDHARA

रसगङ्गाधरः

TEXT WITH ENGLISH TRANSLATION AND CRITICAL STUDY

BY

DHANANJAYA BHANJA

BKP

BHARATIYA KALA PRAKASHAN
DELHI (INDIA)

First Published : 2004

Published by **C.P. Gautam**
BHARATIYA KALA PRAKASHAN
3421-A, IInd Floor Narang Colony, Tri Nagar,
Delhi-110035. Phone : 27393083, 30967505 (O), 27522129 (R)

ISBN : 81-8090-055-X

Laser Type Setting by
A-ONE GRAPHICS
Brahmapuri, Delhi-110053
Phone : 2218 3470

Printed at
Tarun Offset Press
Delhi

DEDICATED

to

My Beloved Parents

पुरोवाक्

अलङ्कारशास्त्रेषु पण्डितराजजगन्नाथविरचितः "रसगङ्गाधरः" एकं प्रमुखं स्थानमलङ्करोति। तत्पूर्ववत्तिनामालङ्कारिकाणां काव्यतत्त्वविषयक मतं सम्यक् परिशील्य जगन्नाथः कुत्रचित् खण्डनात्मकं कुत्रचित् समर्थनात्मकं वा मार्गमनुसरति। अस्मिन् शास्त्रे यावन्ति उदाहरणपद्यानि सन्ति, तानि सर्वाणि तस्य स्वरचितानि। सतद्रसगङ्गाधरात् ज्ञायते। यथा–

"निर्माय नूतनमुदाहरणानुरूपं
काव्यं मयात्र विहितं न परस्य किञ्चित्।
किं सेव्यते सूमनसां मनसाऽपि गन्धः
कस्तुरिकाजननशक्तिभृता मृगेण।"

स्वप्रौढपाण्डित्यं दिदर्शयिषुर्जगन्नाथः अक्षरशः एतद्रसगङ्गाधरे प्रतिपादयति। यस्मिन् स्थले यादृगुदाहरणमावश्यकं तथाविधं सः तस्मिन् स्थले योजयति। रसगङ्गाधरे प्रथमानने द्वितीयानने च सर्वत्र द्रष्टुमेतत् शक्यते। काव्यस्य लक्षणप्रसङ्गे तेनोक्तं यत्–"विशेष्यताऽवच्छेदकं तदितरभेदबुद्धौ साधनं च तल्लक्षणं तावन्निरूप्यते"। तर्हि किन्तावत् काव्यस्य लक्षणमित्याकाङ्क्षायां सपदि सः लिखति–"रमणीयार्थप्रतिपादकः शब्दः काव्यम्" । एतल्लक्षणं परिष्कर्तुं सः पुनः लिखति–रमणीयता च लोकोत्तराह्लादजनकज्ञानगोचरता। "अस्य तात्पर्यमिदं यत्–अलौकिकानन्ददायक ज्ञानवेद्यं रमणीयत्वं भवति, अर्थात् यः आनन्दः साधारणलौकिक भोगात् न लभ्यते, केवलं पुनः पुनः समनुसन्धानेन लभ्यतेस आनन्द एव रमणीयतापदवाच्यः। एवम्भूत आनन्दः केवलं अनुभववेद्यः। अमुमानन्दं जगन्नाथः जात्यन्तर्गतं करोति। नित्यत्वे सति अनेकसमवेतत्वं जातिः इति जातिलक्षणानुसारेणा लौकिकानन्दोऽयं नित्यः। अतः जात्यन्तर्गतत्वमस्य स्वीक्रियते। "पुत्रस्ते

जातः, धनं ते दास्यामि" इतिस्थले बोद्धव्यस्य य आनन्दः संजायते, सः आनन्दः अलौकिकः न भवति, अतः काव्यत्वमत्र नांगीकार्यम्।

अनेन प्रकारेण काव्यस्य समान्यं लक्षणमुक्त्वा जगन्नाथः पुनः काव्यस्य लक्षणं परिष्कर्त्तुं लिखति-"इत्थं चमत्कारजनकभावना विषयार्थ-प्रतिादकं शब्दत्त्वम्, यत्प्रतिपादितार्थ विषयकभावनात्वं चमत्कारावच्छेदकं तत्वम्। स्व विशिष्टजनकताऽवच्छेदकार्थ प्रतिपादकतासंसर्गेण चमत्कारत्व-वत्त्वमेव वा काव्यत्वमिति फलितम्।"

अत्र जगन्नाथः स्वकृतकाव्यलक्षणं त्रिभिः सोपनैः परिष्करोति । प्रथमसोपाने सः लिखिति- चमत्कारस्य जनिका या भावना, तद विषयकस्य अर्थस्य, अर्थात यः अर्थः सहृदयानां मनःसु परां प्रीतिं जनयति, तस्यार्थस्य प्रतिपादकः शब्दः एव काव्यम्। एतस्मिन् लक्षणे कदाचित् कश्चित् दोषमाहिण्ड्यमानः कथयेत-काव्यानन्दज्ञानसमये अनभ्युपगम्यशब्दार्थान्तराणा-मपि ज्ञानं कदाचित् कदाचित् भवति। एतादृशं ज्ञानं समूहालम्बनात्मकं भवति। काव्यानन्दास्वादनकाले एवम्भूतस्यानन्दस्य यः आस्वादः भवति, स आनन्दः काव्यानन्देन सह मिलितः सन् आस्वाद्यते। तर्हि अत्र प्रश्नः जागर्ति किमु एतादृशः आनन्दः काव्यपदवाच्य? एतन्निराकर्तुं जगन्नाथः द्वितीयं सोपानं प्रकाशयति-"यत् प्रतिपादितार्थ.....।" अत्र तात्पर्यमिदं यत्-यदर्थ विषयकभावनात्वं चमत्कारावच्छेदकं तदेव काव्यपदवाच्यम् । अर्थात् समूहावलम्बनज्ञानबलेन यद्यपि काव्यानन्देनसहानावश्यकघटपटादीनां ज्ञानं जायते तथापि पुनः पुनः भावनासमये एतादृशाणां घटादीनां ज्ञानं न जायते। केवलं लोकोत्तरं काव्यानन्दं सामाजिकाः अनुभवन्ति। अतः एतादृशः अलौकिकानन्द एवं काव्यं भवत्ति।

अस्मिन् द्वितीयसोपाने "यत्.....तत्...." इति निर्देशात् काव्यानन्दप्रति-पादक शब्दस्य नैश्चित्यं न ज्ञायते। यथा-केनचित् उच्यते-यः धावन-प्रतियोगितायां प्रथमः भविता सः पुरस्कारस्य प्राप्ता" इत्यत्र धावनसमाप्तितः पूर्वं पुरस्कारप्राप्तृविषये नैश्चित्यं नास्ति तथा काव्यत्वप्रतिपादक शब्द विषये द्वितीयसोपाने नैश्चित्यं नास्ति। अतः स्पष्टरूपेण काव्यत्वप्रसक्तशब्दस्य प्रतिपादनार्थं तृतीयसोपाने जगन्नाथः प्रतिपादयति यत्-स्वविशिष्टजनकता

....."। 'स्वविशिष्ट-जनकता' इत्युक्ते ब्रह्मानन्दज्ञानजनकता। अर्थात् केवलं ब्रह्मानन्दप्रतिपादकसंसर्गित शब्दः एव काव्यमिति। अत्र अन्येषां घटपटादीनां शब्दानां सम्पर्को नास्ति।

रसगङ्गाधरस्य प्रथमानने जगन्नाथः स्वकाव्यलक्षणं प्रतिपाद्य मम्मटादीनां काव्यलक्षणं दूषयति। मम्मटमतखण्डने जगन्नाथः कथयति-काव्यं पठ्यते, काव्यादर्थोऽवगम्यते, काव्यं श्रुतम्, अर्थो न ज्ञातः इत्यादि विश्वजनीनव्यवहारतः प्रत्युत शब्दविशेषस्य एव काव्यपदार्थत्वपंतिपत्तेश्च । अपि च "विनिगमना-भावात् उभयत्र शक्तिरिति प्रत्युक्तम्"।

काव्यस्य भेदकरणे जगन्नाथस्योपरि मम्मटस्य प्रभावः पतितः दृश्यते, मम्मटः काव्यं त्रिविधं मनुते। अन्तिमं भेदमधमं स शब्दार्थ-चित्ररूपेण द्विविधं स्वीकरोति। एतद्भेदद्वयं स्वतन्त्रतया जगन्नाथः मध्यमाधमभेदरूपेण स्वीकरोति। काव्यभेदकरणे सः लिखतितच्चोत्तमोत्तमोत्तममध्यमाधमभेदेन चतुर्धा। उत्तमोत्तमकाव्यस्यालोचनाप्रसङ्गे स अप्पय्यदीक्षितस्य 'निःशेषच्युत-चन्दनम्' इति पद्यगतव्याख्यानं दूषयति।

काव्ये रस मुख्यः। रसस्य उत्पत्तिविषयालोचने सः एकादशमता-न्यालोचयति। एतदालोचनं तस्य सूक्ष्मबुद्धेः परिचायकं भवति। गुणालोचन प्रसङ्गे सः सूक्ष्मविचारं कुर्वन् स्वमतं प्रतिपादयति, अपि च वामनादि-स्वीकृतगुणानां विंशतिभेदान् खण्डयन् त्रीन् भेदान् माधुर्यौजः प्रसादाख्यान् आमनति।

रीतेरालोचनाप्रसङ्गे अमरूकस्य पद्यमेकं "शून्यंवासगृहम्" इति उद्धृत्य तत्र विद्यमानदोषानालोचयति। अत्र जगन्नाथः प्रकाशयति, पद्येऽस्मिन् "उत्थाय किञ्चितशनैः" इति स्थले सवर्णझयद्वयस्य नैकट्येन प्रयोगात् अश्रव्यतादोषः, झयघटितसंयोगपरह्रस्वस्य प्रयोगात् दोषश्च। अर्थात् "उत्थाय", 'किञ्चित्शनैः' इति स्थलयोः त्कारथकारयोः, त्कारशकारयोः, झयप्रत्याहारान्तर्गतवर्णयोः निकटप्रयोगात् अश्रव्यतादोषः। पुनः 'उत्थाय', 'किञ्चिच्छनैः' इति स्थले झयप्रत्याहारवर्णसंयोगात् 'त्थ', 'च्छ' इति पदयोः पूर्वं ह्रस्ववर्णव्यवहारात् दोषः। 'शनैर्निद्राम्, निर्वर्ण्य, 'पत्युर्मुखम्' इति स्थलेषु रेफयुक्तसंयोगात् दोषः। 'विस्रब्धम्' इति स्थले महाप्राणवर्णघटनात्, लज्जा इति स्थले

स्ववर्णद्वयघटनात् झयवर्णसंयोगाच्च दोषः। सर्वोपरि 'क्त्वा' प्रत्ययस्य पञ्चवारप्रयोगः अस्य पद्यस्य स्वारस्यं नाशयति। अपि च 'विलोक्य', आलोक्य इति स्थलयोः 'लोक' क्रियायाः द्विः प्रयोगः कवेः निर्माणसामग्री-दारिद्र्यं प्रकाशयति।

एवं जगन्नाथः भावध्वनिनिरूपणप्रसङ्गे, रसाभासालोचनाप्रसङ्गे सूक्ष्म-दृष्टिनिक्षेपपुरःसरं साहित्यतत्वं निस्काषयति।

एतत् सर्वं डॉ० धनञ्जयभञ्जेन तस्य गवेषणात्मके निबन्धेऽस्मिन् पुङ्खानुपुङ्खरूपेण विचारितमस्ति । रसगङ्गाधरस्य प्रथमाननोपरि जगन्नाथस्य तलस्पर्शिविचारं ये सहृदयाः कलयितुम् इच्छन्ति ते भञ्जकृतगवेषणात्मक-निबन्धात् अस्मात् सर्वं प्राप्स्यन्ति इति दृढं विश्वसिमि। अस्य ग्रन्थस्य बहुलप्रचारं प्रसारञ्च कामये अपि च श्री जगन्नाथस्याशीर्वादः डॉ भञ्जोपरि सर्वदा राजतामिति।

ता० ०१-०१-२००४

डॉ० श्रीनिवास आचार्यः
श्री सदाशिव संस्कृत विद्यापीठम्
(मानित विश्वविद्यालयः)
पुरी, उड़ीसा

ACKNOWLEDGEMENTS

It is with great pleasure and sense of gratitude that I record my obligations to various scholars from whom I have derived invaluable help in the preparation of the thesis.

At the outset I express my deepest feeling of respect and gratitude to myguruji Prof. Srinibas Acharya, who has given me his blessings since my college education and now, in the from of writing the forwarding letter. He was very kind to help me in every aspects from explaining the text to providing all in formations and valuable suggestions in proper time. Secondly I thank to my guide Dr B. K. Dalai, Reader, Pune University for his encourging guidance. I must mention that he allowed me to use his rich personal collections of various useful texts without which it would not have been possible for me to complete the work.

I would like to record my gratitude to the University Grants Commission for awarding me a Fellowship 1992, for a period of four years (1993-1997) to carry out my research work at the University of Pune. The authorities of the University Grants Commission and University of Pune were kind enough to sanction the fellowship in time which made my study at Pune possible.

I am extremely indebted to my elder brother Mr. P.C. Bhanja, who once dreamt me to be at this stage. It is he and his blessings that alone made me reach what I am. I do not know how much I owe to him. I am extremely grateful to my beloved wife Smt. Seema Srivastav (Supriya) for her moral support since the beginning to the final stage of my research work.

I am obliged to the library staff members of BORI, CASS, Jayakar, Deccan College of Pune, Orissa Sahitya Academy, Bhubaneswar, S.K.S.V. Puri for allowing me to make use of their valuable collections:

I thank to Mr. C.P. Gautamji & his indological institution, Bharatiya Kala Prakashan, Delhi, where both are encourging the authors, Sanskrit learners by providing ample opportunities in the form of publishing quality text books. Gautamji, in fact, encourged me a lot and due to him only, this thesis of 1998, comes out in book shape (in two Volumes) and reaches to many hands of Sanskrit Lovers. I must confess that, due to this prakashan, it made possible for me to see this thesis the light.

Dhananjaya Bhanja

ABBREVIATIONS

ABORI	Annals of Bhandarkar Oriental Research Institute, Pune
AD	Appayya Dikṣīta
AK	Alamkāra kaustubha
AL	Amṛtalaharī
AM	Alaṁkāra Muktāvalī
Ama	Amaruśataka
AR	Alaṁkāra ratnākara
AS	Alaṁkārasarvasva
Āvi	Āsafavilāsa
BD	Bhaṭṭoji Dikṣīta
BHU	Banaras Hindu University
BV	Bhāminivilāsa
BVB	Bhāratīya Vidyā, Bombay
CA	Candrāloka
CM	Citramīmāṁsā
CMK	Cītramīmāmsā Khandanam
CSS	Choukhamba Sanskrit Series
CVB	Choukhamba Vidyabhavan, Varanasi
DA	Dhvanyāloka
GL	Gaṅgālaharī

HSP	History of Sanskrit Poetics (Kane, P. V.)
HSP (De)	History of Sanskrit Poetics (De, S. K.)
JASB	Journal of aesthetic Society, Bombay.
JAU	Journal of Annamalai University, Annamalai-nagar
JB	Jagadābharaṇa
JOIB	Journal of Oriental Institute, Baroda
JORM	Journal of Oriental Research, Madras
JP	Jagannāth Paṅḍita
KA	Kāvyādarśa
KL	Karuṇālaharī
KM	Kāvyamīmāṁsā
KP	Kāvyaprakāśa
KR	Kavyarasāyana
KS	Kumārasaṁbhava
KSV	Kāvyālaṁkāra Sūtravṛtti
LL	Laxmīlaharī
Mano	Manoramākucamardana (Mardini)
MLBD	Motilal Banarasidass
NS	Nāṭyasāstra
NSPB	Nirṇayasāgarpress, Bombay
OBA	Oriental Book Agency Pune
OSA	Orissa Sahitya Academy, Bhubaneswar
PB	Prāṇābharaṇa
PKS	PaṇditarājaKāvysaṁgraha
PR/PRJ	Panditarāja Jagannātha
RG	Rasagaṇgādhara

Ru. Kāv.	Rudraṭakāvyālaṁkāra
SKB	Sarasvatī Kaṇṭhābharaṇa
SL	Sūdhālaharī
SPB	Calcutta
SR	Saṅgītaratnākara
SSU	Sampurṇānanda Sanskrit University, Varanasi
TMV	Tilak Maharashtra Vidyapeetha, Pune
RV	Raghuvaṁsa
YVC	Yamunāvarṇanacampū
VIJH	Visvesvarānanda Indological Journal, Hosiar-pur
VĀ	Vāgbhṭṭālaṁkāra
VS	Veṇīsaṁhāra
VV	Vyaktiviveka
(PRSP)	Contribution of PR to Sanskrit Poetics
मदु०	मथुरानाथ शास्त्री और दुर्गाप्रसाद, मुम्बई प्रकाशन
वादु०	वासुदेव और दुर्गाप्रसाद, मुम्बई प्रकाशन
गंगा०	गंगाधर शास्त्री, वाराणसी प्रकाशन
संपु०	केदारनाथ ओझ, संपूर्णानन्द संस्कृत विश्वविद्यालय वाराणसी प्रकाशन
चौ०	चौखम्बा संस्कृत सिरिज्, वाराणसी
म०	डॉ० आठवले, टिलक महाराष्ट्र विद्यापीठ, पूणे
ओ०	डॉ० सूर्यमणि रथ, उड़ीसा साहित्य अकादमी भूवनेश्वर

CONTENTS

TRANSLITRATION FORMAT

अ	a	आ	ā	इ	i	ई	ī	उ	u
ऊ	ū								
ए	e	ऐ	ai	ओ	o	औ	ou	अं	ṅ
अः	ḥ								
क	ka	ख	kha	ग	ga	घ	gha	ङ	ṅ
च	ca	छ	cha	ज	ja	झ	jha	ञ	ñ
ट	ṭa	ठ	ṭha	ड	ḍa	ढ	ḍha	ण	ṇ
त	ta	थ	tha	द	da	ध	dha	न	na
प	pa	फ	pha	ब	ba	भ	bha	म	ma
य	ya	र	ra	ल	la	व	va	श	ś
ष	ṣ	स	sa	ह	ha				
क्ष	kṣa	त्र	tra	ज्ञ	jña				

PART - I

RASGAṄGĀDHARA

TEXT WITH ENGLISH TRANSLATION

RASAGAṄGĀDHARA

(प्रथममाननम्)

स्मृतापि तरुणातपं करुणया हरन्ती नृणा-
मभंगुरतनुत्विषां वलयिता शतैर्विद्युताम्।
कलिन्दगिरि-नन्दिनीतट-सुरद्रुमालम्बिनी
मदीयमतिचुम्बिनी भवतु कापि कादम्बिनी॥१॥

Let the wonderful line of clouds resorting to the divine trees, on the banks of the daughter of Kalinda mountain (the river Yamunā), encircled by hundreds of lightenings of permanent lustre and removing the fresh troubles of men through compassion, even by (mere) rememberance, be the object of my contemplation.

श्रीमज्ज्ञानेन्द्रभिक्षोरधिगतसकल-ब्रह्म-विद्याप्रपञ्चः
काणादीराक्षपादीरपि गहनगिरो यो महेन्द्रादवेदीत्।
देवादेवाध्यगीष्ट स्मरहरनगरे शासनं जैमिनीयं
शेषाङ्कप्राप्तशेषामलभणितिरभूत्सर्वविद्याधरो यः॥२॥
पाषाणादपि पीयूषं स्यन्दते यस्य लीलया।
तं वन्दे पेरुभट्टाख्यं लक्ष्मीकान्तं महागुरुम्॥३॥

(I) pray to that great Teacher, **Perubhaṭṭa** by name, the beloved of **Laxmi,** whose sportive activities even make the stone found nectar, (who has) studied the entire **Vedāntaśātra** under Srimatjñānendra Bhikşu and learned the most difficult **śāśtra** of **Kaṇāda (Nyāya)** and **Akṣapāda (Vaiseṣika)** under **Mahendra,** and studied the **śāstra** expounded by **jaimini (Miṁāṁsā)** under **Deva (Khaṇḍadeva)** in the city of Lord Siva (Kasi) and was educated in faultless **sastra of Seṣa (Patañjali)** under **Śeṣa (Vireśvarapaṇḍita).** who was expert in all **śāstras.**

निमग्नेन क्लेशैर्मननजलधेरन्तरुदरं
मयोन्नीतो लोके ललितरसगङ्गाधरमणिः।
हरन्नन्तर्ध्वान्तं हृदयमधिरूढो गुणवता-
मलङ्कारान्सर्वानपि गलितगर्वान्रचयतु॥४॥

With difficulties, (deeping in) the bottom of the ocean of memory. a charming jewel. the Rasagaṅgādhara was brought out by me, which should illuminate the darkeness by entering the hearts of learned, should also destroy the prides of (alaṅkāra) the works of all (rhetoricians).

परिष्कुर्वन्त्वर्थान्सहृदयधुरीणाः कतिपये
तथापि क्लेशो में कथमपि गतार्थो न भविता।
तिमीन्द्राः संक्षोभं विद्यतु पयोधेःपुनरिमे
किमेतेनायासो भवति विफलो मन्दरगिरेः॥५॥

Let some receptive experts explain the sense (of poetry), still the labour of mine woule not be rendered useless in any way; Similarly, Let these kings of sharks disturb the ocean, does this (disturbance) render the efforts of the mandara mountain (in churning the ocean) fruitless?

निर्मायनूतनमुदाहरणानुरूपं
काव्यं मयात्र निहितं न परस्य किंचित्।
किं सेव्यते सुमनसां मनसापि गन्धः
कस्तूरिकाजननशक्तिभृता मृगेण॥६॥

Composing suitable examples anew, and not utilising (any) of others (poetries), I have quoted the examples (lit. poetries) here (in RG); Does the deer with the power of generating (itself) the fragrance of musk. enjoy the smell of flowers even a little.

मननतरितीर्णविद्यार्णवो जगन्नाथपण्डितनरेन्द्रः।
रसगङ्गाधरनाम्नीं करोति कुतुकेन काव्यमीमांसाम्॥७॥

Jagannatha. the king among scholars crossing the ocean of knowledge by the boat of memory, composes the science of poetry 'Rasagaṅgādhara' by name with great case.

रसगङ्गाधरनामा संदर्भोऽयं चिरं जयतु।
किं च कुलानि कवीनां निसर्गसम्यञ्चिररञ्जयतु॥८॥

Let this text (Sandarbha) Rasagangadhara by name. exist/ prosper for ever, and entertain the entire generation of poets, with its eternal beauty (Charm).

Notes : The first verse stands for a preclude as well as a vendictory to god Kṛṣṇa and further **PR** observes that, only remembrance of Him, all the problems reading the writing/ composition of a text should be removed.

In the second and third verses, **PR** loudly pronounces that, under the proper guidance of his father, Perubhaṭa, he himself got the total knowledge about many sciences. His father was also very wellknown scholar and **PR** says that, his father, whose sportive glances make stones shed nectar.

In the fourth verse, he clearly states that, for the search of jewel like **RG,** he entered into the ocean of that knowledge and brought out with great labour.

In fifth verse, he further adds that the objection from opponents cannot spoil his labour and RG would be accepted by all rehtoricians alike the sharks, those are trying to destroy the ocean and making disturbance, but Mandara, is always fruitful for churning the water.

In the sixth stanza, PR becomes more independent to put example verses according to context in entire RG. So he points out that, unlike other text writers, he does not like to follow others but to create original and new things. It is very clear that, in this RG. the entire examples are made by himself. For this, he further gives a bright example as the deer, who can produce the good smell of musk, never follow the smell of a flower. Alike this PR never followed his predecessors works to get example stanzas.

In seventh verse, PR clarifies that whatever he put in RG, is with great fun only, not at all any burden. He had the calibre to do so. Here the fault may arise that earlier he said that he searched jewel like RG with great pain and again it was written with easy and this needs a brief comparison to clarify this issue.

The 8th and last stanza is for a good will and he tells that RG may prosper for ever and further, give pleasure to whole generations of poet.

RG. 1

तत्र कीर्तिपरमाह्लाद गुरुराज देवताप्रसादाद्यनेक प्रयोजनकस्य काव्यस्य व्युत्पत्ते कविसहृदययोरावश्यकतया गुणालंकारादि भिर्निरुपणीये तस्मिन्विशेष्यतावच्छेदकं तदितर भेदबुद्धौ साधनं च तल्लक्षणं तावन्निरुप्यते-

Trans.: Now (in the present text) that definition (of Poetry) which is the cause of the knowledge of difference from what is other than that, (काव्य) and (which is) the delimitor of the qualifiedness existent (निष्ठा) in the poetry, (determined by the qualificandness) having many purposes namely; fame, ultimate pleasure (highest pleasure), the favour of Teacher, King, God etc., which is defined in terms of गुण and अलंकार etc., the knowledge of which is essential for the poet and the sympathetic reader, is being defined.

Notes : Like other rhetoricians in past, PR proposes the concept of purpose of the poetry in his RG. He writes that fame, ultimate pleasure, i.e. extraordinary pleasure, the favour received from the teachers, kings, Gods etc., are some. **Nāgesa** comments the other purposes as mentioned by **PR** are dravyalābha etc. This refers to receiving of gold like objects, property, beautiful wife, kingdom etc.

RG. 2.

रमणीयार्थप्रतिपादकः शब्दः काव्यम्॥

Trans.: The word(s) which raises the charming sense(s) to comprehension, is poetry.

Notes : After explaining the purpose of the poetry in the preceding text, PR gives his own definition of poetry. He defines poetry as: word(s) that raises the charming sense(s) to comprehension.

It is significant to note here that PR belongs to the school and contribute to the view that only 'śabda' forms the poetry, unlike others who contribute to the view that both **śabda** and **artha** forms the poetry.

In this definition of poetry the following explanation: **ramanīyatā** and **śabda.**

The meaning of **ramaṇīyatā** is being defined and explained by the author himself. We may explain here the purpose of the qualificant namely, **ramaṇīyārthaprati-pādaka** and **sabda.**

If the qualification **ramaṇīya** is dropped then definition of poetry will be **arthapratipādakaḥ sabdakāvyam** and the expressions like **ghaṭamānaya** (bring pot), **gām naya.**

(take away the cow) would become **kāvya**, which is not desirable. if the qualificat '**artha**' is removed, then the definition of poetry will be **ramaṇīya 'śabdaḥ kāvyam'** and then there would be '**ativyāpti**' in the case of grammatical expression (**ramaṇīya sabdapratipādaka**). Further if the word '**sabda**' is excluded or dropped, then there would be '**ativyāti**' in the case of '**ceṣṭā**', etc.

It should not be argued that '**ramaṇīyārthaprati pāda-kaḥ sabdaḥ**' cannot be poetry and the definition suffers from the fault of 'asaṁbhava', in the case of the '**ramaṇī-yārthapratipadakaḥ** sabdaḥ **kāvyam**' should be understood as '**ramaṇīyārthaviṣayakaprattipādijanaka 'sabdajñāna viṣayaka-śabdaḥ-vākyarūpaḥ-kāvyam** Thus the possibility of **asaṁbhava'** can be removed.

This definition is nothing new but an another modified form of Daṇḍin's **Kāvyasarīra.**

Further **PR**'s definition of poetry is short, but its scope is extremely wide.

RG. 2.1

रमणीयता च लोकोत्तराह्लादजनकज्ञानगोचरता।
लोकोत्तरत्वं चाह्लादगतश्चमत्कारत्वापरपर्यायोऽनुभव-
साक्षिको जातिविशेषः।

TRANS : Charmingness (of sense) is the objectness of the knowledge that produces the supernatural transndental pleasure (delight). And the supernaturalness (of pleasure) is the universal, known by ones own experience (enjoyment), which is another synonym (name) of uniqueness (wonderfulness of pleasure) existing in the pleasure.

Notes : In the preceding text, the author has defined poetry in terms of **ramaṇīya.** Thus, in order to understand what poetry is one must be clear about the notion of **ramaṇīyatā.** And hence the author starts to explain the notion of charmingness, *i.e.* **ramaṇīyatā.**

'Charmingness of sense' is the cause of the enjoyment of transdental pleasure due to which the **sahṛdaya** enhoys this transdental pleasure. While explaining the charmingness of sense, PR introduces another concept namely transdentalness (of pleasure) **(lokottaratā).** According to PR, 'lokottaratā' is a universal (**jāti**) proved or realised on the basis of one's own experience, residing in the pleasure, which is nothing but another name of wonderfulness. In otherwords, transdentalness is identical with the wonderfulness of pleasure existing in the pleasure and is known by one's own experience.

It may be noticed that PR has used the term '**jāti**', a universal for **lokottaratā,** deliberately, with a view to include all the causes of charming expression that generates transdental pleasure, which external and one. By the introduction of this notion of universal, the real implication of '**ramanīyatā**' or '**lokottaratā**'was brought out.

RG. 2.2

कारणं च तदवच्छिन्ने भावनाविशेषः पुनः पुनरनुसंधानात्मा। 'पुत्रस्ते जातः,' 'धनं ते दास्यामि' इति वाक्यार्थधीजन्यस्याह्लादस्य न लोकोत्तरत्वम्। अतो न तस्मिन्वाक्ये काव्यत्वप्रसक्तिः।

Trans.: And the cause of (that supernatural/uncommon pleasure or delight) is a special type of imagination, delimited by the (supernaturality) in the form of repeated queries. The pleasure produced from the knowledge (understanding) of the sense of the sentence namely, (the sense of the experssion) 'A son is born to you', 'I shall give you wealth', etc., lack this supernaturalness. Therefore, there is no over-application (of the definition) of poetry in thesee experessions (sentences) (namely, 'A son is born to you...etc.').

Notes : It is stated that the two factors namely, charmingness of expression (**ramaṇīyatā**) based on transdentalness (**lokottaratā**), is poetry. Now the cause of such extraordinary pleasure is being explained.

The point is clarified by the help of two illustrations which produce pleasure but are not treated as poetry.

The two illustrations are; 'a son is born to you' and 'you will get wealth'.

Both these expressions produce pleasure. But they are of common nature and lack '**lokottaratā**'. Thus, these type of expressions do not form poetry.

The causality of that is a kind of knowledge in the form of repeated query, delimited by '**lokottaratā**', which is infact another name of charmingness, as already stated.

This '**ramaṇīyatā**' can be explained as a special kind of the effectness residing in the pleasure delimited by an universal pervaded by all pleasures. The point will be more clear by the diagrams given at the the end of this book.

RG. 2.3

इत्थं च चमत्कारजनकभावनाविषयार्थप्रतिपादकशब्दत्वम्। यत्प्रतिपादितार्थविषयकभावनात्वं चमत्कारजनकतावच्छेदकं तत्त्वम्। स्वविशिष्टजनकतावच्छेदकार्थप्रतिपादकतासंसर्गेण चमत्कारत्ववत्त्वमेव वा काव्यत्वमिति फलितम्।

Trans.: Thus (like this) the words raise the charming sense into comprehension, having imagination as its object, that produces the supernaturalness of pleasure or joy (is poetry).

Or (poetry) is that which raises the charming sense having imagination as its object delimited by the state of being the producer of supernatural pleasure.

Or the extraordinaryness (wonderfulness) of pleasure which is connected with the (words) experssions by the relation of experssiveness (**Pratipādakatā**), which give rise to the sense (**artha**), the delimiter of the generativeness, that generates its own (**sva**) (extraordinaryness of pleasures), is poetry, is the final meaning.

Notes : In the previous text the cause of the charmingness is defined and explained. Now PR proceeds to explain the definition of **kāvya.** It may be noted that **PR** has already given his definition of **kāvya,** which we have already noted. Now he gives three more definitions of poetry. It is significant to note that, these three definitions are new definitions but the modified ones. In these definitions, **PR** imposed upon his original definition of poetry (**kāvya**) by avoiding some faults which might have kept in his definition of poetry. Here we may reproduce these three modified definitions:

1. **camatkārajanakabhāvanāviṣayārthapratipādaka-śabdatvaṁ,**
2. **yatpratipāditārthavisayakabhāvanātvaṁ camatkāra-janakatāvacchedakaṁ tattvaṁ** and
3. **svaviśiṣṭajanakatavacchedakārthapratipādakatā saṁ-sarageṇa camatkāratvavatvameva vā kāvyatvaṁ.**

A careful observation of these definitions suggest that the first definition tries to avoid the fault of '**ativyāpti**' in the original definition of **PR.** This my be explain as follows:

As we can see in this definition, **PR** introduces the term '**bhāvanā**' by inserting it in the place of '**jñāna**'. In the original definition of **kāvya,** there is the possibility of the fault of '**ativyāpti**' and because in the case of '**samuhālaṁ-bana jñāna**', there are many objects of knowledge, out of which, some may be '**ramaṇīya**' and others not. If the worse is produce such knowledge, is treated as '**kāvya**' than the'**śabdas**' producing '**armaṇīyārtha**' would become poetry, which is not desirable. To make it more clear, a knowledge like "the horse is running" or 'a cow is grazing' etc., would become poetry if they form a part of a '**samuhā-laṁbana jñāna**', having some '**ramaṇīyārtha**' expressed through some '**sabdas**'. Such is true in the case of '**satā vadhānis**' or '**sahasrāvadhānis**' who concentrate their minds in more than one objects at a time and their knowledge arises having more than one entity as an object. Thus in order to avoid this fault of '**ativyāpti**', **PR replaces** '**Jñāna**' by '**bhāvanā**'.

Coming to the second modified definition namely, '**yatpratipāditārtha.. etc.,** it must be noted that this is a better definition than the first modified one, already noted. Because, it also avoids the fault of '**ativyāpti**' and incorporates the word '**bhāvanā**' and is presented by adopting **Navyanyāya** techniques. In fact, it is a **Navyanyāya** presen-tation of the same definition.

The same is represented in a more simpler form in the third modified definition. '**kāvyatva**' stated as to be '**camatkāratvavattva**'. The '**camatkāratva**' (charmingness) may exist in '**camatkāra**' by the relation of inherence and hence '**camatkāra**' itself will be the '**kāvya**' and not '**camatkāratvavattva.**' Thus, in the definition, the relation is also maintained namely, **svaviśiṣṭjanakatā .. pratipādaka-tāsaṁsargeṇa.** Thus, **camatkāraavacchinnajanyatānirupitā janakatā nirūpitā** is to be delimited by **viṣayitvasaṁbaṁdha.**

RG. 3

यत्तु प्राञ्चः-'अदोषौ सगुणौ सालंकारौ शब्दार्थौ काव्यम्' इत्याहुः, तत्र विचार्यते-शब्दार्थयुगलं न काव्यशब्दवाच्यम्। मानाभावात्।

काव्यमुच्चैःपठ्यते, काव्यादर्थोऽवगम्यते, काव्यं श्रुतमर्थो न ज्ञातः, इत्यादिविश्वजनीनव्यवहारतःप्रत्युत शब्दविशेषस्यैव काव्य-

पदार्थत्वप्रतिपत्तेश्च। व्यवहार:शब्दमात्रे लक्षणयोपपादनीय इति चेत्, स्यादप्येवम्, यदि काव्यपदार्थतया पराभिमते शब्दार्थयुगले काव्य-शब्दशक्तेः प्रमापकं दृढतरं किमपि प्रमाणं स्यात्, तदेव तु न पश्यामः। विमतवाक्यं त्वश्रद्धेयमेव। इत्थं चासति काव्यशब्दस्य शब्दार्थयुगलशक्तिग्राहके प्रमाणे, प्रागुक्ताद् व्यवहारतः शब्दविशेषे सिद्ध्यन्तीं शक्तिं को नाम निवारयितुमीष्टे। एतेन विनिगमनाभावादुभयत्र शक्तिरिति प्रत्युक्तम्। तदेवं शब्दविशेषस्यैव काव्यपदार्थत्वे सिद्धे तस्यैव लक्षणं वक्तुं युक्तम्, न तु स्वकल्पितस्य काव्यपदार्थस्य।

Trans.: As told the ancient writers (predecessors) namely that "the word and sense which consists poetic embellishments, poetic merits (qualities) and free from poetic blemishes is poetry", is now being critically analyzed.

The twin 'word' and 'sense' together is not fit to be named as poetry. Because, there is no proof (for holding so). Due to the widely accepted expressions (or behavior) namely 'the poerty is read loudly, the sense (meaning) is understood from the poetry'; 'poetry is heard, but the sense (meaning) is not known', etc.....and because the poetry (lit. the category of poetry) is determined in (the case of) a specific type of expressions (words). If it is argued like this namely, the (sense) with regard to any words (expressions), can be obtained by indication (indirect means), let it be like this. If in the combinatioin of word and sense as a category of poetry, propounded by others, there is no strong ground or proof to determine the power of the word (kāvya) denotative. We have no pleasure or liking to accept the statement (or view) of others. Thus when there is no proof to determine the power in the word **kāvya** to express the sense in the unity of word and sense who indeed would like to deny (remove or destroy) the power (or expressing **kāvya** in (the case of) special type of words which is already established (or proved) by expressions, recorded previously. By this (argument) the absence of any uniting factor the view namely, power of expressing **kāvya** in both is refuted (answered to). Thus it is proper to hold that alone as the definition (of poetry) since the category of **kāvya** (the sense of **kāvya**) is with regard to special type of words (or expression) and not the sense of **kavya** as coined (imagined) by some.

Notes : After establishing his own theory of **kāvya, PR** proceeds to examine the definitions of poetry as given by others (*i.e.,*his predecessors), following the well grounded principle of **pradhānamallanirvahaṇa nyāya** *i.e.,* knocking the chief of the wrestler to the ground by which others would automatically be declared defeated). **PR** takes Mammaṭa to ask by questioning the correctness of his definition of poetry. And the refutation of the definition of poetry as given by Mammaṭa, would amount to refuting all those host of rhetoricians, who belong to the group of **śabdārtha** theory as being **kāvya** and follows Mammaṭa. We have already recorded else where that we have two main trends namely **śabdavādi** and **ubhayavādi** or **śabdārthavādi.** Now let us see, how PR refutes the definition of poetry as given by Mammaṭa and in what success.

Mammaṭa defines poetry as follows :

'tadadoṣau śabdārthau saguṇāvanalaṃkṛti punaḥ kvāpi, which means poetry consists of word and sense, free from blemishes, having poetic merits and excellence of style which may at times be without figures of speech. As we can see, this definition has two parts. The main definition and its qualifications. **śabdārthau kāvyaṁ** forms the main part of the definition and **'adoṣausaguṇau'** etc., are the qualifications of '**śabdārthau.**' PR with a view to deny **kāvyatva** to **śabda** and **artha** together, argued :

There is no proof to hold that the **śabda** and **artha,** both together forms poetry (**mānābhāvāt**). The reason he gives in favour of his view is **visvajanī navyavahāraḥ** (*i.e.*, universal expression of the words, **śabda** and **artha**). He says: we have the usage **kāvyamuccaiḥ paṭhyate,** poetry is cited (read) loudly. This valid statement proves that by poetry the preference is made to **śabda** only. Because, what cited or read, is not the sense but the word (**sabda**).

Following the dictum "**mānābhīnā meyasiddhiḥ**' the object is to be proved by means of a valid knowledge and since there is no valid means to prove **sabdār thau** as **kāvya,** Mammaṭa's definition that **sabda** and **artha** together forms poetry is rejected. **PR** quotes many more absurd cases of usages in accepting **sabda** and **artha** as poetry.

1. **kāvyāt artho avagamyate,**

   sense (meaning) is understood from poetry.

2. **kāvyaṁ śrutam artho na jñātaḥ,**

   poetry is heard but sense (meaning) is not understood etc.

These are universal usages or expressions and nobody objects to these expressioins, which makes clear that since something different from poetry and not the part of the poetry. Otherwise the above mentioned usages cannot rightly be justified.

With a view to over come the aforesaid difficulties, the opponent may argue.

To this, **PR** replies: This could have been true if we can get some proof by which **kāvya** will be both **sabda** and **artha.** It is obvious that when there is a **mūkṣyā rthabādha,** that is when **abhidhārtha** fails to convey the sense, one resorts to **lakṣanā.** Thus, in this context, if we have to accept **sabdārthau as kāvya,** which refer to by **śabda** on the strength of **lakṣaṇā,** then we must first establish that the word **kāvya** has the power to express the sense of **śabda** and **artha.** Because, the norms for determining the **abhidhāsakti** do not suggest **kāvya** to mean **śabda and artha.** The norms determining the denotative power of a word, are enumerated in the following couplet,

Śaktigrahaṁ vyākaraṇopamānāt
koṣāptavākyāt vyavahāratasca,
vākyasyaseṣāt vivṛtervadanti
sānnidhyata siddhaḥ pāsya vṛddhāḥ.

And by none of these, we can determine kāvya to mean sabda and artha.

Hence there is no scope to use lakṣaṇā. It should not be argued that, since there is no conclusive proof (**vinigamanā bhāvāt)** in either of the argument, let us accept, either of the two as valid. To this PR says, unlike the opponents, there is conclusive proof in case of his argument to accept, sabda alone as poetry and this proof is in the form of universal usages, as already quoted. Thus, kāvya is determined as sabdaviśeṣa and **PR** proceeds to define that poetry and not any other imaginary concept of poetry of others.

RG. 3.1.

एषैव च वेदपुराणादिलक्षणेष्वपि गतिः। अन्यथा तत्रापीयं दुरवस्था स्यात्।

Trans.: And further, the same fact holds good in case of the definition of **veda,** purāna etc. Otherwise there would arise the (same) difficulty (as already recorded).

Notes : The same argument stands valid in the case of

the definition of **veda, purāṇa** etc. Otherwise the same difficulty would arise in explaining their definitions as well.

In the preceding text, **PR** has refuted that 'word' and 'sense'together cannot be accepted as poetry, as proposed by Mammaṭa etc. Now, and objection or rejoinder is anticipated from the objectors in favour of the view that 'sabda' and 'artha' both together forms poetry. It is as follows:

Generation of '**ānanda**' or **āsvāda** is the ground or cause of treating some thing as poetry or otherwise. And this fact, namely generating poetry is common to both-'**sabda**' and **artha (tatca sabde ca arthe ca avisiṣṭm iti).** If this is accepted as true, that the capacity of generating poetry is common to both 'word and sense' together poetry as is done by us, the followers of the view, namely, '**sabdārthau kāvyaṁ**'.

To this objection, **PR** replies in negative by pointing out this fact that this would give rise to several contingencies.

1. The pleasure is generated from listening the music or melody etc.
2. Pleasure also is generated from the observations of various actions and performances, staged in a drama.

The melodical tones and various accompaniments in dramatic-actions, which are generating pleasure to audiences or readers are not **kāvyas.**

Āsvāda (ānanda) is the next name of pleasure and this āsvāda (pleasure) generates (**udbodhakatva**) the causes for kāvya. Here the word and sense, both are not in a similar position, but word only the generator of pleasure.

So the argument that since, the generation of pleasure is common to both word and sense, let both be poetry, stand refuted.

RG. 4.

यत्त्वास्वादोद्बोधकत्वमेव काव्यत्वप्रयोजकं, तच्च शब्दे चार्थे चाविशिष्टमित्याहुः, तन्न। रागस्यापि रसव्यञ्जकताया ध्वनिकारादि-सकलालङ्कारिकसंमतत्वेन प्रकृते लक्षणीयत्वापत्तेः।

किंबहुना नाट्याङ्गानां सर्वेषामपि प्रायशस्तथात्वेन तत्त्वापत्तिर्दुवारैव।

एतेन रसोद्बोधसमर्थस्यैवात्र लक्ष्यत्वमित्यपि परास्तम्।

Trans.: As is mentioned namely, the state of generating pleasure (**āsvāda**)is the cause of poetry and that is common to both, word and sense, is not correct.

There would arise the contingency of accepting the **rāgas** (music etc) as the definition of the subject defined (i.e. poetry), those being capable of producing pleasure and is accepted by all the rhetoricians including the propounder of **Dhvani** theory (i.e.Ānandavardhana.).

What (to speak) more? It is difficult to debar often all actions and accessories related to dramas from becoming that (**kāvya**) since like that (i. e. producing pleasure).

By this (same argument) the view namely, that which is capable of generating pleasure, as the state of being defined also stands refuted.

RG. 5

अपि च काव्यपदप्रवृत्तिनिमित्तं शब्दार्थयोर्व्यासक्तम्, प्रत्येकपर्याप्तं वा।

नाद्यः। एको न द्वावितिव्यवहारस्येव श्लोकवाक्य न काव्यमिति व्यवहारस्यापत्तेः। न द्वितीयः। एकस्मिन्पद्ये काव्यद्वयव्यवहारापत्तेः।

तस्माद्वेदशास्त्रपुराणलक्षणस्येव काव्यलक्षणस्यापि शब्दनिष्ठतैवोचिता।

Trans.: And again, whether (**kāvyatva**) the ground of the usage of the word 'poetry' exists in 'word' and 'sense' simultaneously taken together (by **paryāpti saṁbandha**) or in each one (of word or sense), (by **samavāya saṁbandha).** The first (alternative) is not (acceptable). Because alike the usage namely, one is not two, there would arise the contingency of not (accepting) using **kāvya** in th case of word or metrical expressions. Because of the contingency of the usage of poetry twice in the metrical composition (**padya**), the second alternative (also) is not true.

Therefore, alike the definitions of **veda, śāstra** and **purāṇa,** it is proper to accept the definition of poetry (**kāvya**) on the basis of words (i. e. word is poetry).

RG. 6.

लक्षणे गुणालङ्कारादिनिवेशोऽपि न युक्तः।

'उदितं मण्डलं विधोः' इति काव्ये दूत्यभिसारिकाविरहिण्यादि-समुदीरितेऽभिसरणविधिनिषेधजीवनाभावादिपरे, 'गतोऽस्तमर्कः' इत्यादौ चाव्याप्त्यापत्तेः।

Trans.: It is also not proper to add (to qualifiy) **guṇa, alaṁkāra** etc., to the definition (of poetry). Because there would arise the contingency of too narrowness in the case of poetry namely 'the sun has set'; 'the moon has arisen' which generates, (the suggested) sense of approaching, denial of approaching and difficult to bear the life in the case of the lady agent (**dutī**), the self approaching lady (**abhisārikā**), woman in separation (**virahiṇī**) etc.

RG. 6.1

न चेदमकाव्यमिति शक्यं वदितुम्। काव्यतयापराभिमतस्यापि तथा वक्तुं शब्यत्वात्। काव्यजीवितं चमत्कारित्वं चाविशिष्टमेव।

गुणत्वालंकारत्वादेरननुगमाच्च। दुष्टं काव्यं इति व्यवहारस्य बाधकं विना लाक्षणिकत्वायोगाच्च।

Trans.: It is not possible to blame (treat) this as '**akāvya**' because, the same can be told in case of poetry though accepted by others. Charmingness as the soul of poetry is not peculiar to that (i.e.charmingness existing in both the examples). Because, there is no uniformity (i. e. one property to inculde all the cases of **guṇas** and all the cases of **alaṁkāras**) in the case of guṇas and alaṁkāras.

And because, in the absence of bādhaka, it is not proper to accept 'indicated sense' in the case of the usage namely, 'duṣṭaṁ kāvyam,' (poetry with blemish).

RG. 6.2

न च संयोगाभाववान्वृक्षः संयोगीतिवदंशभेदेन दोषरहितं, दुष्टिमिति व्यवहारे बाधकं नास्तीति वाच्यम्।

'मूले महीरुहो विहंगमसंयोगी न शाखायाम्' इति प्रतीतेरिवेदं पद्यं पूर्वार्धे काव्यमुत्तरार्धे तु न काव्यमिति स्वरसवाहिनो विश्व-जनीनानुभवस्य विरहादव्याप्यवृत्तिताया अपि तस्यायोगात्।

शौर्यादिवदात्मधर्माणां गुणानाम्, हारादिवदुपस्कारकाणामलंकाराणां च शरीरघटकत्वानुपपत्तेश्च।

Trans.: It cannot be maintained (argued) like this; the tree having conjuction, possesses the absence of contact, like this (expression), there is the absence of defect (blemish), on the basis of the division of parts (hence) there is no difficulty in the expression states namely, defective (poetry) like the cognition namely, the tree has contact with bird in the root (and) not in the branch.

This (piece of poetry) is **kāvya** in the first half (where, there is no fault) but not **kāvya** in the latter half (where, there is full of faults).

Thus, due to the lack of (absence of) univiersal experience, it lacks the fitness to be of incomplete occurrence, also.

Because the qualities in the form of internal properties (**ātmadharma**) like valour, etc., and the ornaments (**alaṁkāra**) which adorns, (the poetry) like necklace, etc., the form (of the poetry) is not accomplished.

Notes : PR gives further reason as to why the qualifications 'adosau' in the definition of **kāvya** as given by Mammaṭa is not proper. For that case, there arises the contingency of calling "the portions of free of fault as **kāvya** and the rest as **akāvya**".

RG. 7

यत्तु 'रसवदेव काव्यम्' इति साहित्यदर्पणे निर्णीतम्, तन्न। वस्त्वलंकारप्रधानानां काव्यानामकाव्यत्वापत्तेः। न चेष्टापत्तिः। महाकविसंप्रदायस्याकुलीभावप्रसङ्गात्। तथाच जलप्रवाहवेगनिपतनोत्पतनभ्रमणानि कविभिर्वर्णितानि, कपिबालादिविलसितानि च। न च तत्रापि यथाकथंचित्परम्परया रसस्पर्शोऽस्त्येवेति वाच्यम्। ईदृशरसस्पर्शस्य 'गौश्चलति,' 'मृगो धावति' इत्यादावतिप्रसक्तत्वेनाप्रयोजकत्वात्। अर्थमात्रस्य विभावानुभावव्यभिचार्यन्यतमत्वादितिदिक्।

Trans.: As is defined, 'the sentence possessed of sentiments is poetry', in Sāhityadarpaṇa (by Viśvanātha), is not (true). Because, there would arise the contingency of nonpoetryness for the objective and rhetoric (figurative) poetries. It cannot be argued. (such) objection is welcome (or favourable to our view). Because there would arise the contingency of uprooting the tradition of great-poets. And again, (the subjects) like 'the flowing;,' 'the speed', 'the fall', 'the rising up', and 'the turning round of the water', are described by poets (in their writings), also the enjoyment of monkeys and youngsters.

It cannot be urged that there (in those subjects) also, **rasa** (sentiment) exists; some how (in some way or the other) indirectly. The presence of such sentiments is not the proof due to the over applicability in the cases like 'the cow moves' (is moving), 'the deer runs (is running)' etc.

Because, every objects, (capable of generating sentiment) is to be one of these, namely, the excitant (**vibhāva**), the ensuant (**anubhāva**) and the transitory moods (**vyab-hicāribhāva**).

RG. 8

तस्य च कारणं कविगता केवला प्रतिभा।

Trans.: The cause of that (poetry) is only intuition (**Pratibhā**) which exists in the poet (**kavigatā**).

RG. 8.1

सा च काव्यघटनानुकूलशब्दार्थोपस्थितिः। तद्गतं च प्रतिभात्वं काव्यकारणतावच्छेदकतया सिद्धो जातिविशेष, उपाधिरूपं वाखण्डम्।

Trans.: And that (**pratibhā**) is the presence (knowledge) of both suitable word and sense, favourable to compose poetry. The intuitionness (**pratibhātva**) existing in that is established as a universal in the form of the delimitor of the causality of poetry or is the form of indivisible imposed property (i. e., not at all fragmentary).

Notes: In this text, PR gives a novel definition of **pratibhā.** He defines **pratibhā** as "**kāvyaghaṭanānukū-lasabdārthopasthitiḥ**[11] Further he defines pratibātva as delimitor of the causality as universal or "**akhaṇḍopādhi**". Universal is defined as that which is one, eternal and existing in many by the relation of **samavāya.**

RG. 8.2

तस्याश्च हेतुः क्वचिद्देवतामहापुरुषप्रसादादिजन्यमदृष्टम्। क्वचिच्च विलक्षणव्युत्पत्तिकाव्यकरणाभ्यासौ।

Trans.: The cause of that (**pratibhā**) is unseen merits, produced (generated or accumulated) due to the grace of deities, great persons some time. Uncommon/distinguished erudition (deep erudition), and the practice of composing poetry (are also the causes), together (form the causes of **pratibhā**).

RG. 8.3

न तु त्रयमेव। बालादेस्तौ विनापि केवलान्महापुरुषप्रसादादपि प्रतिभोत्पत्तेः।

Trans.: (But) not the three, because in the absence of these two (namely, erudition and practice), by the mere blessings of great persons (sages) '**pratibhā**' is seen in the case of children.

Notes : The author refutes the view of some, particularly of Mammaṭa, who proposes three together namely **pratibhā** etc., as the cause of poetry. To him, even in the absence of erudition and practice, one can compose good poetry and this is proved in the case of the child who has acquired **pratibhā** by the grace of great sages or God.

RG. 8.4

न तत्र तयोर्जन्मान्तरीययोः कल्पनं वाच्यम्।

गौरवान्मानाभावात्कार्यस्यान्यथाप्युपपत्तेश्च।

लोके हि बलवता प्रमाणेनागमादिना सति कारणतानिर्णये पश्चादुपस्थितस्य व्यभिचारस्य वारणाय जन्मान्तरीयमन्यथानुपपत्त्या कारणं धर्माधर्मादि कल्प्यते। अन्यथा तु व्यभिचारोपस्थित्या पूर्ववृत्त-कारणतानिर्णये भ्रमत्व प्रतिपत्तिरेव जायते।

Trans.: It cannot be urged that; in that case these two (erudition and practice) be attributed to their previous births, because, there would arise the fault of logical heavy-ness because, there is the absence of any proof (to hold so) and because the effect is generated in the absence of that (cause) (or otherwise).

In common world indeed causality is determined by some powerful means of proof like scripture etc., in order to avoid the fault of deviation arising later, The merits and demerits etc., of the previous births are postulated as cause, in the absence of any other way of justification. Otherwise, there could arise doubt with regard to the validity of the causality determined earlier on the strength of the valid means of proof like the scripture etc., due to the presence of deviation.

RG. 8.5

नापि केवलमदृष्टमेव कारणमित्यपि शक्यं वदितुम्।

कियन्तंचित्कालं काव्यं कर्तुमशक्नुवतः कथमपि संजातयो-र्व्युत्पत्त्यभ्यासयोः प्रतिभायाःप्रादुर्भावस्य दर्शनात्।

तत्राप्यदृष्टस्याङ्गीकारे प्रागपि ताभ्यां तस्याः प्रसक्तेः।

Trans.: it is also not possible to maintain, namely, the unseen (potency) alone is the cause of **pratibhā.** Because it is observed that **pratibhā** is (later) generated in case of one who has some how acquired 'erudition' and 'practice', though was unable to compose poetry for quite some time. If unseen potency is postulated there also, then there would arise the contingency of its presence before as well.

RG. 8.6

न च तत्र प्रतिभायाः प्रतिबन्धकमदृष्टान्तरं कल्प्यमिति वाच्यम्।

तादृशानेकस्थलगतादृष्टद्वयकल्पनापेक्षया क्लृप्तव्युत्पत्त्यभ्यासयोरेव प्रतिभाहेतुत्वकल्पने लाघवात्। अतः प्रागुक्तसरणिरेव ज्यायसी।

तादृशादृष्टस्य तादृशव्युत्पत्त्यभ्यासयोश्च प्रतिभागतं वैलक्षण्यं कार्यतावच्छेदकम्, अतो न व्यभिचारः।

Trans.: It should not be argued, namely, let another unseen potency be postulated as an obstacle (for the emergence of /revelation) of **'pratibhā'.** Because it would be less cumbersome (more economical) to postulate the two, **'pratibhā'** and 'practice', already postulated, as the cause of

'pratibhā' than postulating two (different) unseen potencies depending on the respective cases. Therefore, what is stated by us is proper. And the peculiarity existing in the **'pratibhā'**of the respective 'unseen potency' and 'practice' and **'pratibhā',** is the delimitor or the effectness, hence no fault of deviation.

RG. 9

प्रतिभात्वं च कवितायाः कारणातावच्छेदकं प्रतिभागतवैलक्षण्यमेव वा विलक्षणकाव्यं प्रति[१] इति नात्रापि सः। न च सतोरपि-व्युत्पत्त्यभ्यासयोर्यत्र न प्रतिभोत्पत्तिस्तत्रान्वयव्यभिचार इति वाच्यम्।

तत्र तयोस्तादृशवैलक्षण्ये मानाभावेन कारणतावच्छेदकानवच्छिन्नत्वात्।

पापविशेषस्य तत्र प्रतिबन्धकत्वकल्पनाद्वा न दोषः।

प्रतिबन्धकाभावस्य च कारणता समुदितशक्त्यादित्रयहेतुवादिनः, शक्तिमात्रहेतुतावादिनश्चाविशिष्टा। प्रतिवादिना मन्त्रादिभिः कृते कतिपयदिवसव्यापिनि वाक्स्तंभे विहितानेकप्रबन्धस्यापि कवेः काव्यानुदयस्य दर्शनात्।

Trans.: The **'pratibhātva'** or the extraordinaryness existing in **'pratibhā'** is the delimitor of causality of poetry, for extraordinary poetry; thus, there is no deviation here.

It cannot be urged that, even in the presence of 'erudition' and 'practice', where the **'pratibhā'** is not generated, there is no deviation of mutual agreement (**anvaya-vyabhicāra**). Because of the lack of proof of that extraordinaryness of those two (namely 'erudition' and 'practice') (it) is not delimited by the delimitor of the causality. Or, there is no fault due to the postulation of an obstacle, in the form of demerits. The absence of obstacles in the causality, is common for those. who describe the three together namely, **'śakti'**

---

१. गंगा, चौ, म, –प्रतीति

etc. (as the cause of poetry) and those, who describe **'śakti'** only (as the cause of poetry). Because it is seen that a poet who has composed many poetries (earlier) is unable to compose poetry, when he is made dumb-founded. extending for some days, by opponents, by charm (**'mantra'**) etc.

RG. 10

तच्चोत्तमोत्तमोत्तममध्यमाधमभेदाच्चतुर्धा।

Trans.: And that (poetry) is divided into four namely, super excellent grade (**uttamottama**), excellent grade (**uttama**), middle grade (**madhyama**) and the lowest grade (**adhama**) of poetry.

RG. 11

"शब्दार्थौ यत्र गुणीभावितात्मानौ कमप्यर्थमभिव्यङ्क्तस्तदाद्यम्।"

कमपीति चमत्कृतिभूमिम्। तेनातिगूढस्फुटव्यङ्ग्ययोर्निरासः।

अपराङ्गवाच्यसिद्ध्यङ्गव्यङ्ग्ययोरपि चमत्कारितया तद्वारणाय गुणीभावितात्मानाविति स्वापेक्षया व्यङ्ग्यप्राधान्याभिप्रायकम्।

Trans.: That is the first, (variety of poetry, i. e., super excellent grade) where both the 'word' and the 'sense' together becoming sub-ordinate to its self, (namely), the main idea suggested (to the **vācyārtha**), presents some (**kāmapi**), supernatural charmingness.

Here, some (**kāmapi**) is the object of the experience of the highly poetical composition.

By that, in the cases where the suggested sense is (either) known with great difficulty (**atiguḍha vyaṅgya**) and is on par with expressed sense (**atisphuṭavyaṅgya**) (i. e., highly expressive) are exculded (from becoming super excellent grade poetry). In order to exculde the two also, (namely) the poetry where the suggested sense forms a part of (or becomes subordinate to) something else (i. e., another suggested sense), (**aparāṅgavyaṅgya**) and it becomes a part (complementary) for the expressed sense (**vācyasiddhyaṅgayvyaṅgya**), due to the presence of charmingness, the qualification, namely, 'becoming subordinate to its self', is given (stated), which is indicative of the supposing of suggested sense than its self (expressive sense; 'world' and 'sense').

RG. 11.1

उदाहरणम्-

"शयिता सविधेऽप्यनीश्वरा सफलीकर्तुमहो मनोरथान्।

दयिता दयिताननाम्बुजं दरमीलन्नयना निरीक्षते॥"

अत्रालम्बनस्य नायकस्य, सविधशयनाक्षिप्तस्य रहःस्थानादेरुद्दीपनस्य च विभावस्य, तादृशनिरीक्षणादेरनुभावस्य, त्रपौत्सुक्यादेश्च व्यभिचारिणः संयोगाद्रतिरभिव्यज्यते। आलम्बनादीनां स्वरूपं वक्ष्यते।

Trans.: For example;

'Though a woman, sleeping near her husband, unable to fultill (her) all desires, looking with eyes bit closed to her (husband's) lotus-face'.

Here, the (permanent mood) love is manifested / revealed due to the combination of the sustaintial mood as, the hero (husband), the enhancing mood as the lonely place and sleeping near the husband, the ensuant as, looking like that (eyes bit closed) and the transitory moods namely, the modesty and eagerness etc. The natures (definitions) of **ālambanavibhāva** etc., woule be told later on.

RG. 11.2

न च यद्ययं शयितः स्यात्तदास्याननाम्बुजं[१] चुम्बेयमिति नायिकेच्छाया एव व्यङ्ग्यत्वमत्रेति वाच्यम्। मनोरथान्सफलीकर्तुमसमर्थेत्यनेन

---

१. चौ, ओ, -आननम्

मनोरथाः सर्वेऽस्या हृदि तिष्ठन्तीति प्रतीतेः, स्वशब्देन मनोरथपदेन सामान्याकारेण तादृशेच्छाया अपि निवेदनात्।

Trans.: It cannot be urged thus; here the suggestiveness is in the desire of lady, namely, 'if he (husband) has slept then (I) may kiss his lotus-face. Because, there is the cognition that "all her dlsires are in her heart" by the expression namely, 'unable to fulfill her desires;' (and) also because (her) desires of that kind are expressed in general by its own expression (i. e. by) the word desire (मनोरथ).

RG. 11.3

न च मनोरथपदेन मनोरथत्वाकारेण सामान्येच्छाया अभिधानेऽपि चुम्बेयमिति विषयविशेषविशिष्टेच्छात्वेन व्यङ्ग्यत्वे किं बाधकमिति वाच्यम्। चमत्कारो न स्यादित्यस्यैव बाधकत्वात्। न हि विशेषाकारेण व्यङ्ग्योऽपि सामान्याकारेणाभिहितोऽर्थः सहृदयानां चमत्कृतिमुत्पादयितुमीष्टे। कथमपिवाच्यवृत्त्यनालिङ्गितस्यैव व्यङ्ग्यस्य चमत्कारित्वेनालङ्कारिकैः स्वीकारात्। चुम्बनेच्छाया रत्यनुभावतयैव सुन्दरत्वेन तदव्यञ्जने चुम्बामीति[१] शब्दबलाच्चुम्बनेच्छावदचमत्कारित्वाच्च।

Trans.: It should not be (further) urged like this: even though by the expression, 'desire' (**manoratha**), a desire in genereal, in the form of desireness is expressed, what difficulty (obstacle) is there in accepting a special or specific or qualified desireness, having its object namely (**cumbāmi**), (I would kiss) as being suggested. Because the difficulty would be that it will not generate any charmingness.

Not indeed is it desired that which becomes expressive in general even though is suggestive specially, is capable to generate charmingness in (the heart of) recipient reader; Because the rhetoricians accept that suggested sense as to be charming (containing charmingness) which is no means

१. चौ, ओ, -चुम्बेयम्

pressed (is related to) expressed sense. Further, since (the expression) the desire to kiss is pleasurable as the **anubhava** for (the permanent mood) Love, and in its suggestion from the strength of the expressive words, namely, 'I will kiss' lacks the charmingness like the desire to kiss.

RG. 11.4

एव त्रपाया अपि न प्राधान्येन व्यङ्ग्यत्वम्।

अनुवाद्यतावच्छेदकतया प्रतीतायां तस्यां मुख्यवाक्यार्थत्वायोगात्।

न च दरमीलन्नयनात्वविशिष्टनिरीक्षणं विधेयमिति नानुवाद्यतावच्छेदकत्वं तस्या इति वाच्यम्। एवमपि नयनगतदरमीलनस्य तत्कार्यत्वेऽपि दरमीलन्नयनात्वविशिष्ट निरीक्षणस्य रतिमात्रकार्यत्वात्।

त्रपाया एव मुख्यत्वेन व्यङ्ग्यत्वे निरीक्षणोक्तेरनतिप्रयोजनकत्वापत्तेः। वाच्यवृत्त्या रतेरनुभावे निरीक्षणे त्रपाया अनुभावस्य दरमीलनस्येव व्यंजनया तस्यां तस्या अपि गुणीभावप्रत्ययौचित्यात्।

Trans.: And, 'shyness' also is not primarily suggested here. Because it can not be treated as primary due to it being cognised as being the delimitor of the subjectness."

Objection: It may be argued : The glance qualified by "half-closed-eye-ness" is the predecative, description, hence, it can not be the delimitor of the subjectness "to be expressive-ness."

Answer: Not so. Even in that case, although half closeness of eyes is the effect of that, then glance qualified by the half closed eye is the effect of love in general. And if, the shyness is primarily suggested, then there would arise the contingency of the expression 'looking at being superfluous. As the expressed "half close-ness" made subordinate to the glancing, expressed, by denotation; like that, it is proper to understand the subordinateness of the suggested shyness in the love suggested by suggestion.

RG. 12

यथा वा-

"गुरुमध्यगता मया नताङ्गी निहता नीरजकोरकेण मन्दम्।
दरकुण्डलताण्डवं नतभ्रूलतिकं मामवलोक्य घूर्णितासीत्॥"

अत्र घूर्णितासीदित्यनेनासमीक्ष्यकारिन् किमिदमनुचितं कृतवान-सीत्यर्थसंवलितोऽमर्षश्चर्वणाविश्रान्तिधामत्वात् प्राधान्येन व्यज्यते। तत्र शब्दोऽर्थश्च गुणः।

Trans.: Or, for example:

'The lady, whose limbs were stopping, being gently struck by me, with the bud of a lotus, while she was in the midst of elders, become confused when she saw me with her ear rings slightly shaking and her creeper like eyebrows bent down.'

Here by (the expression), 'moved to otherside,' due to impatience (**amarṣa**) is primarily suggested, based on the sense, namely, 'Oh the ruthless doer, what improper (act) have you done!, due to it being the abode of enjoyment. There (in this verse) the word and the sense are subordinate (i. e. expressive).

RG. 13

यथा वा-

"तल्पगताऽपि च सुतनुःश्वासासङ्गं न या सेहे।
सम्प्रति सा हृदयगतं प्रियपाणिं मन्दमाक्षिपति॥"

इदं च पद्यं मन्निर्मितप्रबन्धगतत्वेन पूर्वसाकाङ्क्षमिति दिङ्मात्रेण व्याख्यायते-या नववधूः पल्यङ्कशयिता श्वासस्यासङ्गमात्रेणापि संकुचि-दङ्गलतिकाऽभूत् सा सम्प्रतिं प्रस्थानपूर्वरजन्यां प्रवत्स्यत्प्रतिका प्रियेण सशङ्केन समर्पितं हृदि पाणिं नववधू-जातिस्वाभाव्यादाक्षिपति, परंतु मन्दम्।

अत्रशनैः स्वस्थानप्रापणात्मना मन्दाक्षेपेण रत्याख्यःस्थायी संलक्ष्य-

क्रमतया व्यज्यते। उपपादयिष्यते च स्थाय्यादीनामपि संलक्ष्यक्रमव्यङ्ग्य-त्वम्। अमुमेवच प्रभेदं ध्वनिमामनन्ति।

Trans.: Or, for example,

'That, lady of beautiful limbs laying on her bed, was unable to bear the fellings of breath (of her husband) earlier, is now removing his (husband's) hand from her chest very slowly.'

Since, this verse occured (there) in another text, composed by me and having the necessity of earlier context, is being explained in brief:

The newly married woman, who moved her body due to the intolerance of (her husband's) breath, is now removing her beloved's hand, put on the chest of the lady, as a woman in the night before the departure day, as it is indicating the nature of newly married woman, but very slowly.

Here, by the 'slow removal of his hand', to place in its proper position, the permanent mood namely, love (**Rati**) is suggested, in a way where the sequence is noticed (संलक्ष्यक्रम).

The suggestiveness of the moods where the sequence is notice, will be shown in the case of other permanent mood etc,

This (super excellent grade) variety (of poetry), is called as ध्वनिकाव्य (suggestive poetry).

RG. 14

यत्तु चित्रमीमांसायामप्पय्यदीक्षितैः 'निश्शेषच्युत्तचंदनम्' इतिपद्यं-ध्वन्युदाहरणप्रसङ्गे व्याख्यातम्-उत्तरीयकर्षणेन चन्दनच्युतिरित्यन्य-थासिद्धिपरिहाराय निःशेषग्रहणम्।ततश्चन्दनच्युतेः स्नानसाधारण्यव्या-वर्तनेन संभोगचिन्होद्घाटनाय तटग्रहणम्। स्नाने हि सर्वत्रचन्दनच्युतिः स्यात्, तव तु स्तनयोस्तट उपरिभागे एव दृश्यते। इयमाश्लेषकृतैव[१]।

१. म.-कृतैवा.

Trans.: Whatever is discussed on the context of the example of **Dhvani,** namely, the verse '**Nissesacyuta**.....etc.' (the removal of Sandalpaste without any remnants), in **CM** by **AD** (is as follows):

(The word) 'without any remnants' is taken to avoid the fault of अन्यथासिद्ध (explaining otherwise), namely, the removal is caused due to the pulling away the upper garments.

Further, a part (a side of the breast) is taken to express (reveal) the signs of love. In the case of bath indeed, there would be the falling of sandalpaste (i. e. from all parts of the breast) entirely; but in your case that is seen (i. e., the falling of the sandalpaste) only on the upper part of your breast, by excluding the bath in general as (the cause of) the removal of sandal paste.

(Thus), this (falling of sandalpaste) is only due to embarassing (at the time of **Saṁbhoga**)

RG. 14.1

तथा निर्मृष्टरागोऽधर इत्यत्र ताम्बूलग्रहणबिलम्बात्प्राचीनरागस्य किञ्चिन्मृष्टतेत्यन्यथासिद्धिपरिहाराय निर्मृष्टराग इति रागस्य निश्शेषमृष्टतोक्ता। पुनःस्नानसाधारण्यव्यावर्तनेन संभोगचिन्होद्घाटनायाधर इति विशिष्य ग्रहणम्। उत्तरोष्ठे सरागेऽधरोष्ठमात्रस्य निर्मृष्टरागता चुम्बन कृतैव,' इत्यादिना, 'इदमपि ध्वनेरुदाहरणम्' 'इत्यन्तेन संदर्भेण तटादिघटिता वाक्यार्थाः स्नानव्यावृतिद्वारा संभोगाङ्गनामाश्लेष चुम्बनादीनां प्रतिपादनेन प्रधानव्यंग्यव्यञ्जने सहायकमाचरन्ति' इति, तदेतदलङ्कारशास्त्रतत्वानवबोधनिबन्धनम्। प्राचीनसकलग्रन्थविरुद्धत्वादुपपत्तिविरोधाच्च।

Trans.: Further, in the case of the expression, namely, the reddish colour of the lips are completely faded away, in order to avoid the fault of अन्यथासिद्ध, that 'due to taking betel for long time before' (or not taking of betel), the earlier reddish colour (in the lips) is bit faded away; it is faded away completely, is stated.

Again, specially the 'lips' is mentioned in order to reveal/ suggest the marks of (signs of) love making by excluding the bath etc., in general.

The state of being faded away of the reddish colour in the lower lip alone, the upper lip being redish, is caused by kissing; By this etc., (and) the sense of the expression तट etc., by expressing, the aids of love like embrassing, kissing etc., become helpful in suggesting the primary suggested sense (love) due to the exclusion of 'bath'; the view namely, this also (**niśśeṣa...**) form an example of suggestiveness is based on the ignorance of the intricacies of the aesthetic science. Because this goes against the view of the all earlier texts; and also it is against justification.

RG. 14.2

तथाहि-पञ्चमोल्लासशेषे 'निश्शेषेत्यादौ गमकतया यानि चन्दनच्यवनादीन्युपात्तानि तानि कारणान्तरतोऽपि भवन्ति, यतश्चात्रैव स्नानकार्यत्वेनोपात्तानीति नोपभोग एव प्रतिबद्धानीत्यनैवकान्तिकानि,' इतिकाव्यप्रकाशकृतोक्तम्। तथा तत्रैव तेन-"भम धम्मिअ वीसत्थो स सुणओ अज्ज मालिदो तेण। गोलाणईकच्छकुडङ्गवासिणा दरिअ-सीहेण॥" इत्यादौ लिङ्गजलिङ्गिज्ञानरूपेणानुमानेन व्यक्ति गतार्थयतो व्यक्तिविवेककृतो मतं प्रत्याचक्षाणेन व्यभिचारित्वेनासिद्धत्वेन च संदिह्यमानादपि लिङ्गाद् व्यञ्जनमभ्युपगतम्।

इत्थमेव च ध्वनिकृताऽपि प्रथमोद्द्योते।

Trans.: To explain the same : Such is the statement of the author of **KP** at the end of the fifth chapter, namely, whatever like the removal of sandalpaste and the like, are taken as the marks (of love) in the case of (the expression), 'without any remnant etc.', those are also possible (to happen) by some other causes; In fact here (in the present case) (those), the removal of sandalpaste and the like, have been described as the effect of bath, and not (definitely) associated with love-enjoyment; hence these (probans) are deserepant.

Further, in the same work he has accepted suggestiveness from the probans though doubtful, due to its being व्यभिचारी (erroneous) and असिद्ध (unproved), by refuting the view that the suggestive sense is obtained by the inference in the form of the knowledge of the probandum generating from the probans in case (of the example), namely,

'O pious man, roam about freely; that dog has been killed today by that fierce lion living in the marshy dells of the Godavari', of the author of **VV**.

And the same also is the view of the expounder of **Dhvani** theory in the first Chapter (of **DA**).

RG. 14.3

एवं च व्यञ्जकानां साधारण्यं प्रतिपादयतां प्रामाणिकानां ग्रन्थैः सहासाधारण्यं प्रतिपादयतस्तव ग्रन्थस्य विरोधःस्फुटः। किं च यदिदं निश्शेषेत्याद्यवान्तरवाक्यार्थानां वापीस्नानव्यावृत्तिद्वारेण व्यङ्ग्यासाधारण्यं संपाद्यते तत्किमर्थमिति पृच्छामः। व्यङ्ग्यस्य व्यञ्जनार्थमिति चेन्न, व्यञ्जकगतासाधारण्यस्य व्यञ्जनानुपायत्वात्।

"औणिद्दं दोब्बल्लं चिन्ता अलसन्तणं सणीससिअम्। महमन्दभाअणीए केरं सहि तुह वि परभवइ॥"

इत्यादौ साधारणानामेवान्निद्र्यादीनां वक्त्रादिवैशिष्ट्यवशादर्थविशेषव्यञ्जकताया अभ्युपगतेः। प्रत्युतासाधारण्यस्यव्याप्त्यपरपर्यायस्यानुमानानुकूलतया व्यक्तिप्रतिकूलत्वाच्च।

Trans.: And thus (in the manner indicated above), the opposition of your text justifying the speciality (uniqueness) of suggestiveness with the texts of those justifying the gererality (of those).

And again, we ask thus: What is the purpose in accepting the uniqueness of suggested sense (love) by excluding the other remaining senses like bathing in the pond in the case of (the expression) 'without any remnants' etc.

If it is answered, namely, to reveal suggested sense, (the uniqueness of the suggested sense is accepted) there we answer:

Not so. Because, the uniqueness of the suggestiveness cannot be the cause (**upāya**) for the expressed sense (love).

Because, the specific-suggestiveness (love making) is attained on the basis of the specific condition of face etc., of the (expression) sleeplessness etc., being in general sense, in case of the verse namely,

"Sleeplessness, weakness, anxiety, idleness and heavy/ long sighs etc., torments you too, because of my unfortunate self, oh (my dear) friend!"

And because, the uniqueness of suggestive sense is favourable (conducive) to inference (of love making) being another synonym of invariable concomitance, and contrary to the emergence of the suggestion (suggestive sense).

RG. 15

अथ तटादिघटितत्वेऽपि न निश्शेषेत्यादिवाक्यार्थानामसाधारण्यम्।

सलिलार्द्रवसनकरणकप्रोञ्छनादिनाऽपि तत्संभवादिति चेत्तर्हि वापीस्नानव्यावर्तनेन कः पुरुषार्थ? एकत्रानैकान्तिकत्वस्येव बहुष्यनैकान्तिकताया अपि जाताया[१] अनुमितिप्रतिकूलत्वाद् व्यक्त्यप्रतिकूलत्वाच्च।

Trans.: Objection: It may be urged further: There is no uniqueness in the sense of the expression, nisshesh etc. though (the sandalpaste is) removed from one side (or the breast).

१. ज्ञाताया in all editions

Because, that (removed from a part/ side) is possible due to the wiping away off by water-wet-germent.

Answer: what is the ultimate gain by excluding, 'bath in the pond,' then it is contrary to inference and also because it is favourable for suggestive sense, for the knower. Because, alike where there is uncertainty (having many purposes) in one case, there is uncertainty in many cases as well.

RG. 15.1

अपि चात्र हि तदन्तिकमेव रन्तुं गतासीति व्यङ्ग्यशरीरे तदन्तिकगमनं रमणरूपफलांशश्चेति द्वयं घटकम्। तत्र तावत्तदन्तिकं गतासीत्यंशस्य त्वन्मते व्यङ्ग्यत्वं दुरुपपादम्। त्वदुक्तरीत्या विशेषणवाक्यार्थानां निश्शेषेति प्रतिपाद्यानां वाच्यार्थे वापीस्नाने बाधितत्वाद्वाच्यकक्षागतप्रधानवाक्यार्थीभूतविधिनिषेधप्रतिपादकाभ्यां गता न गतेति शब्दाभ्यां विरोधिलक्षणया निषेधस्य विधेश्च प्रतीतेरुपपत्तेः।

नहि मुख्यार्थबाधेनोन्मीलितेऽर्थे व्यक्तिवेद्यतोचिता। यथा 'अहो पूर्णं सरो यत्र लुठन्तःस्नान्ति मानवाः' इत्यत्र कर्तृविशेषणानुपपत्त्यधीनोल्लासे पूर्णत्वाभावे।

Trans.: And again here, in the form of the suggested sense, namely, you had gone to him for enjoyment only, too (facts) are suggested, viz, 'going to him,' and 'enjoyment' as its result. Here however, following your view, the suggestiveness of the part namely, 'going to him' (You had gone to him) is kept away (cannot be obtained).

Since, following your explaination, the Qualified/ special senses of the expression (lit. sentences) expressed "निःश्शेषः" (without any remnant etc.), is contradicted in the case of the primary senses, namely, 'bathing in the pond,' the assertion (of going) of prohibition is understood by the help of opposite-indication from the expression that expresses 'assertion' and 'prohibition' namely, (you had) 'gone,' 'not gone' [from a part of] included in primary sense of the sentence being expressive.

Not indeed, it is proper to accept the expressed sense of suggestion, (suggestiveness) in case of the sense expressed by the opposition of the primary sense.

As for example, here in the verse namely, 'the pond is full (with water) where people are bathing being rolled on,' the absence of fullness (of water) is indicated (and not suggested) due to the unsuitability of the qualification/ objective, (being rolled on) of the subject (with fullness of water).

RG. 15.2

अथ तदन्तिकगमनस्य लक्षणावेद्यत्वेपि रमणस्य फलांशस्य लक्ष्यशक्तिमूलध्वननवेद्यत्वमव्याहतमेवेति चेत्, 'अधमत्वमप्रकृष्टत्वं, तच्च जात्या कर्मणा वा भवति। तत्र जात्यापकर्षं नोत्तमनायिका नायकस्य, वक्ति,[१]' इत्यादिना सन्दर्भेणभवतैव तस्यापि[२] अर्थापत्ति वेद्यतायाः स्फुटं वचनात्।

अन्यलभ्यस्य[३] च शब्दार्थताया अस्वीकृतेः।

Trans.: Objection : Well, it cannot be urged that even though 'going to him' is understood by indicative power, yet the suggestiveness (the state of being suggested) depending on the indicative power, (of the suggested sense) namely, 'Love-enjoyment' as a part is not affected.

Answer: Because, 'being revealed by presumption' (of the Love-enjoyment) is clearly stated by you, in the context, namely, the wretchedness, (अधमत्व) is improperness, and that is attributed to ones birth or action. (Out of these two)

१. चौ, वदति

२. गंगा–भवतैवार्थान्निवेद्यताया, तस्यापि is missing in all other editions.

३. चौ, ओ, –अनन्यलभ्यस्य

There a noble lady (heroine) do not speak ill of the hero related to (his) birth. (And) because what (sense) is obtained by something else (other than अभिधा, लक्षणा, व्यंजना) (here presumption) cannot be accepted as conveyed by being state of 'Sound' and 'Sense' (i. e. other indicative or suggestive).

RG. 15.3

अन्यच्च[१] यथाकथञ्चिदङ्गीकुरु वात्र व्यञ्जन व्यापारं तथापि न तवेष्टसिद्धिः। वाच्यानां निश्शेषच्युतचन्दनस्तनतटत्वादीनामधमत्वस्य च त्वदुक्तरीत्या प्रकारान्तरेणानुपपद्यमानतया दूतीसंभोगमात्रनिष्पाद्यत्वेन गुणीभूतव्यङ्गत्वप्रसङ्गात्।

एवं च उपपत्तिविरोधोऽपि स्फुटतर एव।

तस्माद्वाच्यार्थसाधारण्यमेवोचितमतिविदग्धनायिकानिरूपितानां विशेषणवाक्यार्थानाम्।

Trans.: Objection: And further the suggestiveness may be accepted some how.

Answer : Still then, it will not establish your point; because, since the expressive sense like 'the removal of the sandalpaste from the part (side) of the breasts without any remnant etc., and wretchedness etc.,' cannot be explained by any other way, following your view, it would amount to accept it as subordinate suggested sense, due to being effected by the 'love-enjoyment' with the suggested sense.

And like that the opposition with the justification is more visible. Therefore, it would be proper to accept that the specific expression, told by the cvilised maid to be common to expression.

RG. 15.4

तथा हि 'अयिबान्धवजनस्याज्ञातपीडागमे, स्वार्थपरायणे,

---

१. चौ., अपि च

स्नानकालातिक्रमभयवशेन नदीमदीयप्रिययोरन्तिकमगत्वैव वापीं स्नातुमितो ममान्तिकाद्[१] गतासि न पुनस्तस्य परवेदनानभिज्ञतया दुःखदातृत्वेनाधमस्यान्तिकम्। यतो निश्शेषेच्युतचन्दनं स्तनयोस्तटमेव नोरःस्थलम्। वापीगतबहुलयुवजनत्रपापारवश्यादंशंद्वयलग्नाग्रस्वस्तिकीकृतभुजलतायुगलेन तटस्यैवोन्नतया मुहुरामर्षात्[२]। एवं त्वरया सम्यगक्षालनेनोत्तरोष्ठे न निर्मृष्टरागोऽधरस्तु तदपेक्षया गण्डूषजलरदनशोधनाङ्गुल्यादीनामधिकसंमर्दमावहतीति[३] तथा।

किं च सम्यगक्षालनेन नेत्रे जलमात्रसंसर्गाद् दूरमुपरिभाग एवानञ्जने।

शीतवशात्तानवाच्च तव तनुः पुलकितेति। एवं तस्या विदग्धायाः गूढतात्पर्यैवोक्तिरूचिता, अन्यथा वैदग्ध्यभङ्गापत्तेः।

Trans.: The same is explained as follows: "Oh, unknower of the agony of (your) friend, selfish one! on the pretext of being late for bath, not going to the far away river, and to my beloved, you had gone from me to the pond for a bath, but not to that wretched, who gives sorrow and is unable to know the difficulties of other(s).

Because of the repeated rubbing of the side (of the breasts), being raised high, by the end of the creeper like hands forming the design of a **svastika**, touching both the shoulders, due to shyness, caused by the presence of many youths in the pond, the falling of the sandalpaste is (seen) from the part of the breasts (and) not from the (entire) chest.

Further, like that, the redish colour (राग) of the upper lip is not gone (washed off) due to not being properly washed in a haste; how ever, the lower lip looks (darker) than that (upper lip) due to fast movement of fingers for clearing up the teeth, with mouthful of water.

---

१. चौ, - मदन्तिकात्

२. ओ. आमर्शनात्. आमर्शात्-In all other editions

३. म. आहवति

(Further) what more, the existance of collyrium is on the upper sides (of eyes) because of the touch of water in eyes by not washing properly. The horripulation (seen) in your body is because of thinness (of your body) and because of coldness. Like this, the expression with concealed (highly)-desired-sense is proper in case of a cultured lady. Otherwise, there would amount to absence (lit. break of) cleaverness (in her).

RG. 16

एवं साधारणेष्वेषु वाक्यार्थेषु मुख्यार्थे बाधाभावात्तात्पर्यार्थस्य झटित्या (ना?) कलनात्[१] कुतोऽत्र लक्षणावकाशोऽनन्तरं च वाच्यार्थ-प्रतिपत्तेर्वक्तृबोद्धव्यनायकादीनां वैशिष्ट्यस्य प्रतीतौ सत्यामधमपदेन स्वप्रवृत्तिप्रयोजको दुःखदातृत्वरूपो धर्मःसाधारणात्मा वाच्यार्थदशायाम-पराधान्तरनिमित्तकदुःखदातृत्वरूपेण स्थितो व्यञ्जनाव्यापारेण दूतीसंभोग-निमित्तकदुःखदातृत्वाकारेण पर्यवस्यतीत्यालङ्कारिकसिद्धान्तनिष्कर्षः।

Trans.: Like this, since the sense of the expression is made general (i. e., either love-enjoyment or bath as the cause of the removal of sandalpaste etc.), and since there is no मुख्यार्थवाध (difficulty in explaining the primary (or direct meaning) and since the desired meaning is understood easily, there is no scope for the employment of indication. After understanding the primary sense, when the sense is understood from the peculiarity (of expression, condition etc.) of the cultured heroine (lady), the **duti** and the hero by the word अधम, the sense of the state of 'being the giver of sorrow,' the reason of the employment of it (**स्व=अधम**) is understood as the state of 'being the giver of sorrow' (to the heroine) as due to some other bad deeds, as the state of primary sense, becomes the state of 'being the giver of sorrow', due to love-enjoyment with the female-messenger.

---

१. झटित्यनाकलनात् in all other editions.

This is the conclusive view of the rhetoricians (on this point).

RG. 16.1

एतेन 'अधमत्वमपकृष्टत्वं तच्च जात्या कर्मणा वा भवति।

तत्र जात्यापकर्षं नोत्तमनायिका नायकस्य वक्ति।

नापि स्वापराधपर्यवसायिदूतीसंभोगादिहीनकर्मा[१]तिरिक्तेन कर्मणा।

Trans.: By this, what ever is told namely, 'the wretchedness is the inferiority (improperness) and that is attributed to ones birth or action; Here, the noble heroine would not (do not) speak ill of the hero, as of inferior (improper), by birth. Not also by any action other than the bad-deeds like the love-enjoyment with the female-messenger, forming one's own fault; is also refuted.

RG. 16.2

'तादृशं च दूती संप्रेषणात्प्राचीनं सोढमेवेति नोद्धाटनार्हमितीतरव्यावृत्त्या संभोगरूपमेव पर्यवस्यति' इति यदुक्तम्, तदपि निरस्तम्। विदग्धोत्तमनायिकायाः सखीसमक्षं तदुपभोगरूपस्य स्वनायकापराधस्य स्फुटं प्रकाशयितुमतितमामनौचित्येन प्राचीनानामेव सोढानामप्यपराधानामसह्यतया दूतीं प्रति प्रतिपिपादयिषितत्वादिति दिक्।

Trans.: And what ever is told, namely, it amounts to love-enjoyment by excluding other possibilities and also suggested that earlier sending the maid to the heroine had tolerated some faults (of the lover) (for which the would call him अधम) stands refuted. Because of the impropriety of speaking openly the fault of her lover caused by the love-enjoyment with her lover (in front of) her own friend and (due to the) not able to tolerate the earlier faults committed (by him), this expression (i. e. अधम) to the maid, is justified.

---

१. चौ., –word is missing.

RG. 17

यत्र व्यङ्ग्यमप्रधानमेव सच्चमत्कारकारणं तद् द्वितीयम्॥

वाच्यापेक्षया प्रधानीभूतं व्यङ्ग्यान्तरमादाय गुणीभूतं व्यङ्ग्यमादायातिव्याप्तिवारणायावधारणम्। तेन तस्य ध्वनित्वमेव। लीनव्यङ्ग्यवाच्यचित्रातिप्रसङ्गवारणाय चमत्कारेत्यादि।

Trans.: That is the second (variety of poetry viz., excellent grade), where the suggested sense being subordinate, generates (lit.causes) charmingness.

In order to exclude the fault of over application (in the definition of **Uttamakavya**) in case of a suggested sense which is made superior with regard to the expressed sense, and is sub-ordinate with regard to another suggested sense, it (the definition) is restricted (by the expression 'that alone,' '**apradhānameva**'). Therefore, that has suggestiveness. The expression (namely) charmingness etc., are given in order to exclude the cases where the suggested sense is not distinct (i. e., not clearly noticed), and where the expressed sense is the source of charmingness (viz., figurative poetry based on sense).

RG. 17.1

यत्तु 'अतादृशि गुणीभूतव्यङ्ग्यम्' इत्यादिकाव्यप्रकाशगतलक्षणे 'चित्रान्यत्वं' टीकाकारैर्दत्तम्, तन्न। पर्यायोक्तसमासोक्त्यादिप्रधानकाव्येष्वव्याप्त्यापत्तेः। तेषां गुणीभूतव्यङ्गतायाश्चित्रतायाश्च सर्वालङ्कारिकसंमतत्वात्।

Trans.: As is given by the commentators namely, 'other than the figurative poetry' in the difinition (of second variety of poetry) of **KP**, viz., the suggested sense is subordinate to, unlike that etc., is not correct.

Because, there would arise the contingency of under application in cases of poetries having the figures like **paryāyokta** and **samāsokta** etc.

Because, all the rhetoricians are unanimously accepting those (poetries) as '**guṇibhūtavyaṅgya**'and '**citra**'poetries.

RG. 17.2.

उदाहरणम्-

"राघवविरहज्वालासंतापितसह्यशैलशिखरेषु।

शिशिरे सुखं शयानाः कपयः कुप्यन्ति पवनतनयाय॥"

अत्र जानकीकुशलावेदनेन राघवः शिशिरीकृत इतिव्यङ्ग्यमाकस्मिककपिकर्तृकहनूमद्द्वेषयककोपोपपादकतया गुणीभूतमपि दुर्दैववशतो दास्यमनुभवद्राजकलत्रमिव कामपि कमनीयतामावहति।

Trans.: For example; The monkeys get angry with the son of wind-god after having a peaceful sleep (lit. when they are sleeping peacefully) in the cold-autumn on the summits of the '**sahya**' mountain, which was made warm by the flames of the fire in the form of separation of Rāma (from, **Janaki**).'

Here the suggested sense namely, **Rāghava (Rāma)** was passified down by the hearing the well being of **Janaki,** even though subordinate, due to the generation of accidental anger of the monkeys, being the agents for Hanuman, expresses some unique charmingness like the queen who is made a maid by misfortune.

RG. 17.3

नन्वेवं प्रागुक्तमाक्षेपगतं मान्द्यमपि नववधूप्रकृतिविरोधादनुपपद्यमानं व्यङ्ग्येनैवो पपाद्यत इति कथमुत्तमता[१] तस्य काव्यस्येति चेत्, न। यतो ह्यनुदिनसख्युपदेशादिभिरनतिचमत्कारिभिरप्युपपद्यमानं मान्द्यमिदं प्रथमचित्तचुम्बिनीं विप्रलम्भरतिमप्रकाशयन्न प्रभवति स्वातन्त्र्येणपरनिर्वृतिचर्वणागोचरतामाधातुम्।

Trans.: Objection: Well, if this is true, how to account for the super excellentness of that poetry (which is quoted as

१. उत्तमोत्तमता

an example of the super excellent poetry) since, the slowness in the case of removal (of hands), already mentioned, which is not justificable due to its opposition to the nature of a newly married lady, also is justified by suggestion.

Anṣwer : Not so; Because (in the example **'talpa-gatāpi...'** about which the doubt is raised) this slowness (of removing hand) may be due to the repeated advices of the friends (towards her) etc., devoid of charmingness, without expressing the love-in-separation, touching the heart at first, can not generate enjoyment of extraordinary pleasure independently.

RG. 17.4.

इत्थमेव निःशेषच्युतचन्दनमित्यादिपद्येष्वधमत्वादीनि वाच्यानि व्यङ्ग्यातिरिक्तेनार्थेनापाततो निष्पन्नशरीराणि व्यञ्जकानीति न तत्रापि गुणीभावः शङ्कनीय। अनयोर्भेदयोरनपह्नवनीयचमत्कारयोरपि प्रधान्याप्राधान्याभ्यामस्ति कश्चित्सहृदयवेद्यो विशेषः।

Trans.: Like this, in the verse **'nissesacyuta'** etc., the expressed sense of werchedness' can be obtained by some sense, other than the suggested one (i. e., enjoyment of love making) thus, even though the subordinateness (of suggested sense) cannot be doubted. Because, there exist some unique speciality (of charmingness) enjoyable by perceptive (refined) critique (alone) between the primary-ness and secondaryness of these two varieties of poetry (where the charmingness is not concealed).

RG. 17.5.

**यत्तु चित्रमीमांसाकृतोक्तम्..."प्रहरविरतौमध्ये वाह्नस्ततोऽपि परेण वा, किमुत सकले याते वाह्नि प्रिय त्वमिहैष्यसि।
इति दिनशतप्राप्यं देशं प्रियस्य यियासतो,
हरति गमनं बालालापैः सबाष्पगलज्जलैः॥"**

इत्यत्र सकलमहः परमावधिस्ततः परं प्राणान्धारयितुं न शक्नोमीति व्यङ्ग्यं प्रियगमननिवारणरूपवाच्यसिद्ध्यङ्गमतो गुणीभूतव्यङ्ग्यम् इति।

Trans.: Objection: Thus, argued (by) the author of **CM** here in the example- "would you my Lord! Come back to me (lit. to this place) at the end of a **'prahara'** or at middle of the day, or even later than that, or at the end of the day (i. e., sun set) with such child-like utterances with supressed and shedding tears, a lady prevents her husband from his journey to a place reachable in a hundred day, " 'the entire day' (the end of the day i. e. evening) is the latest time (for the beloved to come back), later than this ('I') cannot live (lit. bear my life) is the suggested sense whivh justifies the expressed sense in the form of preventation of the lover from going abroad, hence is (a case of) subordinate suggested sense.

RG. 17.5.1

तन्न। बाष्पगलज्ज[१]लानां प्रहरविरतावित्याद्यालापानामेव प्रियगमननिवारणरूपवाच्यासिद्ध्यङ्गतया व्यङ्ग्यस्य गुणीभावाभावात्।

आलापैरिति तृतीयया प्रकृत्यर्थस्य हरणक्रियाकरणतायाः स्फुटं प्रतिपत्तेः।

Trans.: Answer : That is not true. Because, there is the absence of subordinateness of the suggested sense due to the justification of the expressed sense in the form of 'the preventation of the lover from going abroad,' from the expressed sense of the expression like, (would you) not come back at the end of the day, while shedding tears (profusingly). And because the instrumentality of the words namely (**ālāpaih**) by the expresseion etc.,' of the verb 'preventation from going,' is clear due to the usage in instrumental case ending.

---

१. सबाष्पगलज्ज. in all other editions

RG. 17.6

न च व्यङ्ग्यस्यापि वाच्यसिद्ध्यङ्गतात्र संभवतीति तथोक्तमिति वाच्यम्। निःशेषच्युतचन्दनमित्यादाविवाधमत्वरूपवाच्यसिद्ध्यङ्गताया दूतीसंभोगादौ संभवाद गुणीभावापत्तेः।

Trans.: Objection: It may be contended further: The expressed sense, 'preventation from going' is expressed by the suggested sense, (I would die if you do not come back before the day-end).

Answer: it cannot be argued like that. Because, there would arise the contingency of subordinatensess in case of '**nissesacyuta**'......etc., due to the possibility of the expression of expressed senses, 'the wretchedness', from the suggested sense in the form of the love-enjoyment with the maid-messenger.

RG. 17.7

अस्तु वा ततः परं प्राणान्धारयितुं न शक्नोमीति व्यङ्ग्यस्य वाच्यसिद्ध्यङ्गतया गुणीभावस्तथापि नायकादेर्विभावस्य वाष्पादेरनुभावस्य चित्तावेगादेश्च संचारिणःसंयोगादभिव्यज्यमानेन विप्रलम्भेन ध्वनित्वं को निवारयेत्।

Trans.: Or let the suggested sense namely (I will) die after that (day-end), be subordinate due to its expression of the expressed sense (the preventation from going); still what will prevent this from being the suggested sense of this 'love in separation revealed from the combination of the excitant, the hero etc., the ensuant, the shedding tear etc., and the transitory mood, the mental anxiety etc.

RG. 18.

यत्र व्यङ्ग्यचमत्कारासमानाधिकरणो वाच्यचमत्कारस्तत् तृतीयम्॥

यथा यमुनावर्णने "तनयमैनाकगवेषणलम्बीकृतजलधिजठरप्रविष्ट-हिमगिरिभुजायमानाया भगवत्या भागीरथ्याः सखी" इति। अत्रोत्प्रेक्षा

वाच्यैव चमत्कृतिहेतुः। श्वैत्यपातालतलचुम्बित्वादीनां चमत्कारो लेशतया सन्नप्युत्प्रेक्षा-चसत्कृतिजठरनिलीनो नागरिकेतरनायिकाकल्पितकाश्मीर-द्रवाङ्ग- रागनिगीर्णा निजाङ्गगौरिमेव प्रतीयते। न तादृशोऽस्ति कोऽपि वाच्यार्थो यो मनागनामृष्टप्रतीयमान एव स्वतो रमणीयतामाधातुं प्रभवति। अनयोरेव द्वितीयतृतीयभेदयोर्जागरूकाजागरूकगुणीभूतव्यङ्ग्योःप्रविष्टं निङिलमलङ्कारप्रधानं काव्यम्।

Trans.: That is the third variety of poetry where the charmingness of expressed sense and the charmingness of suggested sense do not occur in the same locus (simultaneously).

For example in the description of **Yamunā** (river) namely "(This is) the friend of golden **Bhāgirathi (Gaṅgā)** looks as if the hands of **Himalaya** (mountain) being strectched long, entered the middle of the ocean to find out (her) son **Maināka.**" Here (in the example) the fancy (**utprekṣā**) presented by the expressed sense is the cause of the charmingness.

Due to the insignificance of charmingness in case of (the suggested sense) like 'coolness', 'touching the netherland' etc; it is merged with the charmingness of the expressed sense of fancy like the charming of a village girl (non-urban lady) which is made colourless (charmless) due to application of some **aṅgarāga** (ointments) in her body.

Further, there is no case of expressed sense that is capable of generating charmingness by itself without touching (i. e. without being related to) the suggested sense a little. And the entire poetries based on a figure (i. e. figurative poetries) are included in these two, the second and third varieties, where the suggested sense is (the cause of) charmingness and not (the cause of) charmingness.

Notes : After the explanation of first two types of poetries now **PR** explains the third one. All the poetries with figures of speech like utprekṣā, etc. come under this group. In this context **PR** writes that even in such alaṁkāras there would be some **vyangya** though negligible and only its presence makes the vācya charming.

To clarify his own view, **PR** states one prose expression from his work, YVC. In this example, the utprekṣā, presented by the 'vācyārtha' is the main cause of the charmingness.

RG. 19

यत्रार्थ चमत्कृत्युपस्कृता शब्दचमत्कृतिःप्रधानं तदधमं चतुर्थम्॥

यथा- "मित्रात्रिपुत्रनेत्राय त्रयीशात्रवशत्रवे।
गोत्रारिगोत्रजत्राय गोत्रात्रे ते नमो नमः॥ इति"
अत्रार्थचमत्कृतिःशब्दचमत्कृतौ लीना।

Trans.: That is the fourth, the **adhama** variety of poetry, where the charmingness of words is predominant than the charmingness of sense. For example:

"I pray to him whose eyes (**netra**) are sun (**mitra**) and moon (**atri-putra**), who is the enemy of the demons of (three Vedas) **trayi,** who is born in the family (**gotra**) of the enemy (**ari**) of the mountains (**gotraḥ**) and the protector of world/cows." Here, the 'charmingness of sense' is merged (is made insignigicant) in the 'charmingness of word'.

Notes : Now, **PR** defines the fourth type of poetry *i.e.* 'adhama kāvya'. Here the charmingness of word is primarily realised and it is more dominant than the charmingness of sense. To prove this predominance of word over sense, **PR** gives a beautiful example where the entire sense or the charmingness or sense is fully merged in the charmingness of word, Further, it is a case of alliteration, which is grouped under **sabdā laṁkāram.**

RG. 19.1.

यद्यपि "यत्रार्थ चमत्कृतिसामान्यशून्या शब्दचमत्कृतिः तत्पञ्च-ममधमाधममपि काव्यविधासु गणचितुमुचितम्।" यथैकाक्षरपद्यर्धावृत्ति-यमकपद्मबन्धादि। तथापि रमणीयार्थप्रतिपादकशब्दतारूपकाव्य-सामान्यलक्षणानाक्रान्ततया वस्तुतः काव्यत्वाभावेन, महाकविभिः प्राचीनपरम्परामनुरुन्धानैस्तत्र तत्र काव्येषु निबद्धमपि नास्माभिर्गणितम्, वस्तुस्थितेरेवानुरोध्यत्वात्।

Trans.: Objection: [Even though] (it may be argued) in the case like the poetry having a single syllable (एकाक्षरपद्य), **Yamaka** where the repetition is in the figuratives like lotus flower etc., it is proper to accept (lit.count) that as '**adhamādhama**,' as the fifth one in the classification of poetry, where the charmingness of word devoid of charmingness of sense is there.

Answer : These (cases of poetries) are not inclusive of the difinition of poetry in general in the form of the poetry the word (s) which raises the charming sense (s) to comprehension due to the lack of poetryness, (in reality) we have not accepted those, on the basis of the facts, though following the ancient traditions, the great poets have composed (placed) in their respective poetries.

RG. 20.

केचिदिमानपि चतुरो भेदानगणयन्त उत्तममध्यमाधमभावेन त्रिविधमेव काव्यमाचक्षते। तत्रार्थचित्रशब्दचित्रयोरविशेषेणाधमत्वमयुक्तं वक्तुम्। तारतम्यस्य स्फुटमुपलब्धेः। को ह्येवं सहृदयं सन् 'विनिर्गतं मानदमात्ममन्दिरात,' 'सच्छिन्नमूलः क्षतजेन रेणु' इत्यादिभिः काव्यैः 'स्वच्छन्दोच्छलद' इत्यादीनां पामरश्लाध्यानामविशेषं ब्रूयात्। सत्यपि तारतम्ये यद्येकभेदत्वं कस्तर्हि ध्वनिगुणीभूतव्यङ्ग्ययोरीषदन्तरयो-र्विभिन्नभेदत्वे दुराग्रहः।

Trans.: Some accept (and argue for) three varieties of poetry in the form of **uttama, madhyama** and **adhama,** without accepting/discarding these four types.

It is not proper to accept (to say) **adhamatva** in the case of (both) the "figurative poetry based on sense" (**arthacitra**) and "the figurative poetry based on word" (**śabdacitra**) on the basis of the similarity. Because the difference is distinctly noticed.

Who indeed (there) being a refined critic would not differntiate (speak of the difference) between 'विनिर्गत,' etc., 'सच्छिन्नमूल' etc., and 'स्वच्छन्द' etc., befitting a layman. Inspite of the difference, (both are) one variety is accepted then, who would like to accept the distinction from **dhvani** and **gunibhutavyangya** having little bit difference.

Notes : Mammata proposed three varieties of poetry. PR strongly declares that due to the clear distinction between the 'sabdacitra' and 'arthacitra', it is essential to accept one more variety. The three examples shown in the text, are given here in full.

(a) *vinirgataṁ mānadamātmamandirād/ bhavatyupasrua yadṛcchyāpi yaṁ/ saṁsabhramendradrutapātitargalā/ nimīlitākṣīva bhiyāmarāvatī."* (KP)

(b) *"sa cchinnamūlaḥ kṣatajena reṇuḥ/ tasyopariṣṭapavan-āvadhutaḥ aṅgāraseṣasya hutāsnasya/ pūrvotthito dhūma ivāvabhāse."* (KP)

(c) *"svacchandocchaladacchakahakuharacchātetarāṁbha-schaṭā/*

mūrcchanmoamaharṣiharṣa vhitasnānāhnikāhnāya vaḥ/ bhindyādudyadāradarduradarī dairghyādaridradruma/ drohodrekamayormīmeduramadā mandākinī manda-tām. (KP)

RG. 21.

यत्र च शब्दार्थचमत्कृत्योरैकाधिकरण्यं तत्र तयोर्गुणप्रधानभावं पर्यालोच्य यथालक्षणं व्यवहर्तव्यम्। समप्रधान्ये तु मध्यमतैव।

यथा-

"उल्लासःफुल्लपङ्करुहपटलपतन्मत्तपुष्पन्धयानां,निस्तारः
शोकदावानलविकलहृदां कोकसीमन्तिनीनाम्।
उत्पातस्तामसानामुपहत-महसां चक्षुषां पक्षपातः,
संघातः कोऽपिधाम्नामयमुदयगिरिप्रान्ततः प्रादुरासीत्॥"

अत्र वृत्त्यनुप्रासप्राचुर्यादोजोगुणप्रकाशकत्वाच्च शब्दस्य प्रसाद-गुणयोगादनन्तरमेवाधिगतस्य रूपकस्य हेत्वलङ्कारस्य वा वाच्यस्य चमत्कृत्योस्तुल्यस्कन्धत्वात्सममेव प्राधान्यम्।

Trans.: And (in the cases) where the poetic charm of word and sense exit in one (poetry) there, after analysing the prominence of the two, those should be accepted as per the definition. However, in the case of equal prominence, (it should be accepted as) the third (variety) only.

For example: "Some uncommon rays of light emerge from the top portion of this mountain; becomes the pleasure (pleasurable condition) for the intoxicated bees while falling (repeatedly) on the sprouting lotuses, the saver of the female curculus melanoleucus (cātaka) whose hearts are terminated due to fire, in the form of sepatation (from their partners), the destroyer of the darkness that obstructs the light and supporter of eyes (the action of seeing)."

Because of the sameness of these two charmingness of the word due to excessiveness of वृत्यनुप्रास and due to the expressive production of florridity (merit) (And) of the sense, due to the application of simplicity (merit) and (due to) the usage of the figure of sense of metaphor (रूपक) and (हेतु) subsequently, the prominence (of word and sense) is equal (strength) indeed.

RG. 22.

तत्र ध्वनेरुत्तमोत्तमस्यासंख्यभेदस्यापि सामान्यतःकेऽपि भेदा निरूप्यन्ते-द्विविधो ध्वनिः, अभिधामूलो लक्षणामूलश्च। तत्राद्यस्त्रिविधः। रसवस्त्वलंकारध्वनिभेदात्। रसध्वनिरित्यलक्ष्यक्रमोपलक्षणाद्रसभावतदाभासभावशान्तिभावोदयभावसंधिभावशबलत्वानां ग्रहणम्।

द्वितीयश्च द्विविधः। अर्थान्तरसंक्रमितवाच्योऽत्यन्ततिरस्कृतवाच्यश्च।

एवं पञ्चात्मके ध्वनौ परमरमणीयतया रसध्वनेस्तदात्मा रसस्तावदभिधीयते–

Trans.: (With regard to that) of the suggestion of Super Excellent (poetry), even though, there are innumerable varieties (still), a few (important) varieties are to be defined (here) in general. The suggestion is of two types, (suggestion) based on expression (अभिधा) and indication (लक्षणा). Out of these two; the first namely (अभिधा) has three varieties namely, the suggestion of the sentiment (**rasadhvani)**, the suggestion of mere fact (वस्तुध्वनि) and the suggestion of figures (अलंकारध्वनि). Because of the metaphorical expression of (असंलक्ष्यक्रम), that where the order (between the suggestion and something suggested) is not distinct of the suggestion of the sentiment (रसध्वनि), the sentiment, the mood, their semblance, the pacification of the moods, the rise of the moods, the variegation of the moods etc., are included (in it).

And the second has two varieties namely, अर्थान्तरसंक्रमित (i. e., the expressed sense is transferred (extended) to another sense) and अत्यन्ततिरस्कृत (i. e., the expressed sense is altogether (neglected) abandoned. (And) where the suggestion is of these five varieties (like this), due to the extraordinary charmingness of suggestive sentiment (**rasadhvani**) the suggestion as being its soul, is now taken for analysis (difined).

Notes : After explaining the varieties of poetry, now PR proceeds to explain rasasūtra, which is the most important part of RG. There are eleven interpretations of the rasasūtra following the tradition of NS. It starts from Abhinavagupta's interpretation. Here. before coming to that first interpretation, PR gives a general information regarding the dhvani. This 'dhvani' is of two types namely abhidhā and **lakṣaṇā;** further these two types of dhvani are divided into five types. Abhidha, at first, is of three types according to senti-ment, mere fact and alaṁkāra. Like this the **lakṣanā** is of two types i.e. **arthāntara saṁkramita vācya** and **atyantati-raskṛtavācya.**

RG. 23.

समुचितललितसंनिवेशचारुणाकाव्येनसमर्पितैः सहृदयहृदयं प्रविष्टैस्तदीयसहृदयतासहकृतेनभावनाविशेषमहिम्नाविगलितदुष्यन्त-रमणीत्वादिभिरलौकिकविभावानुभावव्यभिचारि-शब्दव्यपदेश्यैः शकुन्तलादिभिरालम्बनकारणैश्चन्द्रिकादिभिरुद्दीपनकारणैरश्रुपाता-दिभिःकार्यैश्चिन्तादिभिःसहकारिभिश्च संभूय प्रादुर्भावितेनालौकिकेन व्यापारेण तत्कालनिवर्तितानन्दांशावरणाज्ञानेनात एवं प्रमुष्टपरिमित-प्रमातृत्वादिनिजधर्मेण प्रमात्रा स्वप्रकाशतया वास्तवेन निजस्वरूपानन्देन सह गोचरीक्रियमाणः प्राग्विनिविष्टवासनारूपो रत्यादिरेव रसः॥

Trans.: Presented in the charming poetry due to appropriate and sweet expressions, touched the heart of the connoissure, and by the special power of **bhāvanā** (repeated brooding) about that along with the respective connoisseurness (residing in him) and by the sustaintial mood like **Śakuntalā** etc, the enhancing mood like moon light etc., the ensuant like shedding of tears etc, and transitory mood like anxiety etc., expressed as of extraordinary excitant, ensuant and transitory like the 'beloved of **Duṣyanta**' of 'lover of **Śakuntalā**' etc, (coming together), flashes some extraordinary functions by which the covering of ignorance is removed that moment, and in the enjoyer, devoid of its personal qualities like having limited knowledgeness etc., due to the manifestation of the soul, the love etc., laying lattent in the form of previous impressions, enjoyable by the real experience of the enjoyment of knowledge alone are enjoyed as sentiment (**Rasa**).

RG. 24.

तथा चाहुः- 'व्यक्तः स तैर्विभावाद्यैः स्थानीभावो रसः स्मृतः' इति। व्यक्तो व्यक्तिविषयीकृतः। व्यक्तिश्च भग्नावरणा चित्। यथाहि शरावादिना पिहितो दीपस्तन्निवृत्तौ संनिहितान् पदार्थान् प्रकाशयति, स्वयं च प्रकाशते, एवमात्मचैतन्यं विभावादिसंवलितान् रत्यादीन्। अन्तः करणधर्माणां (केवल)[१] साक्षिभास्यत्वाभ्युपगतेः।

Trans.: Further (it is) said thus: 'the permanent mood, manifested through excitant (determinant moods) etc., is sentiment (**rasa**). Manifested means something made the object of suggestion. And suggestion (means) devoid of (any) covering of knowledge (in the form of ingnorance).

As for example; A lamp covered by a shallow cup etc., and after removal of that, visualises (reveals) the nearer objects as well as to its self. Alike this, the universal soul shows the pleasure (**Rati**) etc., which are menifested by excitants etc. Because, the pleasure etc., (**ratyādi**), the property of the internal organs are postulated to be self-realisation.

RG. 25.

विभावादीनामपि स्वप्नतुरगादीनामिव रङ्गरजतादीनामिव साक्षि[२]-भास्यत्वमविरुद्धम्। व्यञ्जकविभावादिचर्वणया आवरणभङ्गस्य वोत्पत्तिविनाशाभ्यामुत्पत्तिविनाशौ रसे उपचर्येते। वर्णनित्यतायामिव व्यञ्जकताल्वादिव्यापारस्य गकारादौ, विभावादिचर्वणावधित्वादा-वरणभङ्गस्य, निवृत्तायां तस्यां प्रकाशस्यावृतत्वाद्विद्यमानोऽपि स्थायी न प्रकाशते।

Trans.: In the case of **vibhāva** etc., (excitant etc.) there

---

१. केवल- is missing in all other editions.

२. म., इव वा साक्षि.

is no contradiction in the realisation alike (the cognition of) the dream-horse (Horse seen in dream), and the conch (**rangarajata**). The production and destruction (of **rasa**) is secondarily applied to '**rasa**' due to the production and destruction of the removal of the covering, (in the form of ignorance) by the enjoyment of excitant etc., the revealer (of **rasa**); as in the case of the syllable '**ga**' etc., due to the function of palate etc., the revealer of the syllables though the syllables are eternal. Because the tenure of the 'removal of the covering' in the form of ignorance in the time of the enjoyment of excitant etc., when this causes to exist the permanent mood though excitant is not revealed because of the covering of the revealing factor (**prakāśa**).

RG. 26.

यद्वा भावनाविशेषमहिम्ना सहृदयस्य निजसहृदयतावशोन्मिषितेन विभावादिसंसृष्ट तत्तत्स्थाय्युपहितस्वस्वरूपानन्दाकारा समाधाविव योगिनः चित्तवृत्तिरुपजायते। तन्मयीभवनमिति यावत्। आनन्दो अयं न लौकिकसुखान्तसाधारणः। अनन्तकरणवृत्तिरूपत्वात्। इथंच मम्मट[१]भट्टादिग्रन्थस्वारस्येन भग्नावरणचिद्विशिष्टो रत्यादिः स्थायीभावो रस इति स्थितम्।

Trans.: Or there arises from the respective permanent moods an experience of the nature of eternal pleasure in the appreciative critic, by virtue of his own appreciative quality and the power of some experience of the enjoyment of the combination of the **vibhāva** etc., like the mental state of Yogis in **samādhi.** (And that is) a state of oneness (i. e., emerging in that). This pleasure indeed is not common to the other ordinary pleasure, because, it is in the form of (the eternal pleasure) not generated by the association of internal organs. And thus, the permanent mood like love etc., devoid

---

१. अभिनवगुप्त मम्मट in all other editions.

of covering (of ignorance) is proved to be **rasa**, following the text of **Mammaṭa** etc.

RG. 27.

वस्तुतस्तु वक्ष्यमाणश्रुतिस्वारस्येन रत्याद्यवच्छिन्ना भग्नावरणा चिदेव रसः।

सर्वथैव चास्या विशिष्टात्मनो विशेषणं विशेष्यं वा चिदंशमादाय नित्यत्वं स्वप्रकाशत्वं च सिद्धम्।

रत्याद्यंशमादाय त्वनित्यत्वमितरभास्यत्वं च। चर्वणा चास्य चिद्गतावरणभङ्ग एव प्रागुक्तातदाकारन्तःकरणवृत्तिर्वा। इयं च परं ब्रह्मास्वादात् समाधेर्विलक्षणा, विभावादिविषयसंवलितचिदा नन्दालम्बनत्वात्। भाव्या च काव्यव्यापारमात्रात्।

Trans.: As a matter of fact, 'cit' alone conditioned by the removal of coverings (of ignorance) delimitted by love etc., is **rasa.** At any rate, the eternity and universality or self-realisation of this (**rasa**) (is proved) accepting either the qualifierness or qualificantness of 'cit'. And accepting the component pleasure etc., (as **rasa**) the transitoriness and realisation by other means, is proved. And the enjoyment (**carvaṇā**) of this (**rasa**) is the removal of coverings (in the form of ignorance) of Soul, or the (function) experience of the internal state of being like that as state before. This (enjoyment) is different from the meditation in the form of the state of Supreme-Soul;because of its inclusiveness with pleasurable state based on the collection of objects in like exctant etc. And this should be understood from the suggestions of poetry/ the poetical approachment.

RG. 28.

अथास्यां सुखांशभाने किंमानमिति चेत्समाधावपि तद्भाने किं मानमिति पर्यनुयोगस्य तुल्यत्वात्। "सुखमात्यन्तिकं यत्तदबुद्धिग्राह्यमतीन्द्रियम्, इत्यादिःशब्दोऽस्ति तत्र मानमिति चेदस्त्यत्रापि 'रसो वै

सः," 'रसं ह्येवायं लब्ध्वानन्दीभवति' इति श्रुतिः, सकलसहृदय प्रत्यक्षं चेति प्रमाणद्वयम्। येयं द्विजीयपक्षे तदाकार- चित्तवृत्त्यात्मिका रसचर्वणोपन्यस्ता सा शब्दव्यापारभाव्यत्वाच्छाब्दी। अपरोक्षसुखा-लम्बनत्वाच्चापरोक्षात्मिका। तत्त्वं वाक्यजबुद्धिवत्। इत्याहुरभिनव-गुप्ताचार्यपादाः।

Trans.: Objection: Well. It may be argued thus: 'What is the proof of experiencing pleasure in it?'

Answer: then 'What is the proof of experiencing (pleasure) that in meditation' would be (our) counterquestion, because of the similarity of omitting to blame what ought to be blamed.

Objection: It may be argued further thus: there is proof in the form of words (Scriptures) namely; highest pleasure is grasped by intellect which is beyond the range of sense-organs etc.

Answer: In that case (there are) also two proofs viz. thus goes the Vedic statement that indeed is **rasa,** and this **rasa** alone varily becomes pleasurable attaining that state, etc. And it is experienced by the entire refined sympathetic critics.

Thus, says **Abhinava**: In the second alternative, whatever is established as enjoyment of **rasa** in the form of that (तदाकारवृत्ति), is verbal understanding, because that is understood by the usage of words. And because of being dependent on direct pleasure/ experience, it is in the form of a direct experience, like the understanding from the verbal expression, namely, 'you (are) that', (tattvamasi).

RG. 29

भट्टनायकास्तु 'ताटस्थ्येन रसप्रतीतावनास्वाद्यत्वम्। आत्मगतत्वेन तु प्रत्यतो दुर्घटः। शकुन्तलादीनां सामाजिकान्प्रत्यविभावत्वात्। विना

भावमनालम्बनस्य रसादेरप्रतिपत्तेः। न च कान्तात्वं साधारणं विभावतावच्छेदकमत्राप्यस्तीति वाच्यम्। अप्रामाण्यनिश्चयानालिङ्गितागम्यात्वप्रकारकज्ञानविरहस्य विशेष्यतासंबन्धावच्छिन्नप्रतियोगिताकस्य विभावतावच्छेदककोटाववश्यं निवेश्यत्वात्। अन्यथा स्वस्त्रादेरपि कान्तात्वादिना तत्त्वापत्ते। एवमशोच्यत्वकापुरुषत्वादिज्ञानविरहस्य तथाविधस्य करुणरसादौ।

Trans.: Bhattanayaka, however holds: If '**rasa**' is experienced by the charmed spectator, it can (not) be enjoyed. The experience by one's own (i. e., the character) however is not possible, because, '**Śakuntalā**' etc., are not the excitants for the spectators. Because, the **rasa** cannot be experienced without depending on excitant etc. It cannot be argued that there is (quality) the delimitor of the excitantness, common to the state of being a charming lady! Because, by the absence of knowledge which is free from definite erroneous cognition having non-enjoyable-ness as its qualifier and delimited by the relation of qualifiedness, is to be added as the delimitor of the excitantness.

Otherwise, there would arise the excitantness (of love) in the cases of beautiful ladies as (**own**) sister etc. Further, in the cases like pathos etc., that type of ignorance/ without prior knowledge, regarding presons as unthinkable (he may be remembered), cowardness (he may be a hero) etc., will arise.

Notes : The interpretation of **rasasūtra** following **Bhattanāyaka** is presented in this text. Here PR has recorded some objections from the point of view of **Bhattanāyaka.** According to **Bhattanāyaka** if the seat of rasa is taken to be the original character of the actor, then it cannot be enjoyed by the audience. Because the character etc., cannot form the excitant etc., for audience and the absence of excitant, no rasa can be realised. This objection is raised against the view of Bhattalollaṭa.

RG. 30

तादृशज्ञानानुपादस्तु तत्प्रतिबन्धकान्तरनिर्वचनमन्तरेण दुरुपपादः। स्वात्मनि दुष्यन्ताद्यभेदबुद्धिरेव तथेति चेन्न। नायके धराधौरेयत्वधीरत्वादे रात्मनि चाधुनिकत्वकापुरुषत्वादेर्वैधर्म्यस्य स्फुटं प्रतिपत्तेरभेदबोधस्यैव दुर्लभत्वात्।

Trans.: However, the non-generation of that type of knowledge in the absence of the expression of the respective obstacles, cannot be avoided.

Objection: It may argued: In one's mind (lit.heart), the knowledge of identity with **Duṣyanta** etc., is considered as that.

Answer: Not so (is the answer). Because, the knowledge of indentity is impossible due to the clear cognition of dissimilarities in one's self, with hero possessed of the quality of being the lord of earth and the steadyness etc., and the modernness and cowardness etc.

RG. 30.1

किं च केयं प्रतीतिः। प्रमाणान्तरानुपस्थानाच्छाद्बीति चेत् न। व्यावहारिकशब्दान्तरजन्यनायकमिथुनवृत्तान्तवित्तिनामिवास्या अप्यहृद्य-त्वापत्तेः। नापि मानसी, चिन्तोपनीतानां तेषामेव पदार्थानां मानस्याः प्रतीतेरस्या वैलक्षण्योपलम्भात्। न च स्मृतिः, तथा प्रागननुभवात्। तस्मादभिधया निवेदिताःपदार्था भावकत्वव्यापारेणागम्यात्वादिरस विरोधिज्ञानप्रतिबन्धद्वारा कान्तात्वादिरसानुकूलधर्मपुरस्कारेणावस्थाप्यन्ते।

Trans.: Objection: And it may be asked; what is this **pratiti** (designated as **rasa**)?

Answer and its refutation: It may be argued: Due to its non-emergence by other means of proof (viz.perception etc.) it is verbal-understanding. Not so, because there would arise the contingency non-experiencing, of that knowledge arising from the common expressions and the conversation of a couple (hero and heroine).

(And) because of the distinction between the realisation of this (**rasa**) from mental perception, and the knowledge which comes after repeated thinking, is clearly visible so not also the mental perception.

(And) because of the lack of its prior experience (of those actors and actress) not also the memory.

Conclusion: Therefore, the functionary objects as presented in poetry are propounded due to the imaginary function and by avoiding the negative experience regarding **rasa** as 'unreachable' etc., and due to the association of positive nature (experience) of **rasa** as 'charming beauty' etc.

RG. 31

एवं साधारणीकृतेषु दुष्यन्त शकुन्तलादेशकालवयोवस्थादिषु पङ्क्तौ पूर्वव्यापारमहिमनि तृतीयस्य भोगकृत्त्वव्यापारस्य महिम्ना निगीर्णयो रजस्तमसोरुद्रिक्तसत्त्वजनितेन निजचित्स्वभाव निर्वृतिविश्रान्तिलाक्षणेन साक्षात्कारेण विषयीकृतो भावनोपनीतः साधारणात्मारत्यादिः स्थायी रसः।

Trans.: In this manner, the permanent mood namely, love etc., in the form of universal state, after reaching the pleasurable imagination, due to its (**abhidhā**) universalisation of **Duṣyanta-Śakuntalā**- Place - Season (time) - Age- Situation (condition) etc., being ceased to function itself due to the earlier stage (i. e., imagination), and by the power of third- functioning stage, namely, enjoyment (or experience) and due to its dominance of **sattva** over **rajas** and **tamas,** and by the form of retiring of one's own consciousness nature (is called as) **rasa.**

Notes : The realisation of **rasa** is explained by PR from the point of view of Bhaṭṭanāyaka. Bhaṭṭanāyaka has proposed two more powers of poetic languages in the name of **Bhojakatva and Bhāvakatva.** By the power of first one,

sattvaguna dominance over **raja and tamas.** And by the power of latter, one, the permanent mood is enjoyed as **rasa**, in a generalized manner, **bhogakṛtvavyāpārasyamahimnā sādhāraṇātmā ratyādi rasaḥ.**

RG. 32

तत्र भुज्यमानो रत्यादिः, रत्यादि भोगो वेत्युभयमेव रसः। सोऽयं भोगो विषयसवंलनाद् ब्रह्मास्वादसविधवर्तीत्युच्यते, एवं च त्रयोंऽशाः काव्यस्य।

'अभिधा भावना चैव तद्भोगीकृतिरेव च' इत्याहुः।

मतस्यैतस्य पूर्वस्मान्मताद्भावकत्वव्यापारान्तस्वीकार एव विशेषः।

भोगस्तु व्यक्तिः। भोगकृत्त्वं तु व्यञ्जनादिविशिष्टम्। अन्या तु सैव सरणिः।

Trans.: Both are **rasas** namely, 'love etc., being enjoyed' or 'enjoyment of love etc,' (is the conclusion).

And due to its inclusiveness with pleasurable state based on the collection of worldly objects is called, as nearer to the (enjoyment in the form of the state of) Superme-Soul (ironically even it is quite different). And thus, the poetry has three components—as is stated namely '**Abhidhā**'—the form of primary understanding (indication in secondary sense), '**Bhāvanā**'—the instrumental to convert later into universalisation, and '**Bhogikṛta** of that'—by which, the enjoyment of **rasa** through love etc., (takes place).

The speciality of this view from the earlier view is the acceptance of the employment of different (other) repeated thoughts (thinking). The enjoyment of **rasa** is suggestion. The state of being enjoyed is indeed not different from suggestiveness. The rest follows the same way of interpretation.

Notes : Against the view of Bhaṭṭnāyaka, PR explains: there is no need to accept two more powers of poetic language.

Bhojakatva is nothing but vyanjanā. **Bhogàstu vyaktiḥ** and **bhāvakatva** is the very enjoyment.

RG. 33

नव्यास्तु- 'काव्ये नाट्ये च कविना नटेन च प्रकाशितेषु विभावादिषु व्यञ्जनव्यापारेण दुष्यन्तादौ शकुन्तलादिरतौ गृहीतायामनन्तरं च सहृदयतोल्लासितस्य भावनाविशेषरूपस्य दोषस्य महिम्ना कल्पित-दुष्यन्तत्वावच्छादिते स्वात्मन्यज्ञानावच्छिन्ने शुक्तिकाशकल इव रजत-खण्डः समुत्पद्यमानोऽनिर्वचनीयः साक्षिभास्यः शकुन्तलादिविषय-करत्यादिरेव रसः।

Trans.: The modern poeticians however, hold: due to the poet & the actor in a poetry and a drama respectively, the (knowledge regarding) excitant etc., generates, then with the help of the suggestive functions, the love of **Duṣyanta** etc., for **Śakuntalā** etc., are cognised. Further, due to the fult in the form of a special type of imagination of a 'refined critic', an imaginary **Duṣyanta** imposed on one's own soul (as 'I am **Duṣyanta**'; not a reader or an audience); due to ignorance like a piece of pearl looks like a peice of silver (from its brightness), an indescribable revealed by one's sight, occures which is the (permanent) love towards (having **Śakuntalā** as its **visaya)** **Śakuntalā** is called as **rasa.**

Notes : PR records the view of some latter rhetoricians. According to this view, when the excitant etc. like Duṣyanta etc. are presented the first knowledge arises that Duṣyanta is in love with Śakuntalā or as the case may be. Afterwards there is subsequent awareness which is in fact a fault (defective one), and on the power of that fault the audience's mind is endowed with imaginary Duṣyanta and he understands himself to be real character. And thus, in him arises the love towards Śakuntalā. **Bhāvanā visesarupasyadosasyamahimnā.** This experience cannot be explained as either real or unreal and its nature cannot be explained properly. This peculiar mental state is **rasa,** which is realised due to the fault stated earlier (**ayaṁ ca kārya doṣasya....**) and when this fault is removed then the realisation of **rasa** ceases. And when, the identity is established between the real love of Duṣyanta towards Śakuntalā and the love realised due to the fault one term it as suggested and described by the poet.

RG. 33.1.

अयं च कार्यो दोषविशेषस्य। नाश्यश्च तन्नाशस्य।

स्वोत्तरभाविना लोकोत्तराह्लादेन भेदाग्रहात्सुखपदव्यपदेश्यो भवति।

स्वपूर्वोपस्थितेन रत्यादिना तदग्रहात्तद्रतित्वेनैकत्वाध्यवसानाद्वा व्यङ्ग्यो वर्णनीयश्चोच्यते।

अवच्छादकं दुष्यन्तत्वमप्यनिर्वचनीयमेव। अवच्छादकत्वं च रत्यादिविशिष्टबोधे विशेष्यतावच्छेदकत्वम्। एतेन दुष्यन्तादिनिष्ठस्य रत्यादेरनास्वाद्यत्वान्नरसत्वम्। स्वनिष्ठस्य तु तस्य शकुन्तलादिभिर-तत्संबन्धिभिः कथमभिव्यक्तिः। स्वस्मिन् दुष्यन्ताद्यभेदबुद्धिस्तु बाधबुद्धि-पराहतेत्यादिकमपास्तम्।

Trans.: This is the effect of (that) type of fault which is removed in the removal of that.

The **rasa** is expressed / designated as affording pleasure, because of the non-cognition of the difference with the extra-ordinary charmingness which occurs upon (**Śakuntalā**) by one's own-self.

(This is **rasa**) declared to be suggestive and describable due to (its) the non-cognition of the difference (with the) love etc., presented earlier in the one's own-self, or due to the cognition of identify (oneness) in the love of that (character).

Dusyntaness, which is imposed (overpowered) over one's own self is also indescribable. And the "imposedness" is (the state of being imposed), the delimiter-ness of the qualificandness is case of the qualified cognition of love etc. By this (above) argument, the following, namely, the love etc, which is entitled in **Duṣyanta** etc., is not (to be taken as) **rasa.** How, indeed that, love etc, exists on one's own-self is revealed, **Śakuntalā** etc. (other actors etc.) with any other they are not related.

The cognition of identity with **Duṣyanta** etc., with ons's ownself, is removed by the knowledge of qualified cognition, stands refuted.

RG. 34.

यदपि विभावादीनां साधारण्यं प्राचीनैरुक्तं तदपि काव्येन शकुन्तलादिशब्दैः शकुन्तलात्वादिप्रकारकबोधजनकैःप्रतिपाद्यमानेषु दोषविशेषकल्पनं विना दुरुपपादम्।,

अतोऽवश्यकल्प्ये दोषविशेषे तेनैव स्वात्मनि दुष्यन्ताद्यभेदबुद्धिरपि सूपपादा। नन्वेवमपि रतेरस्तु नाम दुष्यन्त इव सहृदयेऽपि सुखविशेष-जनकता, करुणरसादिषु तु स्थायिनःशोकादेर्दुःखजनकतया प्रसिद्धस्य कथमिव सहृदयाह्लादहेतुत्वम्। प्रत्युत नायक इव सहृदयेऽपि दुःखजनन-स्यैवौचित्यात्।

Trans.: Though, the universalisation of excitant etc, are accepted by ancients, yet, it is impossible, to justify without the imagination of a special type of fault in **Śakuntalā** etc., which are presented by the expressions **Śakuntalā** etc., and by the generator of the realisation having **Śakuntalātva** as its qualifierness in the poetry. Therefore, the imagination of special type of fault is significantly necessary, And by that alone the cognition of indentity with **Duṣyanta** etc., in one's own-self is well explained.

Well, let the state of being the generator of some extraordinary pleasure in enjoyer also, then how the permanent mood with regard to love etc., as in the case of **Duṣyanta**. However, in the case of Pathos etc., where the state of being the generator of griefness of the premanent mood, sorrow etc., are largly accepted (well experienced).

How, the account for its causality with regard to the pleasurableness of enjoyer, on the contrary, the experience (lit. the generator) of griefness in case of the enjoyer alike the hero etc., is proved.

RG. 35.

न च सत्यस्य शोकादेर्दुःखजनकत्वं क्लृप्तं न कल्पितस्येति नायकानामेव दुःखम्, न सहृदयस्येति वाच्यम्।

रज्जुसर्पादेर्भयकम्पाद्यनुत्पादकतापत्तेः। सहृदये रतेरपि कल्पितत्वेन सुखजनकतानुपपत्तेश्चेति चेत्। सत्यम्।

शृङ्गारप्रधानकाव्येभ्य इव करुणप्रधानकाव्येभ्योऽपि यदि केवलाह्लाद एव सहृदयहृदयप्रमाणकस्तदा कार्यानुरोधेन कारणस्य कल्पनीयत्वाल्लोकोत्तरकाव्यव्यापारस्यैवाह्लादप्रयोजकत्वमिव दुःखप्रतिबन्धकत्वपि कल्पनीयम्।

Trans.: Objection: It cannot be argued that the generation of griefness etc., of the permanent moods like sorrow etc., in reality is accepted by all and not in the case of imaginant (i. e. imaginary sorrow), though the griefness is with regard to the actual hero alone and not of the enjoyer; Because, there would arise the contingency (absurdity) of the non-experience (non-generation) of fear, tremor etc., from (the cognition of) the rope-serpent. And because of the pleasure etc., of (the permanent mood) the love etc., also in the enjoyer, cannot be explained due to its being imaginary.

Answer: (Whatever is said) is true. If the heart of the enjoyer (that experiences pleasure etc.) is the proof (for the enjoyment) of pleasure alone, also from the poetries having the dominance of Pathos (pathos-dominant-poetries) as in the case of poetries having the dominance of erotics/love. then since the cause is determined on the basis of the effect, as the non-worldy activity (i. e, supernormal behaviour etc.) is the case (of the enjoyment) of pleasure, the contradictory factor (for the enjoyment) of sorrow is to be postulated.

RG. 36.

अथ यद्याह्लाद इव दुःखमपि प्रमाणसिद्धं तदा प्रतिबन्धकत्वं न कल्पनीयम्। स्वस्वकारणवशाच्चोभयमपि भविष्यति। अथ तत्र कवीनां कर्तुम्, सहृदयानां च श्रोतुम्, कथं प्रवृत्तिः। अनिष्टसाधनत्वेन निवृत्ते-रुचितत्वात्। इति चेत्। इष्टस्याधिक्यादनिष्टस्य च न्यूनत्वाच्चन्दन-द्रवलेपनादाविव प्रवृत्तेरुपपत्तेः। केवलाह्लादवादिनां तु प्रवृत्तिरप्रत्यूहैव। अश्रुपातादयोऽपि तत्तदानन्दानुभवस्वाभाव्यात्। न तु दुःखात्।

अत एव भगवद्भक्तानां भगवद्वर्णनाकर्णनादश्रुपातादय उपपद्यन्ते। न हि तत्र जात्वपि दुःखानुभवोऽस्ति।

Trans.: Further, if alike pleasure, giref also is established by experience (of the enjoyer) (lit. valid means of knowledge) then, the state of being a contradictory factor should not be postulated. Both occur on the basis of their respective causes.

Objection: Well, it may be argued: How then, there is an inclination of poet and enjoyer to compose and listen respectively (to those pathetic poetries)? Because, due to its non-desirableness, withdrawal (from those) is indeed proper.

Answer: The inclination is justified like the application of sandal paste etc., due to the profuseness of desireablity and the limitedness of non-desirbility. For those, subscribing to the view that, pleasure alone is experienced (in case of pathos etc.) there is no difficulty (for the explanation) of the inclination. Shedding of tear etc., also peculiar due to the nature of the experience of respective pleasurable activities and not due to grief etc. Therefore, the shedding of tear etc., occur in the case of the devotees by the naration and listening (of the greatness) of God, and not indeed there is a little bit experience of sorrow.

RG. 37.

न च करुणरसादौ स्वात्मनि शोकादिमद्दशरथादितादात्म्यारोपे यद्याह्लादस्तदा स्वप्नादौ संनिपातादौ वा स्वात्मनि तदारोपेऽपि स स्यात्। आनुभविकं च तत्र केवलं दुःखम्। इतीहापि तदेव युक्तमिति वाच्यम्। अयं हि लोकोत्तरस्य काव्यव्यापारस्य महिमा, यत्प्रयोज्या अरमणीया अपि शोकादयः पदार्था आह्लादमलौकिकं जनयन्ति। विलक्षणो हि कमनीयः काव्यव्यापारज आस्वादः प्रमाणान्तरजादनुभवात्।

Trans.: Objection: It may be argued: In case of Pathos etc., if by the imposition of identity with Dasaratha etc., possessed of grief etc., in one's self, then in dream of colapsing condition etc., even in the imposition of that in one's soul, the result would be that (the enjoyment of pleasure). (As a matter of fact) the object of experience is sorrow (unhappyness) only there. The same is true in the present case as well.

Answer: Not so. This indeed in due to the power of extra-ordinary function of poetry, by (the power of) which the object griefness etc, even though not pleasurable, generate non-worldly pleasure etc. Unique indeed is the enjoyments, generated from the charming function of poetry, is special (different) from the enjoyment generated from the other means (of enjoyment).'

RG. 38.

जन्यत्वं च स्वजन्यभावनाजन्यरत्यादिविषयकत्वम्।
तेन रसास्वादस्य काव्यव्यापाराजन्यत्वेऽपि न क्षतिः।
शकुन्तलादावगम्यात्वज्ञानोत्पादस्तु स्वात्मनि दुष्यन्ताद्यभेदबुद्ध्या प्रतिबध्यते' इत्याहुः।

Trans.: The generatedness is the state of being the object, namely love etc., generated from the imagination generated from that self (काव्यव्यापार).

Thus (by that), there is no harm if the enjoyment of **rasa** is not (accepted to be) generated from the function of poetry. And thus is concluded: The knowledge of non approchableness in the case fo **Śakuntalā** etc., arising is protected due to the knowledge of indentity with **Duṣyanta** etc. in one's own-self (काव्यव्यापार).

RG. 39.

परेतु' व्यञ्जनव्यापारस्यानिर्वचनीयख्यातेश्चानभ्युपगमेऽपि प्रागुक्तदोषमहिम्ना स्वात्मनि दुष्यन्तादितादात्म्यावगाही शकुन्तलादि-विषयकरत्यादिमदभेदबोधो मानसःवि[१]लक्षणविषयताशाली रसः। स्वाप्नादिस्तु तादृशबोधो न काव्यार्थचिन्तनजन्मेति न रसः। तेन तत्र न तादृशाह्लादापत्तिः। एवमपि स्वस्मिन्नविद्यमानस्य रत्यादेरनुभवः कथं नाम स्यात्। मैवम्। नह्ययं लौकिकसाक्षात्कारो रत्यादेः, येनावश्यं विषयसद्भावोऽपेक्षणीयः स्यात्। अपि तु भ्रमः। आस्वादनस्य रसविषय-कत्वव्यवहारस्तु रत्यादिविषकत्वालम्बनः इत्यपि वदन्ति।

Trans.: Some others propose this: Even though, the suggestiveness (regarding the love of **Duṣyanta** etc., for **Śakuntalā** etc.) and the indescribable factors (regarding love generation in one's own self) is not accepted, due to the power of the fault (i. e. **bhāvanā**) as stated earlier, the mental cognition of identity generated from the repeated thinking of poetry, in one's own self, that generates the knowledge of identity with **Duṣyanta** etc., possessing love for **Śakuntalā** etc., having some non wordly (pleasure) as it's **viṣaya,** is **rasa**. In the state of dream etc., the experience (knowledge) of that kind is not generated from the thinking of poetic sense, though, is not (to be accepted as) **rasa.** Therefore, there is no contingency of (the experience of) that kind of enjoyment there (in the state of dream etc).

Objection: In this manner, how then, there would be the experience of love etc, in one's ownself, which is not there.

---

१. काव्यार्थाभावनाजन्मा विलक्षण...in all other editions.

Answer: No so. This indeed is not the normal experience of love etc., for which, there would be the expectancy of the presense of the object (i. e. **rasa**). But is illusion. However, the reference experession of the enjoyment as **rasa** is dependant (on) love etc., as its object.

Notes : After giving the view of **Navya,** now PR quotes the others views in the interpretation of sentiment with regard to Bharata's **rasa-sūtra**. Accordingly, these statements are minor ones and present minor impotances also. Rightly V.A.R. Sastri, declares that the exponents of some of these views do not accept the function of suggestiveness and says that the audience by virtue of his **sahṛdayatva** on witnessing the successful personation of the sustaintial like Duṣyanta and Śakuntalā by an expert actor indentifies himself with the real character, 'Duṣyanta', in his love to Śakuntalā and that the realisation or mental experience of this indentification gives him a thrill of pleasure Further the term **rasa nispatti** also would mean the generation of a knowledge of the indentity of the audience with the real character.

RG. 40.

एतैश्चस्वात्मनि दुष्यन्तत्वधर्मितावच्छेदकशकुन्तलादिविषयकरतिवैशिष्ट्यावगाही, स्वात्मत्वविशिष्टे शकुन्तलादिविषयकरतिविशिष्ट-दुष्यन्ततादात्मावगाही, स्वात्मत्वविशिष्टे दुष्यन्तत्वशकुन्तलाविषय-करत्योर्वैशिष्ट्यावगाही, वा त्रिविधोऽपि बोधो रसपदार्थतयाभ्युपेयः। तत्र रतेर्विशेषणीभूतायाः शब्दादप्रतीतत्वाद्व्यञ्जनायाश्च तत्प्रत्यायिकाया अनभ्युपगमाच्चेष्टादिलिङ्गकमादौ विशेषणज्ञानार्थमनुमानभ्युपेयम्।

Trans.: Following these views, the knowledge of the following three forms, namely (i) I am possessed of that, the love towards '**Śakuntalā**' etc., residing in '**Duṣyanta**' delimited by '**Duṣyanta**-ness. (ii) I am not different from that '**Duṣyanta**' having **Śakuntalā** as the object of its love. (iii) I am possessed of '**Duṣyanta**-ness and the love having '**Śakuntalā**' as its object; are to be accepted as '**rasa**.' The necessity of inference for the knowledge of love etc. in this view is explained: Since 'love etc', occur here (in all these three kind of knowledges which are to be called **rasa**) as qualifiers, and (they) cannot be known by words, and since the suggestive power is not acceptable to the followers of these (views), for the prior knowledge of the qualification, one has to resort to inference basing the probans like the action (of the character).

RG. 41.

'मुख्यतया दुष्यन्तादिगत एव रसो रत्यादिः कमनीयविभा -वाद्यभिनयप्रदर्शनकोविदे दुष्यन्ताद्यनुकर्तरि नटे समारोप्य साक्षात्क्रियते इत्येके'। मतेऽस्मिन्साक्षात्कारो दुष्यन्तोऽयं शकुन्तलादिविषय-करतिमानित्यादिः प्राग्वद्धर्म्यंशे लौकिक आरोप्यांशे त्वलौकिकः।

Trans.: Some proposed thus: Primarily, the **rasa** (namely) love etc., existing in **Duṣyanta** etc., (for **Śakuntalā**) is enjoyed after imposing (it) on the actor, expert in the presentation of charming excitant etc., who is immitating **Duṣyanta** etc. In this view, the enjoyment namely 'this is **Duṣyanta**, having love for **Śakuntalā** etc. 'alike in the earlier case, is worldly (normal) in the part of the possesson of the attribute (i.e. **Duṣyanta** etc.) and is non-worldly (i.e. super-normal) in the part of the locus of the imposition (i.e., the actor etc).

RG. 41.1

'दुष्यन्तादिगतोरत्यादिर्नटेपक्षे दुष्यन्तत्वेन गृहीते विभावादिभिः कृतिमैरप्यकृत्रिमतया गृहीतैर्भिन्ने विषयेऽनुमितिसामाग्र्या बलवत्त्वा-दनुमीयमानो रसः' इत्यपरे।

Trans.: Others hold thus: The love etc, existing in **Duṣyanta** etc., when experiences in the charactor takes as being

Duṣyanta and which is being inferred by the collection of (the factor of) inference due to the strength with regard to different objects when it is accepted as non-artificial, even though (it is) artificial, by the excitant etc., is **rasa.**

RG. 41.2

'विभावादयस्त्रयः समुदिता रसाः' इति कतिपये।

Trans.: The combination of the three being presented namely the excitant, (the ensuant and the transitory) etc., is **rasa**, is the view of some.

RG. 41.3

'त्रिषु यः एव चमत्कारी स एव रसोऽन्यथा तु त्रयोऽपि न' इति बहवः।

Trans.: That alone is **rasa** which is most charming among the three, otherwise, (in the absence of that charm) eventhough there (combination) is not (**rasa**) is the view of many.

RG. 41.4

'भाव्यमानो विभाव एव रसः' इत्यन्ये।

Trans.: According to some others: the excitant alone in which the permanent mood etc., are being thought after repeatedly, is **rasa.**

RG. 41.5

'तथा अनुभावस्तथा इतीतरे'।

Trans.: And the ensuant alone in which the permanent mood etc., are being thought after, repeatedly is **rasa**, is the view of still others.

RG. 42.

तत्र 'विभावानुभावव्यभिचारिसंयोगाद्रसनिष्पत्तिः' इति सूत्रं तत्तन्मतपरतया व्याख्यायते-'विभावानुभावव्यभिचारिभिःसंयोगाद् व्यञ्जनाद्र-

सस्य चिदानन्दविशिष्टस्थाय्यात्मनः स्थाय्युपहितचिदानन्दात्मनो वा निष्पत्तिः स्वरुपेण प्रकाशनम्' इत्याद्ये।

Trans.: Now the sutra namely, 'from the correlation of 'excitant', 'ensuant' and 'transitory moods', the **rasa** comes into being', is being explained following the respective ways of interpretations. According to the first view, due to the combination i. e. donate due to the suggestion of excitant, ensuant and transitory moods the "**rasa**" is experienced, which is in the form of eternal pleasure qualified by Love etc., or the 'Love' qualified by eternal pleasure etc.

RG. 42.1

'विभावानुभावव्यभिचारिणां सम्यकसाधारणात्मतया योगाद्भावकत्वव्यापारेण भावनाद्रसस्य स्थाय्युपहितसत्त्वोद्रेक प्रकाशितस्वात्मानन्दरूपस्य निष्पत्तिर्भोगाख्येन साक्षात्कारेण विषयी कृतिः' इति द्वितीये।

Trans.: Following the second view; Due to the combination i. e. the experience by the special power of poetic expression called भावकत्व the excitant, ensuant, transitory moods in the form of proper generalisation, the "Rasa", of the nature of the pleasure of sell realisation, latent in the form of permanent mood, and manifested in the dominance of 'सत्वगुण'.

RG. 42.2.

'विभावानुभावव्यभिचारिणां संयोगाद्भावनाविशेषरूपात्दोषाद्रसस्यानिर्वचनीयदुष्यन्तरत्याद्यात्मनो निष्पत्तिरुत्पत्तिः' इति तृतीये।

Trans.: Following the third view : Due to the combination of excitant, ensuant and transitory moods, i. e. due to the defect of the special type of experience, the "Rasa" in the form of unexpressable love of '**Duṣyanta**' etc., are experienced.

RG. 42.3.

विभावादीनां संयोगाज्ज्ञानाद्रसस्य ज्ञानविशेषात्मनो निष्पत्तिरुत्पत्तिः इति चतुर्थे।

Trans.: Following the fourth view: Rasa is generated in the form of a special type of experience, from the 'samyoga', namely the knowledge of the correlated excitant etc.

RG. 42.4.

'विभावादीनां संबन्धाद्रसस्य रत्यादेर्निष्पत्तिरारोपः' इति पञ्चमे।

Trans.: Following the fifth view, '**niṣpatti**' namely imposition, of **rasa** i. e. love etc., from the correlation of excitant etc.

RG. 42.5.

विभावादिभिः कृत्रिमैरप्यकृत्रिमतया गृहीतैः संयोगादनुमानाद्रसस्य रत्यादेनिष्पत्तिरनुमितिर्नटादौ पक्ष इति शेषः इति षष्ठे।

Trans.: Following the sixth view: Due to the combination i. e. (due to the) experience of the excitant etc. assuming as true or real which are not real, the "Rasa" in the form of Love etc., are experienced i. e. inferred in the subject, the actor etc.

RG. 42.6.

'विभावादीनां त्रयाणां संयोगात्समुदायाद्रसनिष्पत्ती रसपदव्यवहारः' इति सप्तमे।

Trans.: Following the seventh view : 'Rasa **niṣpatti**' namely to be designated as **rasa**, from the 'saṁyoga' i.e. from the collection of correlated of the three namely excitant etc.

RG. 42.7

'विभावादिषु सम्यग्योगाच्चमत्कारात्' इत्यष्टमे। तदेवं पर्यवसित-स्त्रिषु मतेषु सूत्रविरोधः।

Trans.: Following the eighth view: 'saṁyogāt' means from the proper union (of excitant etc), i. e. charming in excitant etc., (**rasa** to be experienced).

Like this, In the three (remaining) views, the contradiction with the sutra, is seen.

RG. 43.

विभावानुभावव्यभिचारिणामेकस्य तु रसान्तरसाधारणतया नियतरसव्यञ्जकतानुपपत्तेः सूत्रे मिलितानामुपादानम्।

एवं च प्रामाणिके मिलितानां व्यञ्जकत्वे यत्र क्वचिदेकस्मादेवा-साधारणाद्रसोद्बोधस्तत्रेतदद्वयमाक्षेप्यम्। अतो नानैकान्तिकत्वम्। इत्थं नानाजातीयाभिः शेमुषीभिर्नानारूपतयावसितोऽपि मनीषिभिः परमाह्लादा-विनाभावितया प्रतीयमानः प्रपञ्चेऽस्मिन्रसो रमणीयतामावहतीति निर्विवादम्।

Trans.: Due to the non-realisatioin of the invariable suggestiveness, of any one of excitant, ensuant and tranistory moods, for any one sentiment, or due to the lack of (any one of these three) being the suggestive of 'sentiments' in general, (the qualification) "due to the combination of", is given in the '**rasasūtra**'. Like this, when it is stated that the three together becomes suggestive (of **rasa**) where from extraordinary one, the sentiment is suggested, then the other forms are to be attributed (on that) hence, no fault of plurality of causes (for the suggestion of sentiment) would arise. Like this, though, the sentiment is defined differently by scholars of different intelects, still there is no difference of opinions on the fact that, it contain charmingness and is enjoyed as identical with the extraordinary pleasure.

RG. 44.

स च--शृङ्गारः करुणः शान्तो रौद्रो वीरोऽद्भुतस्तथा।
हास्यो भयानकश्चैव बीभत्सश्चेति ते नव॥

इत्युक्तेर्नवधा। मुनिवचनं चात्र मानम्[१]।

केचित्तु-शान्तस्य शमसाध्यत्वान्नटे च तदसंभवात्।
अष्टावेव रसा नाट्ये न शान्तस्तत्र युज्यते।। इत्याहुः।

Trana.: And that is of nine types when it is said thus:

Those (**rasas**) are nine (in number) namely, the erotic, the pathetic, the quietism. the furious, the heroic, the wonderful, the comic, the terrific and the disgustful. And the statement of the ancient (Bharatamuni) is the-proof (to hole so).

Some, however, hold (lit. said) like this; In dramatic composition, there are eight **rasas**: the quietism is not proper there (in drama). The quiestism is generated by detachment and is impossible in the destruction of that (in the character or actor).

Notes : Here PR discusses about the number of **rasas.** To him, the rasas are nine including quietism. He establishes quietism as a separate sentiment even in a dramatic act, on the authority of Bharata- **munivacanaṁ atra mānaṁ.** He records the view of some critics who holds that quiestism and its permanent mood **śama,** cannot be accepted in the case of dramatic act because, the dramatic accompaniments-music, dance etc., go against the nature of **śama,** which is defined by detachment from worldly affairs.

RG. 44.1

तच्चपरे न क्षमन्ते। तथाहि-नटे शमाभावादिति हेतुरसंगतः।

नटे रसाभिव्यक्तेरस्वीकारात्। सामाजिकानां शमवत्त्वेन तत्र रसोद्बोधे बाधकाभावात्। न च नटस्य शमाभावात्तदभिनय प्रकाशकत्वानुपपत्तिरिति वाच्यम्। तस्य भयक्रोधादेरप्यभावेन तदभिनयप्रकाशकताया अप्यसंगत्यापत्तेः। यदि च नटस्य क्रोधादेरभावेन वास्तव-

---

१. चौ, ओ, -प्रमाणम्

तत्कार्याणां बधबन्धादीनामुत्पत्त्यसंभवेऽपि कृत्रिमतत्कार्याणां शिक्षाभ्यासादित उत्पत्तौ नास्ति वाधकमिति नीरीक्ष्यते, तदा प्रकृतेऽपि तुल्यम्।

Trans.: That is not tolerated by others. It is like this-the ground namely, there is the absence of detachmentness, in the actor is not correct, because, the manifestation of sentiment in the actor is not accepted. There is the absence of difficulty for the enjoyment of sentiment in the case of audience since (they) posses detachment. It should not be argued thus; due to the absence of detachmentness in the character, the expression by action is not possible to generate that. Because, there would arise the contingency of improperness in the expression by action, due to the (similar) absence of fear, anger, of that (character).

And it is observed thus: there is no obstacle for generation of action, eventhough, the real actions like killing, arresting etc., are not possible due to the absence of anger etc., in case of the character, but, it is to be generated by the (helf of) learning, practicing of those artificial actions. Then the argument is like: in the case of the sentiment in question (i. e. quietism), (the generation of actions) will be similar (to those other sentiments).

RG. 45

अथ नाट्ये गीतवाद्यादीनां विरोधिनां सत्त्वात्सामाजिकेष्वपि विषयवैमुख्यात्मनः शान्तस्य कथमुद्रेक इति चेत्, नाट्ये शान्तरसमभ्युपगच्छद्भिः फलबलात्तद्गीतवाद्यादेस्तस्मिन्विरोधिताया अकल्पनात्। विषयचिन्तासामान्यस्य तत्र विरोधित्वस्वीकारे तदीयालम्बनस्य संसारानित्यत्वस्य तदुद्दीपनस्य पुराणश्रवणसत्सङ्गपुण्यवन तीर्थावलोकनादेरपि विषयत्वेन विरोधित्वापत्तेः।

Trans.: Objection: Well, It may be urged: how then there would be the experience of quietism which is of the nature 'of indifference towards wordly objects, in the audience in case of dramatic presentation due to the pressure of contradictory elements like song, music etc.

Answer: Those who accept the quietism sentiment in the dramatic presentation donot accept the contradicotry characters of the song, music etc., presented there in that (dramatic presentation), on the basis of the effect (of the 'quietism sentiment'). And if the "univerasality of knowledge of wordly object" is accepted as contradictory to (the experience of quietism sentiment) then, there would arise the contingency of accepting the transitory characters of the universe, its sustaintial mood (cause) and the listining of scriptures, association with noble beings, visiting a sacred place etc., its ehancing mood (cause) as contradictory.

RG. 45.1

अत एव चरमाध्याये संगीतरत्नाकरेः–"अष्टावेव रसा नाट्येष्विति केचिदचूचुदन्। तदचारु यतः कंचिन्न रसं स्वदते नटः॥"

इत्यादिना नाट्येपि शान्तो रसोऽस्तीति व्यवस्थापितम्।

यैरपि नाट्ये शान्तो रसो नास्तीत्यभ्युपगम्यते तैरपि बाधकाभावान्महाभारतादिप्रबन्धानां शान्तरसप्रधानतया[१]।

अखिललोकानुभवसिद्धत्वाच्च काव्ये सोऽवश्यं स्वीकार्यः।

Trans.: Thus, there is **śāntarasa** also in the drama, is established by this namely, "some held that there are eight **rasas** in dramas, it is not proper, because the actor does not enjoy any **rasa** at all etc", in the last chapter of **Saṅgīta-ratnākara** (=SR). And those who do not accept the **śāntarasa** in dramas, they also, due to the absence of any contradiction and due to its acceptance by the experience of many and due to the pre-dominance of **śāntarasa** in Mahābhārata etc., that ought to be accepted in poetry.

१. चौ, म, संपू, मदु–प्रधानताया

RG. 45.2

अत एव 'अष्टौ नाट्ये रसाः स्मृताः' इत्युपक्रम्य 'शान्तोऽपि नवमो रसः' इति मम्मटभट्टा अप्युपसमहार्षुः।

अमीषां च-

'रतिः शोकश्च निर्वेदक्रोधोत्साहश्च विस्मयः।
हासो भयं जुगुप्सा च स्थायिभावाः क्रमादमी'॥

Trans.: Therefore, Mammaṭabhaṭa also starting from that statement namely, "there are eight **rasas**." And of these (nine **rasas**), the permanent moods are love, sorrow, detachment, anger, energy, wonder, laughter, gear and disquiet respectively.

Notes : Ultimately, PR establishes quietism as the ninth **rasa** following Mammaṭa etc., - śāntopi navamaḥ rasaḥ.

RG. 46

रसेभ्यः स्थायिभावानां घटादेर्घटाद्यवच्छिन्नाकाशादिव प्रथम-द्वितीययोर्मतयोः, सत्यरजतस्यानिर्वचनीयरजतादिव तृतीये, विषयस्य (रजतादेः) ज्ञानादिव चतुर्थे भेदो बोध्यः। तत्र आ प्रबन्धं स्थिरत्वादमीषां भावानां स्थायित्वम्। न च चित्तवृत्तिरूपाणामेषामाशुविनाशित्वेन स्थिरत्वं दुर्लभम्, वासनारूपतया स्थिरत्वं तु व्यभिचारिष्वतिप्रसक्तमिति वाच्यम्। वासनारूपाणाममीषां मुहुर्मुहुरभिव्यक्तेरेव स्थिरपदार्थत्वात्। व्यभिचारिणां तु नैव, तदभिव्यक्तेर्विद्युदुद्योतप्रायत्वात्।

Trans.: The difference of the permanent moods from the sentiments are to be understood as of the pot etc. from the sky, delimited by the pot following the first and second views. of the real silver from the imaginary silver (where shell is wrongly cognised as silver), in the third view, of the object (like silver etc.) for the experience in the fourth view. The permanecy of these moods are due to their remaining in fact from the beginning of the poetry (till the enjoyment of the sentiments).

Objection: it may be argued: The permanency of these, is not possible to justify, because they are destroyed immediately (after the enjoyment) since they are the nature of mental states. And if however, the permanency (of these) are accepted as in the form of impressions, there, it would wrongly be extended to transitory moods.

Answer: Not so. Because, the permanency of these in the form of (previous) impressions is due to the repeated manifestation (of those) only. On the otherhand, the transitory moods are not like that, because the manifestation of that is like the flash of the lightening and uninterrupted.

Notes : The distinction between sentiment and permanent mood is not possible at any condition, **Ratyadi avacchinna caitanya** is different from ratyadibhoga **rasaḥ.** It is quite similarly discussed by Abhinav and Bhaṭṭnāyaka with the case of a pot and sky. Here both objects are far from similarity. **Ākāsavacchinnaghaṭaḥ** is not used anywhere unlike the use of **ghaṭādyavacchinna ākāsa.** According to the view of third group of scholars, sentiment is different from permanent mood like the case of real silver and imaginary silver. The fourth group shows the difference that, the knowledge is different from the subject i.e., **visayasya-jnanadiva sthāyibhāvasya rasāt bhedaḥ.**

RG. 47.

यदाहुः-'विरुद्धैरविरुद्धैर्वा भावैर्विच्छिद्यते न यः।
आत्मभावं नयत्याशु स स्थायी लवणाकरः॥
चिरं चित्तेऽवतिष्ठन्ते संबध्यन्तेऽनुबन्धिभिः।
रसत्वंये प्रपद्यन्ते प्रसिद्धाः स्थायिनोऽत्र ते'॥

चिरमिति व्यभिचारिवारणाय। अनुबन्धिभिर्विभावाद्यैः। तथा 'सजातीयविजातीयैरतिरस्कृतमूर्तिमान्'।

यावद्रसं वर्तमानः स्थायिभाव उदाहृतः॥ इति।

Trans.: As is said (by ancients) which does not differentiate from the similar or dissimilar moods, and instantly transforms then into its won form, that is permanent (mood) like the mine of salt (ocean). Though, which stay for a long duration in heart. are associated with the connectors and attained the state of **rasa**, they are known as permanent (mood) here. The expression namely 'ciram' is to exclude the transitory mood. 'With the connectors' means with the excitant etc. Thus, which is not affected by the favourable and unfavourable moods; excitant along with the **rasa** is called as permanent mood.

RG. 48.

केचित्तु रत्याद्यन्यतमत्वं स्थायित्वमाहुः। तन्न। रत्यादीनामेकस्मिन्प्ररूढेऽन्यस्याप्ररूढस्य व्यभिचारित्वोपगमात्। प्ररूढत्वाप्ररूढत्वे वह्वल्पविभावजत्वे। तदुक्तं रत्नाकरे-

'रत्यादयः स्थायिभावाः स्युर्भूयिष्ठविभावजाः।
स्तोकं[१]र्विभावैरुत्पन्नास्त एव व्यभिचारिणः॥ इति।

एवं च वीररसे प्रधाने क्रोधो, रौद्रे चौत्साहः, श्रृङ्गरो हासो व्यभिचारी भवति, नान्तरीयकश्च। यदा तु प्रधानपरिपोषार्थं सोऽपि बहुविभावजः क्रियते तदा तु रसालंकार इत्यादि बोध्यम्।

Trans.: The state of being permanent (i. e. permanentness) is being one of the love etc., is the view of some. That is not true. Because, in the dominance of one of the love etc., the other which is non-dominant would be vyabhicari. And the condition of being dominant and non dominant is governed by being produced from profuseness and scarcity of excitant etc., respectively.

The same is stated in SR, namely: the love etc., are the

---

१. चौ, म, संपू, -स्तोकैः

permanent moods, produced from the profuseness of excitant etc., and produced from less excitants are transitory moods. And thus, the dominance of 'Anger' in the heroic sentiment, 'Enthusiasm' in the furious, 'Laughter' in erotic become transitory, and are not to be separated.

However, when, for the accompishment of the main (permanent mood), that also is presented by profuseness of excitant, then it should be understood as the case of रसवदलंकार etc.

RG. 49.

तत्र—स्त्रीपुंसयोरन्योन्यालम्बनः प्रेमाख्याश्चित्तवृत्तिविशेषो रतिः स्थायिभावः॥ गुरुदेवतापुत्राद्यालम्बनस्तु व्यभिचारी।

Trans.: Out of these (nine) the permanent mood, love, is the state of mental feeling (activity) called love, receprocally dependant on the (beloved) woman and (lover) man. However the lover is dependant on (the woman and her lover) teacher, God, Son etc. would be transitory mood.

RG. 49.1

पुत्रादिवियोगमरणादिजन्मा वैक्लव्याख्याश्चित्तवृत्तिविशेषः शोकः॥

स्त्रीपुंसयोस्तु वियोगे जीवितत्वज्ञानदशायां वैक्लव्यपोषिताया रतेरेव प्राधान्याच्छृङ्गारो विप्रलम्भाख्यो रसः। वैक्लव्यं तु संचारिमात्रम्।

मृतत्वज्ञानदशायां तु रतिपोषितस्य वैक्लव्यस्येति करुण एव। यदा तु सत्यपि मृतत्वज्ञाने देवताप्रसादादिना पुनरुज्जीवनज्ञानं कथंचित्स्यात्, तदालम्बनस्यात्यन्तिकनिरासाभावाच्चिरप्रवास विप्रलम्भ एव न स करुणः। यथा चन्द्रपीडं प्रति महाश्वेतावाक्येषु। केचित्तु रसान्तरम् एवात्र करुणविप्रलम्भाख्यमिच्छन्ति।

Trans.: The state of mental feeling (activity) called patheticness generated from the separation, death of son etc. is sorrow.

In the condition of separation of beloved (woman) and lover (man), in the knowledge of (the lover & beloved) 'being alive', the erotic sentiment, due to the predominance supported by pathosness is called love-in-separation. But the pathosness, is transitory only. In the knowledge of (beloved or lover) 'being dead', the patheticness supported by love, is indeed Pathos. However when even in the knowledge of (beloved or lover) 'being dead', if there is the knowledge of the possibility of 'being alive', again, some how, due to the blessing of God etc., then (in that case), because of the absence of absolute denial of the dependant, that is not Pathos, but is love-in-separation, like staying away for long. For example: in the expression of **Mahāśvetā** towards **Candrāpiḍa**. However, some hold this as a distinct sentiment (**rasa**) in the name of "love-in-separation with Pathos."

RG. 49.2

नित्यानित्यवस्तुविचारजन्मा विषयविरागाख्यो[१] निर्वेदः॥
गृहकलहादिजस्तु व्यभिचारी।

Trans.: The mental feeling in the name of non-enjoyment of worldly objects generated from decissive thoughts of mortal and imortal (objects) is detachment. But those generating from the quarrel in house. etc, is transitory mood.

RG. 49.3

गुरुबन्धुवधादिपरमापराधजन्मा प्रज्वलनाख्यः क्रोधः॥

अयं च परविनाशादिहेतुः। क्षुद्रापराधजन्मा तु पुरुषवचना-संभाषणादिहेतुः। अयमेवामर्षाख्यो व्यभिचारीति विवेकः।

Trans.: The state of mental feeling, called inflamation, generated from highest crimes, like the killing of (one's) teacher, (one's) friend etc., is anger.

---

१. म, -विरामाख्यो

This anger is the cause of killng of others or enemy etc. But if generated from a minor crime, is the cause of hard speech, not speaking (properly) etc.

This (anger) is the transitory mood namely, indignation (**अमर्ष**), thus is the difference.

RG. 49.4

परपराक्रमदानादिस्मृतिजन्मा औन्नत्याख्य उत्साहः॥

Trans.: The mental feeling called progressiveness generated from the memory like the 'bravery of enemy', 'the donating by some one', etc. is energy.

RG. 49.5

अलौकिकवस्तुदर्शनादिजन्मा आश्चर्याख्यो विस्मयः॥

Trans.: The mental feeling called astonishment, generated from the sight of non worldly objects (extraordinary things) etc., is wonder.

RG. 49.6

वागङ्गादिविकारदर्शनजन्मा विकासाख्यो हासः॥

Trans.: The mental feeling called developments generated frm the sight of the deformity of speech, limbs etc., is laughter.

RG. 49.7

व्याघ्रदर्शनादिजन्मा परमानर्थविषयको वैक्लव्याख्यः स भयम्॥

परमानर्थविषयकत्वाभावे तु स एव त्रासो व्यभिचारी।

अपरे तु औत्पातिकप्रभवस्त्रासः, स्वापराधद्वारोत्थं भयमिति भयत्रासयोर्भेदमाहुः।

Trans.: The mental feeling in the name of feebleness, generated from the sight of the tiger etc., having some utter-misfortune as its object, is fear. That (fear) is a transitory mood namely '**trāsa**' where the utter-misfortune is not its object. However other accept the difference between fear and **trāsa** thus: **trāsa** is caused by natural calamities (where as) fear is generated from one's own-fault (crime made by own-self)

RG. 49.8

कदर्यवस्तुविलोकनजन्मा विचिकित्साख्यश्चित्तवृत्तिविशेषो जुगुप्सा॥

Trans.: The mental feeling in the name of hatredness generated from the sight of some unpleasant (ugly) objects, is disgust.

RG. 50.

एवमेषां स्थायिभावानां लोके तत्तन्नायकगतानां यान्यालम्बन-तयोद्दीपनतया वा कारणत्वेन प्रसिद्धानि तान्येषु काव्यनाट्ययोर्व्यज्यमानेषु विभावशब्देन व्यपदिश्यन्ते॥

विभावयन्तीति व्युत्पत्तेः।
यानिच कार्यतया तान्यनुभावशब्देन॥

अनु पश्चाद्भाव उत्पत्तिर्येषाम्। अनुभावयन्तीति वा व्युत्पत्तेः।
यानि सह चरन्ति तानि व्यभिचारिशब्देन॥

Trans.: And those which are known as causes in the from of sustaintial or enhancing moods of these permanent moods, residing in the respective heros in common life, are expressed by the term **vibhāva** (i. e. excitant) when presented in poetry and drama. This is on the basis of the etymology, namely (they) specifically help in the attainment (of permanent mood).

Those which are (known as) effect, are (expressed) by, the term **anubhāva** (i. e. ensuant).

Because of the etymology namely, they are effected afterward (or 'anu' means afterward) and **bhāva** means 'affecting' of those. Those, which coexists (with excitant and ensuant) are (expressed) by the term 'vyabhicāri' (i. e. transitory moods).

RG. 51.

तत्र शृङ्गारस्य स्त्रीपुंसावालम्बने चन्द्रिकावसन्तविविधोपवन-पवनरहस्थानादय उद्दीपनविभावाः। तन्मुखावलोकनतद्गुणश्रवण-कीर्तनादयोऽन्ये सात्त्विकभावाश्चानुभावाः। स्मृतिचिन्तादयो व्यभिचारिणः।

Trans.: In the case of erotic sentiment, the **ālaṁbanas** are beloved and loved (for each other), the moon light, the spring season, various gardens, the breeze, the lonely place etc., are **uddipanavibhāvas**. The (beautiful) sight of face (of the hero by the heroine or vice-versa), the uttering and listening of his merits (human qualities) etc., and the सात्त्विक moods are ensuants. The recollection, anxiety etc., are transitory moods.

RG. 51.1

करुणस्य बन्धुनाशादय आलम्बनानि। तत्संबन्धिगृहतुरगाभरण-दर्शनादयस्तत्कथाश्रवणादयश्चोद्दीपकाः। गात्रक्षेपाश्रुपातादयोऽनुभावा, ग्लानिक्षयमोहविषादचिन्तौत्सुक्यदीनताजडतादयो व्यभिचारिणः।

Trans.: The death of the friend etc., are alambanas of Pathos. The seeing of (one's) own house, (his) horse, (his) ornaments etc., and the listening of ones' (past) stroy etc. (of one for the others) are **uddīpakas.** The rubbing the body (due to sorrow), the shedding of tear etc., are the ensuants and pallor, weakness, perplexity, depression, anxiety, longing, wretchedness, insensitiveness etc., (सात्विक) are the trasitory moods.

RG. 51.2

शान्तस्यानित्यत्वेन ज्ञातं जगदालम्बनम्। वेदान्तश्रवणतपोवन-तापसदर्शनाद्युद्दीपनम्। विषयारुचिशत्रुमित्राद्यौदासीन्यचेष्टाहानि-नासाग्रदृष्ट्या दयोऽनुभावाः। हर्षोन्मादस्मृतिमत्यादयो व्यभिचारिणः।

Trans.: The realisation of the world as transitory is the

ālaṁbana to quietism. The listening fo Vedic texts, the sight of the forest (the sight) with asetic etc., are **uddīpanas**. The hesitation towards worldly desires, the indifference for friend or (and) foe, disinterested for any activities, concetring on one's nose (meditating) etc., are the ensuants. The joy, madness, recollection, judgement etc., are the transitory moods.

RG. 51.3

रौद्रस्यागस्कृत्पुरुषादिरालम्बनम्। तत्कृतोऽपराधादिरुद्दीपकः।

वधबन्धादिफलको नेत्रारुण्यदन्तपीडनपरुषभाषणशस्त्रग्रहणा-दिरनुभावः। अमर्षवेग्रौग्य्रचापलादयः संचारिणः।

एवं यस्याश्चित्तवृत्तेर्यो विषयः स तस्या आलम्बनम्। निमित्तानि चोद्दीपकानीति बोध्यम्।।

Trans.: The sinful person etc., are the sustantial (mood) of the furious (sentiment). The sins etc., committed by one, are enhancing (mood). The reddish eyes, biting teeth, harsh speech, holding weapon etc., with the purpose of killing, arresting etc. are ensuants. And the resentment, excitement, ferocity, unsteadiness etc., are transitory moods. Like this, whatever is the object of (whatever) mental fellings, those are the sustantial (moods) of those, And, (there) the causes (should be) understood as enhancing (moods).

RG. 52.

तत्र शृङ्गारो द्विविधः। संयोग विप्रलम्भश्च। रतेः संयोगकाला-वच्छिन्नत्वे प्रथमः। वियोगकालावच्छिन्नत्वे द्वितीयः, संयोगश्च न दम्पत्योः समानाधिकरण्यम्।

एकतल्पशयनेऽपीर्ष्यादिसद्भावे विप्रलम्भस्यैव वर्णनात्। एवं वियोगोऽपि न वैयधिकरणम्। दोषस्योक्तत्वात्। तस्माद्द्वौबिमौ संयोग-वियोगाख्यावन्तः करणवृत्तिविशेषौ।

यत्संयुक्तो वियुक्तश्चास्मीति धीः। तत्राद्यो यथा शयिता सविधेऽप्यनीश्वरा इत्यत्रः निरूपितः।

Trans.: Out of those, the erotic is of two types (namely), love-in-union and love-in-separation. The love by the delimitted time of union is the first. When delimitted by the time of separation (it) is the second. And the union (lit. contact) is not the state of being co-existance of the lover and the beloved, Because, even in the case of sleeping in one bed, the description of love in separation is seen due to the presence of envy etc., Similarly, (the love in) separation is not the state of being existing in different places due to the fault as told. Thus, these two namely 'saṁyoga' and 'viyoga' are the special type of metal feelings (states) of internal qualities, which creates the feelings (lit. knowledge) namely, being united and being separated. Out of these two, the example for first is explained here namely, "sleepling nearer to her husband (beloved) one, yet unable..." (in the RG. 11.1)

Notes : The erotic sentiment is basically divided into two categories. The first one is love-in-union and the other one is love-in-separation. However, in some editions, **vipralaṁbha** is replaced by the term 'viyoga' and the meaning is constant. we can accept vipralaṁbha as the appropriate term to this context, because, here love remains as permanent mood where, vipralaṁbha causes one variety of erotic sentiment. Interestingly, in the case of the division of heros, one type of hero is called as vipralabdha, which is partially similar with the term vipralaṁbha. Thus, according to some scholar like Madhusudana Sastri, if vipralaṁbha is used in the proper context, it will cause the fault. But if these **vipralaṁbha** is explained with its proper definition, then there is no harm.

RG. 52.1

यत्तु चित्रमीमांसायाम्–'वागर्थाविव संपृक्तौ', इत्यत्र रसध्वनिः, निरतिशयप्रेमशालिताव्यञ्जनात् तद्ध्वनिमार्गानाकलननिबन्धनम्। पार्वतीपरमेश्वरविषयककविरतौ प्रधाने निरतिशयप्रेम्णो गुणीभावात्। न हि गुणीभूतस्य रत्यादे रसध्वनिव्यपदेशहेतुत्वं युक्तम्। 'भिन्नो रसाद्यलंकारादलंकार्यतया स्थितः' इति सिद्धान्तात्।

Trans.: Whatever is said in **CM** namely, in the case "like the union of word and sense etc., (**vāgarthau**)." is a case of **rasadhavni**, because of the suggestion of possesing deep love (**niratiśaya**) is due to not understanding properly the principles of suggestiveness (**Dhvanimārga**).

Because, since the poet's love having its objects as Parvati ans Siva is dominating (primary), the deep love (of Siva and Parvati) becomes sub-ordinate. Indeed, it is not proper to hold the love etc., which are subordinate as the cause of the expression of **rasadhvani**. Because of the conclusive opinion namely, **rasavadālaṁkāra** is placed separately from alaṁkārya (i. e. **Dhvani**).

RG. 52.2

द्वितीयो यथा-'वाचो माङ्गलिकीः प्रयाणसमये जल्पत्यनल्पं जने/ केलीमन्दिरमारुतायनमुखे विन्यस्तवक्त्राम्बुजा// निःश्वासग्लपिताधरोपरिपतद्बाष्पार्द्रवक्षोरुहा/ बाला लोलविलोचना शिव शिव प्राणेशमालोकते'//

अत्राप्यालम्बनस्य नायकस्य निःश्वासाश्रुपातादेरनुभावस्य, विषादचिन्तावेगादेश्च व्यभिचारिण, संयोगाद्रतिरभिव्यज्यमाना वियोगकालावच्छिन्नत्वाद्विप्रलंभरसव्यपदेशहेतुः।

Trans.: The second is as follows: "The young lady, keeping her louts-face on the window of their meeting home, with heavy breaths and moving eyes, shedding tears on breasts, looks to her husband (with heart rending condition), when the relatives (of her husband) made much farewell speeches at his departed time."

Here also, the love being menifested by the co-relation of the sustantial like husband (beloved), the ensuants like the heavy breaths and shedding of tear etc, and the transitory moods like the depression, anxiety, excitement etc, is the casue for the expression of love in separation due to it being delimitted by the time of separation.

RG. 52.3

यथा वा- 'आविर्भूता यदवधि मधुस्यन्दिनी नन्दसूनोः/ कान्तिः काचिन्निखिलनयनाकर्षणे कार्मणज्ञा// श्वासो दीर्घस्तदवधि मुखे पाण्डिमा गण्डयुग्मे/ शून्या वृत्तिः कुलमृगदृशां चेतसि प्रादुरासीत्'//

यथा वा- 'नयनाञ्चलावमर्शं या न कदाचित्पुरा सेहे।
आलिङ्गितापि जोषं तस्थौ सा गन्तुकेन दयितेन'॥

इहापि सहजचांचल्यनिवृत्तिर्जडता चानुभावव्यभिचारिणौ।

इमं च पञ्चविधं प्राञ्चः प्रवासादिभिरुपाधिभिरामनन्ति॥

ते च प्रवासाभिलाषविरहेर्ष्याशापानां विशेषानुपलम्भान्नास्माभिः प्रपञ्चिताः।

Trans.: Or for example: "A long sigh from the mouth, pallor on the cheek and a vancant mood of the mind were experienced by high-born ladies from the time that they saw the knew inexpressible beauty of the son of Nanda, that dropped honey (i.e., was sweet like honey) and the magic of attracting all eyes."

Or again as follows: "She, who could never before bear even the contact of a glance, remained silent even though embraced by her lover who intended to go away (to some distance)."

In this case also, the non-interested looking is ensuant and the insensitiveness is transitory mood.

To these, by the imposes properties like foreign residence

etc., the old theorists called as five varieties. And they are namely foreign residence (of lover), longing, isolation, Jealousy, curse are not elaborated by us due to the absence of any speciality.

RG. 53.

करुणो यथा– 'अपहाय सकलबान्धवचिन्तामुद्वास्य गुरुकुल-प्रणयम्। हा तनय विनयशालिन्कथमिव परलोकपथिकोऽभूः'॥

अत्र प्रमीततनय आलम्बनम्। तत्कालावच्छिन्नबान्धवदश नाद्युदी-पनम्। रोदनमनुभावः। दैन्यादयः संचारिणः।

Trans.: The illustration of Pathos is as follows:

"Abandoning cares for all kinsmen and discarding affection for his family, parents etc., how have you; oh (my) devoted Son ! become a guest (lit-traveller) of the other world."

Here, the dead son is sustaintial mood and the sight of relatives etc, at that situation is enhancing moods. The crying is ensuant and the state of pityness etc., are transitory moods.

RG. 54.

शान्तो यथा–'मलयानिलकालकूटयो रमणीकुन्तलभोगिभोगयोः।

श्वपचात्मभुवोर्निरन्तरा मम जाता परमात्मनि स्थितिः'॥

अत्र प्रपञ्चः सर्वोऽप्यालम्बनम्। सर्वत्र साम्यमनुभावः।

मत्यादयः संचारिणः। यद्यपि प्रथमार्धे उत्तमाधमयोरुपक्रमा-द्द्वितीयार्धेऽधमोत्तमवचनं क्रमभङ्गमावहति, तथापि वक्तुर्ब्रह्मात्मक-तयोत्तमाधमज्ञानवैकल्यं संपन्नमिति द्योतनाय क्रमभङ्गो गुण एव।

Trans.: The illustration of quietism (sentiment) is as follows:

"Between the **Malaya** wind and the **Kālakuṭa** poison, the lady's lock of hair and the hood of snake, and a **Cāṇḍāla** and **Brāhmin,** there is no difference for me, having attained the state of Supreme Soul."

Here the entire phenomenal world is sustaintial mood, the identity in all cases is ensuant mood and the judgement etc, are transitory moods.

Even though, in the first half (of the verse) due to its beginning in sequence of superior and inferior (objects) and in the second half with inferior and superior (objects), it bears the fault of 'not following the sequence', yet, that lack of sequence is merit to show that as the speaker has attented in the sate of Superme Soul, lacks the knowledge of superiority and inferiority.

RG. 54.1

इदं पुनर्नोदाहार्यम्– 'सुरस्त्रोतस्विन्याः पुलिनमधितिष्ठन्नयनयो-र्विधायान्तर्मुद्रामथ सपदि विद्राव्य विषयान्। विधूतान्तर्ध्वान्तो मधुरमधुरायां चिति कदा, निमग्नः स्यां कस्यांचन नवनभस्याम्बुदरुचि'॥

अत्रापि यद्यपि विषयगणालम्बनः सुरस्त्रोतस्विनीतटाद्युद्दीपितो नयननिमीलनादिभिरनुभावितः स्थायी निर्वेदः प्रतीयते, तथापि भगव-द्वासुदेवालम्बनायां कविरतौ गुणीभूत इति न शान्तरसध्वनिव्यपदेशहेतुः। इदं च पद्यं मन्त्रिर्मितायां भगवद्भक्तिप्रधानायां करुणालहर्यामुपनि-बद्धमिति तत्प्रधानभावप्रधन्यमेवार्हति। शान्तरसाननुगुणश्चायमोजस्वी गुम्फे इति चानुदापहार्यमेवैतत्। पूर्वपद्ये तु परमात्मनि स्थितीः इत्यनेन तत्ताद्रूप्यावगमाद्रतेरप्रतिपत्तिः।

Trans.: This again is not to be illustrated (as **Śāntarasa**) "when shall I merge with the charmful Superme Soul like the newly arrived attractive cloud on the sky, after rejecting entire worldly desires and removing ignorance, by sitting near the bank of Gaṅgā, the river of Gods, with closed eyes."

Here also, even though, the permanent mood detachment is revealed from the sustaintial mood like worldly objects, the enhancing moods like the bank etc., of river Ganga, the ensuant mood like the closing eyes, yet, it is not the cause of the expression, namely, **Rasadhavani** of quietism (sentiment) due to the sub-ordination of love of the poet having sustaintial mood like lord **Vāsudeva.**

And this verse is included in **KL**, composed by me, primarily based on devotion to God: Thus, it becomes capable for the predominance of that mood (Bhagavat Bhakti). further, this cannot be illustrated as an example of the quietism sentiment, due to its composition with vigourous as a negative merit for **Śāntarasa.** In the earlier verse, however, by the experssion, '**paramātmani sthitiḥ...**etc'., the love is not revealed due to the cognition of indentity.

RG. 55.

रौद्रो यथा– 'नवोच्छलितयौवनस्फुरदखर्वगर्वज्वरे/ मदीयगुरु-कार्मुकं गलितसाध्वसं वृश्चति। अयं पततु निर्दय दलितदृप्तभूभृद्गल/ स्खलद्रुधिरघस्मरो मम परश्वधो भैरवः'//

अत्र तदानीं रामत्वेनाज्ञातो गुरुकार्मुकभञ्जक आलम्बनम्।

अत एव विशेष्यानुपादानम्। गुरुद्रुहो नामग्रहणानौचित्यात्, क्रोधाविष्काराद्वा। ध्वनिविशेषानुमितो निःशङ्कधनुर्भङ्ग उद्दीपकः।

पुरुषोक्तिरनुभावः। गर्वोग्रत्वादयः संचारिणः। एषा च धनुर्भङ्गध्वनि-भग्नसमाधेर्भार्गवस्योक्तिः।

Trans.: The illustration of **Raudrarasa** is as follows:

"On him highly proud of his blooming youth and breaking without fear my teacher's bow may fall my terrible axe, wet with the blood of the vain of kings."

Here, the breaker of bow of his guru, unknown as being Rāma at that time is sustaintial mood. Therefore. the specific name is not mentioned, (or) due to the improperness of uttering the name of one, disregarding one's guru or due to the anger.

The breaking of the bow without fear inferred from the peculiar sound is enhancing mood. The speech with harsh words is ensuant mood. The pride, the violence etc, are the transitory moods. This is the speech of Parasurama, whose meditation was broken by the sound for the break of bow.

RG. 55.1

वृत्तिरप्यत्र महोद्धता रौद्रस्य परमौजस्वितां परिपुष्णाति। अन्यत्र गुरुस्मरणे सत्यहंभावविगमस्यावश्यकतया प्रकृते चाजहत्स्वार्थलक्षणा-मूलध्वननेन मदीयेत्यनेन गर्वोत्कर्षस्यैव प्रकाशानात्स्फुटं गम्यमानेन विवेकशून्यत्वेन क्रोधस्याधिक्यं गम्यते।

Trans.: The highly agitated style (of composition) is, here supportive to the excessive florridity of furious (sentiment). At other cases, the necessity of avioding the arrogance due to the rememberance of teacher would arise. (i. e. furious sentiment cannot take place). Yet by the experssion namely मदीय as it is included with the **ajahatsvārthalakṣaṇā** and the superiority of **garva** is suggestive and (hence), the superiority of anger also is suggested due to the clear realisation of विवेकशून्यता i. e. the lack of proper judgement.

RG. 55.2

इदं तु नोदाहार्यम्–'धनुर्विदलनध्वनिश्रवणतत्क्षणाविर्भवन्महा-गुरुवधस्मृतिः श्वसनवेगधूताधरः। विलोचनविनिः सरद्बहलवि-स्फुलिङ्गव्रजो रघुप्रवरमाक्षिपञ्जयति जामदग्न्यो मुनिः'॥

अत्राप्यपराधास्पदेन रघुनन्दनेनालम्बितो धनुर्विदलन ध्वनिश्रवणे-नोद्दीपितो निःश्वासनेत्रज्वलनादिभिरनुभावितो महागुरुवधस्मृति-गर्वोग्रत्वादिभिश्च संचारितः क्रोधो यद्यपि व्यज्यते, तथाप्यसौ तत्प्रभाव-वर्णनबीजभूतायां कविरतौ गुणीभूत इति न रौद्ररसध्वनिव्यपदेशहेतुः। काव्यप्रकाशगतरौद्ररसोदाहरणे तु "कृतमनुमतं दृष्टं वा यैरिदं गुरु-पातकम्" इति पद्ये रौद्ररसव्यञ्जनक्षमा नास्ति वृत्तिः, अतस्तत्कवेरशक्तिरेव।

Trans.: This is not to be illustrated as (an example of **raudra rasa**): "The memory of the killing of (his) master (जामदग्नी) awakened at once by listening the sound form the breaking of the bow, the lower lip trembled due to the long breathings; the forceful fire like reddish eyes brightened, and in these conditions, Paraśurām, indicated his superiority ot Rāma, the successor of Raghu.

"Here also even though the anger (**krodha**) is expressed by having the sustaintial mood like the successor of Raghu, who has comitted sin, the enhancing mood like the listening of the sound of bow breaking the ensuant mood like the breathing, reddish eyes etc., and the transitory moods like the recollection of the killing of Master, pride, ugratā etc, yet, is not the cause of the expression as **rasadhvani** of Raudra, becuase of being sustaintial to the poet's love which is the root-cause for the narration of his glory.

On the other hand, in the illustrative verse of **Raudrarasa** in **KP**, namely, कृतमनु....there is no style of producing the suggestion of **Raudrarasa**, and therefore, that is only due to the lack of poet's intuition.

RG. 56.

वीरश्चतुर्धा। दानदयायुद्धधर्मैस्तदुपाधेरुत्साहस्य चतुर्विधत्वात्।

तत्राद्यो यथा–'कियदिदमधिकं मे यद्द्विजायार्थयित्रे/कवचमरमणीयं कुण्डले चार्पयामि। अकरुणमवकृत्य द्राक्कृपाणेन निर्य/द्वहलरुधिरधारं मौलिमावेदयामि॥

एषा द्विजवेषायेन्द्राय कवचकुण्डलदानोद्यतस्य कर्णस्य तद्दानविस्मितान्सभ्यान्प्रत्युक्तिः। अत्र याचमान आलम्बनम्। तदुदीरिता स्तुतिरुद्दीपिका। कवचादिवितरणं तत्र लघुत्वबुद्ध्यादिकं चानुभावः।

मे इत्यर्थान्तरसंक्रमितवाच्यध्वन्युत्थापितो गर्वः स्वकीयलोकोत्तरपितृजन्यत्वादिस्मृतिश्च संचारिणौ।

Trans.: The Heroic sentiment is of four types. Because of their imposed properties of **utsāha** (as permanent mood) as being four, namely, **dāna, dayā, yuddha** and **dharma.**

The example for the first type out of these four is:

"What is this enough I am offering to the Brahmins, with an ordinary armour and ear-rings? (I) can offer my head withfull of blood, after cutting by a cruel sword."

This is the expression of Karṇa, ready to offer his armour and ear-rings as gifts to Indra, in the pretent of an ascetic; towards the audience, surprised by the offering of armour and ear-rings. Here, the seeker (Indra) is sustaintial mood, the praising by him (Indra to Karna) is enhancing mood. The sense of littleness in giving away the armour etc., is ensuant mood. The word 'my' reflects the **'arthāntarasaṁkramita-vācya' dhvani**, which generates pride and the recollection of being born of his super-humaṇ forefather, are transitory moods.

RG. 56.1

वृत्तिरप्यत्रतत्तदर्थानुरूपोद्गमविरामशालितया सहृदयैकचमत्कारिणी।

तथाहि-उत्साहपोषकं कवचकुण्डलार्पणयोर्लघुत्वनिरूपणं विधातु पूर्वार्धे तदनुकूलशिथिलबन्धात्मिका। उत्तरार्धे तु मौलितः प्राग्वक्तृगतगर्वोत्साहपरिपोषणायोद्धता। ततः परं ब्राह्मणे सविनयत्वं प्रकाशयितुं तन्मूलीभूतं गर्वराहित्यं ध्वनयितुं पुनः शिथिलैव। अत एवावेदयामीत्युक्तम्। न तु ददामि वितरामीति वा।

Trans.: The style here also is pleasurable to refined critic due to its development and the termination favouring to those senses. Accordingley, in the first half (of the verse), it is in the form of loose-word-compounds fovourable to those, to make the offer of armour and ear-rings etc. as insignificant (not very important) which are supportive of enthusiasm (**utsāha**). In the latter half, however, beginning from the expression **maulī** etc., for the proper development, there is enthusiasm and pride etc., of the earlier speaker (i. e. Karna).

Again, afterthat, in order to show modesty, and to suggest pride-less-ness in Brahmins, the loose-compunds (are used). Therefore, the expression is आवेदयामि; 'I offer', and not (I) 'give' or (I) 'distribute.'

RG. 56.2

इदं तु नोदाहरणीयम्– 'यस्योद्दामदिवानिशार्थिविलसद्दान प्रवाह-प्रथामाकर्ण्यावनिमण्डलागतवियद्बन्दीन्द्रवृन्दाननात्। ईर्ष्यानिर्भर-फुल्लरोमनिकरव्यावल्गदूधस्स्रवत्पीयूषप्रकरैः सुरेन्द्रसुरभिः प्रावृट्पयो-दायते'॥

अत्रेन्द्रसभामध्यगतसकलनिरीक्षकालम्बनः अवनिमण्डला-गतविषयबन्दीन्द्रवदनविनिर्गतराजदानवर्णनोद्दीपितः, ऊधःप्रस्नुत-पीयूषप्रकरैनुभावितः, असूयादिभिः संचारिभिः परिपोषितोऽपि कामगवीगत उत्साहो राजस्तुतिगुणीभूत इति न रसव्यपदेशहेतुः।

Trans.: This cannot be illustrated: "The newly produced milk continued to flow like the seasonal rain from Kamdhenu, the cow of the Indra, being horripilated due to jealousness, after listening the fame of the givingness towards the seekers in days and nights continiously from the voices (lit. mouth) of the वन्दीजनाः, (those praising God and Goddess)."

Here the enthusiasm residing in Kamadhenu is made subordinate to the praising of the king, thus, not the cause of the expression as **rasa**, even though, supported by the sustaintial mood like the entire obsevers presented in the Indra's meeting palace, the enhancing mood like the narration of the continious offerings from the mouth of heavenly bards, came from the earth, the ensuant mood like flowing of necter from heaven and the transitory mood like envy etc.

RG. 56.3

अत एवेदमपि नोदाहरणम्– 'साब्धिद्वीपकुलाचलां वसुमतीमाक्रम्य सप्तान्तरां/ सर्वां द्यामपि सस्मितेन हरिणा मन्दं समालोकितः/

प्रादुर्भूतपरप्रमोदविदलद्रोमाञ्चितस्तत्क्षणं/ व्यानम्रीकृतकंधरोऽसुरवरो मौलिं पुरो न्यस्तवान्'॥

इह च भगवद्वामनालम्बनः, तत्कर्तृकमन्दनिरीक्षणोद्दीपितः रोमाञ्चादिभिरनुभावितः, हर्षादिभिः पोषितः, उत्साहो व्यज्यमानोऽपि गुणः। प्रागन्यगतस्येव प्रकृते राजगतस्यापि तस्य राजस्तुत्युत्कर्षकत्वात्। एतेन त्यागः सप्तसमुद्रमुद्रितमहीनिर्व्याजदानावधिः इति श्रीवत्सलाञ्छनोक्तमुदाहरणं परास्तम्। तस्य गुणीभूतव्यङ्ग्यत्वेन रसध्वनिप्रसङ्गेऽनुदाहरणीयत्वात्।

Trans.: "In the same manner, therefore the following also cannot be illustrated: "After covering oceans, islands, all mountains, earth, the sky; when Hari looked with sweet smile (towards) Valī the king of demons, horripilated and delighted with great pleasure at once and offered his head by bending down his shoulders."

And here, the enthusiasm though being suggested, becomes sub-ordinate having the sustaintial mood as Lord Vāmana, the enhancing mood as the seeing with little closed eyes by him (Vāmana), the ensuant mood like horripulation etc., and the transitory mood like joy etc.

Because, alike the existance in other (i. e. different) case (example), in the present case also, though existing in the king, that makes of the praise of the king.

Because of its illustration in the case of **Rasadhvani** (as it is) already illustrated in the case of sub-ordinated suggestion, the example given by Srivatsalanchhana (in his comm. on **KP**) is defeated namely, "by the dame logic."

RG. 56.4

ननु 'अकरुणमवकृत्य'-इत्यत्रापि प्रतीयमानस्य दानवीरस्य कर्णस्तुत्यङ्गत्वात्कथं ध्वनित्वमिति चेत्, सत्यम्। अत्र कवेः कर्णवचनानुवादमात्रतात्पर्यकत्वेन कर्णस्तुतौ तात्पर्यविरहात्, कर्णस्य च

महाशयत्वेनात्मस्तुतौ तात्पर्यानुपपत्तेः स्तुतिरवाक्यार्थ एव। परं तु वीररसप्रत्ययानन्तरं तादृशोत्साहेन लिङ्गेन स्वाधिकरणे सानुमीयते।

राजवर्णनपद्ये तु राजस्तुतौ तात्पर्याद्वाक्यार्थतैव तस्याः।

Trans.: Objection: Well, it may be argued in the expression, namely, "akaruṇamavakṛtya...etc." (vide. RG. 56) also its suggestiveness of the cognised **dānaviratva,** due to it being sub-ordinate to praise of Karna.

Answer: (This view seems to be) correct. Because of absence of intention with regard to the prasie of Karṇa, due to the intention of the poet only to present the expression of Karṇa; And again the intention of self-praise is not accountable in the case of Karṇa being a noble-person, here, the praising is not the intended sense of the sentence.

However, that is inferred in its locus by the probans in the form that enthusiasm after the realisation of heroic sentiment. However, in the verse of **rājavarṇana** (vide RG. 56.2) due to the intention of the praise of the king, that is the sense of the expression.

RG. 56.5

द्वितीयो यथा–'न कपोत भवन्तमणवपि स्पृशतुश्येनसमुद्भवं भयम्। इदमद्यमया तृणीकृतं भवदायुःकुशलं कलेवरम्'॥

अथवैवं विन्यासः-'न कपोतकपोतकं तव स्पृशतु श्येन! मनागपि स्पृहा। इदद्य मया समर्पितं भवते चारुतरं कलेवरम्'॥

एषा शिबेः कपोतं श्येनं प्रति चोक्तिः। अत्र कपोत आलम्बनम्। तद्गतं व्याकुलीभवनमुद्दीपनम्। तस्य कृते स्वकलेवरार्पणमनुभावः।

न चात्र शरीरदानप्रत्ययाददा। नवीरध्वनित्वापत्तिरिति वाच्यम्। श्येनकपोतयोर्भक्ष्यभक्षकभावापन्नत्वेन शिबिशरीरस्या र्थिनोऽभावात्तद-प्रतिपत्तेः। श्येन शरीरनिवेदनस्य कपोतशरीरत्राणोपाधिकतया विनिमय-पदवाच्यत्वात्।

Trans.: The illustration of the second type (of **Virarasa**) is as follows:

"Oh dove! Let there be no fear from the eagle (generated by eagle). Because, I have given up my body, favourable to your life, today (my body is made use-less)".

Or, it can be explained like this as:

"Oh eagle ! Let there be no little desire by you for the baby-dove. Here now, I have offered my handsome body to you (for your satisfication)."

This is the speech of king Sivi to the dove and eagle. Here, dove is sustaintial mood, the anxiety with him (dove) is enhancing mood, the offering of one's body for the sake of him (dove/eagle) is ensuant mood.

It cannot be argued in the present case that due to the knowledge of offering of one's body, let there be the contingency of calling it as a sense of the suggestion of being **dānavīra** (the heroic sentiment having the offering qualities).

That (contingency) would not arise because of the absence of the seeking of body of 'Sivi'due to the relation of 'eater' and 'the eatable' between the dove and the eagle.

(And) Because, it is to be rightly called as (a case of) exchange in the form of offering the body to eagle for the saving at the life of the dove (and not a case of **dānavīra**).

RG. 56.6

तृतीयो यथा–'रणे दीनान्देवान्दशवदन विद्राव्य वहति/ प्रभाव-
प्रागल्भ्यं त्वयि तु मम कोऽयं परिकरः/
ललाटोद्यज्ज्वालाकवतिलतजगज्जालविभवो/ भवो मे कोदण्ड-
च्युतविशिखवेगं कलयतु'//

एषा दशवदनं प्रति भगवतो रामस्योक्तिः।

इह भव आलम्बनम्। रणदर्शनमुद्दीपनम्।

दशवदनावज्ञानुभावः[१]। गर्वः संचारी। वृत्तिरत्र देवानां प्रस्तावे तद्गतकातर्यप्रकाशनद्वारा वीररसानालम्बनत्वावगतयेऽनुद्धतैव[२]।

दशवदनप्रस्तावे तु देवदर्पदमनवीरत्वप्रतिपादनायोद्धतापि तस्यावज्ञया रामगतोत्साहानालम्बनत्वेन तदालम्बनस्य रसस्याप्रत्ययान्न प्रकर्षवती। भगवतो भवस्य तु परमोत्तमालम्बनविभावत्वात्तत्प्रस्तावे तदालम्बनस्यौजस्विनो वीररसस्य निष्पत्तेः प्रकृष्टोद्धता।

Trans.: The illustration of the third is:

Oh you ten faced one, who carries false-pride of velour by defeating (the helpless) Gods in the war, what indeed would be my efforts. Let Lord Śiva, capable to cover entire world by the flames arising from his fore-head, tolerate the speed of arrow released from my bow."

The is the speech of Lord Rāma to ten-faced one (Rāvaṇa). Here, the entire world is sustaintial mood; the sight of war is enhancing mood; the disregard towards the **Dasavadana** is ensuant mood; and pride is the transitory mood. The style, here, is not developed, for the understanding of the non-sustaintness of heroic sentiment by showing the pityness in those in the cases of Gods.

In the context of '**Dasavadana**', however the style meant for the expression of heroism in the form of surpassing the pride of the Gods, due to the उद्धता, non-realisation of the sentiment of that sustaintial mood not being the sustaintial of enthusiasm existings in Rāma, the उद्धता is not excellent. However, in that case, because of the Lord Siva being the best and atmost sustaintial excitant, for the manifestation of heroic sentiment having florridity based on that is the proper style of उद्धता.

---

१. चौ, अनुभव

२. चौ, अवगतयो, ओ, अवगतया

RG. 56.7

चतुर्थोयथा– 'सपदि विलयमेतु राज्यलक्ष्मीरुपरि पतन्त्वथवा कृपाणधाराः।

अपहरतुतरां शिरः कृतान्तो मम तु मतिर्न मनागपैति धर्मात्'॥

एषाऽधर्मेणापि रिपुर्जेतव्य इति वदन्तं प्रति युधिष्ठिरस्योक्तिः।

अत्रधर्मविषयक आलम्बनम्। न जातु कामान्न भयान्न लोभा-द्धर्मंत्यजेत्जीवितस्यापि हेतोः इत्यादिवाक्यालोचनमुद्दीपनम्।

शिरश्छेदाद्यङ्गीकारोऽनुभावः। धृतिः संचारिणी। इत्थं वीररसस्य चातुर्विध्यं प्रपञ्चितं प्राचामनुरोधात्।

Trans.: The illustration for fourth one is (as follows):

"May the prosperity of my state come to an end at once, may the sword fall upon (on me), may the God of death take away my head, still my mind would not go a step away, from righteousway (i. e. **dharma**)."

This is the speech of Yuddhiṣṭhira for them, who told namely "the enemy should be captured by sinful actions also." Here, the object of **dharma** is sustaintial mood; The analysis etc., with expression namely not indeed to give up one's '**dharma**' to fulfill the sensual desires or due to fear or due to greediness, even for the cause of one's life, is enhancing mood. The acceptance of cutting off one's head etc., is ensuant and **dhṛti** is transitory mood. In this way, the four fold of **Virarasa** is narrated in detail, following the tradition of the predecessors.

RG. 56.8

वस्तुतस्तु बहवो वीररसस्य शृङ्गारस्येव प्रकारा निरूपयितुं शक्यन्ते। तथा हि प्राचीन एव 'सपदि विलयमेतु' इत्यादि पद्ये 'मम तु मतिर्न मनागपैतुसत्यात्' इति चरमपादव्यत्यासेन पद्यान्तरतां प्रापिते सत्यवीरस्यापि संभवात्। न च सत्यस्यापि धर्मान्तर्गततया धर्मवीररस एव तद्वीरस्याप्यन्तर्भाव इति वाच्यम्। दानदययोरपि तदन्तर्गततया तद्वीरयोरपि धर्मवीरात्पृथग्गणनानौचित्यात्।

Trans.: As a matter of fact, it is possible to define many varieties of heroic sentiment as in the cases of erotic sentiment. Accordingly, in the earlier verse namely "सपदि विलयमेतु" etc., by replacing the last line (i. e. **mama tu matiḥ na manāgapaitu dharmāt**) by "mama tu matih na manāgapaitu satyāt", when it becomes state of a different verse, it forms an example of **Satyavīra**.

Objection: The expression '**satya**' being included in **dharma** in the sentiment of **dharmavira** also, the sentiment of **satyavīra** should be included.

Answer: Not so. because of the inclussiveness of dāna, dayā, in that (dharma), the sentiment dānavīra and dayārvīra should be expressed as different from dharmavīra.

RG. 56.9

एवं पाण्डित्यवीरोऽपि प्रतीयते।

यथा-'अपि वक्ति गिरां पतिःस्वयं यदि तासामधिदेवतापि वा।
अयमस्मिपुरो हयाननस्मरणोल्लङ्घितवाङ्मयाम्बुधिः॥'

अत्र बृहस्पत्याद्यालम्बनः सभादिदर्शनोद्दीपितो निखिलविद्वत्तिरस्कारानुभावितो गर्वेण संचारिणा पोषित उत्साहो वक्तुः प्रतीयते। ननु चात्र युद्धवीरत्वम्। युद्धत्वस्य वादसाधारणस्य वाच्यत्वात्, इति चेत्, क्षमावीरे किं ब्रूयाः।

यथा-'अपि बहलदहनजालं मूर्ध्नि रिपुर्मे निरन्तरं धमतु।
पातयतु वासिधारामहमणुमात्रं न किंचिदाभाषे॥'

क्षमावत् उक्तिरियम्।

Trans.: Like this, the heroic sentiment possessed of knowledge is also realised. The example follows:

"I am steady to cross the ocean of speech in the remembrence of Lord Hayānana, eventhough, the lord of the speech (i. e. Gurubṛhaspati) or the supreme Gooddess (i. e. Sarasvatī) of those speak (themsleves) (in the time of शास्त्रार्थ)".

Here, the enthusiasm of the speaker is reflected by having the sustaintial mood like Bṛhaspati etc., the enhancing mood like the sight of literary meetings etc., the ensuant like the insulting the entire scholars and the transitory mood like pride.

Objection: Well, one can argue for **yuddhavīratva**, due to the similar expression of arguments and counter-arguments of war.

Answer: If, so, then, what can be told in the case of the heroic sentiment possessed of endurance (क्षमा)? For example: "Even though, the enemy burns fire over my head continiously or strike with sword, yet, I would not speak a single word (in protest)." This is the speech of a person having patience to tolerate.

RG. 56.10

बलवीरे वा किं समादध्याः।

यथा–'परिहरतु धरां फणिप्रवीरः सुखमयतां कमठोऽपि तां विहाय। अहमिह पुरुहूत! पक्षकोणे निखिलमिदं जगदक्लमं वहामि॥'

पुरुहूतं प्रत्येषा गरुत्मतः उक्तिः। ननु अपि वक्ति-परिहरतु धराम्-इति पद्यद्वये गर्व एव नोत्साहः। मध्यस्थपद्ये तु धृतिरेव ध्वन्यते इति भावध्वनय एवैते न रसध्वनयः इति चेत्, तर्हि युद्धवीरादिष्वपि गर्वादिध्वनितामेव किं न ब्रूयाः। रसध्वनिसामान्यमेव वा किं न तद्व्यभिचारध्वनेन गतार्थयेः। स्थायिप्रतीतिर्दुरपह्नवा चेत्तुल्यं प्रकृतेऽपि। अनन्तरोक्तपद्ये तु नोत्साहःप्रतीयते। दयावीरादिषु प्रतीयत इति तु राज्ञामा (राजा) ज्ञामात्रम्[१]।

Trans.: Or what can be the explanation in case of the heroic sentiment of power: For example:

"Oh Puruhūta, to this entire world, I can hold on the

१. चौ, गंगा, ओ, –राजाज्ञामात्रम्

corner of my wing without any efforts, Let the Sesanāga, the king among serpents leave the world, also the tortoise happily stay away leaving her."

This is the speech of Garuda to Puruhūta.

Objection: Well, it my be argued: There is no enthusiasm, but pride indeed in the two illustrative verses (given earlier) namely,'अपि वक्ति...'and' परिहरतु धराम्...'Further धृति in suggested in the verse coming in between (i. e. अपि बहल...) and therefore, these are the cases of भावध्वनि and not रसध्वनि.

Answer: If so, then, in the case of युद्धवीर, why not to accept the suggestiveness of pride etc.? Or why not accept the रसध्वनि in general, the suggestiveness of those transitory moods?

If it is argued- the realisation of the permanent mood would not be avoided, then, the same is true in the present case as well. However, the enthusiasm is not realised in the verse occuring next. Further, this is suggested in the cases of दयावीर etc., as it is only the order of king (but no arguments made here after).

RG. 57

अद्भुतो यथा–'चराचरजगज्जालसदनं वदनं तव।
गलद्गगनगाम्भीर्यं वीक्ष्यास्मिहृतचेतना॥'

कदाचिद्भगवतो वासुदेवस्य वदनमालोकितवत्या यशोदाया इयमुक्तिः। अत्र वदनमालम्बनम्। अन्तर्गतचराचरजगज्जालदर्शनमुद्दीपनम्। हृतचेतनत्वम्, तेन गम्यं रोमाञ्चनेत्रस्फारणादि चानुभावः। त्रासादयो व्यभिचारिणः। नैवात्र विद्यमानापि पुत्रगता प्रीतिः प्रतीयते। व्यञ्जकाभावात्। प्रतीतायां वा तस्यां विस्मयस्य गुणत्वं न युज्यते। एवं कश्चिन्महापुरुषोऽयमिति भक्तिरपि तस्याः पुत्रो ममायं बाल इति निश्चयेन प्रतिबन्धादुत्पत्तुमेव नेष्टे। अतस्तस्यामपि विस्मयस्य गुणीभावो न शङ्क्यः।

Trans.: To illustrate the wonderful sentiment: "I fall unconscious, seeing your face, deep as the sky, the abode of the entire animate and inanimate worlds?"

This is the speech of **Yośodā**, while looking at the face of Lord **Vāsudeva** in some occasion.

Here, the face (of **Vāsudeva**) is sustaintial mood, the sight of entire world being inside (the mouth) is enhancing mood, the state of unconscious (ness) and due to that, the horripilation, spreading of the eyes (of **Yaśodā**) etc., are ensuants and the fear etc., are transitory moods.

Here, eventhough, there is the affection towards (her) son is not realised, due to the absence of suggestiveness. Or, even, if it is realised, it is not proper to accept the wonder as sub-ordinate (to devotion). And also, the devotion of her, namely, 'this is some great-soul' cannot arise due to the obastacle in the form of the conclusive knowledge that 'this child is my son.' Therefore, there also, one need not doubt the sub-ordinateness of विस्मय (in devotion).

RG. 57.1

यत्तु सहृदयशिरोमणिभिः प्राचीनैरुदाहृतम् चित्रं महानेष तवावतारः, क्व कान्तिरेषाभिनवैव भङ्गिः। लोकोत्तरं धैर्यमहो प्रभावःकाप्याकृतिर्नूतन एष सर्गः॥ इति, तत्रेदं वक्तव्यम्-प्रतीयतां नामात्र विस्मयः, परं त्वसौ कथंकारं (अद्भुतरस) ध्वनिव्यपदेशहेतुः। प्रतिपाद्यमहापुरुषविशेष-विषयायाः प्रधानीभूतायाः स्तोतृगतभक्तेः प्रकर्षकत्वेनास्य गुणीभूतत्वात्। यथा महाभारते गीतासु विश्वरूपं दृष्टवतः पार्थस्य पश्यामि देवांस्तव देव देहे सर्वांस्तथा भूतविशेषसंघान् इत्यादौ वाक्यसंदर्भे। इत्थं चास्य रसालंकारत्वमुचितम्। भक्तिर्नैवात्र प्रतीयत इति चेत्दरमुकुलितलोचनं विदांकुर्वन्तु सहृदयाः।

Trans.: Regarding the illustration, namely,

"What a wonder ! What a great immutability is this !

What a splendour ! Novel, indeed, is the appearance! Extra-ordinary is the equanimity ! Oh, what a spell; and what a figure ! Novel, indeed, is this creation." by the ancient great critics; this (following views) is to be said. Let the wonder be suggested (some how), but how to account for its causality for the expression of अद्भुतरसध्वनि.

Because, due to the superiority of the devotion existing in the devotess, which is made primary, having its विषय as some great soul as stated, (the विस्मय)is made sub-ordinate to this.

As for, in the context of the expression of Pārtha in **Gītā** of Mahābhārata, while seeing the Universal sight (of Kṛṣṇa) namely, "O God ! I am seeing all the Gods and also creatures of different types in your body" etc. Like this, it is proper to hold as a case of रसालंकार. It is urged that the devotion is not suggested here, then the sympathetic readers may realise it by the posture of halfclosing-eye-sights.

RG. 58

हास्यो यथा–"श्रीतातपादैर्विहिते निबन्धे निरूपिता नूतनयुक्तिरेषा।
अङ्गं गवां पूर्वमहो पवित्रं न वा कथं रासभधर्मपत्न्याः॥"

तार्किकपुत्रोऽत्रालम्बनम्। तदीया निःशङ्कोक्तिरुद्दीपिका।
रदनप्रकाशादिरुद्वेगादयश्चानुभावव्यभिचारिणः।

Trans.: The illustration of the comic is (as follows):

"In the text, composed by (my) revered father, the following new argument is made:- The front part of the body of the cows is pure and scared, why is that of a she-donkey (female) is not pure?"

Here, the son of the logician is the sustaintial mood; his speech without a tinge of doubt is enhancing mood; the showing of teeth etc., are the ensuants and excitement etc., are the transitory moods.

RG. 58.1

अत्राहुः- आत्मस्थः परसंस्थश्चेत्यस्य भेदद्वयं मतम्।
आत्मस्थो द्रष्टुरुत्पन्नो विभावेक्षणमात्रतः॥
हसन्तमपरं द्रष्टुः विभावश्चोपजायते।
योऽसौ हास्यरसस्तज्ज्ञैः परस्थः परिकीर्तितः॥
उत्तमानां मध्यमानां नीचानामप्यसौ भवेत्।
त्र्यवस्थः कथितस्तस्य षड्भेदाः सन्ति चापरे॥
स्मितं च हसितं प्रोक्तमुत्तमं पुरुषे बुधैः।
भवेद्विहसितं चोपहसितं मध्यमे नरे॥
नीचेऽपहसितं चातिहसितं परिकीर्तितम्।
ईषत्फुल्लकपोलाभ्यां कटाक्षैरप्यनुल्बणैः॥
अदृश्यदशनो हासो मधुरः स्मितमुच्यते।
वक्त्रनेत्रकपोलैश्चे दुत्फुल्लैरुपलक्षितः॥
किंचिल्लक्षितदन्तश्च तदा हसितमिष्यते।
सशब्दं मधुरं गालगतं वदनरागवत्॥
आकुञ्चिताक्षि मन्द्रंच विदुर्विहसितं बुधाः।
निकुञ्चितांसशीर्षश्च जिह्मदृष्टिविलोकनः॥
उत्फुल्लनासिको हासो नाम्नोपहसितं मतम्।
अस्थानजः साश्रुदृष्टिराकम्पस्कन्धमूर्धजः॥
शार्ङ्गदेवेन गदितो हासोऽपहसिताह्वः।
स्थूलकर्णकटुध्वानो बाष्पपूरप्लुतेक्षणः।
करोपगूढपार्श्वश्च हासोऽतिहसितं मतम्॥ इति।

Trans.: Here it is stated: This is of two types, namely, of one's own and of others. Among these two, the first type namely आत्मस्थ, is that which is generated after immediate sight of the excitants in the द्रष्टा. That is called परसंस्थ by the experts of comic sentiment the excitants which is generated by seeing sombody laughing.

And that is said to have three types based on the best, the common and lowest class. And according to others that is of six types.

Smiles (स्मित) and slight laughter (हसित) are characteristic of the best characters, open laughter (विहसित) and mocking laughter (उपहसित)are among common characters and loud laughter (अपहसित) and excessive laughter (अतिहसित) belong to the lowest characters, is the view of experts.

The sweet laughter (which) is the characteristic of best characters in which, the cheeks are a little expanded, and one's glances are elegantly suggestive, the teeth are not quite visible, is called as smile (स्मित).

That state, where the eyes begin to dilate, the cheeks are puffed out and the mouth is slightly open, the teeth are also partially visible is called slight laughter (हसित).

That state (of sweet laughter) is called open laughter (*i.e.* विहसित) by scholars, in which, the eyes are slightly contracted (आकुंचित) and the cheeks fully distended, the sound of the laughter is soft and the face is coloured.

In the mocking laughter (*i.e.* उपहसित) the nostrils are distended, the eyes squint and the shoulders and head are bent.

when, one laughterout of place, with tear in eyes, and the shoulders and head are shaking (with laughter) to this शांर्गदेव, tells to be loud laughter (*i.e.* अपहसित).

When, the eyes are swollen and bathed in tears, and there are loud and violent cries and one holds one's sides with one's hands, is called as excessive laughter (*i.e.* अतिहसित).

RG. 59

भयानको यथा–श्येनमम्बरतलादुपागतं शुष्यदाननबिलो विलोकयन्। कम्पमानतनुराकुलेक्षणः स्पन्दितुं नहि शशाक लावकः॥

अत्र श्येन आलम्बनम्। सवेगापतनमुदीपनम्। आननशोषादयोऽनुभावाः। दैन्यादयः संचारिणः।

Trans.: To illustrate the terrific sentiment:

"Seeing the vulture coming nearby from the sky, the लावक (bird) with its pale face, throbbing body and anxious looks, could not stir out."

Here, 'the vulture' is sustaintial mood, (his) 'sudden falling' (from the sky) is enhancing mood, 'the pale face' is ensuant mood and 'the wretchedness etc.' are the transitory moods.

RG. 60

बीभत्सो यथा-"नखैर्विदारितान्त्राणां शवानां पूयशोणितम्।
आननेष्वनुलिम्पन्ति हृष्टा वेतालयोषितः॥"
शवा इहालम्बनम्। आन्त्रविदारणाद्युद्दीपनम्।
आक्षिप्ता रोमाञ्चनेत्रनिमीलनादयोऽनुभावाः।
आवेगादयः संचारिणः।

Trans.: To illustrate the disgustful sentiment;:

"The wives of ghosts became happy when they drank the blood from the corpses, with intenstines completely dislocated and torn off with nails."

Here, 'the dead bodies' are sustaintial mood, 'the tearing of the intenstines' is enhancing mood, 'the closing of eyes' and 'horripilation etc.', due to happiness are the ensuant mood and the 'excitement etc', are the transitory moods.

RG. 60.1

ननु रतिक्रोधोत्साहभयशोकविस्मयनिर्वेदेषु

प्रागुदातेषुयथा–लम्बनाश्रययोः संप्रत्ययः, न तथा हासे जुगुप्सायां च। तत्रालम्बनस्यैव प्रतीतेः। पद्यश्रोतुश्च रसास्वादाधिकरणत्वेन लौकिकहास जुगुप्सा श्रयत्वानुपत्तेरिति चेत्। सत्यम्। तदाश्रयस्य द्रष्टृपुरुषविशेषस्य तत्राक्षेप्यत्वात्। तदनाक्षेपे तु श्रोतुः स्वीयकान्ता-वर्णनपद्यादिव रसोद्बोधे बाधका- भावात्।

Trans.: Objection: well, it may be argued: As the realisation of sustaintial mood and आश्रय, in the cases of love, anger, enthusiasm, fear, grief, wonder, and detachment as illustrated earlier, is not like that, in the cases of laughter and disgust. Because, the sustaintial mood only is realised in those cases (two, namely laughter and disgust). And the श्रोता of the poetry cannot be the substratum of worldly laughter and disgust, due to the substratum of the enjoyment of **rasa**.

Answer: This (argument) is true. (But) the substratum-ness of certain audience has to be super-imposed on that. In the absence of imposition of that, there would be difficulty for the realisation of sentiment from the poem, describing one's own beloved. (lady).

RG. 61

एवं संक्षेपेण निरूपिता रसाः। एषां प्राधान्ये ध्वनिव्यपदेशहेतुत्वम्, गुणीभावे तु रसालंकारत्वम्। केचित्तु प्राधान्य एवैषां रसत्व-मन्यथा–लंकारत्वमेव। रसालंकारव्यपदेशस्त्वलंकारध्वनिव्यपदेशवत्। ब्राह्मण- श्रमण-न्यायात्। एवमसंलक्ष्यक्रमतायामेव[१]। अन्यथा तु वस्तुमात्रम्, इत्याहुः। एते चासंलक्ष्यक्रमव्यङ्ग्याः, सहृदयेन रसव्यक्तौ झगिति जाय- मानायां विभावानुभावव्यभिचारिविमर्शक्रमस्य सतोऽपि सूचीशतपत्रशत- वेधक्रमस्येवालक्षणात्। न त्वक्रमव्यङ्ग्याः। व्यक्तेस्तद्धेतूनां च हेतुहेतुमद्भावासंगत्यापत्तेः।

Trans.: Like this, the sentiments are explained in brief.

---

१. चौ, –क्रमव्यङ्ग्यतायामेव

In the dominance of these (sentiments), remains the causality of being named as suggestive, otherwise, in its state of being sub-ordinate, (it is) called रसालंकार.

Some, however hold like this: In case of the dominance of these, would be (called) sentiment; Otherwise, **alaṁkāra.** However, the expression of रसालंकार is like expression of अलंकारध्वनि, on the logic of the saying of ब्राह्मणश्रमण. Like this, similar is the case with असंलक्ष्यक्रम. Otherwise, it is only (the suggestion of) mere fact. And these are the cases of suggestion, not marked distinctly in sequence. Because, eventhough, the knowledge regarding sequence of excitant, ensuant and transitory moods in existing, yet, the quick realisation of sentiment (and the various moods) by refined critics comes at once like the non-realisation of the sequence of speering by a needle in the hundred petals (lotus leaf). However, this cannot be अक्रमव्यंग्य *i.e.*, the suggestiveness is not in sequence. Because, there would arise the contingency of improperness in the realisation of cause and effect of moods and sentiments respectively.

RG. 62

अथ कथमेते एव रसाः। भगवदालम्बनस्य रोमाञ्चाश्रुपातादिभिरनुभावितस्य हर्षादिभिः परितोषितस्य भागवतादिपुराणश्रवणसमये भगवद्भक्तैरनुभूयमानस्य भक्तिरसस्य दुरपह्नवत्वात्। भगवदनुरागरूपा भक्तिश्चात्र स्थायिभावः। नचासौ शान्तरसेऽन्तर्भावमर्हति। अनुरागस्य वैराग्यविरुद्धत्वात्। उच्यतेभक्तेर्देवादिविषयरतित्वेन भावान्तर्गततयारसत्वानुपपत्तेः।

"रतिर्देवादिविषया व्यभिचारी तथाञ्जितः।
भावः प्रोक्तस्तदाभासा ह्यनौचित्यप्रवर्तिताः॥"
इति हि प्राचां सिद्धान्तात्।

Trans.: Objection: Well, How is it that these are the

only sentiments. Because, it is difficult to discard the sentiment of devotion being realised by the devotess of God, at the time of listening to Puranic texts, namely. भागवत etc., menifested by the sustaintial mood like 'God', ensuants like 'the horripilation', 'shedding tears etc', and the transitory moods like 'joy etc.' In this case the devotion in the form of love for God is the permanent mood. Because of the opposition conflict between रति and वैराग्य, it cannot be included in the quietism sentiment.

Answer: Now answer; The 'devotion' cannot be (treated as) sentiment, due to its inclusion in mood as the love for God etc. (lit. having God etc., as its object). Because following indeed is the view of the ancient theorist, namely, 'love' having its object God etc., and the expressed transitory moods, are called as moods. They are called apparent when used without propriety.

Notes : PR records an objection who proposes 'bhakti' as a distinct sentiment which cannot be included either in any of these nine sentiments. To him 'bhakti' cannot be accepted as a sentiment. It is included under **bhāva** and the authority of distinguishing and naming something as **bhāva** or **rasa** is based on the statement of Bharatamuni.

RG. 63

न च तर्हि कामिनीविषयाया अपि रतेर्भावत्वमस्तु, रतित्वाविशेषात्, अस्तु वा भगवद्भक्तेरेव स्थायित्वम्, (कामिन्यादिरतीनां च भावत्वम्,) विनिगमकाभावात्, इति वाच्यम्। भरतादिमुनिवचनानामेवात्र रसभावत्वादिव्यवस्थापकत्वेन स्वातन्त्र्यायोगात्[१]। अन्यथा पुत्रादि विषयाया अपि रतेः स्थायिभावत्वं कुतो न स्यात्, न स्याद्वा कुतः शुद्ध भावत्वं जुगुप्साशोकादीनाम्, इत्यखिलदर्शनव्याकुली स्यात्। रसानां नवत्वगणना च मुनिवचननियन्त्रिता भज्येत, इति यशाशास्त्रमेव ज्यायः।

---

१. चौ, संपू, वादु, मदु, ओ, -स्वातन्त्र्ययोगात्

Trans.: Objection: Well, in that case, let the love having its object 'a beautiful lady' be mood. Because the loveness is common to both. Or the 'love for God'/ 'devotion for God' be permanent mood, (and the love for a beautiful lady be mood), due to the lack of any unifing property.

Answer: It cannot be argued like this. because, the statements of the sages like भरत etc., are alone the ground for the classification of sentiments and moods etc. Otherwise, why not to accept the love for son etc. (lit. love having its object as one's son etc.) be not accepted as permanent mood. Or again, why not to accept the independentness of disgust and grief etc. Then, the entire philosophy of poetry will be disturbed. Thus, the enumeration of the sentiments to be nine is maintioned by the statement of the sage. Thus, is the conclustion as per the **śāstra.**

RG. 64

एतेषां परस्परं (कैरपि सहाविरोधः) कैरपि विरोधः। तत्र वीर शृङ्गारयोः, शृङ्गारहास्ययोः, वीरोद्भुतयोः, वीररौद्रयो; शृङ्गाराद्भुतयोश्चाविरोध। शृङ्गारबीभत्सयोः, शृङ्गारकरुणयोः वीरभयानकयोः, शान्तरौद्रयोः शान्त शृङ्गारयोश्च विरोधः। अत्र[१] कविना प्रकृतरसं परिपोष्टुकामेन तदभिव्यञ्जके काव्ये तद्विरुद्धरसाङ्गानां निबन्धनं न कार्यम्। तथा हि सति तदभिव्यक्तौ विरुद्धः प्रकृतं बाधेत। सुन्दोपसुन्दन्यायेन चोभया[२]रुपहतिः स्यात्। यदि तु विरुद्धयोरपि रसयोरेकत्र समावेश इष्यते तदा विरोधं परिहृत्य विधेयः।

Trans.: Among these (there are) mutual reconcilation between some, (and) mutual concilation between some. Out of these, there is mutual reconciliations between, 'heroic and erotic,' 'erotic and comic', 'heroic and wonderful', 'heroic

१. चौ, ओ,- तत्र

२. चौ, गंगा, मदु, ओ, -वोभयो

and furious', and 'erotic and wonderful' sentiments. And there is mutual conciliations (oppositions) between 'erotic and disgustful', 'erotic and pathos', 'heroic and terrific' and 'quietism and erotic' sentiments. In this case, the poet with the intention of the proper development of the primary sentiment (main रस in question) should not utilise the opposing sub-ordinate sentiment in a poetry suggesting these (sentiments).

Accordingly, if that opposing (sub-ordinate sentiments) are suggested, it would obstruct (the proper development of) the primary sentiments. And both the sentiments (primary and subordinate) would be destroyed following the logic of सुन्द and उपसुन्द sentiment.

If, however, the application of two sentiments is intended then, it should be done after avoiding the opposing sentiments.

RG. 65

तथा हि- विरोधस्तावद्द्विविधः। स्थितिविरोधो ज्ञानविरोधश्च। आद्यस्तदधिकरणावृत्तितारूपः। द्वितीयस्तज्ज्ञानप्रतिबद्धज्ञानकत्वलक्षणः। तत्राधिकरणान्तरे विरोधिनः स्थापने प्रथमो निवर्तते। यथा नायकगतत्वेन वीररसे वर्णनीये प्रतिनायके भयानकस्य। रसपदेनात्र प्रकरणे तदुपाधिः स्थायिभावो गृह्यते। रसस्य सामाजिकवृत्त्वित्वेन नायकाद्यवृत्तित्वात्। अद्वितीयानन्दमयत्वेन विरोधाभावाच्च। उदाहरणम्- "कुण्डलीकृत-कोदण्डदोर्दण्डस्य पुरस्तव। मृगाररातेरिव मृगाः परे नैवावतस्थिरे॥"

Trans.: Now, the conflict is of two types, conflict with regard to their locus and the conflict with regard to their knowledge. The first type is in the from of being non-existant in its (proper sentiment) locus. The second type is in the form of 'obstructing knowledge' of that knowledge (of the proper). Out of these two, the first, can be avoided by placing and conflicting sentiments at different locus. As for the example, while narrating the heroic sentiment existing with hero, (placement of) the terrific in villian. Here, in this context, the permanent mood is understood by the expression, "sentiments", which is its property. Because, it does not reside in the character etc., (Lit. locus etc.) due to its existance in the audience. And because of the absence of conflict of the nature of extra-ordinary highest pleasure. The example for the first type follows :

"(O King !) In your presence (lit. in front of you) who has bent the bow like a circle by mighty arms, the enemies could not stand, like the deer before the lion.

RG. 65.1

रसान्तरस्याविरोधिनः संधिकर्तुरिवान्तरालेऽवस्थाने द्वितीयोऽपि निवर्तते। यथा मन्निर्मितायामाख्यायिकायां कण्वाश्रमगतस्य श्वेतकेता र्महर्षेः शान्तरसप्रधाने वर्णने प्रस्तुते किमिदमनाकलितपूर्वं रूपम्, कोऽयमनिर्वाच्यो वचनरचनाया मधुरिमा इत्यद्भुतस्यान्त रवस्थापनेन वरवर्णिनीं प्रत्युनुरागवर्णने।

यथा वा–"सुराङ्गनाभिराश्लिष्टा व्योम्नि वीरा विमानगाः।
विलोकन्ते निजान्देहान्फेरुनारीभिरावृतान्॥"

अत्र सुराङ्गनामृतशरीरालम्बनयोः शृङ्गारबीभत्सयोरन्तः स्वर्गलाभाक्षिप्तो वीररसो निवेशितः। अन्तर्निवेशश्च तदुभयचर्वणाकालान्तर्वर्तिकालगतचर्वणाकत्वम्। तच्च प्रकृतपद्ये प्रथमार्ध एव शृङ्गारचर्वणोत्तरं वीरस्य चर्वणादनन्तरं च द्वितीयार्धे बीभत्सस्येति स्फुटमेव। "भुरेणुदिग्धान्" इत्यादि काव्यप्रकाशगतपद्यकदम्बेषु तु प्रथमश्रुतबीभत्ससामग्रीवशाद्बीभत्सचर्वणोत्तरं तत्सामग्र्याक्षिप्तनिः शङ्कप्राणत्यागादिरूपसामग्रीकस्य वीरस्य चर्वणे शृङ्गारचर्वणेति विवेकः। इत्थं चोदासीनचर्वणेन प्रतिबन्धकज्ञाननिवृत्तो निष्प्रत्यूहः प्रतिबध्यचर्वणोदय इति फलितोऽर्थः।

Trans.: The second type of conflict also, can be avoided by placing a non conflicting sentiment in between (two conflicting sentiments) like a compromiser. As in the case of the naration of affection towards the lady, by placing the wonderful sentiment in between, namely, "What a figure is this which has not yet come within human comprehnsion; extraordinary sweetness does (her) speech possess ! etc.," in the context of narration of quietism as primary at the time of the arrival of श्वेतकेतु, in the कण्वाश्रम, in the अख्यायिका, composed by me.

Or for example: "The heroes sitting in the aerial cars in the sky, being embraced by devine damsels, look at their own bodies surrounded by she-jackals."

Here, the heroic sentiment, indicated by ascendency in heaven is 'placed in between' the erotic and disgustful having the sustaintial like heaven-harlots and dead bodies respectevely. And the, अन्तर्निवेश, 'placing in between' in the state of being enjoyed, condition by the time of enjoyment of these confliced two. And that also, in case of the present verse, the enjoyment of erotic in the first half is followed by the enjoyment of heroic, and then, in the second half, the enjoyment of disqustful is visible.

However, there is the enjoyment of erotic with the enjoyment of heroism on the basis of the collection of its causes like the fearless death etc., brought forth or presented by the colletcion of causes of that after the enjoyment of the disgustfulness (again) on the basis of the collection of the causes of disgust heard first in the collection of verses occuring in **KP** namely." This is the difference in interpretation (from that). Hence, the ultimate sense arrived at each. In this manner, by the removal of the obstructing knowledge in the case of indifferent audience, the enjoyment of the obstructed (sentiment) arises भूरेणूदिग्धान्...etc.

RG. 66

अङ्गाङ्गिनोरङ्गिन्यन्यस्मिन्नङ्ग्योर्वा न विरोधः।

अङ्गत्वानुपपत्तिप्रसङ्गात्। "यथा–प्रत्युद्गता सविनयं सहसा सखीभिः/ स्मेरैः स्मरस्य सचिवैः रससावलोकैः/ मामद्य मञ्जुरचनैर्वचनैश्च बाले/ हा लेशतोऽपि न कथं वद सत्करोषि/"

इयं च पुरो निपतितां प्रमीतां नायिकां प्रति नायकस्योक्तिः।

इह नायिकालम्बना, अश्रुपातादिभिरनुभावैरावेगविषादादिभिः-संचारिभिश्च व्यज्यमाना नायकगता रतिस्तुल्यसामग्र्यभिव्यक्ते प्रकृतत्वात्प्रधानीभूते तद्गत एव शोके प्रकर्षकत्वादङ्गम्।

यदि तु नायकगता रतिर्नात्र प्रतीयते, किं तु निरुक्तसामग्र्या शोक एव प्रकृतत्वादित्यागृह्यते तदा नायकालम्बना प्रत्युद्गमाद्यनुभाविता हर्षादिभिः पोषिता नायिकाश्रया रतिरेव तत्राङ्गमस्तु। नायिकागतरतेर्नायकशोकप्रकर्षहेतुतायाः सर्वसंमतत्वात् न च नायिकाया नाशात् तद्गताया रतेरसंनिधानात्कथं अंगतेति वाच्यम्। संनिधानस्याङ्गतायामतन्त्रत्वेन स्मर्यमाणायास्तस्या अङ्गत्वोवपत्तेः।

Trans.: And there is no contradiction either between the primary and the subordinate sentiments or between one primary and the subordinate sentiments of others. Because, there would arise the contingency of non-acceptance of subordinateness.

For the example: "Alas ! how is it that you, O love, do not, suddenly coming forth with modesty (to receive me) as before, gladden (lit. cool) me even in the slightest degree by means of your smiling and affectionate looks and your sweet words, which are the ministers of love?"

This is the speech of the lover to the dead beloved, laying infront of him. Here, the love of the lover being manifested by sustaintial like 'the beloved lady', the enhancing like 'shedding the tears etc.' the transitory moods like 'excitement' and 'depression' etc., made subordinate due to it being superior exsting in that grief, which is primary, because of it being proper to express similar causes. And if, however the love exsting in lover is not realised, due to it being the subject of grief alone, is expressed by the cause already stated, then, in that case, let the subordinate lover existing in the beloved manifested by the sustaintial like 'the lover', the enhancing like 'welcoming' etc., and (the transitory moods like) 'joy' etc. Because, the causality of the love, residing in the beloved, is with regard to the deep grief of the lover, is well accepted by all.

Objection: How to account for the sub-ordinate-ness of the love existing in her, in the case of the death of the beloved, due to its absence?

Answer: It cannot be argued. Because, the sub-ordinate-ness of that is possible, by remembering her, since being present, is not the ground for something been treated as subordinate.

RG. 67

अङ्ग्योर्यथा-

"उत्क्षिप्ताः कबरीभरं, विवलिताः पार्श्वद्वयं न्यक्कृताः, पादाम्भोजयुगं, रूषा परिहृता दूरेण चेलाञ्चलम्।

गुहृणन्ति त्वरया भवत्प्रतिभटक्ष्मापालबामभ्रुबां, यान्तीनां गहनेषु कणटकचिताः केके न भूमीरुहाः॥"

अत्र समासोक्त्यवयवाभ्यां तरुकामिकर्तृकरिपुकामिनीकबर्यादिग्रहणरूपाभ्यां प्रकृताप्रकृतव्यवहाराभ्यां व्यक्तयोः करुणशृङ्गारयो राजविषयकरतिभावाङ्गत्वम्।

Trans.: The example of opposition between subordinates is as:

O king, What are the trees full of thorns indeed which

at once donot catch held of the braid of hairs while lifting up, both the arms (lit. sides) while putting aside, both the lotus like feet while placing down and the corner of the silk garments while throwing with anger, of the wives of your rival kings running away in the derse forest (out of your fear)."

Here, both the pathos and the erotic become the subordinate of the love with regard to the king by the knowledge of the expression of the real and the imposed (knowledge) in the form of the catching of the कबरी etc., of the wives of the rivals by the trees and (by the) lover etc., the components of condensed speech (*i.e.* समासोक्ति).

RG. 67.1

किं च प्रकृतरसपरिपुष्टिमिच्छता विरोधिनोऽपि रसस्य बाध्यत्वेन निबन्धनं कार्यमेव। तथा हि सति वैरिविजयकृता वर्ण्यस्य कापि शोभा संपद्यते। बाध्यत्वं च रसस्य प्रबलैर्विरोधिनो रसस्याङ्गै र्विद्यमानेष्वपि स्वाङ्गेषु निष्पत्तेः प्रतिबन्धः। व्यभिचारिणो बाध्यत्वं तु तदीयरसनिष्पत्तिप्रतिबन्धमात्रात्। न त्वनभिव्यक्त्या। अभिव्यक्तौ बाधकाभावात्।

Trans.: Moreover, one who intends the proper development of the primary sentiment should utilise, eventhough, the opposing sentiment as being obstractable. And in doing so, (as) some extraordinary prosperty (lit.beauty) of the king, who have won over his rival, is attained.

And बाध्यत्व is the obstacle for the manifestation of the primary रस even in the presence of its subordinates, due to the many opposing subordinate sentiments. However, the state of being obstructable, of the transitory moods, is in the form of the obstacles for the manifestation of the respective sentiments, not indeed due to it because there is non-realisation, due to the obstacle for the realisation (of those).

RG. 67.2

न च विरोध्यङ्गाभिव्यक्त्या प्रतिबन्धान्नाभिव्यक्तिरिति वाच्यम्। तद्व्यञ्जकशब्दार्थज्ञानसमये विरोध्यङ्गाभिव्यञ्जकशब्दार्थ ज्ञानस्यासंनिधानात्। प्रतिबध्यप्रतिबन्धकभावकल्पने मानाभावात्। भावशबलताया उच्छेदापत्तेश्च। रसनिष्पत्तेः प्रतिबन्धस्त्वनुभवसिद्ध इति तां प्रत्येव विरोध्यङ्गानां बलवतामभिव्यक्तेः प्रतिबन्धकत्वं न्याय्यम्। अपि च यत्र साधारणविशेषणमहिम्ना विरुद्धयोरभिव्यक्तिस्तत्रापि विरोधो निवर्तते।

यथा–"नितान्तं यौवनोन्मत्ता गाढरक्ता सदाहवे।
वसुंधरां समालिङ्ग्य शेरते वीर तेऽरयः॥"

Trans.: Objection: Well, it may be argued: due to the obstacle by the knowledge (of the अंगs) of the opposing sentiment, there is no knowledge of the transitory moods (of the primary sentiment).

Answer: Not so. Because. durıng the time of the knowledge of the meaning suggesting tnat (transitory moods) (of the primary sentiment) there is the absence of the knowledge of the sense that suggesting the अंगs (transitory moods) of the opposing sentiments.

Because, there is no ground for the postulation, the relation of 'obstacle and being obstructed' (between the transitory mood of the primary and the transitory moód of the opposing sentiments).

And because, there would arise the contingency of discarding (the principle of) veriagition between emotions. The obstacleness for the realisation of sentiment, howerver, is proved by (common) experience. Thus, for (the realisation of) that, it is proper to accept, the expression of the powerful अंगs (transitory moods) of the opposing sentiments as obstacles. And further, when the two opposing sentiments are expressed due to common qualifications, there also the opposition is removed. For example: "O brave ! Your enemies, those, over-powered with duly youthness and shedding blood by regular battles, are sleeping by embrassing the earth."

RG. 68

इत्थमविरोधसंपादनेनापि निबध्यमानो रसो रसशब्देन शृङ्गारादिशब्दैर्वा नाभिधातुमुचितः। अनास्वाद्यतापत्तेः। तदास्वादश्च व्यञ्जन मात्रनिष्पाद्य इत्युक्तत्वात्। यत्र विभावादिभिरभिव्यक्तस्य रसस्य स्वशब्देनाभिधानं तत्र को दोष इति चेत्, व्यङ्ग्यस्य वाच्यीकरणे सामान्यतो वमनाख्यदोषस्य वक्ष्यमाणत्वात्। आस्वाद्यतावच्छेदकरुपेण प्रत्ययाजानकतया रसस्थले वाच्यवृत्तेः कापेयकल्पत्वेन विशेषदोषत्वाच्च।

Trans.: Like this, it is not proper to express sentiment even either by the term sentiment or erotic, etc., though being composed by non-conflicting अंगऽ. Because, there would arise the contingency of non-enjoyments, because it is accepted thus the enjoyment of that sentiment is the result of suggestiveness only.

Objection: It may be argued: And where, the sentiment is expressed by its own term, manifested by excitant etc., what would be the fault ?

Answer: Because, there would arise the general fault called, 'वमन', which will be explained later on, in converting of suggested into expressed. Since the realisation of sentiment is not (in the form of) in case of the sentiment enjoybleness, delimitted by suggestiveness being expressed (by the term रस etc.) it would amount to the specific fault, like the efforts of a monkey (indulged in futile and foolish activites).

Rg. 68.1

एवं स्थायिव्यभिचारिणामपि शब्दवाच्यत्वं दोषः। एवं

विभावानुभावयोरसम्यक्प्रत्यये विलम्बेन प्रत्यये वा न रसास्वाद इति तयोर्दोषत्वम्। समबलप्रबलप्रतिकूलरसाङ्गानां निबन्धनं तु प्रकृतरसपोषप्रातीपिकमिति दोषः। प्रबन्धे प्रकृतस्य रसस्य प्रसङ्गान्तरेण विच्छिन्नस्य पुनर्दीपने सामाजिकानां न सामग्र्येण रसास्वाद इति विच्छिन्नदीपनं दोषः। तथा तत्तद्रसप्रस्तावनार्हेऽवसरे प्रस्तावः। विच्छेदानर्हे च विच्छेदः। यथा संध्यावन्दनदेवयजनादिधर्मवर्णने प्रसक्ते कयापि कामिन्या सह कस्यचित्कामुकस्यानुरागवर्णने। यथा च समुपस्थितेषु महाहवदुर्ममेषु प्रतिभटेषु मर्मभिन्दिवचनान्युद्गिरस्य नायकस्य संध्यावन्दनादिवर्णने चेत्युभयमनुचितम्। एवमप्रधानस्य प्रतिनायकादेर्नानाविधानां चरितानामनेकविधायाश्च संपदो नायकसंबन्धिभ्यस्तेभ्यो नातिशयो वर्णनीयः। तथा सति वर्णयितुमिष्टो नायकस्योत्कर्षो न सिध्येत्। तत्प्रयुक्तो रसपोषश्च न स्यात्।

Trans.: Similarly, the direct expression in words in case of permanent moods, transitory moods also, fault. Further, in the cases like, the improper realisation, or untimely realisation of excitant, ensuant etc., there is no enjoyment of the sentiment. Thus, these two are caused for fault. The composition of equal, powerful and opposite subordinate sentiment in a poetry opposes the proper development of the primary sentiment. Further, the fault namely, विच्छिन्नदीपन, occurs in the text, where the primary sentiment is discontinued by interrupation of some other incidents, because the enjoyment of sentiment in entirity is not possible for the audience. And the narration at the time not fit for its presentation and the discontinution at the time not fit for the discontunuation, are to be faults of the respective sentiments.

For example: The narration of love-making by some one with a lady at the time of the narration of religious act like संध्यावर्णन, देवयजन etc. And (again) for example: the narration of संध्यावर्णन by the hero at the time of the use of rivalry dialouges between opponents on the battle ground, and thus, the both (cases) are improper (to adopt).

Like this, the excessive narration of the villians etc., and his different deeds and manifold prosperty in compare to the hero should not be described.

In that case, (*i.e.* such narrations is done), the excellancy of hero which is desired for the narration cannot be attained. And the sentiment grounded on that, would not be (properly) realised.

RG. 68.2

न च प्रतिनायकोत्कर्षस्य तदभिभावकनायकोत्कर्षाङ्गत्त्वात्कथमवर्णनीयत्वमिति वाच्यम्। यादृशस्य प्रतिनायकोत्कर्षवर्णनस्य तदभिभावकनायकोत्कर्षाङ्गतासंपादकत्वं तादृशस्येष्टत्वात्। तद्विरोधिन एव निषेध्यत्वात्। न च प्रतिपक्षस्य प्रकृतापेक्षया वर्ण्यमानोऽप्युत्कर्षः स्वाश्रयहन्तृतामात्रादेव प्रकृतगतमुत्कर्षमतिशाययेत्, अतो न दोषावह इति वाच्यम्। एवं हि सति महाराजं कमपि विषशरक्षेपमात्रेण व्यापादितवतो वराकस्य शबरस्येव प्रकृतस्य नायकस्य न कोऽप्युत्कर्षः स्यादिति।

Trans.: Objection: It may be argued: Since, excellenceness of the villain is supportive of, and subordinate to, the excellenceness of the hero, how it should not be described.

Answer: Not so. Because, the description of that kind of excellenceness of the villain is desired, which is responsible for making it subordinate to, and the supportive of the excellenceness of the hero. And what is contray to that alone, is prohibited here.

Objection: It may be argued thus: The excellenceness of the villain from the hero, (which is) being narrated, would enhance the excellenceness with regard to the hero, due to the state of being the destroyer of its superstratum, hence does not carry any fault.

Answer: Not so. If that is ture, like the poor hunter, who has killed some king merely hitting by a poisonous arrow, there would not be any excellenceness in case of the hero.

RG. 68.3

तथा रसालम्बनाश्रययोरनुसंधानमन्तरान्तरा न चेद्दोषः।

तदनुसंधानाधीनाहि रसप्रतिपत्तिधारा तदननुसंधाने विरता स्यात्। एवं प्रकृतरसानुपकारस्य वस्तुनो वर्णनमपि प्रकृतरसविरामहेतुत्वाद्दोष एव। अनौचित्यं तु रसभंङ्गहेतुत्वात्परिहरणीयम्।

भङ्गश्च पानकादिरसादौ सिकतादिनिपातजनितेवारुंतुदता। तच्च जातिदेशकालवर्णाश्रमवयोवस्थाप्रकृतिव्यवहारादेः प्रपञ्चजातस्य तस्य तस्य यल्लोकशास्त्रसिद्धमुचितद्रव्यगुणक्रियादि तद्भेदः।

Trans.: It is a poetic fault if the description of both the sustaintial and dependance of (आश्रय) sentiment does not take place in regular intervals. The flow of the realisation of sentiment is dependant on the description (in regular intervals) of that and in case of the non-description, it supressed. Like this, the narration of the factors unfavourable for the development of the primary sentiment also, are called faults due to its being the cause of the obstruction of the primary sentiment. And the impropriety indeed is to be avioded due to its being the cause of the obsetruction for the realisation of sentiment. And the obstruction, in enjoyment of sentiment is like the mental distress caused by the mixing of the sand etc., in the drinkable sweet juice etc. And that (lack of proprity) is to be different from those, which is proper substance, quality, action etc., established by common behaviour and **śāstra,** with regard to the respective worldly objects entirely like race, place. time caste, house, age, condition, nature, behaviour etc.

RG. 69

जात्यादेरनुचितं यथा-गवादेस्तेजोबलकार्याणि पराक्रमादीनि, सिंहादेश्च साधुभावादीनि। स्वर्गे जराव्याध्यादि, भूलोके सुधासेवनादि। शिशिरे जलविहारादीनि, ग्रीष्मे वह्निसेवा। ब्राह्मणस्य मृगया, बाहुजस्य प्रतिग्रहः, शूद्रस्य निगमाध्ययनम्। ब्रह्मचारिणो यतेश्च ताम्बूलचर्वणम्, दारोपसंग्रहः। बालवृद्धयोः स्त्रीसेवनम्, यूश्चश्च विरागः। दरिद्राणामाढ्याचरणम्, आढ्यानां च दरिद्राचारः। प्रकृतयो दिव्याः, अदिव्या, दिव्यादिव्याश्च। धीरोदात्तधीरोद्धतधीरललितधीरशान्ता उत्साहक्रोधकामिनीरतिनिर्वेदप्रधाना उत्तममध्यमाधमाश्च। तत्र रत्यादीनां भयातिरिक्तस्थायिभावानां सर्वत्र समत्वेऽपि रतेः संभोगरूपाया मनुष्येष्विवोत्तमदेवतासु स्फुटीकृतसकलानुभावर्णनमनुचितम्। क्रोधस्य च लोकभस्मीकरणपटोर्दिनरात्रिव्यत्ययाद्यनेकाश्चर्यकारिणो दिव्येष्विवादिव्येषु। आलम्बनगताराध्यत्वस्यानुभावगतमिथ्यात्वस्य च रसानुल्लासापत्तेः।

Trans.: The impropriety in case of the race etc., is:

The (description of) powerful actions, the strength etc, in the case of cows, and the innoceances etc., of lion etc. The (description of) old age, the diseases etc., in heaven and the drinking of nectar on earth; The (discription of) water-sports etc., in winter and the enjoyment of fire in summer; The (discription of) hunting in case of a Brahmana, acceptance of gifts in case of a Kṣatriya and the reciting of **veda** in case of a sūdra. The chewing of bettle, attachment with women etc., in case of Brahmacari, Yati; The enjoyment of ladies in case of childern and old persons and the non-attachment with ladies in case of youth; The (description of) behaviour of a poor like a rich man and (the description of) a rich like a poor man etc.

The nature (of the hero) are devine, धीरोदात्त, धीरोद्धत्त, धीरललित, धीरशान्त, humanbeing and semi-devine. And (they are) by the dominance of enthusiasm, anger, love for lady and detachment are called as best, common and lowest (also).

Out of these, the clear narration of the entire ensuants in the case of devines, like the human beings of the permanent mood love etc., other than the fear, is not proper, even though, the love in the form of enjoyment is same in all cases. (cannot be narrated for devines).

Further, for anger, the description of many a wounderful deeds like the power of demolishing the world, changing the day into night and vice varsa, (lacks propriety) in case of human beings like the devine beings. Because, there would arise the contingency of non-realisation of sentiment from the object of being worshiped, residing in the sustaintial mood and false-hoodness, residing in the ensuants.

RG. 69.1

न च साधारणीकरणादाराध्यत्वज्ञानानुत्पत्तिरिति वाच्यम्। यत्र सहृदयानां रसोद्बोधः प्रमाणसिद्धस्तत्रैव साधारणीकरणस्य कल्पनात्। अन्यथा स्वमातृविषयकस्वपितृरतिवर्णनेऽपि सहृदयस्य रसोद्बोधापत्तेः। जयदेवादिभिस्तु गीतगोविन्दादिप्रबन्धेषु सकलसहृदयसंमतोऽयं समयो मनोन्मत्तमतङ्गजैरिव भिन्न इति न तन्निदर्शनेनेदानींतनेन तथा वर्णयितुं सांप्रतम्। तथा विद्यावयोवर्णाश्रमतपोभिरुत्कृष्टैः स्वतोऽपकृष्टेषु न सबहु-मानेन वचसा व्यवहर्तव्यम्। व्यवहर्तव्यं चापकृष्टैरुत्कृष्टेषु। तत्रापि तत्रभवन्भगवन्नित्यादिभिः संबोधनैर्मुनिगुरुदेवताप्रभृतय एव न राजादयः, जात्योत्तमैर्द्विजैरेव, नाधमैः शूद्रादिभिः, परमेश्वरेत्यादिसंबोधनैश्चक्रवर्तिन एव, न मुनिप्रभृतयः संबोध्याः। तथा चाहुः–

"अनौचित्यादृते नान्यद्रसभङ्गस्य कारणम्।
प्रसिद्धौचित्यबन्धस्तु रसस्योपनिषत्परा॥" इति।

Trans.: Objection: It may be argued like this: The knowledge of the object of being worshiped would not arise by the process of universalisation.

Answer: It is not so. When the realisation of sentiment is established by expreience by refined critics, the universalisation is to be postulated there. Ohterwise, there would arise the contingency of the accepting the realisation of sentiment, by refined critics, even in the cases like the narration of love to one's ownfather, with regard to one's own mother.

This poetic covention (rule) which is accepted by all (authorities) in the case like that, of the texts like **Gīta govinda** etc., composed by Jayadeva etc, thus, is different like in the modern poets showing that as ground / following this (the behaviour) of a intexticated king elephant.

Those are superior due to their knowledge, age, race, meditation, should not treat with respectable address with those, interior to them. And the interior should treat the superior (due to their knowledge, age etc,) with respectable address).

And there also, the expression like, तत्रभवन्, भगवन्, etc., are used for address to the sage, teacher, God etc. and not for the king etc. The emperors alone and not the sages etc. The highclasstwice borns alone and not the low-borns are to be addressed by the expression परमेश्वर. Thus (it is) told:

There is no other cause for a breach in sentiment except improprietyness (indecorum). The greater secret about sentiment is conformity to well known consideration of proprietyness (decorum) etc.

RG. 69.2

यावता त्वनौचित्येन रसस्य पुष्टिस्तावत्तु न वार्यते। रसप्रतिकूलस्यैव तस्य निषेध्यत्वात्। अत एव "ब्रह्मन्नध्ययनस्य नैषसमयस्तूष्णीं बहिः स्थीयतां, स्वल्पं जल्प बृहस्पते ! जडमते ! नैषा सभा वज्रिणः। वीणां संहर नारद! स्तुतिकथालापैरलं तुम्बुरो!, सीतारल्लकभल्लभग्नहृदयः

स्वस्थो न लङ्केश्वरः।" इतिकस्यचिन्नाटकस्य पद्ये विप्रलम्भ शृङ्गाराङ्गीभूतवीरसाक्षेपकपरमैश्वर्यपरिपोषकता स्थितदौवारिकवचनस्य ब्रह्माद्यधित्तेपपस्यानौचित्यं नदोषः। एवमेव "अले ले सद्दःसमुप्पाडिअहरियकुसग्गन्थि, मयाच्छमालापइवित्तिविस्यम्भिअवालविवन्दः कअणा वम्हणा" इत्यादि विदूषकवचनेऽपि रे शब्दादिप्रयोगस्य तत्तथा। हास्यानुगुणत्वात्। एषा हि दिगुपदर्शिता। अनया सुधीभिरन्य- दप्यूह्यम्।

Trans.: In so far as the nourishment of sentiment is there, even in the lack of propriety, we does not object. Because, what is objected (as fault) is the unfavourable factors of the (respective sentiment).

Therefore, the lack of proprity following the insult of ब्रह्मा etc., in the speech of the warder, namely :

"O Brahmā ! stand outside siliently, this is not the proper time for recitation of **Vedas**, foolish Bṛhaspati ! speak little, this is not the assembly of Indra; O Narada ! stop playing (your) Viṇā, O Tumbura ! enough of your sweet-praise. Because, the Lord of Lanka, whose heart is broken by the सिन्दुर mark in the from of a weapon, in the forhead of Sītā, is not well," in a verse of some drama. is not a fault due to it being hie supportive of the profound prosperity, suggestive of heroic sentiment which is subordinate to the primary sentiment, the love-in-separation. Like this, in the speech of the confindential friend of the king also, the use of the words रे, रे, etc., in the expression namely:

O lowest graded Brahimns ! creater of faith रुद्राक्षमाला in the minds of child-widows by counting, made from newly snatced green racred grass etc. (is not improper), because of its being favourable to laughter (sentiment).This way, the presentation (of the concept of sentiment) is completd. By following this, scholars should realise others.

RG. 70

रसेषु चैतेषु निगदितेषु माधुर्योजःप्रसादाख्यांस्त्रीन्गुणानाहुः। तत्र "शृङ्गारे संयोगाख्ये यन्माधुर्यं ततोऽतिशयितं करुणे, ताभ्यां विप्रलम्भे, तेभ्योऽपि शान्ते। उत्तरोत्तरमतिशयितायाश्चितद्रुतेर्जननात्" 'इति केचित्। 'संयोगशृङ्गारात्करुणशान्तयोस्ताभ्यामपि विप्रलम्भे इत्यपरे।' 'संयोग शृङ्गारात्करुणविप्रलम्भशान्तेषु निरतिशयितमेव न पुनस्तत्रापि तारतम्यम्' इत्यन्ये। तत्र प्रथमचरमयोर्मतयोः 'करुणे विप्रलम्भे तच्छान्ते चातिशयान्वितम्' इति प्राचां सूत्रमनुकूलम्। तस्योत्तरसूत्रगतस्य क्रमेणेति पदस्यापकर्षानपकर्षाभ्यां व्याख्याद्वयस्य संभवात्। मध्यस्ते तु मते करुणशान्ताभ्यां विप्रलंभस्य माधुर्यातिशये यदि सहृदयानामनुभवोऽस्ति साक्षी तदा स प्रमाणम्।

Trans.: Three merits, namely, Sweetness, florridity and smiplicity are accepted (by experts). The expression of sweetness in the case of pathos is more than that the sentiment called love-in-union. Still more than these two (namely pathos and love-in-union) in love-in-separation, even more from all these (three) in quietism. This is because of the dominance of the mental state being mented, in the subsequent sentiment, is the view of some. According to some other, from the love-in-union, it is more in Pathos and quietism, and these two, still more in love-in-separation. In Pathos, love-in-union and quietism, it is more from the love-in-separation, still different (among their status) is the view of some others. Out of these, the 'first' and the 'last' views namely, the association with excessive (of sweetness) goes with the (view as stated in the) view of the ancient theorist. Because, the two interpretations are possible either by excluding or including the word "in a sequence" occuring in the next view, with regard to the second view, namely, the excessive of sweetness in case of love-in-separation from 'Pathos' and 'quietism' if there is the realisation in the form of exprience, of the critics, then that is the proof.

RG. 70.1

वीरबीभत्सरौद्रेष्वोजसो यथोत्तरमतिशयः। उत्तरोत्तरमतिशयिता-याश्चित्तदीप्तेर्जननात्। अद्भुतहास्यभयानकानां गुणद्वययोगित्वं केचि-दिच्छन्ति। अपरे तु प्रसादमात्रम्। प्रसादस्तु सर्वेषु रसेषु सर्वासु रचनासु च साधारणः।

Trans.: The expression of flooridity in heroic, disgustful and furious sentiments is higher in sequence of their occurrances. The cause of the excessive (and more) in the succeedings from the preceedings, occurring in a sequence is the mental state (in the form of) brilliant expansion of heart. Some desires to associate two merits with the sentiments like wonderful, comic and terrific. However, still some others intent the association of simplicity alone. Simplicity is common to all kind of expressions and in all types of sentiments.

RG. 71

गुणानां चैषां द्रुतिदीप्तिविकासाख्यास्तिस्रश्चित्तवृत्तयः क्रमेण प्रयोज्याः। तत्तद्गुणविशिष्टरसचर्वणाजन्या इति यावत्। एवमेतेषु गुणेषु रसमात्रधर्मेषु व्यवसितेषु 'मधुरा रचना', 'ओजस्वी बन्ध' इत्यादयो व्यवहारा 'आकारोऽस्यशूर' इत्यादिव्यवहारवदौपचारिका इति मम्मट-भट्टादयः।

Trans.: The Three (*i.e.* mental states) namely 'being softened', 'brightness' and development of these merits should be employed respectively in sequence. Thus, the (expressions) are produced, from the enjoyment of sentiment, having respective merits. The usage namely 'the sweet composition', 'style having florridity' etc., in these merits are like the usage namely, 'his form alone is heroic' etc., in case of these merits having sentiment alone as its soul, is the view of Mammaṭ-abhaṭṭa etc.

RG. 71.1

येऽमी माधुर्योजःप्रसादा रसमात्रधर्मतयोक्तास्तेषां रसधर्मत्वे किं

मानम्, प्रत्त्यक्षमेवेति चेत्, न। दाहादेः कार्यादनलगतस्योष्णस्पर्शस्य यथा भिन्नतयानुभवस्तथा द्रुत्यादिचित्तवृत्तिभ्यो रसकार्येभ्योऽन्येषां रसगतगुणानामननुभवात्। तादृशगुणविशिष्टरसानां द्रुत्यादिकारणत्वा-त्कारणतावच्छेदकतया गुणानामनुमानमिति चेत्, नो; प्रातिस्विक-रूपेणैव रसानां कारणतोपपत्तो गुणकल्पने गौरवात्।

Trans.: Objection: And whatever is told that these merits namely sweetness, florridity and simplicity are the inseparable attributers of sentiment alone, what is the proof of those being only the attributers of sentiment?

Clarification: It cannot be perception indeed. Because as the merits residing in sentiments in the mental state of 'being softened' etc., is not realised distinctly as the hot touch residing in the fire, is realised distinclty, from the effect 'burning.' And if (it is argued for) the inference of merits due to the causes as 'being softened' etc., of sentiments with those merits respectively, it cannot be so. Because, there would arise the contingency of heavyness in imaginary merits in the case of accepting the causes of sentiments by specific attributing nature.

RG. 71.2

श‍ृङ्गारकरुणशान्तानां माधुर्यवत्त्वेन द्रुतिकारणत्वं, प्रातिस्वि-करुपेण कारणत्वकल्पनापेक्षया लघुभूतमिति तु न वाच्यम्। परेण मधुरत्व मधुरतरत्वादि (रसधर्माणां) गुणानां पृथग्द्रुतत्वद्रुततरत्वादिकार्य तारतम्यप्रयोजकतयाभ्युपगमेन माधुर्यवत्त्वेन कारणताया गुरुभूतत्वात्। इत्थं च प्रातिस्विकरूपेणैव कारणत्वे लाघवम्।[१]

Trans.: It cannot be argued that it would be less in numbers by accepting the causes as individual forms, than (the acceptance) of the causes for 'being soften etc., by sweetness etc., in cases of erotic, pathos and quietism

१. This orginal text is composed with different readings. The syllable त्व is missing.

sentiments respectively. Because. there would arise the (contingency of accepting) heavyness of the causes as being sweetness, emerging by the application of the differences between effects (and causes) of merits namely individual softness and more softness in the cases like sweetness and more sweetness respectively, is the view of some others (*i.e.* Mammaṭa). As a matter of fact, the number (of causes) would be less by following the individual form (is the view of first group of scholars).

RG. 71.3

किं चात्मनो निर्गुणतयात्मरूपरसगुणत्वं माधुर्यादीनामनुपपन्नम्। एवं तदुपाधिरत्यादिगुणत्वमपि, मानाभावात्, परीत्या गुणे गुणान्तरस्यानौचित्याच्च। अथ 'शृङ्गारो मधुर' इत्यादिव्यवहारः कथमिति चेत्, एवं तर्हि द्रुत्यादिचित्तवृत्तिप्रयोजकत्वम्, प्रयोजकतासंबन्धेन द्रुत्यादिकमेव वा माधुर्यादिकमस्तु। व्यवहारास्तु वाजिगन्धोष्णेति व्यवहारवदक्षतः। प्रयोजकत्वं चादृष्टादिविलक्षणं शब्दार्थरसरचनागतमेव ग्राह्यम्। अतो न व्यवहारातिप्रसक्तिः। तथा च शब्दार्थयोरपि माधुर्यादेरीदृशस्य सत्त्वादुपचारो नैव कल्प्य इति तु मादृशाः।

Trans.: However, the sweetness etc., as the merits (soul) of the sentiments, connot be realised because, there is no shape of soul. Like this, the merits of the love etc, being the imposed properities of those (sentiments) also cannot be realised due to the lack of any proof. And due to the improprietyness of other merits in one merit, according to the view of others (*i.e.* logician). As a matter of fact, how then, the usage namely, the erotic in sweet etc., (are accepted). Then (it can be accepted that) the sweetness etc., are the generator of the mental states like 'being soften' etc., or (It can be accepted as). Let these, 'being softness' etc., are sweetness etc., alone by the relation of generatedness. However, the usages are not interrupted like the indicative usage 'the medicine is hot' etc.

The term should be understood as the generation of word, sense, sentiment, composition from the extraordinary unseen favours. Thus, the over-application of the usage is not here. Like this, as a matter of fact, according to our view, it cannot be imagined (like the view of Mammaṭa) that 'the existance of sweetness etc., in word and sense are to be understood by indicative sense."

RG. 72

जरत्तरास्तु–'श्लेषः प्रसादः समता माधुर्यं सुकुमारता।
अर्थव्यक्तिरुदारत्वमोजः कान्तिसमाधयः॥'
इति दश शब्दगुणान्, दशैव चार्थगुणानामनन्ति।
नामानि पुनस्तान्येव, लक्षणं तु भिन्नम्।

Trans.: However, ancient theorits postulated ten merits of word namely coalescence (श्लेष), simplicity (प्रसाद), uniformity (समता), sweetness (माधुर्य), softness (सुकुमारता), lucidity (अर्थव्यक्ति), raciness (उदारता), florridity (ओजस्), brilliancy (कान्ति) and symometry (समाधि) and also ten merits of sense. And the names (of these merits) are same (like the merits of word) but the natures (lit. definitions) are different.

RG. 72.1

तथा हि- शब्दानां भिन्नानामप्येकत्वप्रतिभानप्रयोजकः संहितयैक-जातीयवर्णविन्यासविशेषो गाढत्वापरपर्यायः श्लेषः॥

यदाहुः–'श्लिष्टमस्पष्टशैथिल्यम्' इति।

यथा–'अनवरतविद्वदद्रुमद्रोहिदारिद्र्यमाद्यद् द्विपोद्दामदर्पौंधवि-द्रावणप्रौढपञ्चाननः' इति।

Trans.: Accordingly, "placing of words of one type of close-connection, which is responsible for the knowledge of oneness, even in case of different words, another synonym of 'thickness' *i.e.* गाढता is coalescence." As told the ancient that the inistinctness of distinctive (between words) is the state of being coalesence. Example: "Here the brave five-face, capable of driving away the prides of the elephant, made by the rut in the form of poverty, quarrels continuously against the trees in the form of wise-persons.

Rg. 72.2

गाढत्वशैथिल्याभ्यां व्युत्क्रमेण मिश्रणं बन्धस्य प्रसादः॥
यथा– 'किं ब्रूमस्तव वीरतां वयममी, यस्मिन्धराखण्डल!
क्रीडाकुण्डलितभ्रुशोणनयनं दोर्मण्डलं पश्यसि।

माणिक्यावलिकान्तिदन्तुरतरैर्भूषासहस्त्रोत्करै, र्विन्ध्यारण्य गुहागृहा वनिरुहास्तत्कालमुल्लासिताः॥'

अत्र यस्मिन्नित्यन्तं शैथिल्यम्, भ्रुशब्दान्तं गाढत्वम्, पुनर्नयनेत्यन्तं प्रथममित्यादि बोध्यम्।

Trans.: "The combination of boldness and loseness (of words), without any sequence in a compostion is simplicity. "Example: "O king, Indra of earth ! What can we speak ofyour braveness!! When you fix your red eyes; when the eye brows are made bent play fully, the trees are brightened immedeately in the darken area of बिन्ध्यगुहा like a house as the rows of gems focusing (on those trees)."

Here, it should be understood as the losseness (of expression) are upto यस्मिन् and the boldness upto भ्रू (and) again, upto (नयने) is like first (*i.e.* looseness) etc."

RG. 72.3

उपक्रमादासमाप्ते रीत्यभेदः समता॥

यथा वक्ष्यमाणमाधुर्योदाहरणे। तत्र ह्युपनागरिकयैवोपक्रमसंहारौ।

Trans.: "Uniformity consists in the non-difference of style from the begining to end." As in case of the example of sweetness to be given. There (in the verse), it starts and ends in उपनागरिका sytle.

RG. 72.4

संयोगपरह्रस्वातिरिक्तवर्णघटितत्वे सति पृथक्पदत्वं माधुर्यम्।।
यथा– "नितरां परुषां सरोजमाला न मृणालानि विचारपेशलानि।
यदिकामलता तवाङ्गकानामथ का नाम कथापि पल्लवानाम्।।"

Trans.: "The State of being free from compounds and formed by the syllables of other than those short syllables, occuring after the conjuncts is sweetness."

Example: "When the tenderness of your limbs (is being spoken off) then a row of lotuses is extremely rough; the lotus stalks are not tender enough for consideration; and (lastly) what mention should be made of the foliage?"

Notes : The term **pṛthakpadatva** is given for the realisation of those compositions, free from compounds. The long compound sentences do not give pleasure to readers. To avoid the long compounds, this term is composed. As in **Madhusudanī** it is commented namely, **atra samāsadīrghatā pariharaṇīyeti bhāvaḥ.**

RG. 72.5

अपरुषवर्णघटितत्वं सुकुमारता।।

यथा-"स्वेदाम्बुसान्द्रकणशालिकपोलपालि, दोलायितश्रवण-कुण्डलवन्दनीया।

आनन्दमङ्कुरयति स्मरणेन कापि, रम्या दशा मनसि मे मदिरेक्षणायाः।।" अत्र पूर्वार्धे। उत्तरार्धे तु माधुर्यमपि।

Trans.: "The state of being formed by sofd syllables is softness." Example:

"The inexpressible charming state of my beloved endowed with fascinating eyes, produces delight in my mind when remembered; the state, which deserves to be praised (Lit. saluted) on account of the ear-rings dangling over the surface of the cheecks adorned with a network and drops of perspirtation." Here the first-half (is the example of) softness and the latter half is also of the sweetness.

RG. 72.6

झगिति प्रतीयमानार्थान्वयकत्वमर्थव्यक्तिः॥

यथा 'नितराम्' इत्यादौ।

Trans.: "The quick apprehension of the connection of sense is lucidity." As in the verse namly." नितरां परुषां सरोजमाला. ...." etc., (as quoted earlier).

RG. 72.7

कठिनवर्णघटनारूपविकटत्वलक्षणोदारता॥

यथा– "प्रमोदभरतुन्दिलप्रमथदत्ततालावली, विनोदिनी विनायके डमरुडिंड्डिमध्वानिनि। ललाटतटविस्फुटन्नवकृपीटयोनिच्छटो, हठोद्धतजटोद्भटो गतपटो नटो नृत्यति॥"

"पदानां नृत्यत्प्रायत्वं विकटता" इति काव्यप्रकाशटीकाकारा व्याचक्षते। उदाहरन्ति च "स्वचरणविनिविष्टैर्नूपुरैर्नर्तकीनां झटिति रणितमासीत्" इत्यादि। तत्र तेषामेतादृशीं विकटत्व लक्षणामुदारतामोजस्यन्तर्भावयन्काव्यप्रकाशकारःकथमनुकूल इति ते एव जानन्ति। नह्यत्रौजसो वैपुल्येन प्रतिभानमस्ति। 'विनिविष्टैर्नूपुरैर्नर्त'-इत्यत्र सन्नप्योजसो लवो न चमत्कारी। नापि तत्र नृत्यत्प्रायत्वं वर्णानामनुभवन्ति सहृदयाः। अंशान्तरे तु माधुर्यमेव।

Trans.: "Raciness is विकटता in the form of arrangement of harsh syllables." Example :"Nude Lord Siva started ताण्डव dance, from the edge of whose fore head, the blaze of the fire was coming out, (being) forceful, due to (his) matted hair forcefully standing on his head, when विनायक (Gaṇeśa) was dancing; making the sound of 'Dim' 'Dim', supported by the clapping sound of Pramatha's, cheerfully showing his belly, being fill in pleasure."

The commentator of **KP**, holds thus: विकटता is "the dancing state of words." And the example given is: The lady dancers suddenly became soundful having नूपुर on their feet ets." Only they know how this would be favourable for them, whom, the author of **KP**, wants to include raciness in the form of harsh syllables. And here, florridity is not realised in abundance. Here, in the verse namely, 'the lady dancers etc.', even though there is little florridity, (Yet) it is not charming. And again, the refined critics donot experience the dancing state of syllables there. In the rest part (of this verse) there is sweetness alone.

Notes : Jagannath does not accept that the Vikaṭatā involved here is due to a swing of words (padānāṁnrtyatprāyatvaṁ) as enjoyed by Vāmana. He appears to hold that Mammaṭa could not have included the earlier theorist's Udāratā under Ojas, had he understood this vikaṭatva to be due to a peculiar swing of words.

RG. 72.8

संयोगपरह्रस्वप्राचुर्यरूपं गाढत्वमोजः॥

यथा–"साहंकारसुरासुरावलिकराकृष्टभ्रमन्मन्दरक्षुभ्यत्क्षीर धिवल्गु-वीचिवलयश्रीगर्वसर्वंकषाः। तृष्णाताम्यदमन्दतापसकुलैः सानन्दमा-लोकिताभूमीभूषण! भूषयन्ति भुवनाभोगं भवत्कीर्तयः॥" यथा वा 'अयं पततु निर्दयम्' इत्यादिप्रागुहाहृते।

Trans.: "Florridity is the deepness in the form of abundance of vowels, followed by conjunct consonants."

Example: "O king of earth ! Your fame, the destroyer of the pride of the beauty in tides of ocean of milk resulted by the churning of the Mandara mountain, by the hands of the group of proudy Gods and demons, (and) looked happily by the group of ascetics, those are termented by thirst, adorns the entire world." Or as in the verse, illustrated earlier namely, 'अयं पततु निर्दयम्...' etc."

Notes : Ojas is one variety of merits of word. Vāmana declares as **gāḍhabandhatvamojaḥ** whereas PR's definition consists **gāḍhabandhatvam.** The gāḍhatva means the conjunct syllables in a position where it looks sometimes like long compounds as in the example verse, given by PR.

RG. 72.9

अविदग्धवैदिकादिप्रयोगयोग्यानां पदानां परिहारेण प्रयुज्यमानेषु पदेषु लोकोत्तरशोभारूपमौज्ज्वल्यं कान्तिः॥ यथा नितराम् इत्यादि प्रागुदाहृते।

Trans.: "The brilliancy is the brightness in the from of extraordinary beauty in the words being utilised, by avoiding the words (which) fit to be used by the inexperienced ritualists (not conversant with poetic expression). "The example verse namely, नितरां परुषां सरोजमाला etc." quoted earlier.

RG. 72.10

बन्धगाढत्वशिथिलत्वयोः क्रमेणावस्थापनं समाधिः॥

अनयोरेव प्राचीनैरारोहावरोहव्यपदेशः कृतः।

क्रम एव हि तयोः प्रसादादस्य भेदकः। तत्र हि तयोर्व्युत्क्रमेण वृत्तेः। यथा–"स्वर्गनिर्गतनिरर्गलगङ्गातुङ्गभङ्गुरतरंगसखानाम्।

कवेलामृतमुचां वचनानां यस्य लास्यगृहमास्यसरोजम्॥"

अत्रारोहः प्रथमेऽर्धे। तृतीयचरणे त्ववरोहः। गङ्गेत्यादौ माधुर्यस्य व्यञ्जकेषु वर्णेषु सत्स्वपिः, दीर्घसमासान्तःपातितया न तस्य प्ररोहः। उत्तरार्धे तु सोऽपि। एते दश शब्दगुणाः।

Trans.: "The placement of 'boldness' and 'loosseness' in style, in a sequence is symmetry. "These two (*i.e.* boldness and looseness in style) are called as ascending high (आरोह) and descending down (अवरोह) by the predecessors (like Vamana etc.). The sequence of style of these two ascend and descend is indeed the distinguishing factor of this from Simplicity. Because., there (in the case of Simplicity), they occur in the reverse order. Example: "Whose louts-like face is the seat of sport; the speeches like nectar alone, and like the high breaking tides of Ganga, falling continiously from the heaven.

Here, in the first half (of this verse) there is asscend, (*i.e.* tone is high). But in the third line, there is descend. Eventhough, there are suggestive syllables expressing sweetness, in the expression, गंगा तुंग भंगुर तरंग etc., yet due to it being of long compound, it is not supportive of that (sweetness). However, in the latter half, that (sweetness) exists. These are the ten merits of words (discussed).

RG. 73

एवं क्रियापरम्पराया विदग्धचेष्टितस्य तदस्फुटत्वस्य तदुपपादकयुक्तेश्च सामानाधिकरण्यरूपः संसर्ग श्लेषः॥

Trans.: And "the Coalescence is an association in the form of co-existance of an artful demeanour, its incongruity (lit. indistictness) and the arguments to show that, by the means of series of actions."

RG. 73.1

यावदर्थकपदत्वरूपमर्थवैमल्यं प्रसादः॥

यथा– 'कमलानुकारि वदनं किल तस्याः' इत्यादि। प्रत्युदाहरणं तु 'कमलकान्त्यनुकारि वक्त्रम्' इत्यादि।

Trans.: "The clearness of sense in the form of word (s) expressing desired sense (s) alone, is the Simplicity.

Example: "Her face is like (immitating) lotus indeed etc." A counter example (of this) is: "The face is like (immitating) the brightness of lotus etc.

RG. 73.2

प्रक्रमाभङ्गेनार्थघटनात्मकमवैषम्यं समता॥

यथा– "हरिं पिता हरिर्माता हरिर्भ्राता हरि सुहृत्।

हरिं सर्वत्र पश्यामि हरेरन्यन्न भाति मे॥"

अत्र विष्णुर्भ्रातेत्यादिनिर्माणे प्रक्रमभङ्गात्मकं वैषम्यम्।

Trans.: "The harmony in the form of placing the sense, without interrupting the sequence (of expression from beginning to end) is Uniformity." Example: "Hari is (my) Father, Hari is Mother, Hari is Brother, Hari is Friend, Everywhere (I) see hari and nothing attract me other than Hari.

Here, (in the present verse) the dis-harmony in the form of interruption of the sequence world arise by composing., "Viṣ ṇu" is Brother etc. (*i.e.* replacing the world Hari by Viṣhṇu).

RG. 73.3

एकस्या एवोक्तेर्भङ्ग्यन्तरेण पुनः कथनात्मकमुक्तिवैचित्र्यं माधुर्यम्॥

यथा–"विधत्तां निःशङ्कं निरवधिसमाधिं विधिरहो सुखं शेषे शेतां हरिरविरतं नृत्यतु हरः।

कृतं प्रायश्चित्तैरलमथ तपोदानयजनैः।

सवित्री कामानां यदि जगति जागर्ति भवती॥"

अत्र विध्यादिभिर्नास्ति किमपि प्रयोजनमित्येषोऽर्थः समाधिविधानादिप्रेरणारूपेणोक्तिवैचित्र्येणाभिहितः। अन्य थानवीकृतत्वापत्तेः।

Trans.: "The charming speech, repeated by different style of one speech, is called Sweetness." Example: "If the Goddess of all desires is awaken (for me) then Let Lord Brahmā continue the ceaseless meditation without anxiety, Let Lord **Viṣṇu** pleasurely sleep on **Śeṣa** (the king of serpents), Let Lord **Śiva** dance contineously. There is no need of any atonement (प्रायश्चित), by performing religious autsterities' , donation and sacrificial rites."

Here, the sense like 'there is no need of Brahmā etc., is expressed by charming style in the form of urge to do meditation etc. Otherwise, there would arise the fault of absence of novelity here.

RG. 73.4

अकाण्डे शोकदायित्वाभावरूपमपारुष्यं सुकुमारता॥

यथा– "त्वरया याति पान्थोऽयं प्रियाविरहकातरः।"

'प्रियामरणकातरः' इत्यत्र तु शोकदायिनो मरणशब्दस्य सत्त्वा-त्पारुष्यम्। इदं चाश्लीलतादोषव्याप्यम्।

Trans.: "The absence (of hardness) in the form of the absence of the description of pathetic sense etc., in improper time (place) is Softness."

"This traveller, unhappy of being separated from (his) beloved is moving fast." However, here in the expression 'unhappy due to the 'death' of his beloved, due to the presence of the term मरण that causes शोक, is a case of hardness. And this is pervacive of fault of being Vulgarity (अश्लील).

RG. 73.5

वस्तुनो वर्णनीयस्यासाधारणक्रियारूपयोर्वर्णनमर्थव्यक्तिः॥

यथा– "गुरुमध्ये कमलाक्षी कमलाक्षेण प्रहर्तुकामं माम्।

रदयन्त्रितरसनाग्रं तरलितनयनं निवारयांचक्रे॥"

अयमेवेदानींतनैः स्वभावोक्त्यलंकार इति व्यपदिश्यते॥

Trans.: "The description of extraordinary deed and form of the object of description is Lucidity." Example "The lotus-eyed one, prevented me, who inteneded to strike her in the midst of her elders with pieces of a clod of earth, (from doing so) holding the tip of her tongue. between (the two rows of) her teeth and by rolling her eyes." The modern scholars describe this (Lucidity) as a case of svabhāvokti (figure of speech).

RG. 73.6

"चुम्बनं देहि मे भार्ये कामचाण्डालतृप्तये" इत्यादिग्राम्यार्थपरिहार उदारता॥

Trans.: "Raciness is avoiding vulgar sense." For example: 'Oh darling wife ! Give me kiss for satisfication of sensual desire etc."

RG. 73.7

एकस्य पदार्थस्य बहुभिः पदैरभिधानं बहुनां चैकेन, तथैकस्य वाक्यार्थस्य बहुभिर्वाक्यैर्बहुवाक्यार्थस्यैकवाक्येनाभिधानं विशेषनां साभिप्रायत्वं चेति पञ्चविधमोजः।।

यहादुः-"पदार्थे वाक्यचरना वाक्यार्थेच पदाभिधा।
प्रौढिर्व्याससमासौ च साभिप्रायत्वमस्य च।।" इति।

पूर्वार्धप्रतिपाद्यं द्वयं व्याससमासौ चेति चतुष्प्रकारा प्रौढिः, साभिप्रायत्वं चेति पञ्चप्रकारमोज इत्यर्थः। प्रौढिः प्रतिपादनवैचित्र्यम्।

Trans.: Florrdity is of five types namely, a) the expression of one word by a series of words, b) of many (words) by one word, c) and like that expression of the sense of one sentence by many sentences, d) of many (sentences) by one (sentence) and e) the appropriateness of the usage of qualifications. "As is told (by ancients):

The boldness in the expression (of sense) are the use of a series of words instead of a single word and, the use of a single word in order to convey the sense of a sentence, the analytic expression (of sense by a diffuseness in which the self-same sense is sought to be expressed in more ways than one), the synthetic expression (of sense by a brevity in which several sentences are joined together in one integrated whole through the use of suffixes) and the appropriateness of sense."

The प्रौढि is of four types: the two presented in the first half (and the other two) namely, the analytic expression and the synthetic expression. And (including) appropriatness, the florridity is of five types. The style of uncommon presentation is called प्रौढि.

RG. 73.7.1

"यथा—सरसिजवनबन्धुश्रीसमारम्भकाले/ रजनिरमणराज्ये नाश-माशु प्रयाति। परमपुरुषवक्त्रादुद्गतानां नराणां/ मधुमधुरगिरां च प्रादु रासीद्विनोदः॥"

अत्रोषसीत्येकपदार्थस्याभिधानाय प्रथमचरणः।

इत्याद्यग्रेऽपि बोध्यम्।

Trans.: The example (for the first type of florridity): "The charmingful honey-like-sweet chanting of the people, born from the mouth of Superme Lord ब्रह्मा, producing pleasure, at the time of the destruction of the kingdom of night emporer Moon, suddenly, at the time of the arrival of the prosperity (rays) of the louts-friend Sun."

Here, for the expression of one single word namely, 'in the morning' the entire first line (is given). The same may be understood for the rest.

RG. 73.7.2

"खण्डितानेत्रकञ्जालिमञ्जुरञ्जनपण्डिताः।
मण्डिताखिलदिक्प्रान्ताश्चण्डांशोर्भान्ति भानवः॥"

अत्र 'यस्याः पराङ्गनागेहात्पतिः प्रातर्गृहेऽञ्चति इति' वाक्यार्थे खण्डितापदाभिधानम्।

Trans.: The example (for the second type of florridity) as:

"The rays of Sun, expert in making reddish the bunch of lotus-eyes of खण्डिता lady (those are neglected by their respective husbands) are spread over in all directions looks beautiful."

Here, the only word खण्डिता is used, for the sense of the complete sentence whose husband returns home in the morning from the abode of other lady.

RG. 73.7.3

"अयाचितः सुखं दत्ते याचितश्च न यच्छति।
सर्वस्वं चापि हरते विधिरुच्छृङ्खलो नृणाम्॥"

अत्र दैवाधीनं सर्वमित्येकस्मिन्वाक्यार्थे नानावाक्यचरनात्मको व्यासपदवाच्यो विस्तरः।

Trans.: The example (for the third type of florridity) as "The unsteady fate gives prosperity without seeking for it, donot give, being sought for, and also takes away everything of people."

Here, for the expression of the sense of one sentence, namely, 'everything is under the control of fate' there is elaboration called analytic expression in the form of expression having many sentences.

RG. 73.7.4

"तपस्यतो मुनेर्वक्त्राद्वेदार्थमधिगत्य सः।
वासुदेवनिविष्टात्मा विवेश परमं पदम्॥"

अत्र मुनिस्तपस्यति, तद्वक्त्रात्स वेदार्थमधिगतवान्, तदनन्तरं वासुदेवे परब्रह्मणि मनः प्रावेशयत्, ततश्च मुक्तोऽभूदिति वाक्यार्थ-कलापाः शतृ-क्त्वाबहुव्रीहिभिस्तिङ्न्तेन चानुवाद्यविधेयभावेनैकवाक्यार्थीकृतः।

Trans.: The example (for the fourth type of florridity) as:

"He attained the highest state (Liberation) concentring his soul on **Vāsudeva**, learning the Veda from the mouth of sage, engaged in meditation."

Here, these series of expressions, namely, 'the sage is meditating,' 'he learnt the **Veda** from his mouth,' and then 'concentrated (hiṣ) mind wiht Supreme God **Vāsudeva**', and after that "he attained salvation." These series of expressions are roped in one sentence by शतृ, क्त्वा, बहुब्रीहि, तिङ्न्त by description and described.

RG. 73.7.5

साभिप्रायत्वं च प्रकृतार्थपोषकता।

यथा– गणिकाजामिलमुख्यानवता भवता बताहमपि।

सीदन्भवमरुगर्ते करुणामूर्ते ! न सर्वथोपेक्ष्यः॥

अत्रोपेक्षाभावे करुणामूर्तित्वं पोषकम्। पापिष्ठत्वात्करुणाया अभावे प्रकृतेस्याः संपादनाय गणिकेत्यादि सीदन्निति च।

Trans.: "Appropriateness is the state of being the supportive of the sense in question." The example (for this fifth type of florridity) as:

"O the incarnation of Pityness ! Never ignore me, (I am) spoiling due to the falling in the worldly deserted well, at the time your protection to the noterious '**Piṅgala**' and **Ajāmila**'.

Here, the expression of 'the incarnation of pityness is the supportive (ground) for the absence of ingnorance. For the absence of pityness due to being a sinner and with a view to justify its (promises) the expresions like '**Gaṇikā**', '**Sidantī** ' etc., are employed.

RG. 73.8

दीप्तरसत्वं कान्तिः॥

तच्च स्फुटप्रतीयमानरसत्वम्। उदाहरणं च वर्णितमेव रसप्रकरणे। वर्णयिष्यते च।

Trans.: "Brilliancy is the clear reflection of the sentiment." And that (reflection) is the distinct realisation of sentiment. The example of this is narrated in the context of sentiment and would be narrated further.

RG. 73.9

अवर्णितपूर्वोऽयमर्थः पूर्ववर्णितच्छायो वेति कवेरालोचनं समाधिः॥

ज्ञानस्य विषयतासंबन्धेनार्थनिष्ठत्वादर्थगुणता।

आद्यो यथा 'तनयमैनाकगवेषण' इत्यादौ, द्वितीयस्तु प्रायशः सर्वत्रैवेत्याहुः।

Trans.: "The symmetry is the discussion made by poet namely, 'either this sense is not narrated earlier' or 'is similar to the earlier narration else where." The knowledge is a case of the merit of sense, because (bound to) ground on sense, by the realisation of objectness. The example of first type is: तनय मैनाक गवेषण etc. The example of the second type is said to be seen in all poetries often.

RG. 74

अपरे त्वेषु गुणेषु कतिपयान् प्रागुक्तै स्त्रिभिर्गुणैर्वक्ष्यमाणादोषा-भावालंकारैश्च गतार्थयन्तः, कांश्चिद्वैचित्र्यमात्ररूपतया, क्वचिद्दोषतया च मन्यमाना न तावतः स्वीकुर्वन्ति।

Trans.: Some other, however, donot accept some (merits) out of these (ten) by including in the three merits, mentoned earlier, taking it as the absence of faults, or cases of **alaṁkāras**, and some as only having the charmingness only and some are having faults (blemishes).

RG. 74.1

तथाहि श्लेषोदारताप्रसादसमाधीनामोजोव्यञ्जकघनायामन्तर्भावः। न च श्लेषोदारतयोः सर्वांशेगाढबन्धात्मनोरोव्यञ्जकघटनात्मर्भावोस्तु नाम, प्रसादसमाध्योस्तु गाढशिथिलात्मनोरंशनौजोव्यञ्जकान्त र्भावेऽप्यं-शान्तरेण कुत्रान्तर्भाव इति वाच्यम्। माधुर्याभिव्यञ्जके प्रसादाभिव्यञ्जके वेति सुवचत्वात्।

Trans.: Likewise, the merits (of words) namely, Coalescence, Raciness. Simplicity, Symmetry are included with the compostion, suggestive of florridity.

Objection: It may be argued: Let Coalescence and Raciness as bold syllables in each components be included in the compostion suggestive of florridity. However, in case of simplicity and symmetry having (both) bold and loose syllables, they are inclusive in the suggestive (composition) of florridity, yet in other parts, where it would be included?

Answer: Not so. It is well established that either in suggestive expression of sweetness or suggestive expression of simplicity, it can be included.

RG. 74.2

माधुर्यं तु परेषामस्मदभ्युपगतमाधुर्यव्यञ्जकमेव। एवं च सर्वत्र व्यञ्जके व्यङ्ग्यशब्दप्रयोगो भाक्तः। समता तु सर्वत्रानुचितैव। प्रतिपाद्योद्भटत्वानुद्भटत्वाभ्यामेकस्मिन्नेव पद्ये मार्गभेदस्येष्टत्वात्।

यथा– "निर्माणे यदि मार्मिकोऽसि नितरामत्यन्तपाकद्र वन्मृद्विका-मधुमाधुरीमपरीहारोद्धुराणां गिराम्। काव्यतर्हि सखे ! सुखेन कथय त्वं संमुखे मादृशां, नो चेदुष्कृतमात्मना कृतमिव स्वान्ताद्बहिर्मा कृथाः॥"

अत्र पूर्वार्धे तृतीयचरणे च लोकोत्तरनिर्माणप्रतिपादके यो मार्गो, न स चतुर्थचरणे कदर्यकाव्यप्रतिपादक इति वैषम्यमेव गुणः ग्राम्यत्वकष्टत्वयोत्स्यागात्कान्तिसौकुमार्ययोर्गतार्थता। प्रसादेन चार्थव्यक्ते-व्यक्तेरिति।

Trans.: However, the sweetness, accepted by other, is the suggestor of sweetness, as accepted by us. And thus, the expression of suggestiveness, is used secondarily as suggestor in all (cases). However, the use of uniformity is improper every where. Because the desiredness of inversion or alternate composition in a particular verse with (composition of) boldness and looseness, which is to be presented.

Example: "If you have the best skill in composing poem, capable of surpassing the excessive sweetness of the juice dropping from every ripe grapes, then alone should you, Oh friend ! repeat your poem fearlessly, before persons like me. Otherwise donot bring it out of your heart as a sin committed by yourself.

Here, non-similarity alone is the merit, namely, the style that represents the extraordinary composition (of poetry) is (followed) in the first half and in the third line as well, that (style) is not (followed) in the fourth line as that represent a bad-composition (of poetry). In the removal of vulgarity and difficultiness (blemishes), is the acceptance of (merits) brilliancy and softness. And also, by simplicity, the lucidity is included.

RG. 75

अर्थगुणेष्वपि-श्लेषः, ओजसः आद्याश्चत्वारो भेदाश्च उक्तिवैचित्र्यमात्ररूपा इति न गुणान्तर्भावमर्हन्ति।

अन्यथा प्रतिश्लोकमर्थवैचित्र्यवैलक्षण्याद्, गुणभेदापत्तेः। अनधिकपदत्वात्मा प्रसादः, उक्तिवैचित्र्यवपुर्माधुर्यम्, अपारुष्यशरीरं सौकुमार्यम्, अग्राम्यत्वरूपोदारता, वैषम्याभावलक्षणा समता, साभिप्रायत्वात्मकः पंचम ओजसः प्रकारः, स्वभाव स्फुटत्वात्मिकार्थव्यक्तिः,स्फुटरसत्वरूपा कान्तिश्च,अधिकपदत्वानवीकृतत्वामङ्गलरूपाश्लीलत्वग्राम्यत्वभग्नप्रक्रमत्वा पुष्टार्थत्वरूपाणांदोषाणांनिराकरणेन स्वभावोक्त्यलंकारस्य रसध्वनिरसवदलंकारयोश्च स्वीकरणेन गतार्थानि। समाधिस्तु कविगतः काव्यस्य कारणं न तु गुणः, प्रतिभाया अपि काव्यगुणत्वापत्तेः। अतस्त्रय एव गुणा इति मम्मटभट्टादयः।

Trans.: And in case of the merits of sense also, the coalesence and the first four varieties of florridity are not be included, being in the form of mere charmful expression. Otherwise there would arise the contingency of accepting many varieties of merit due to the existance of charming sense in each poetry.

Simplicity in the form of not too many words; sweetness in the form of charmful speech; Softness in the form of without hardness (in words); Raciness in the form of non-vulgrity (of words); Uniformity in the form of absence of non-similarity, and the fifth type of florridity in the form of supportive of necessary qualifications (adjectives) are accounted for, by avoiding the faults namely अधिकपदता, अनवीकृतता, अश्लीलता, ग्राम्यता, भग्नप्रक्रमता and अपुष्टार्थता respectively. And Further, अर्थव्यक्ति in the form of presentation of natural speech and कान्ति in the form of the visible reflection of sentiment are, accounted for by accepting the स्वभावोक्तिअलंकार, रसवदलंकार and रसध्वनि respectively.

However, समाधि is the case of the poetry residing with poet and (heance) not a merit. Otherwise, there would arise the contingency of accepting प्रतिभा, 'the poetic talent' or 'intiution' as a merit. Therefore, Mammaṭa and others accept only three merits.

RG. 76

तत्र टवर्ग वर्जितानां वर्गाणां प्रथमतृतीयैः शर्भिरन्तस्थैश्च घटिता, नैकट्येन प्रयुक्तैरनुस्वारपरसवर्णैः शुद्धानुनासिकैश्च शोभिता, वक्ष्यमाणैः सामान्यतो विशेषतश्च निषिद्धैः संयोगाद्यैरचुम्बिता, अवृत्तिर्मृदुवृत्तिर्वा रचनानुपूर्व्यात्मिका माधुर्यस्य व्यञ्जिका। द्वितीयचतुर्थास्तु वर्ग्यागुणस्यास्य नानुकूला नापि प्रतिकूला; दूरतया संनिवेशिताश्चेत्। नैकट्येन तु प्रतिकुला अपि भवन्ति। यदि तदायत्तोनानुप्रासः[१]। अन्ये तु वर्गस्थानां पञ्चानामप्यविशेषेण माधुर्यव्यञ्जकतामाहुः।

उदाहरणम्–

"तां तमालतरुकान्तिलङ्घिनीं किंकरीकृतनवाम्बुदत्विषम्।
स्वान्तमेकलय शान्तये चिरं नैचिकीनयनचुम्बितां श्रियम्॥"

यथा वा–

"स्वेदाम्बुसान्द्रकणशालिकपोलपालिरन्तःस्मितालसविलोकनवन्दनीया।

१. चौ, म, संपू, वादू, मदू, ओ, –अनुप्रास

आनन्दमंकुरयति स्मरणेन कापि रम्यमा दशा मनसि मे गदि-रेक्षणायाः॥"

प्रथमे पद्येहतिशथयोक्त्यलंकृतस्य गवह्दयानौत्सुक्यस्य भगवद्वि-षयकतेर्वाध्वन्ममानायाः शान्त एव पर्यवसनात्त द्गतमाधुर्यस्या-भिव्यञ्जिका रचनेयम्। द्वितीये तु स्मृत्युपष्टब्ध शृङ्गारगतस्य।

Trans.: There (in those merits), the first and third letters (mutes as k, g, c, j, t, d, p, b) of all वर्ग except the letters of the ट वर्ग, combined with the letters, श, ष, स, य, व, र, ल, adorns by 'm' with short vowels; परसवर्ण, pure अनुनासिक, and not touched by general and specific combined consonants; which are to be explained, the composition with either in absence of compouonds or presence of small compunds are farvourable for माधुर्य.

However, the second and fourth letters of the वर्गs are not favourable for this merit. Also not unfavourable due to the placement in long distances. If they form any aliteration, then, even used in nearby, are also not favourable. However, some accept that the all letters resting in five वर्गs are generally favourable.

Example: "O my mind, remember to that charm of Him, which surpassed the beauty of the तमाल plants, defeated the beauty of the newly arrived cloud and seen in the eyes of cows."

"The inexpressible charming state of my beloved endwed with facinating eyes, produces delight in my mind when remembered; the state, which deserves to be praised (lit. saluted) on account of the ear-rings dangling over the surface of the cheecks adorned with a network and drops of perspiration."

In the first verse, it is composed with favourable (letters) for माधुर्य in that of (शान्त) queitism alone, which is suggestive of either eagerness of meditation of lord or pleasure regarding Lord (कृष्ण), bascd on hyperbolic (अतिशयोक्ति), a figure of speech. However, in the second verse, (it is expressed) with erotic (शृंगार), favourable to recollection (of the earlier condition of the beloved).

RG. 77

नैकट्येन द्वितीयचतुर्थवर्गवर्णटवर्ग जिह्वामूलीयोपध्मागानीयविसर्ग सकारबहुलैर्वर्णैर्घटितो झयरेफान्यतरघटितसंयोगपरह्रस्वैश्च नैकट्येन प्रयुक्तैरालिङ्गितो दीर्घवृत्त्यात्मा गुम्फ ओजसः। अस्मिन्पतिताः प्रथमतृतीय-वर्ग्या गुणास्यास्य नानुकूला नापि प्रतिकूलाः संयोगाघटकाश्चेत्। तद्घटकास्त्वनुकूला एव। एवमनुस्वारपरसवर्णाअपि।

यथा– 'अयं पततु निर्दयं दलितदृप्त-' इत्यादौ प्रागुदाहृते।

Trans.: Further, the composition having the second and fourth letters of all serieses as well as all letters of ट वर्ग जिह्वामूलीय and उपध्मानीय letters, विसर्ग, स, झय (*i.e.* झ, भ, घ, ढ, ध, ज, ब, ग, ड, द, ख, फ, छ, ठ, थ, च, ट, त, क, प) and रेफ letters with long compunds, are favorable for ओजस्.

And if, the first and third letters of above are included, in this merit, then, cannot be favourable factors. Further, due to the non-attachment of संयोग letters, it is not unfavourable also. It is favourable indeed by the संयोग letters. Like this, अनुस्वार and परसवर्ण letters also.

Example: As illustrated earlier in the experssion namely 'अयं पततु निर्दयम्....' etc.

RG. 78.

श्रुतमात्रा वाक्यार्थ करतलबदरमिव निवेदयन्ती घटना प्रसादस्य।

अयं च सर्वसाधारणो गुणः। उदाहरणान्यत्र प्रायशो मदीयानि सर्वाण्येव पद्यानि। तथापि यथा–

"चिन्तामीलितमनसो मनसिजः सख्यो विहीनप्रभाः/ प्राणेशः प्रणयाकुलः पुनरसावास्तां समस्ता कथा। एतत्त्वां विनिवेदयामि मम चेदुक्तिं हितां मन्यसे/ मुग्धे मा कुरु मानमाननमिदं राकापतिर्जेष्यति॥"

अत्र सर्वावच्छेदेन प्रसादाभिव्यञ्जकत्वमंशभेदेन तु माधुर्योजोभिव्यञ्जकत्वमपि। मनसिजान्तस्य मा कुर्वादेश्च माधुर्योभिव्यक्ति हेतुत्वात्। सख्य इत्यादेरोजोगमकत्वात्।

Trans.: The composition of प्रसाद (merit) is expressed by the sense of the sentence after listening only, like the realisation of berry-nut which is on the palm.

And this a common merit. The examples are mostly of my entire verses quoted at other contexts. However one example:

"The God of love has his mind vacant with anxiety (*i.e.* does not know what to do to influence your mind); your friends have lost their splendour (since they cannot presuade you); and the lord of your life is distressed on account of his love, but let all this consideration be set aside. This, however, I tell you, if you think my advice to be beneficial, that you should not, O foolish one, be headstrong; Otherwise the husband of Rākā (moon) will vanquish (surpass) this face of yours."

Here (in this verse) the suggestor of प्रसाद is in entire parts. However, the suggestor of ओजस् are also parttally seen.

Upto चिन्ता......मनसिज and मा कुरु.......जेष्यति, there are suggestors for माधुर्य. In सख्यो...प्रभा. etc., there are suggestors for ओजस.

RG. 78.1

नन्वत्र शृङ्गाराश्रयस्य माधुर्यस्याभिव्यक्तये तदनुकूलास्तु नाम रचना, ओजसस्तु कः प्रसङ्गो यदर्थं तदनुकूलवर्णविन्यास इति चेत्।

नायिकामानोपशान्तये कृतानेकयत्नायास्तदीपं हितमुपदिशन्त्याः सख्याः सक्रोधत्वस्य व्यञ्जनीयतया तथाविन्यासस्य साफल्यात्।

किं बहुना रसस्यौजस्विनोऽमर्षादेर्भावस्य चाविवक्षायामपि वक्तरि क्रुद्धतया प्रसिद्धे वाच्ये वा क्रूरतरे आख्यायिकादौ प्रबन्धे वा परुष-वर्णघटनेष्यते। यथा वाः-"वाचा निर्मलया सुधामधुरया यां नाथ शिक्षामदा/ स्तां स्वप्नेऽपि न संस्पृशाम्यहमहंभावावृतो निस्त्रपः।

इत्यागःशतशालिनं पुररपि स्वीयेषु मां विभ्रतस्त्वत्तो नास्ति दयानिधिर्यदुपते मत्तो न मत्तः पर॥"

अत्र गुणान्तरासमानाधिकरणः प्रसादः।

Trans.: Objection: Well, Let there the composition having favourable letters to that for the expression of माधुर्य as it manifasted by शृंगार. But how it is proper in the case of ओजस, by accepting it as the favourable for that ?

Answer: Because of the succesive composition like that, by the suggested anger of friend for giving good advices who did a lot to controll the anger of the beloved lady.

Whats more ? it is desired to compose harsh letters in आख्यायिका, if the speaker is expressing in anger or is the cruel (words) are intended in प्रवन्ध, where, the clear/visible expresion of sentiments with ओजस् and mood with अमर्ष are not possible.

"O Lord !, A shameless creature, being filled with pride, do not, even in dream remember the advice (contained in the उपनिषद etc.) which you imparted to me by pure words sweet like nectar. Even though I have thus committed hundreds of faults, you still count me as one of your own. O Lord of Yadus ! there is no store of mercy greater than yourself, nor is there a person more arrogant than myself."

Or as : Here, it is a case of pure प्रसाद, due to the lack of other merits.

RG. 79.

इदानीं तत्तद्गुणव्यञ्जनक्षमाया निर्मितेः परिचयाय सामान्यतो विशेषतश्च वर्जनीयं किंचिन्निरूप्यतेवर्णानां स्वानन्तर्यं सकृदेक पदगतत्वे किंचिदश्रव्यम्। यथा 'ककुभसुरभिः, विततगात्रः,' 'पललमिवाभाति' इत्यादौ। असकृच्चेदधिकम्। यथा– 'विततततरस्तरुरेष भाति' भूमौ एवं भिन्नपदगतत्वेपि यथा–'शुक करोषि कथं विजने रुचिम्' इत्यादौ। सकृद्भिन्नपदगतत्वे ततोऽप्यधिकम्। यथा– 'पिक ककुभो मुखरीकुरु प्रकाकम्।' एवं स्व समानवर्ग्यानन्तर्यं सकृदेकपदगतत्वे किंचिदश्रव्यम्। यथा 'वितथस्ते मनोरथः'। असकृच्चेदधिकम्। यथा– 'वितथतरं वचनं तव प्रतीमः'। एवं भिन्नपदगतत्वे। यथा 'अथ तस्य वचः श्रुत्वा' इत्यादौ। असकृत्भिन्नपदगतत्वे तु ततोप्यधिकम्। 'अथ तथा कुरु येन सुखं लभे'।

Trans.: And now for the recognisation of those compositions having power in suggestive merits respectively, some avoiding (compositions) are being explained in general and particular. It is inaudible in general in the case like the ulterance of some letter in one word once only as क, क, (in ककुभसुरभि), त, त, (in विततगात्र), ल, ल, (in पललमिवाभाति) etc. And particularly if uttered many times as त, त, त (in विततततरस्तरुरेष भाति भूमौ).

Like this, the ulterance of one letter in separate words as क, क, (in शुक करोषि कथं विजने रुचिम् etc.). It is more (inaudible) also in case of repeated ulterance of one letter (in पिक ककुभो मुखरीकुरुप्रक्राममम्) separate words as क, क, क.

Further, if the letters of a particular वर्ग are ultered in one word (is also a fault) as त, थ (in वितथस्ते मनोरथः) and if uttered many times as त, थ, त, (in वितथतरं वचनं तव प्रतीमः), then become more inaudible.

Like this, if the letters of a particular वर्ग are uttered in many words as त, थ (in अथ तस्य वचः श्रुत्वा etc) and if uttered more than one time in many words the fault increases as त (in अथ तथा कुरु येन सुखं लभे).

RG. 80.

एतच्च वर्गाणां प्रथमद्वितीययोस्तृतीयचतुर्थयोरानन्तर्यम्। प्रथमतृतीययोद्वितीयतृतीययोर्वांनन्तर्यं तु तथा नाश्राव्यम्।

किंत्वीषन्निर्माणमार्मिकैकवेद्यम्। एतदप्यसकृच्चेत्ततोऽधिक -त्वात्साधारणैरपि वैद्यम्। खग कलानिधिरेष विजृम्भते। इति वदति दिवानिशं धन्यः। पञ्चमानां मधुरत्वेन स्ववर्ग्यांनन्तर्यं न तथा। यथा-तनुते तनुतां तनौ। स्वानन्तर्यं त्वश्रव्यमेव। यथा मम महती मनसि व्यथा-विरासीत्। एतानि चाश्रव्यत्वानि गुरुव्यवायेनापोह्यन्ते। संजायतां कथंकारं काके केकाकलस्वनः।

Trans.: The (inaudible) fault rests on first and second and third and fourth syllables in sequence, of all serieses (वर्ग). However, the composition with first and third, and second and third, syllables are not so much but partially inaudible, to be called as fault. But it is realised by the experts, composing poetries. And again, if this sequence is repeatedly done, it causes for much (inaudible) fault, thus this is realised by common readers. The example: 'खगः कलानिधिरेष विजृम्भते and इति वदति दिवानिशं धन्यः'

However, the fifth syllables of serieses (*i.e.* ञ, म, ङ, ण, न) are not so much inaudible by the sweet utterance in the sentence as in the expression namely तनुते तनुतां तन्तौ. If this utterance repeatedly used, then becomes inaudible as मम महती मनसि व्यथाविरासीन्. These usages are avoidable by the interpretation of long syllables as in the sentence संजायतां कथंकारं काके केकाकलस्वनः।

RG. 80.1

यथा वा–

यथा यथा तामरसायतेक्षणा मया सरागं नितरां निषेविता।

तथा तथा तत्त्वकथेव सर्वतो विकृष्य मामेकरसं चकार सा॥

इदंतु दीर्घव्यवाये। संयोगपरव्यवाये तु "सदा जयानुषङ्गाणामङ्गानां संगरस्थलम्। रङ्गाङ्गणमिवाभाति तत्तत्तुरगताण्डवैः॥"

इदं तु बोध्यम्-गुरुर्ययोर्व्यवधायकस्तयोरेव वर्णयोरानन्तर्य कृतम-श्रव्यत्वमपवदति। तेनात्र थकारतकारानन्तर्यकृतदोषापवादेऽपि तकार-थकारान्तर्यकृतमश्रव्यत्वमनपोदितमेव। एवं त्र्यादीनां संयोगोऽपि प्रायेणाश्रव्यः। राष्ट्रे तवोष्ट्र्यः परितश्चरन्ति इत्येवमादयः श्रुतिकाटवभेदा अन्येऽप्यनुभवानुसारेण बोध्याः।

Trans.: Or in the example: "When I enjoyed that (concentred) lotus-eyed-one, pleasurely, she attracted me towards her and made me one with enjoyment like a spiritual discourse."

This is an example of the 'employment of long syllables in distance, which donot amount to the fault of inaudibleness. However, in the case of long syllable caused by the following consonants, the example is: "The battle ground of the army of the अंग region, interested for winning, looks like a theatre-state, by the तांडव dance, of horses and by their steps."

Here, this is to be understood, if two syllables of same group of aspirated are differenciated by a long syllable, then the inaudible, due to the recitation after that, is removed. Thus, in the example, even though, there is the possibility of the fault of inaudibleness, due to the presence of त, थ, still, there is no fault. And if three new syllables are connected, it amount to the fault of inaudible in most cases. For example: राष्ट्रे तवोष्ट्र्यः etc., the variety of 'harsh expression (श्रुतिकटु) are to be understood according to the experiences.

RG. 81

अथ दीर्घानन्तर्यं संयोगस्य भिन्नपदगतस्य सकृदप्यश्रव्यम्। असकृत्तु सुतराम्।

"हरिणीप्रेक्षणा यत्र गृहिणी न विलोक्यते।
सेवितं सर्वसंपद्भिरपि तद्भवनं वनम्॥"
एकपदगतस्य तु तथा नाश्रव्यम्।

यथा–"जाग्रता विचितः पन्थाः शात्रवाणां वृथोद्यमः।" परसवर्णकृतस्य तु संयोगस्य सर्वथा दीर्घाद्भिन्नपदगतत्वा भावान्मघूरत्वाच्चानन्तर्यं न मनागप्यश्रव्यम्,

यथा–"तान्तमालतरुकान्ति"–इत्यादिपद्ये।

अत्र तामित्यत्र नीमित्यत्र च परसवर्णस्य पूर्वपदभक्ततया न संयोगो भिन्नपदगतः। प्रत्येकं संयोगसंज्ञेति पक्षेऽपि भिन्नपदगतः संयोगो न दीर्घादव्यवहितपरः।

नवाम्बुदेत्यत्र त्वेकादेशस्य पदद्वयभक्ततया दीर्घाद्भिन्नपदगतत्वे सत्यव्यवहितोत्तरत्वं यद्यपि परसवर्णकृत संयोगस्य भवति तथाप्यत्र भिन्नपदगतत्वमेकपदगतभिन्नत्वं विवक्षितमित्यदोषः। असकृत्तु सुतराम्।

यथा–"एषा प्रिया मे क्व गता त्रणकुला। इदं चाश्रव्यत्वं पंगुत्वमिव प्रतीयते।

Trans.: Further, if long syllables, followed with the combined syllables in different words at one place, it forms the fault of inaudibleness. And if this type of usage occurs frequently, then caused for that fault indeed.

Example: "The house adorned with all properities, looks like a jungle, if the deer-eyed lady (wife) is not seen."

And if this fault occurs in one word, then it cannot be inaudible. Example: जाग्रता विजितः पन्थाः शात्रवाणां वृथोद्यमः (The ways of the useless enemies have been discovered (by me). Due to the long syllables only in fault of combined words and due to the absence of separate words and ...so due to their sweetness, there is no inaudibleness (fault) at all in the cases of (परसवर्ण) as in the verse namely तान् तमालतरुकान्ति etc.

Here, in the term like तान्त and नींकि, the परसवर्ण syllables become subordinate to the proceeding words, thus, cannot be called as separated from संयोगपद.

All are to be designated as (is the view of पतंजलि) and so the words are to be accepted distinicitly but cannot be called long syllables due to the non-placement of long syllables in middle. Due to the use of two words in one word namely नवाम्बुद (नव+अम्बुद), as a case of एकादेश according to the grammatical statement, even, having idstinct words form the long syllables and made it combined (one) after conjuntcion , still, these distinct words are made only one word and thus there is no fault, and if this type of usage is made very often (more than once) there indeed arises this fault. As the example. एष प्रिया मे क्व गता त्रपाकुला (here प्र in प्रिया and त्र in त्रपाकुला are संयोगपद and used twice). And this inaudibleness (fault are reflecting the lamness (state) of the poetry.

RG. 82

अथ स्वेच्छया संध्यकरणं सकृदप्यश्रव्यम्। यथा-'रम्याणि इन्दुमुखि ते किलकिञ्चितानि। प्रगृह्यताप्रयुक्तं त्वसकृदेव। अहो अमी इन्दुमुखीविलासेः। एवमेवच य-व-लोप्रयुक्तम् अपर इषव एते कामिनीनां दृगन्ता।

कथं तर्हि-

"भुजगाहितप्रकृतयो गारुडमन्त्रा इवावनीरमण।
तारा इव तुरगा इव सुखलीना मन्त्रिणो भवतः॥"

इति भवदीयं काव्यमिति चेदकृत्वैव यलोपं पाठान्न दोषः।

एवं रोरुत्वस्य हलि लोपस्य यणगुणवृद्दिसवर्णदीर्घपूर्वरूपादीनां

नैकट्येन बाहुल्यमश्रव्यताहेतुः। एवमिमे सर्वेऽप्यश्रव्यभेदाः काव्यसामान्ये वर्जनीयाः।

Trans.: Further, the deliberate avoidence of '**sandhi'** (combination of syllables) even once, amount the fault of inaudibleness.

Example: 'O moon like faced one, charming is your expressions', However, the non-employment of '**sandhi**' in case of प्रगृह्य repeatedly, amount to that (fault). viz "The charm of moon-like face etc". Like this, if the composition is dropping य, व (in the expression namely) 'the charming eyes of these ladies are some other arrows." (it will amount to the same fault). How then, there is no fault in your poetry, without dropping य namely "O the king of earth! your ministers are living pleasurely like stars, like horses and like those charms in the form of Garuda, for the serpents in the form of enemies."

Further the placing of उत्व in the place of रु, the हल्लोप the excessive use of यण्, गुण, वृद्धि, सवर्ण दीर्घ, पूर्वरूप, etc. in nearest compounds, amount, to the fault of inaudibleness. And these various 'inaudible' faults should be avoided in poetry in general.

RG. 83

अथ विशेषतो वर्जनीयाः। तत्र मधुररसेषुये विशेषतो वर्जनीया अनुपदं वक्ष्यन्तेते एवौजस्विष्वनुकूलाः, ये चानुकूलतयोक्तास्ते प्रतिकूला इति सामान्यतो निर्णयः। मधुररेषु दीर्घसमासं झयुघटित-संयोगपरह्रस्वस्य विसर्जनीयादेशसकारजिह्वामूलीयोपधमानीयानां टवर्ग-झयां रेफट्टकारान्तरघटितसंयोगस्य हलां ल-म-न-भिन्नानां स्वात्मना संयोगस्य युद्वयघटितसंयोगस्य चासकृत्प्रयोगं नैकट्येन वर्जयेत्। सवर्ण-झयुद्वयघटित संयोगस्य शर्भिन्नमहाप्राणझ घटितसंयोगस्य सकृदपीति संक्षेपः।

Trans.: Now starts the explanation of the specific faults, to be avoided: Out of these, those are to specifically avoided just to be narrated, in case of the group of मधुररस (i.e. श्रृंगार, शांत, करुण), they are supportive of florridity. And those are, told as supportive for, (ओज) are non supportive of others (गुणा:), is the general theory.

In case of the sweet sentiments, the long compound, (दीर्घ समास), झयूघटितसंयोगपरहस्व, विसर्गप्राचुर्य, जिह्वामूलीया, उपध्मानीय, टवर्गझय् झयूद्वयघटितसंयोग, सर्वणझयूद्वयघटितसंयोग, शर्भिन्नमहाप्राणसंयोग the compositions are to be avoided.

RG. 84

दीर्घसमासो यथा–

"लोलालकावलिवलन्नयनारविन्द लीलावशंवदित लोकविलाच-नाया:/ सायाहनि प्रणयिनो भवनं व्रजन्त्या/ श्वेतो न कस्य हरतेगतिर-ङ्गनाया://"

झयघटितसंयोगपरहृस्वानां प्राचुर्यं नैकट्येन यथा–

"हीरस्फुरद्रदनशुभ्रिमशोभि किं च/ सान्द्रामृतं वदनमेणविलोच-नाया:/ वेधा विधाय पुनरुक्तमिवेन्दुबिम्बं/ दरीकरोति न कथं विदुषां वरेण्य://"

अत्र भ्रिशब्दपर्यन्तं शृङ्गाराननुगुणम्। शिष्टं तु रमणीयम्।

उत्तरार्धे ककारतकाररूपझयूद्वयसंयोगस्य सत्त्वेऽपि प्राचुर्या भावान्न दोष:। यदितु दन्तांशुकान्तमरविन्दरमापहारि सान्द्रामृतम्," इत्यादि क्रियते तदा सर्वमेव रमणीयम्।

Trans.: The example for 'Long compound' follows: "Whose hearts are not attracted by the gait of the lady, going to the lovers home in evening, who has captured the eyes of people by the charm of her lotus-eyes and the curling hairs on her forehead."

The example for the use of excessive unstressed syllables of combined words forming झय in near (ness):

"Why did Brahma, worshipped by scholars, not remove the circle of moon, after creating the face of the deer-eyed one, having bright teeth like diamonds and full of nectar, as in the case पुनरुक्त."

Here, the expression upto the term, भ्रि is not favourable for erotic (sentiment). However, the remaining compositions are charming. In the latter half (of the verse), even there is the existance of क, त, which are syllables of झय yet, due to the absence of excessive compositions, it is not a fault. However, if the composition like, दन्ताशुकान्तमरविन्ध etc., is done, (in the first line of the verse), then the entire verse can present charmingness (sense).

RG. 84.1

विसर्गप्राचुर्यं यथा–

"सानुरागाः सानुकम्पाश्चतुराश्शीलशीलताः।
हरन्ति हृदयं हन्त कान्तायाः स्वान्तवृत्तयः॥"

अत्र शकारद्वयसंयोगान्तं पूर्वार्धं माधुर्याननुगुणम्।

जिह्वामूलीयप्राचुर्यं यथा–

"कलितकुलिशघाता केऽपि खेलन्ति वाता कुशलमिह कथं वा जायतां जीविते में। अयमपि बत गुञ्जन्नालि माकन्दमौलौ, चुलुकयति मदीयां चेतनां चञ्चरीकः॥"

अत्र द्वितीयजिह्वामूलीयपर्यन्तमननुगुणं माधुर्यस्य। यदि च कथय कथमिवाशा जायतां जीविते मे मलयभुजगवान्ता वान्ति वाताःकृतान्ताः इति विधीयते, तदा नायं दोषः।

Trans.: The example for the excessive use of विसर्गः. "The affection, sympatheticness, cleverness, behaviour etc., as being the mental states of my beloved, Alas ! are tormenting my heart."

Here, the first half being connected with two श, which is not favouring sweetness (merit).

Example for the excessive use of guttural syllables (specifically the विसर्ग before क and ख).

"O my friend ! the thunder like wind is playing (havoc for me); how can be there goodness in my life ? And this bee, sitting on the top of the mango there, collapsing my consciousness, by making sound." Here, the composition upto the second guttural syllables, are not favourable of sweetness (merit).

And if the expression made like, कथय कथमिवाशा जायतां जीविते etc., then this cannot be a fault.

RG. 84.2

उपध्मानीयप्राचुर्यं यथा–

"अलकाः फणिशावतुल्यशीला नयनान्ताःपरिषुङ्खितेषुलीलाः।
चपलोपमिता खलु स्वयं या बत लोके सुखसाधनं कथं सा।।"
अत्र द्वावुपध्मानीयावेव न शान्तानुगुणौ।

टवर्गझ यां प्राचुर्यं यथा–

"वचने तव यत्र माधुरी सा हृदि पूर्णा करुणा च कोमलेऽभूत्।
अधुना हरिणाक्षि हा कथं वा कटुता तत्र कठोरताविरासीत्।।
अधुना सखि तत्र हा कथं वा गतिरन्यैव विलोक्यते गुणानाम्

इति त्वनुगुणम्। रेफघटितसंयोगस्यासकृत्प्रयोगो यथा–

"तुलामनालोक्य निजामखर्वं गौराङ्गि गर्वं न कदापि कुर्याः।
लसन्ति नानाफलभारवत्यो लताः कियत्यो गहनान्तरेषु।।"

यदि तु "तुलामनालोक्य महीतलेऽस्मिन्" इति निर्मीयते तदा साधु।

Trans.: Example for the excessive use of उपध्मानीय (the विसर्ग pronounced before प, फ) syllables:

"How can such a lady be worthy one in this world, whose hairs are similar with the body of the serpent; whose eye-corners are adorned like the wings of arrows and whose behaviour itself is similar to lightining."

Here the two उपध्मानीय syllables (*i.e.* काफ, न्ता:प) are not favourable for erotic (sentiment).

Example for the excessive use of ट series and झय: "O my deer-eyed lady ! The sweetness in your voice and soften heart was there in with you. Alas ! How the harshness and cruelty (in voice and heart) is established there in now ?"

However, if the compositon made like, अघुना सखि तत्र हा कथं वा गतिरन्यैव विलोक्यते गुणानाम् then, it may be favourable.

Example for the repeated use of रेफ "O bright lady ! Never be so greedy yourself by not comparing with others. In this thickest jungle, many more trees are bented down with lot of fruits." However, if it is composed with the expression namely., "तुला मनालोक्य महीतलेस्मिन्" then it would be proper.

RG. 84.3

हलां ल-म-न-भिन्नानां स्वात्मना संयोगस्याकृत्प्रयोगो-

यथा–"विगणय्य मे निकाय्यं तामनुयातोऽसि नैव तन्नन्नाय्यम्।"

ल-म-नानां स्वात्मनासंयोगस्तु न तथा पारुष्यमावहति। यथा "इयंमुल्लसिता मुखस्य शोभा परिफुलं नयनाम्बुजद्वयं ते।

जलदालिमयंजगद्वितन्वन्कलितः क्वापि किमालि नीलमेघः॥"

झयुद्वयघटितसंयोगस्य यथा–

"आ सायं सलिलभरे सवितारमुपास्य सादरं तपसा।

अधुनाब्जेन मनात्तव मानिनि तुलना मुखस्याप्ता॥"

अत्र द्वितीयार्धमरम्यम्। सरसिजकुलेन संप्रति भामिनि ते मुखतुलाधिगता इति तु साधु।

Trans.: The example for the frequent use of combined हल् consonants except 'ल', म and 'न.'

"It is not proper for you to follow her by leaving my house." If the connected ल, म, न, syllables are used there, then the fault will not caused so much harsh. As in the example:

'O friend ! the charm of your face is brightened, the both lotus-eyes are developed. Have you seen that cloud, coloured blue (like कृष्ण), which has covered entire world."

The example for the frequent use of combined series syllables (other than the fifth series) : (two झय)

"O beautiful lady ! The lotus attained a little similarity in your face by worshipping (hence) meditating with love to Sun God, in the pond till the evening."

Here the second half (of the verse) is not charming. However, if the verse is composed with the expression such as., सरसिजकुलेन संप्रति भामिनि ! ते मुखतुलाधिगता, then it would present the charmingness.

RG. 84.4.

झयुद्वयघटितसंयोगस्य सकृत्प्रयोगो यथा–

"अयि मन्दस्मितमधुरं वदनं तन्वङ्गि यदि मनाक्कुरुषे।
अधुनैव कलय शमितं राकारमणस्य हन्त साम्राज्यम्॥"

नन्वत्र ककारद्वयसंयोगस्य हल्घटितस्वात्मसंयोगत्वेनैव निषेधात्क-खसंयोगस्य महाप्राणसंयोगनिषेधविषयत्वात्तृतीयसंयोगस्य चासंभवात्स-वर्णझयुद्वयसंयोगनिषेधो निरवकाश इति चेत्, न।

सकृत्प्रयोगविषयत्वेनास्य पार्थक्यात्। अन्यथा मनाक्कुरुषे इति निर्दोषं स्यात्। महाप्राणघटितसंयोगो यथा–

'अयि मृगमदबिन्दुं चेद्भाले बाले समातनुषे।'
उत्तरार्धं तु प्राचीनमेव।

Trans.: The use of combination of series letters other than the fifth ones (*i.e.*ञ, म, ङ, ण, and न) as.

"O beautiful lady ! If you smile a little with sweet and charmingful (attitude), Alas ! then now only the kingdom of moon, the king of night, will be destroyed (come to an halt)."

Objection: Well, It may be argued that, there is no scope to avoid the use of "combination of series syllables other than the fifth ones, because of the contradiction of using two syllables with each other (in the case of मनाक्कुरुषे) having हल्, and because of the (further) denial objects as the combined महाप्राण syllables are inclusive in combined क and ख syllables, and because of the immposible interpratation of third group of combined syllables.

Answer: Not true. Because, it is different as it is used only once with combined syllables. Otherwise, the expression namely मनाक्कुरुषे will be free from fault.

The example for the use of combined महाप्राण syllables:

"O beautiful lady ! If you put musk on forehead…etc," However, the latter half of this verse is alike the verse given earlier.

RG. 85.

एवं त्वप्रत्ययं यङन्तानि, यङ्लुगन्तान्यन्यानि च शाब्दिक प्रियाण्यपि मधुररसे न प्रयुञ्जीत। एवं व्यङ्ग्यचर्वणातिरिक्त योजना विशेषापेक्षानापततोऽधिकचमत्कारिणोऽनुप्रासनिचयान्यमकादींश्च-संभवतोऽपि कविर्न निबध्नीयात्। यतो हि ते रसचर्वणायामनन्तर्भवन्तः सहृदयहृदयं स्वाभिमुखं विदधाना रसपराङ्मुखं विदधीरन्। विप्रलम्भे तु सुतराम्। यतो मधुरतमत्वेनास्य निर्मलसितानिर्मितपानकरसस्येव

तनीयानपि स्वातन्त्र्यमावहन्पदार्थः सहृदयहृदयारुंतुदतया न सर्वथैव सामानाधिकरण्यमर्हति।

Trans.: Like this, however, the suffix, यङ्न्त, यङ्लुगन्त and such other types of usage (like कृदन्त, तद्धित etc.) are favourable to grammarians, yet should not be employed in the (composition having) sweet sentiments (by poets). Further, the poets should not compose those (poetries) by which, eventhough, the excessive charmingness with alliteration and repetition or paronomasia (यमक) **alaṁkāras**, realised than the late realisation of suggestion. Accordingly, if those occur excessively and primarily, they cannot be included in the realisation of suggestion and (they) can turn away the minds (hearts) of refined critics from the sentiments. In the case of love-in-separation, it must be (avoided). As a matter of fact, it is not proper to make generalisation of there objects with this sentiment (विप्रलम्भ), due to its hurting quality for refined critics as its excessive sweetness (accepted) like the juice made out from the pure sugar candy.

RG. 85.1

यहादुः–"ध्वन्यात्मभूते शृङ्गारे यमकादिनिबन्धनम्।
शक्तावपि प्रमादित्वं विप्रलम्भे विशेषतः॥"

ये तु पुनरक्लिष्टतयानुनन्नतस्कन्धतया च न पृथग्भावनामपेक्षन्ते, किं तु रसचर्वणायामेव सुसुखं गोचरीकर्तुं शक्याः, न तेषामनुप्रासादीनां त्यागो युक्तः।

यथा–"कस्तूरिकातिलकमालि विधाय सायं/स्मेरानना सपदि शीलय सौधमौलिम्। प्रौढिं भजन्तु कुमुदानि मुदामुदारा/मुल्लासयन्तु परितो हरितो मुखानि॥"

इत्थमेते प्रसङ्गतो मुधररसाभिव्यञ्जिकायां रचनायां संक्षेपेण निरूपिता दोषाः।

Trans.: As (it is) told :

"Even though, (the poet) has poetic talent (to compose), it is (one's) ngeligenceness to include '**Yamaka**' etc. in the erotic compostion, which is suggestive to poetry and in case of the sentiment; love in separation, (विप्रलम्भ श्रृंगारकाव्य)is particularly (the poet's) carelessness."

However, those alliteration etc, should not be avoided, those never depend on distinct manifestation (of themselves) due to non-difficultness and due to not so high uses, but capable of realisation with proper charm at the time of the realisation of sentiment.

Example: "O friend, having applied a 'tilaka' mark of musk (to your forehead), mount the top of the turret with a smiling face in the evening, and so let night lotuses have a good deal of delight and let the quarters gladden their faces all around."

RG. 86.

'एभिर्विशेषविषयैः सामान्यैरपि च दूषणै रहिता।
माधुर्यभारभङ्गुरसुन्दरपदवर्णविन्यासा।।
व्युत्पत्तिमुद्गिरन्ती निर्मातुर्या प्रसादयुता।
तां विबुधा वैदर्भी वदन्तिवृत्तिं गृहीतपरिपाकाम्।।'

अस्यामुदाहृतान्येव कियन्त्यपि पद्यानि।

यथा वा–

"आयातैव निशा निशापतिकरैः कीर्णं दिशामन्तरं/ भामिन्यो भवनेषु भूषरणगणैरूल्लासयन्ति श्रियम्। वामेमानगपाकरोपि न मनागद्यापि रोषेण ते/ हा हा बालमृणालतोऽप्यतितमां तन्वीतनु- स्ताम्यतिं।।"

Trans.: The composition without these general and specific faults (as told earlier), crisped with excessive sweetness (merit), adorned with beautiful words and syllables, made by talented poets in lucidity (merits), is called as high quality 'Vaidarbhi', by the scholars. So many verses are given as example for this style. Or one more as.

"The night has come, the space between the quarters is pervaded by the rays of the lord of the night (moon), and other women are adoring their bodies with numbers of ornaments, in their houses, still you, O lady ! do not lessen your haughtiness even in the slightest degree. (And). Alas ! your body much more slender than even a young lotus-stalk, is distressed by your anger,"

RG. 86.1.

अस्याश्च रीतेर्निर्माणे कविना नितरामवहितेन भाव्यम्।

अन्यथातु परिपाकभङ्गःस्यात्।

यथामरुककविपद्ये–"शून्यं वासगृहं विलोक्य शयनादुत्थाय किंचिच्छनैर्निद्राव्याजमुपागतस्य सुचिरं निर्वर्ण्य पत्युर्मुखम्। विस्त्रब्धं परिचुम्ब्य जातपुलकामालोक्य गण्डस्थलीं लज्जा नम्रमुखी प्रियेण हसता बालाचिरं चुम्बिता॥"

अत्रोत्थाय किंचिच्छनैरित्यत्र सवर्णझयूद्वयसंयोगस्तत्रापि नैकट्यनेति सुतरामश्रव्यः। एवं झयूघटितसंयोगपरह्रस्वस्यापि। तथा शनैर्निद्रेत्यत्र, निवणर्य पत्युर्मुखमित्यत्र च रेफघटितसयोगस्य, झयूघटित संयोग-परह्रस्वस्य च प्राचुर्यम्। विस्त्रब्धमित्यत्र महाप्राणघटितस्य, लज्जेत्यत्र स्वात्मसवर्णझयूद्वयघटितस्य, मुखी प्रियेणेत्यत्र भिन्नपदगतदीर्घानन्तरस्य संयोगस्य, तथा क्त्वाप्रत्ययत्य पञ्चकृत्वः, लोकतेश्चधातोर्द्विःप्रयोगः कवेनिर्माणसामाग्रीदारिद्र्यं प्रकाशयति। इत्यलं परकीयकाव्यविमर्शनेन। इति संक्षेपेण निरूपिताः रसा।

Trans.: And at the time of composition of this style, the poet should be very careful. Otherwise, there may arise the break of charmingness in sentiments. As in the verse composed by Amaruka:

"Finding the bed chamber secluded, the young bride rising gently and slowly from her couch and having scanned for very long the face of her Lord feigning sleep, imprinted a kiss without fear or hesitation; on preceiving his cheeks horripilated, her head bend down in bashfulness while the smiling lover kissed her for long."

Here, it is inaudible indeed in the expression namely, उत्थाय and किंचिन्छनैः due to the frequent use of combined सवर्ण झय syllables. Like this, the use of low pitched syllables also become faults. Further, in the expression namely, शनैः निद्रा and निर्वर्ण्य पत्युर्मुखम् are inaudible due to and excessive use of low-pitched syllables. In the expression विस्रब्ध, लज्जा, मुखीप्रियेण the faults occuring for महाप्राण, ie., fricative syllables, combination of two similar syllables (लज्जा), and high pitched syllables respectively. The suffix क्त्वा is used five times and लोकु धातु is used two times as these are expressing the poorness (non-capability) of the poet to compose good poetry. Any how, it is not good to criticise others composition. And thus, the concept of sentiment is explained in brief.

RG. 87.

अथ भावध्वनि निरूप्यते-अथ किं भावत्वम्। विभावानुभाव-भिन्नत्वे सति रसव्यञ्जकत्वमिति चेत्। रसकाव्यवाक्येऽतिव्याप्त्यापत्तेः। अर्थद्वारा शब्दस्यापि व्यञ्जकत्वात्। द्वारान्तरनिरपेक्षत्वेनव्यञ्जकत्वे विशेषिते त्वसंभवः प्रसज्येत। भावस्यापिभावनाद्वारैव व्यञ्जकत्वात्। भावनायामतिव्याप्त्यापत्तेश्च। अत एव च विभावानुभावभिन्नत्वस्येव शब्दिभिन्नत्वस्यापि तद्विशेषरणत्वे न निस्तारः। प्रधानध्वन्यमानभावे रसव्यञ्जकताभावादव्याप्त्यापत्तेश्च।

Trans.: Now starts the explanation of the suggestion of transitory moods. Well. what is transitory mood? It is said to be the state of being the suggestive sentiment, being different from excitant and ensuant, then there would arise the contingency of over-application in case of expression of poetries-dominated by sentiment. Because, the expression (of word) also become suggestive through the suggested sense (to avoid the fault of over application). If the suggestiveness is qualified by 'non-dependent of some other means, then this would amount to be the fault of non-application (असम्भव). Because, the transitory mood becomes suggestive through realisation. And also it would amount the fault of over-application in case of भावना. Therefore. there is no way than making (the addition) "being different from words" also as the qualification of that like "being different form excitant and ensuant." Because, it would amount to the fault of under-application due to the absence of the suggestiveness of 'sentiment', where the 'transitory mood' (itself) is primarily suggested.

RG. 87.1.

न च तत्रापि प्रान्ते रसोऽभिव्यज्यत एवेति वाच्यम्। भावध्वनिविलोपप्रसङ्गात्। भावचमत्कारप्रकर्षाद्भावध्वनित्वम्। रसस्तु तत्र व्यज्यमानोऽप्यचमत्कारित्वान्न ध्वनिव्यपदेशहेतुरित्यपि न शक्यं वदितुम्। चमत्काररहितरसव्यक्तौ मानाभावात्। रसेहि धर्मिग्राहकमानेनानन्दांशाविनाभावस्य प्रागेवादेदनात्।

Trans.: Objection to opponents: It may be argued:

In that case also, the manifestation of sentiment is realised later.

Answer: Not true, Because, this supposition would lead to the complete extinction of the transitory suggestion.

Further Objection: It may be further argued:

Due to the superiority of the charmingness of transitory mood, the suggestion of transitory mood is realised. However, even though , the sentiment is suggested there, still, due to its noncharmingness, it cannot be called as the suggested idea.

Answer: It cannot be argued so. Because, there is no such proof for accepting the menifestation of sentiment, devoid of charmingness. And it is stated earlier, the experience of the substratum and the experience fo charmingness stands in the relation of invariable existance in sentiment.

RG. 87.2.

अस्तु वा प्राधान्येन ध्वन्यमानस्यापि भावस्य प्रान्ते रसाभिव्यञ्ज-कत्वम्। तथापिदेशकालवयोवस्थादिनानापदार्थघटिते पद्यवाक्यार्थे तथाप्यतिव्याप्तिः। तस्य विभावानुभावभिन्नत्वे सति रसाभिव्यञ्जकत्वात्। नापिरसाभिव्यञ्जकचर्वणाविषयचित्तवृत्तित्वं तत्त्वम्। भावादिचवर्णाया-मतिप्रसङ्गवारणाय चर्वणाविषयतेति चित्तवृत्तिविशेषणमिति वाच्यम्।

"कालागुरुद्रवं सा हालाहलवद्विजानती नितराम्।
अपिनीलोत्पलमालां बाला व्यालावलिं किलामनुते॥"

इत्यत्र हालाहलसदृशत्वप्रकारकज्ञाने अतिव्याप्तेः। तस्य विप्रल-म्भानुभावत्वेन रसाभिव्यञ्जकचर्वणाविषयत्वात्, चित्तवृत्तित्वाच्च। नाप्य-खणडम्, तन्त्वे मानाभावात्।

Trans.: Or let there be the manifestation of sentiment later, though the transitory mood is primarily suggested. Still, there would be the fault of over application in case of sense of the poetic expression comprises of various objects like place, time, age, condition etc. Because, that suggests the sentiment being different from excitant, ensuant.

Objection: The mental state, having the enjoyment of the suggestion of sentiment, as its object, is that (भाव). In order to avoid the fault of over-application, in the case of the enjoyment of transitory mood etc., the enjoyment it self may be added as the qualification of the mental state.

Answer: Not so. Because there would arise the fault of over-application in the knowledge having the state of being similar to poison as its qualifier, in the expression namely, "that lady, congnised the black fragnant paste as poison and also (she) sees the garland of blue-lotuses as a group of serpents."

Because, that becomes the object of the enjoyment, in suggestiveness of sentiment as the ensuant of the sentiment, love-in separation. And also because, that is a mental state. Due to the absence of proof, it (भाव) cannot be indivisible properly (अखड).

RG. 88

अत्रोच्यते "विभावादिव्यज्यमानहर्षाद्यन्यतमत्वं तत्त्वम्॥"

यदाहुः—व्यभिचार्यञ्जितो भावः इति। हर्षादीनां च सामाजिकगतानामेव स्थायिभावन्यायेनाभिव्यक्तिः, सापि रसन्यायेनेति केचित्।

व्यङ्ग्यान्तरन्यायेनेत्यपरे मन्यन्ते। विभावानुभावौ चात्र व्यञ्जकौ। न त्वेकस्मिन्व्यभिचारिणि ध्वन्यमाने व्यभिचार्यन्तरं व्यञ्जकतयावश्यमपेक्ष्यते। तस्यैव प्राधान्यापत्तेः।

Trans.: Answer follows: (Now the definition of transitory mood is being explained here by):

"Thatness (भावत्व) is the state of being anyone of (३४ भाव) joy (हर्ष) etc, being suggested by excitant etc."

As (it is) told: 'That suggested by Transitory mood is भाव. The joy etc., residing in the audiences are also manifested (as in the case of) like the premanent mood (lit. following the logic of the manifestation of भाव). And according to some, that (manifestation) is like (the manifestation of) sentiment. (And) still some others hold thus, that (भाव) is manifested like the other suggestive factors (natures) (i.e. वस्तुध्वनि and अलंकारध्वनि). The both 'excitant' and 'ensuant' are the suggestive here.

It is not that, some other transitory mood, is necessary as the suggestive, when one transitory mood is suggested. Because, there would arise the contingency of that being primary.

RG. 89.

वस्तुतस्तु प्रकरणादिवशात्प्राधान्यमनुभवति कस्मिंश्चिद्भावे तदीयसामग्रीव्यङ्ग्यत्वेन नान्तरीयकतया तन्निमानमावहतो व्यभिचार्यन्तरस्याङ्गत्वेऽपि न क्षतिः। यथा गर्वादावमर्षस्य, अमर्षादौ वा गर्वस्य। न चैवं सति गुणीभूतव्यङ्ग्यत्वापत्तिः। पृथग्विभावानुभावाभिव्यक्तस्य, अत एवाऽनान्तरीयकस्य भावस्य, भावान्तरगुणीभूतस्यैव गुणीभूतव्यङ्ग्यव्यपदेशहेतुत्वात्। विभावस्त्वत्र व्यभिचारिणो निमित्तकारणसामान्यम्। न तु रसस्येव सर्वथैवालम्बनोद्दीपने अपेक्षिते। यदि तु क्वचित्संभवतस्तदा न वार्येते।

Trans.: As a matter of fact, eventhough, some transitory moods are primary, due to the context, becomes subordinate to some other transitory mood by becoming forceful, not being so, due to the absence of interruption; as suggested (suggestive) factors. There is no harm as in the case like the 'resentment' etc. in 'arrogance' and the arrogance etc., in 'resentment.'

It cannot be argued, in that case, that this would amount to the contingency of accepting it as subordinate suggestion.

Those transitory moods, which are expressed by different 'excitants' and 'ensuants' and hence not interrupted, and is subordinate to some other transitory moods, is the casue (namely) subordinate suggestion.

The 'excitant' here is only general instrumental cause of the transitory mood. And like 'sentiment' it does not depend on 'sustaintial' And enhancing' moods invariably. However, if it occurs, at times, then there is no harm.

RG. 90.

हर्षादयस्तु-हर्षस्मृतिव्रीडामोहधृतिशङ्काग्लानिदैन्यचिन्ताम दश्रम-गर्वनिद्रामतिव्याधित्राससुप्तबिबोधामर्षावहित्थोग्रतोन्मादमरणवितर्क-विषादौत्सुक्यावेगजडतालस्यासूया पस्मारचपलताः। प्रतिपक्षकृतधिक्कारादिजन्मा निर्वेदश्चेति त्रयस्त्रिंशद्व्यभिचारिणः। गुरुदेवनृपपुत्रादिविषया रतिश्चेति चतुस्त्रिंशत्। एतेन वात्सल्याख्यं पुत्राद्यालम्बनं रसान्तरमिति परास्तम्। उच्छृङ्खलताया मुनिवचनपराहतत्वात्।

Trans.: The Transitory moods namely joy etc., are thirty-three (in number), known as: Joy, Rocollection, Bashfulness, Perplexity, Steadiness, Apprehension, Weakness, Wertchedness, Anxiety, Intoxication, Fatigue, Arrogance, Sleeping, Judgement, Sickness, fright, Dreaming, Awakening, Resentment, Dissimulation, Ferocity, Madness, Moribundness, Deliberat on despair, Longing, Excitement, Stuper, Indolence, Envy, Epilepsy, Inconstancy and Despondency (nirveda) generates from the insult etc., caused by an opponent. The thrity-forth is love (**Rati**) with regard to (ones) Teacher, God, King, Son etc.

By this, the other sentiment namely, tenderness (वात्सल्य) having sustaintial mood as son etc., stands refuted. Because, there would arise the contingency of disobeying to the theories as given by sages (भरतमुनि etc.)

RG. 91.

तत्र इष्टप्राप्त्यादि जन्मा सुखविशेषो हर्षः॥

तदुक्तम्–"देवभर्तृगुरुस्वामिप्रसादः प्रियसंगमः।
मनोरथाप्तिरप्राप्यमनोहरधनागमः।
तथोत्पत्तिश्च पुत्रादेर्विभावो यत्र जायते।
नेत्रवक्त्रप्रसादश्च प्रियोक्तिः पुलकोद्गमः॥
अश्रुस्वेदादयश्चानुभावा हर्ष तमादिशेत्॥" इति।

उदाहरणम्–

"अवधौ दिवसावसानकाले भवनद्वारि विलोचने दधाना।
अवलोक्य समागतं तदा मामथ रामा विकसन्मुखी बभूव।।"

अत्रावधिकाले प्रियागमनं विभावः। मुखविकासोऽनुभावः।

Trans.: Out of these, the special type of pleasure, generated by the attainment of desired objects etc. is joy.

As (it is) told: (Where) the blessings of God, Protector, Teacher, Superior, the union with beloved, getting the desired object, receiving the pleasurable wealth (and) also the birth of son etc., become the excitant. And the happy emotions of eyes, face, the dialogues of beloved, erection of the hairs (due to delight rather than by fear), the tearing and sweating etc., become ensuants. That is called joy.

Example: "The beautiful lady, who had directed her eyes towards the gate of the house in the evening which was the appointed time (of my arrival), had her face delighted on seeing me coming."

Here, "the arrival of lover in the appointed time" is excitant. Delighted face is ensuant.

RG. 92.

संस्कारजन्यं ज्ञानं स्मृतिः।।

यथा-"तन्मञ्जु मन्दहसितं श्वसितानि तानि/ सा वै कलङ्कविधुरा मधुराननश्रीः। अद्यापि मे हृदयमुन्मदयन्ति हन्त/ सायंतनाम्बुजसहोदर-लोच- नायाः।।"

चिताविशेषोऽत्रविभावः। भ्रून्नतिगात्रनिश्चलत्वादय आक्षेपगम्या अनुभावाः। यद्यप्यत्रास्या एव स्मृतेः संचारिण्या, नायिकारूपस्य विभावस्य, हन्तपदगम्यस्य हृदयवैकल्यरूपानुभावस्य संयोगाद्विप्रलम्भ रसाभिव्यक्ते रसध्वनित्वं शक्यते वक्तुम्। तथापि स्मृतेरेवात्र पुरः स्फूर्तिकत्वाच्चमत्कारित्वाच्च तद्ध्वनित्वमुक्तम्।

Trans.: The knowledge generated from previous impressions is Recollection.

Example: Alas ! that sweet and gentle smile, those sighs and that spotless and charming beauty of the face of the lady, whose eyes appeared like an evening lotus (*i.e.,* closed) still madden my heart.

Here the special type of anxiety is excitant. The raising of eye-brows, unsteadiness of the body etc., understood from indication are ensuants.

Even though, it is proper to hold the suggestiveness of the sentiment, the sentiment of love-in-separation, by the combination of the excitant as the hero (lover), of the ensuant as the wretchedness of the mental state in the expression हन्त and of the transitory mood as recollection, yet, it is a case of suggestiveness of mood (instead of sentiment), due to the first realisation of recollection alone, and also due to the charmingness (of that) here.

RG. 92.1

तदादेर्बुद्धिस्थ प्रकारावच्छिन्न शक्तिरिति नये बुद्धेः शक्यतावच्छेदकानुगमकतया न वाच्यतासंस्पर्शः। बुद्धिस्थत्वं शक्यतावच्छेदकमिति नयेऽपि स्मृतित्वेन स्मृतेर्व्यक्तिवैद्यतैव। तस्याश्चात्र वाक्यवेद्यत्वेऽपि पदस्यैव कुर्वद्रूपत्वात्पदध्वनिविषत्वम्। एतेन भावानां पदव्यङ्गत्वे न वैचित्र्यमिति परास्तम्। सायंतनाम्बुजोपमानेन नयनयोरुत्तरोधिकनिमीलनोन्मुखत्वध्वननद्वारा तस्या आनन्दमग्नताप्रकाशः।

Trans.: Following in view namely, the expression, 'that' (तदादे) etc., has denotative power of the idea (वस्तु) residing in the knowledge, due to the cognition being the delimitor of the denotative sense, the recollection of the would not be a case of expressiveness. Even, following the view namely, the state of being residing in the cognition is the delimitor of the expressive, then, in the form of recollection, (the recollection) would be a case of suggestiveness. Hence, even though that is suggested from 'the full sentence', still due to the function of the 'word', it becomes the object of the suggestion of word. On the same ground, there is no charmingness of moods though suggested by word, stands refuted. By giving the simile of 'evening lotus', by the suggestion of the 'clossing of the eyes' more and more gradually, the expression of her being charmed with pleasure, is reflected.

RG. 92.2

"दरानमबत्कधरबन्धमीषन्निमीलितस्निग्धविलोचनाब्जम्।
अनल्पनिःश्वासभरालसाङ्गं स्मरामि सङ्गंचिरमङ्गसानायाः॥"

इत्यत्र स्मृतिर्न भावः। स्वशब्देन निवेदनादव्यङ्ग्यत्वात्। नापि स्मरणालंकारः। सादृश्यामूलकत्वात्। सादृश्यमूलकस्यैव स्मरणस्यालंकारत्वम्, अन्यस्य तु व्यञ्जितस्य भावत्वमिति सिद्धान्तात्। किं तु विभाव एव सुन्दरत्वात्कथंचिद्रसपर्यवसायी।

Trans.: Example: "I long remember the (sexual) intercourse of my beloved where in her neck was a little bent down, her lotus-like and affectionate eyes were slightly closed, and her limbs were languised on account of a number of heavy breathings."

Here, the recolletion is not a case of transitory mood, due to being non suggestive by expressing in its own form (स्मरामि) itself. Further, not also a case of the figure-of-speech called स्मरण, beacuse it is not based on similarity. The figure of speech स्मरण is based on similarity alone. But, in other cases of suggestiveness (where similarity is not there), would be a case of suggestive-transitory mood, is the rule.

However, the excitant, indeed, is same as sentiment, somehow, due to the charmingness (resting in this).

RG. 93

स्त्रीणां पुरुषमुखावलोकनादेः पुसां च प्रतिज्ञाभङ्गपराभवादेरुत्पन्नो वैवर्ण्याधोमुखत्वादिकारणीभूतश्चित्तवृत्तिविशेषो व्रीडा॥

यथा–

"कुचकलशयुगान्तर्मामकीनं नखाङ्कं/ सपुलकतनु मन्दं मन्दमालोकमाना/ विनिहितवदनं मां वीक्ष्य बाला गवाक्षे/ चकितनतनताङ्गी सद्म सद्यो विवेश//"

अत्र प्रियस्य दर्शनं, तेन नायिकाकर्तृकस्वकुचा[१]न्तर्वर्तिप्रियनखक्षतावलोकनजन्यहर्षावेदकतत्पुलकादेर्दर्शनं च विभावः। सद्यः सदनप्रवेशोऽनुभावः।

Trans.: A mental state having, the change of colour, looking downwards etc., as the cause, caused by seeing the face of men etc., in the women and the fault of not keeping (ones) promise etc., in the case of men is Bashfulness.

Example: 'The young lady, with her body all horripilated, looking at the marks of my nails between her two jar-like breasts, at once entered the house, with limbs expressing fear and bent down, when she saw me with my face placed in ạ window (looking at her)'.

Here, seeing the lover, and by that, notcing the horripilation etc. in the form of producing joy, generated by looking at the nail-marks of lover in her own breasts, marked by lover, is excitant. The sudden enterance to house is ensuant.

RG. 93.1

यथा वा– "निरुद्ध्य यान्तीं तरसा कपोतीं कूजत्कपोतस्य पुरो ददाने। मयि स्मितार्द्रवदनारविन्दं सा मन्दमन्दं नमयांबभूव॥"

पूर्वत्र त्रास इवात्रापि हर्षो लेशतया सन्नपि व्रीडाया अनुगुण

१. तत्कुच is found in other editions.

एव। प्रियकर्तृकं कपोतस्याग्रे कपोत्याः समर्पणं विभावः। वदननमन-मनुभावः।

Trans.: Or as:

"When I placed before the cooing pigeon, his mate that was going away by stopping her forcibly, she (my beloved) slowly bent down her smiling lotus-like face towards me."

'Here also, alike alarm (त्रास) in the earlier (verse), eventhough, joy exists, due to its pousity, is subordinate to bashfulness. Leaving the female pigoen before, by the lover is excitant. Bending down of the face, is ensuant.

RG. 94.

भयवियोगादिप्रयोज्या वस्तुतत्त्वानवधारिणी चित्तवृत्तिर्मोहः॥

'अवस्थान्तरशबलितसा तथा' इति तु नव्याः।

उदाहरणम्–

"विरहेण विकलहृदया विलपन्ती दयित दयितेति।
आगतमपि तं सविधे परिचयहीनेव वीक्षते बाला॥"

अत्रकान्तवियोगो विभावः। इन्द्रियवैकल्यं लज्जाद्यभावश्चानुभावः।

यथा वा–

"शुण्डदण्डं कुण्डलीकृत्य कूले कल्लोलिन्याः किंचिदाकुञ्चिताक्षः।
नैवाकर्षत्यम्बु नैवाम्बुजालिं कान्तापेतः कृत्यशून्यो गजेन्द्रः॥"

Trans.: The mental state, unable to recognise the reality of object, caused by fearfulness, separation etc., is perplexity. According to modern theorists:" Mental state supported by various situations is that (*i.e.* Perplexity).

Example: "The young lady whose heart was afflicted with separation and who was crying out 'my dear lover', 'my dear lover', looks at him, even when he comes near, like one that has no acquaintance with him."

Here, the separation of lover is excitant, the pathetic conditions of sensual organs and lack of shyness etc., are ensuants. Or as: "Separated from (his) beloved (she-elephant), the king of elephant giving up all activites, looking with half closed eyes on the bank of the river, making his trunk a circle, neither drinking water (lit-drawing water) nor eating lotuses."

RG. 95.

लोभशोकभयादिजनितोपप्लवनिवारणकारणीभूतश्चित्तवृत्ति विशेषो धृतिः॥

उदाहरणम्–

"संतापयामि हृदयं धावं धावं धरातले किमहम्।
अस्ति मम शिरसि सततं नन्दकुमारः प्रभुःपरमः॥"

अत्र विवेकश्रुतसंपत्त्यादिर्विभावः। चपलाद्युपशमोऽनुभावः। ननुचोत्तरार्धे चिन्ता नास्तीति वस्तुनोऽभिव्यक्तेः कथमस्य धृति भावध्वनित्वमिति चेत्, तस्य धृत्युपयोगितयैवाभिव्यक्तेः।

Trans.: The mental state having the removal of desturbances, as the cause, caused by greediness, grief, fearness etc., is Steadiness.

Example: "Why do I harass my mind by struggling after everything in this world. There is one to watch always over me, it is the son of Nanda, the Supreme Lord."

Here, the discriminative power, the knowledge of **śāstra**'s etc., are excitants. The removal of fickleness is ensuant.

Objection: Well. How can it be a case, where the transitory mood of contentment is suggested in the expression of the fact namely, there is no anxiety at all, in the latter half (of the verse).

Answer : Because, the expression of the absence of anxiety alone is supportive of that Steadiness.

RG. 96.

किमनिष्टं मम भविष्यतीत्याकारश्चित्तवृत्तिविशेषः शङ्का॥

उदाहरणम्–

"विधिवञ्चितया मया न यातं सखि संकेतनिकेतनं प्रियस्य।
अधुना वत किं विधातुकामो मयि कामो नृपतिः पुनर्न जाने।"

अत्रराजापराधो विभावः। मुखवैवर्ण्यादय आक्षेप्या अनुभावाः।
इयं तु भयाद्युत्पादनेन कम्पादिकारिणी, न तु चिन्ता।

Trans.: A mental state in the form of 'What would be inauspicious for me' is Apprehension.

Example: "O my friend ! I did not go to the meeting place of (my) lover, being cheated by fate now, I donot know, what will the "King of love" (*i.e.* Cupid) wants to do for me.

Here the mistake done towards the king (by not attending his wish) is excitant. The change of colour in the face etc., are ensuants.This is due to thrilling etc., caused by fear etc., only, but not due to anxiety.

RG. 97.

आधिव्याधिजन्यबलहानिप्रभवो वैवर्ण्यशिथिलाङ्गत्व दृग्भ्रमणादिहेतुर्दुःखविशेषो ग्लानिः॥

यथा–

"शयिता शैवलशयने सुषमाशेषा नवेन्दुलेखेव।
प्रियमागतमपि सविधे सत्कुरुते मधुरवीक्षणैरेव॥"

अत्र प्रियविरहो विभावः। मधुरवीक्षणैरेवेत्येवकारेण बोध्यमाना प्रत्युद्गमचरणनिपतनाश्लेषादीनां निवृत्तिरनुभावः।

Trans.: The unhappiness caused by the change of colour, lazyness, unsteadiness of eyes etc., generated from the collapse of the energy due to mental and physical conditions is Weakness.

Example: 'She, who, like the digit of the new moon, has only her beauty still remaining, lying on a bed of moss, receives her lover, although, he comes near, only with her sweet glances.'

Here, the separation of lover is excitant. The non-doing of coming again to him, falling under the feet etc., understood by the expression 'only' (एव) in the verse मधुरवीक्षणैरेव is ensuant.

RG. 97.1.

न चात्र श्रमः शङ्क्यः। कारणाभावात्। केचित्तु "व्याध्यादिप्रभव-बलनाशं ग्लानिमाहुः"। तेषां मते चित्तवृत्त्यात्मकेषु भावेषु नाशरुपाया ग्लानेः कथं समावेश इति ध्येयम्। 'यद्यपि बलस्यापचयो ग्लानिरा-धिव्याधिसमुद्रवः'। इति लक्षणवाक्यादपचयशब्देन नाश एव प्रतीयते, तथापि प्रागुक्तानुपपत्त्या बलनाशजन्यं दुःखमेव बलापचयशब्देन विवक्षितम्।

Trans.: And here, the 'Fatigue' is not to be doubted, due to absence of any proof. However, some accept that the collapse of energy due to disease etc., is Weakness.

According to their view, how Weakness in the form of collapsing to be included in the mood in the form of mental state, is to be thought over.

Eventhough, from the expression, namely, the loss of energy alone, caused by mental and physical conditions is Weakness (ग्लानि), by the word loss (अपचय), collapsed alone is understood. Still, due to absence of reconciliation which is stated earlier, the unhappiness alone caused by the collapse of energy, is intended by the expression, losing (बलापचय).

RG. 98.

दुःखदारिद्र्यापराधादिजनितः स्वापकर्षभाषणादिहेतुश्चित्तवृत्ति-विशेषो दैन्यम्॥

उदाहरणम्–

"हतकेन मया वनान्तरे वनजाक्षी सहसा विवासिता।
अधुना मम कुत्र सा सती पतितस्येव परा सरस्वती॥"

सीतां परित्यक्तवतो भगवतः श्रीरामभद्रस्येयमुक्तिः।
अत्रसीतापरित्यागरूपोऽपराधस्तज्जन्यं दुःखं वा विभावः।
पतितसाम्यरूपस्वापकर्षभाषणमनुभावः।

Trans.: The mental state caused by expressing one's own fault etc., generated by sorrow, poverty, crime etc., is Wretchedness.

Example: 'The lotus-eye (Sita) is exiled by me, being हतक. and now, where shall I get that devoted lady like the Saraswati (lit. **Veda**) is restricted to पतित (a man is fallen by his moral conducts).'

This is the speech of Lord रामचन्द्र, after rejecting Sita (exiling Sita in jungle). Here, the crime (sin) in the form of rejecting Sita or the sorrow caused by this is excitant. Expressing (his) own fault similar to a पतित, is ensuant.

RG. 98.1

यदाहुः–

"चिन्तौत्सुक्यान्मनस्तापाद्दौर्गत्याच्च विभावतः।
अनुभावात्तु शिरसोऽप्यावृत्तेर्गात्रगोरवात्॥
देहोपस्करणत्यागाद्दैन्यं भावं विभावयेत्॥ इति।"
'दौर्गत्यादेरनौजस्यं दैन्यं मलिनतादिकृत्।' इति च।

अत्र हतकेन मया विवासिता न तु विधिनेत्येतस्यार्थस्यपतितोपमयैव परिपोषः, न तु शूद्राद्युपमया। यतः शूद्रस्य जात्यैव श्रुतिदौर्लभ्यं विधिना कृतम्। पतितस्य तु ब्राह्मणादेर्विधिना श्रुतिसुलभत्वे स्वभावेन कृतेऽपि तेनैव तथाविधं पापमाचरता स्वतःश्रुतिदूरीकृतेति तस्य पतितेन साम्यम्। तस्याश्च श्रुत्येत्युपमालंकारो दैन्यमेवालंकुरुते। तथा

मयेति सेति चोपादानलक्षणामूलध्वनिभ्यां कृतघ्नत्वकृत ज्ञात्वनिर्दयत्वदयावतीत्वाद्यनेकधर्मप्रकाशनद्वारा तदेव परिपोष्यते। सेति स्मृत्या च लेशतः प्रतीयमानया।

Trans.: As is told: The mood, Wretchedness developed, due to the excitants namely, anxiety, impatience, sorrowfulness, miserable state and due to the ensuants like, moving the head, feeling heavyness in body, and due to the removal of ornaments etc.

And also Wretchedness is the absense of lusture due to the misfortune that causes dirts. Here, (in the illustrative verse), the sense is realised by simile with पतित, fallen man (by conducts) by the standard of composition of this expression that she is exiled by me, a हतक, but not (realised) by fate. Because the non-availability of Vedic Texts for शूद्र, is restricted by 'Brahmā,' by their caste.

However, in the case of ब्राह्मण etc., the **Veda**, was available to them, fallen by conducts, yet, the **Veda** was denied from him by conducting sin, and therefore, he has similarity with पतित, a fallen man (by conducts).

The comparision of her with **'sṛti'** (in smile) adorning the 'Wretchedness.' And further, the expression 'by me', and 'she', by the suggestion of, उपादानलक्षणा, being with various natures like cheat (कृतघ्न), gratefulness (कृतज्ञ), cruel (निर्दय), kindhearted (दयावती), etc., enhancing that Wretchedness. And, by the expression 'she', the faint recollection (of her) realised further.

RG. 99.

इष्टाप्राप्त्यनिष्टप्राप्त्यादिजनिता ध्यानापरपर्यायावैवर्ण्य भूलेखनाधोमुखत्वादिहेतुश्चित्तवृत्तिविशेषश्चिन्ता॥

यदाहुः–

“विभावा यत्र दारिद्र्यमैश्वर्यभ्रंशनं तथा।
इष्टार्थापहृतिः, शश्वच्छ्वासोच्छवासावधो मुखम्।”
संतापः स्मरणं चैव कार्श्यं, देहानुपस्कृतिः।
अधृतिश्चानुभावाः स्युः, सा चिन्ता परिकीर्तिता॥
‘वितर्कोऽस्या क्षणे पूर्वे पाश्चात्येवोपजायते॥’ इति।
‘ध्यानं चिन्ता हितानाप्तेः संतापादिकरी मता।’ इति च।

उदाहरणम्–

‘अधरद्युतिरस्तपल्लवा मुखशोभा शशिकान्तिलङ्घिनी।
अकृतप्रतिमा तनुः कृता विधिना कस्य कृते मृगीदृशः॥’

अत्र तदप्राप्तिर्विभावः। अनुतापादय आक्षेप्या अनुभावाः।

न चात्रौत्सुक्यध्वनिरिति वाच्यम्। कस्य कृत इत्यनिर्धारित-धर्म्यालम्बनायाश्चिन्ताया एव प्रतीयमानतया सतोऽप्यौत्सुक्यस्यैतद्वाक्येन प्राधान्येनानवबोधनात्[१]।

Trans.: The mental state caused by the change at colours, nailing on earth, looking with face downward etc., the synonym of constant thinking, generated by the non-fulfillment of (one's) desire, facing un-desirables etc., is Anxiety.

As (it is) told: This is known as Anxiety, the poverty, lost of property (highness); stealing of desired object etc, are excitants and heavy breathing, looking with face downwards, unhappiness, rememberance, thickness, and uglyness of body, impatience etc, are the ensuants.

And alternating thoughts (deliberation) appear at the preceeding and succeeding moments of this. Further, the thoughts for not getting desired objects, is called as Anxiety, which generates unhappiness is the view of some.

---

१. वादु, –प्राधान्येनाबवोधनात्, But in all other editions प्राधान्येनाबोध-नात्

Example: "The grace of the lower lip abscuring (the redness of) the tenderness of sprouts, the beauty of the face surpassing that of the moon, and the incomparable body of her whose eye brows are beautiful; all this does not speak of the creation of this creator (*i.e.* this must have been the creation of some other creator).'

Here, the non-getting of that (beautiful lady) is excitant (and) repenting etc., ensuants.

Objection: It may be argued that here it is a case of suggstiveness of longing.

Answer: Not so. Because, by the expression 'for whom etc.' the longing is not understood primarily, even though, in the sentence having longing, by the realisation of Anxiety alone in the expression having some uncertion perosn, as sustaintial mood, (for whom, this (lady) is created).

RG. 100.

मद्याद्युपयोगजन्मा उल्लासाख्यःशयनहसितादिहेतुश्चित्तवृत्तिविशेषो मदः॥

यदाहुः–

"संमोहानन्दसंभेदो मदो मद्योपयोगजः।" इति।

तत्रोत्तमे पुरुषे स्वापोऽनुभावः। मध्यमे हसितगाने।

नीचे तु रोदनपरुषोक्त्यादि। अयं च मदस्त्रिविधः। तरुणमध्यमाधमभेदात्। अव्यक्तासंगतवाक्यैः सुकुमारस्खलद्गत्या च योऽभिनीयेते स आद्यः। भुजाक्षेपस्खलितघूर्णितादिभिर्मध्यमः। गतिभङ्गस्मृतिनाशहिक्काछर्द्यादिभिरधमः।

Trans.: The mental state caused by sleeping, laughing etc., generated by the drinking of wine etc., called उल्लास is Inoxication.

As (it is) told: that Intoxication generated by the drinking of wine, is mixture of pleasure with preplexity. And there, in the case of noble person, sleeping, in (the case of) common (person), laughter and singing, and further in (the case of) lowest (person), crying, speaking of harsh words etc., are ensuants. This intoxication, is of three types namely, तरुण, मध्यम and अधम.

Which is acted with indistinct and improper sentences, slipping action with proper manner is called as तरुण (type of intoxication). By indicating hands, by falling here and there, moving around etc., is called as मध्यम. and the अधम is by (acting with) breaking the motion, loss of memory, hiccups and vomiting etc.

RG. 100.1

उदाहरणम्– "मधुरतरं स्मयमानः स्वस्मिन्नेवालपनशनैः किमपि।
कोकनदयेस्त्रिलोकीमालम्बनशून्यमीक्षते क्षीबः॥"

अत्र मादकद्रव्यसेवनं विभावः। अव्यक्तालापाद्यनुभावः। अत्र मत्तस्वभाववर्णनस्य तन्निष्ठमदव्यञ्जनार्थत्वान्मदभाव एव प्रधानमिति न स्वभावोक्त्यलंकारस्य प्राधान्यम्, अपि तु तद्ध्वन्युपस्कारकत्वमेव।

इदं वा पुनरुदाहरणम्–

"मधुरसान्मधुरं हि तवाधरं तरुणि मद्वदने विनिवेशय।
मम गृहाण करेण कराम्बुजं पपपतामि हहा भभभूतले॥"

अत्रापि स एव विभावः। अधिकवर्णोच्चारणादिरनुभावः।

पूर्वार्धगता ग्राम्योक्तिरुत्तरार्धे च तरुणाकरोम्बुजोपमेयतया निरूपणीये स्वकरस्य तदुपमेयतया निरूपणं च मदमेव पोषयतः।

Trans.: "A drunked smiling sweetly, uttering something to himself very slowly, making eyes reddish like the red-lotuses, is looking aimlessly to all directions. Here, the drinking of intoxicated drinks is excitant. The indistinct utterances etc., are ensuants.

Here, due to the suggestive sense of intoxication, residing in that of the description of the behaviour of a drunked, the mood of intoxication is primarily suggested and thus, not the figure of speech स्वभावोक्ति. But it is a supportive factor of that (mood of intoxication) or this may be another illustration:

"O beautiful lady: Please keep your lips, sweeter than honey, on my face, Take my lotus like hands by (your) hands, I am (Fa Fa) falling on the (Ga Ga) ground."

Here, that also (intoxictated drinks) is excitant. The uttering of unnecessarily irrelivant syllables etc., are ensuants. The indiscent speech in the first half and in the latter half (of verse), making his own hands as उपमेय of that (lotus), instead of making the hands of the lady (as उपमेय) are supporting the (mood of) Intoxication.

RG. 101.

बहुतरशारीरव्यापारजन्मा निःश्वासाङ्गसंमर्दनिद्रादिकारणीभूतः खेदविशेषः श्रमः।।

यदाहुः—

"अध्वव्यायामसेवाद्यैर्विभावैरनुभावकैः।
गात्रसंवाहनैरास्यसंकोचैरङ्गमोटनैः।।
निःश्वासैर्जृम्भितैर्मन्दैः पादोत्क्षेपैः श्रमो मतः।।" इति। 'श्रमः खेदोऽध्वरत्यादेर्निद्राश्वासादिकृन्मतः।' इति च।

अयं च सत्यपि बले जायते। शारीरव्यापारादेव च जायते। न तु ग्लानिः। अतो ग्लानेः श्रमस्य भेदः।

Trans.: The weariness caused by breathing, exhauted limbs, sleeping etc., generated by excessive physical activities, is Fatigue.

As (it is) told thus: Fatigue is said (to be caused) by the excitants like walking, exercising etc., and (by) the ensuants like pressing (one's) own body, closeness of the face, stretching one's own body, breathing, hiccups, lifting feet with slow motion etc. And again told: The weariness caused by walking, sexual activities, breathing, sleeping etc., are called as Fatigue.

This (Fatigue) is generated, even if the energy exists (in body) and also generated due to the physical activities alone. But not the weakness (generated). Therefore, Fatigue is different from Weakness (ग्लानि).

RG. 101.1.

उदाहरणम्–

"विधाय सा मद्वदनानुकूलं कपोलमूलं हृदये शयाना।

चिराय चित्रेलिखितेवतन्वी न स्पन्दितुं मन्दमपि क्षमासीत्॥"

अत्र विपरीतसुरतरूपः शारीरव्यापारो विभावः। स्पन्दराहित्यशयनादयोऽनुभावाः। न चात्र निद्राभावध्वननेन गतार्थतेति शङ्क्यम्। सुषुप्तौ हि ज्ञानराहित्येनैव यत्नराहित्यान्मन्दमपि स्पन्दितुं न क्षमासीदित्यस्यानतिप्रयोजनकत्वापत्तेः। शीङाभिहिततया तस्या व्यङ्ग्यत्वानुपपत्तेश्च। श्रमे त्वानुगुण्यमुचितम्।

Trans.: Example: "That lady, holding (her) forehead towards my face, slept on (my) chest for a long time not able to move a little like a painted statue."

Here, the physical activities in the form of love making in opposite style is excitant. Sleeping motionless etc., are ensuants.

Objection: It may be doubted that here, this (Fatigue) be included in (निद्रा) sleeping, due to the suggestive mood of sleeping.

Answer: Not so, Because, due to the lack of efforts in the absence of the knowledge, in deepsleep, there would arise the contingency of senselessnes of that expression namely, "was not able to move a little even."

And also, because of the non-realisation of the suggetiveness of that due to the expression with 'sin' (शीङ्) as a verbal form. It is proper to be supportive in the case of Fatigue (in stead of sleeping).

RG. 102.

रूपधनविद्यादिप्रत्युक्तात्मोत्कर्षज्ञानाधीनपरावहेलनं गर्वः॥

उदाहरणम्–

"आ मूलाद्रत्नसानोर्मलयवलयितादा च कूलात्पयोधे/ र्यावन्तः सन्ति काव्यप्रणयनपटवस्ते विषङ्कं वदन्तु/ मृद्वीकामध्यनिर्यन्मसृणरसझरीमाधुरीभाग्यभाजं/ वाचामाचार्यतायाः पदमनुभवितुं कोऽस्ति धन्यो मदन्यः//"

अत्र स्वकीयकविताया अनन्यसाधारणताज्ञानं विभावः। पराधिक्षेपैरेतादृशवाकयप्रयोगोऽनुभावः। इमं चासूयापि लेशतः-पुष्णाति। उत्साहप्रधानो गूढगर्वो हि वीररसध्वनिः, अयं तु गर्वःप्रधान इति तस्यादस्य विशेषः।

Trans.: Disobedience to others caused by the knowledge of superiority in (one's) own self due to beauty, prosperity, learing etc., is Arrogance.

Example: "Let all those persons, skillful in composing poems, from the foot of the मेरु mountain down to the shores of the ocean sorrounded by the मलय mountain, declare openly if there is any other person besides me, who is furtunate enough to enjoy the postion of being the master of the speech which has the good luck of possessing the sweetness of the flow of the sweet juice, coming out of the interior of the grapes."

Here, the extraordinary knowledge with regard to one's own composition is excitant. The use of that type of expression having challange to others is ensuant. And envy also is supporting to this a little. In case of suggestive heroic sentiment indeed, enthusiasm is primary, and Arrogance is secondary; However, here, this Arrogance is primarily (existing) thus, this is different from that.

RG. 102.1

तथा हि वीररसप्रसङ्गे प्रागुदाहृते 'यदि वक्ति' इत्यादि पद्ये गीष्पतिना गिरामधिदेवतयापि साकमहं वदिष्यामीति वचनेनाभिव्यक्तस्योत्साहस्य परिपोषकतया स्थितः सर्वेभ्यः पण्डितेभ्योऽहमधिक इति गर्वः। न तु प्रकृतपद्य इव नास्त्येव महीतले मदन्य इति स्फुटोदितेन सोलुण्ठवचनेनानुभावेन प्राधान्येन प्रतीयमानः।

Trans.: As a matter of fact, the Arrogance is here, suggested in the expression namely. 'I am the most learned perosn than all scholars, 'to menifaste the enthusiasm which is expressed namely, 'I will speak even with the Supreme Lord of speech from the verse, earlier illsutrated as यदि वक्ति. ..etc., in the context of heroic sentiment. However, the Arrogance is not suggested primarily by the ensuants like the clear expression namely, 'No body is there in this world other than me' in the present verse.

RG. 103.

श्रमादिप्रयोज्यं चेतः संमीलनं निद्रा॥
नेत्रनिमीलनगात्रनिष्क्रियत्वादयोऽस्यानुभावाः।
उदाहरणम्–
"सा मदागमनबृंहिततोषा जागरेण गतिमाखिलदोषा।
बोधितापि बुबुधे मधुपैर्न प्रातराननजसौरभलुब्धैः॥"
रात्रिजागरणश्रमोऽत्र विभावः। मधुपैर्बोधाभावोऽनुभावः।

Trans.: The steadiness of mental state caused by fatigue etc., is 'sleeping'. The closeness of eyes, activelessness of body etc., are its ensuants.

Example: "She passed whole night without sleep, delighted in my arrival, and later, even awakened by bees, greedy for smell of lotus-like morning face, (she) slept."

Here, the fatigue, due to not sleeping during night is excitant. The not-awakening by the bees is ensuant.

RG. 104.

शास्त्रादिविचारजन्यमर्थनिधारणं मतिः॥

अत्र निःशङ्कतदर्थानुष्ठानसंशयोच्छेदादयोऽनुभावाः।

उदाहरणम्-

"निखिलं जगदेव नश्वरं पुनरस्मिन्नितरां कलेवरम्।

अथ तस्य कृते कियानयं क्रियते हन्त मया परिश्रमः॥"

शरीरमेतज्जलबुद्बुदोपमं-इत्यादिशास्त्रपर्यालोचनमत्र विभावः।

हन्तपदगम्या स्वनिन्दा, राजसेवादिविरतिर्वितृष्णता चानुभावः।

झगिति मतेरेव चमत्काराद्ध्वनिव्यपदेशहेतुता, न शान्तस्य; विलम्बेन प्रतीतेः।

Trans.: The determination of the sense by the analysis of शास्त्र etc., is Judgement.

Here the remove of doubt etc., employment of the sense with out any doubt is ensuant.

Example: "The entire world is mortal, and again to take birth (lit. कलेवर) here always, alas ! How much labour am I doing for that?"

Here, the analysis of scriptures namely, 'Life is like a drop of water' etc., is excitant. The hate of one's ownself, understood from the expression हन्त, not attached with the service of king, non affection etc., are ensuants. The charmingness of Judgement only, realised instantly, is the cause for it to be called **Dhvani.** And it cannot be **Dhavni** of quietism (शान्त) sentiment due to the late realisation.

RG. 105.

रोगविरहादिप्रभवो मनस्तापो व्याधिः॥

गात्रशैथिल्यश्वासादयोऽत्रानुभावाः।
यदाहुः– "एकैकशो द्वन्द्वशो वा त्रयाणां वा प्रकोपतः।
वातपित्तकफानां स्युर्व्याधयो ये ज्वरादयः॥
इह तत्प्रभवो भावो व्याधिरित्यभिधीयते॥"
उदाहरणम्–"हृदये कृतशैवलानुषङ्गा मुहुरङ्गानि यतस्ततः क्षिपन्ती।
तदुदन्तपरे मुखे सखीनामतिदीनामियमादधाति दृष्टिम्॥"
विरहोऽत्र विभावः। अङ्गक्षेपादिरनुभावः।

Trans.: The mental anguish, caused by disease, separation etc., is Sickness. Lazyness of body, breathing etc, are ensuants here.

As (it is) told: "The mental state arising from those which are the diseases like fever etc., generating from the influence of either one or two or three of the वात, पित्त, कफ, is called Sickness."

Example: "Placing moss on her bosom, and often tossing her limbs (here and there), this lady directs extermely helpless glance on the face of her friends when they utter the name of her lover."

Here, the separation (from lover) is excitant, tossing of limbs (here and there) etc., are ensuants.

RG. 106.

भीरोर्घोरसत्त्वदर्शनस्फूर्जथुश्रवणादिजन्मा चित्तवृत्तिविशेषस्त्रासः॥
अनुभावाश्चास्य रोमाञ्चकम्पस्तम्भादयः।
यदाहुः– 'औत्पातिकैर्मनः क्षेपस्त्रासः कम्पादिकारकः।'
उदाहारणम्–"आलीषु केलीरभसेन बाला मुहुर्ममालापमुपालपन्ती।
आरादुपाकर्ण्य गिरं मदीयां सौदामिनीयां सुषमामयासीत्।"
अत्र पत्या स्ववचनाकर्णनं विभावः। पलायनमनुभावः।
न चात्र लज्जाया व्यङ्ग्यत्वमाशङ्कनीयम्। शैशवेनैव तस्या निरासात्।
इदं वा विविक्तमुदाहरणम–

"मा कुरु कशां कराब्जे करुणावति कम्पते मम स्वान्तम्।
खेलन्न जातु गोपैरम्ब विलम्बं करिष्यामि॥"

एषा भगवतो लीलागोपकिशोरस्योक्तिः।

Trans.: The mental state generated by the sight of a dreadful being, listening the sound of thunderbolt etc., in the case of coward is Fright. Horripilation, thrilling, paralyzing etc., are the ensuants of this.

As (it is) told: "The mental agony that causes thrilling etc., by natural calamity etc., is Fright."

Example: "The young lady, often imitating my words to her friends under the impulse of sport, assumed the beauty of the lightining (*i.e.* disappeared immediately) on hearing my voice from a distance."

Here the listening of the own voice (speech) by one's husband, is excitant, Running away is ensuant. The suggestiveness of basuhfulness cannot be doubted here. Because of the lack of that (bashfulness) by the expression बाला, as it represents the childhood, Or the example for (further) clarification:

"O my mother, O Kindhearted one !" Do not cane me by (your) lotus hands. My heart is trumbling. Never shall I make late after playing with the Gopa boys."

This is the speech of Lord, the young Kṛṣṇa who is fond of play.

RG. 107.

निद्रावि (ना) भावोत्थज्ञानं सुप्तम्॥

स्वप्न इति यावत्। अस्यानुभावः प्रलापादिः॥ नेत्रनिमीलनादयस्तु निद्राया एवानुभावा न त्वस्य। अनिदंजन्यत्वात्। यत्तु प्राचीनैः "अस्यानुभावा निभृतगात्रनेत्रनिमीलनं–" इत्याद्युक्तं तदन्यथासिद्धानामपि तेषामेतद्भावव्यापकत्वादिति ध्येयम्।

उदाहरणम्– "अकरुण मृषाभाषासिन्धो विमुञ्चममांचलं, तव परिचितः स्नेहः सम्यङ्मयेत्यनुभाषिणीम्। अविरलगलद्बाष्पां तन्वीं निरस्तविभूषणां, क इह भवतीं भद्रे निद्रे विना विनिवेदयेत्।।"

एषा प्रवासगतस्य स्वप्नेऽपि प्रियामेवंभाषिणीं दृष्टवतो निद्रां प्रति कस्यचिदुक्तिः। यद्यप्येवंभूतायाः प्रियतमावस्थाया निवेदनेन निद्रे मम भवत्या महानुपकारः कृत इति वस्तु, विप्रलम्भशृङ्गारश्चात्र प्रतीतिपथमवतरति, तथापि पुरः स्फूर्तिकतया स्वप्नध्वननमत्रोदाहृतं, न प्रान्ते तयोर्ध्वननंनिदोद्धुमीष्टे।

Trans.: The knowledge generated by the excitant, in the form of sleeping, is Dreaming.

This is termed as dream (**svapna**). The utterance etc., is ensuant of this. The rubbing of eyes etc., however,, are ensuants of sleeping only and not of this (Dreaming), due to its generation (of these activites) in dream.

Whatever the ancient theorists told namely, 'tossing limbs (here and there), rubbing of eyes are ensuants of this (**svapna**), etc., that holds good due to its prevasiveness of that, which are established otherwise.

Example: "O happy sleep, who indeed but you can win over to me, the slender-bodied one who has cast off her ornaments, who is continuously shedding tears, and who reproaches me with the words, 'O you, ruthless and ocean of false words, leave off the end of my garments. I have seen well what your love is."

This is the speech of, some one, staying away (from home), to 'sleep' after seeing (lit. Listening) his beloved speaking like this, in dream. Eventhough, by the presentation of the condition like this of the beloved, the realisation of love-in-separation and the suggestive fact namely. "O sleep ! you have done a great favour to me, 'comes to one's mind, still, it is illustrated as (the example of) the suggestion of

Dream due to its quick realisation. And later on, the suggestion of those (mere fact and love in separation) connot be refuted, if realised.

RG. 108.

निद्रानाशोत्तरं जायमानोबोधो विबोधः॥

निद्रानाशश्च तत्वपूर्तिस्वप्नान्तबलवच्छ्ब्दस्पर्शादिभिर्जायत इति त एवात्र विभावाः। अक्षिमर्दनगात्रमर्दनादयोऽनुभावाः।

तत्र संक्षेपेणोदाहरणम्–

"नितरां हितयाद्य निद्रया मे बत यामे चरमे निबेदितायाः।

सुदृशो वचनं शृणोमि यावन्मयि तावत्प्रचुकोप वारिवाहः।"

अत्र गर्जितश्रवणं विभावः। प्रियावचनश्रवणोल्ला सनाशोऽनुभावस्तून्नेयः। केचिदविद्याध्वंसजन्यमप्यमुमामनन्ति। तेषां मते 'नष्टो मोहः स्मृतिर्लब्धा त्वत्प्रसादान्मयाच्युत।

स्थितोऽस्मि गतसंदेहःकरिष्ये वचनं तव॥'

इति गीतापद्यमुदाहार्यम्। न तु वारिवाहविषयाया असूयाया एवात्र वाक्यार्थतेति शङ्क्यम्। विबोधप्रतीतौ हि सत्यां तस्मिन्ननौचित्यावगमे सत्यनुचितविबोधजनकत्वेन वारिवाहेऽसूयाया विलम्बेन प्रतीतेः परमुखनिरीक्षकत्वात्। स्यादपि तस्या अपि प्राधान्यम्, यदि वारिवाहे निष्करुणत्वादिबोधकं किंचिदपि स्यात्।

नापि स्पप्नस्य। वारिवाहनादेन तन्नाशस्यैव प्रतिपत्तेः।

अस्तु वा स्वप्नभावप्रशमेनासूयया च सहास्य संकरः।

Trans.: The knowledge arising after the end of sleep is awakening. And the end of sleep. caused by the fulfillment of that, end of the dream, the loud voice, touching etc., and these are the excitants here. Rubbing of eyes, rubbing the body etc., are ensuants.

The example is given here in brief: "When, at the last quarter of the night, I was pleasurely enjoying the voice of my beloved, by the favour of sleep, the cloud became angry with me."

Here, the listening of the sound of the cloud in excitant. The end of the pleasure through the listening of beloved voice is ensuant. Some accept this as to be caused by the destruction of ignorance. According to their view, the following verse is illustrated from **Gītā**: "Destroyed is the confusion, and through your grace, I have regained a proper way of thinking with doubts dispelled. I stand ready to do your bidding."

Objection: It may be doubted that the primary suggestion of envy towards the cloud is understood in this sentence.

Answer: Not so. Because, after the knowledge of awakening indeed, there arises the konwledge of impropriety (and) the envy towards the cloud as the cause of untimingly awakening, is generated leasurely (*i.e.* not instantly), due to its dependanceness on the knowledge some thing else (*i.e.* awakening). That would have been primary suggestion, if there would, however, been some expression suggesting the sense of cruelty etc. And also (it is) not a case of suggestion of dream, due to the destruction of the (dream) by the sound of cloud. Or let there be the existance of this with envy, by the end of dream.

RG. 108.1.

इदं तु नोदाहार्यम्-

"गाढमलिङ्ग्य सकलां यामिनीं सह तस्थुषीम्।

निद्रां विहाय स प्रातरालिलिङ्गाथ चेतनाम्॥"

विबोधस्य चेतनापदवाच्यत्वात्। यथा कश्चित्सत्यप्रतिज्ञो द्वाभ्यां नायिकाभ्यां द्वौ कालावुपभोगार्थं दत्त्वा यथोचिते काल एकामुपभुज्य कालान्तरे प्रवृत्ते तां विहायापरां भुङ्क्ते, तथैवायं रात्री निद्रां, प्रातश्चेतनामिति समासोक्तेरेवेह प्रकाशनात्।

Trans.: And the following cannot be an example (of awakening) due to the expression of the term चेतना.

"Some one, slept the whole night by deeply embrashing (to 'sleep') and in the morning, embrashed, 'consciousness' by leaving 'sleep'."

And, there, the figure namely 'condensed speech (समासोक्ति) is realised that, this person spent night with 'sleep' and with 'Consciousness' in the morning, as in the case like some one, keeping his words, giving alternative times for two beloveds for love making, and in proper time, enjoying with one and later leaving her, enjoys another (beloved).

RG. 109.

परकृतावज्ञादिनानापराधजन्यो मौनवाक्पारुष्यादिकारणी भूत श्चित्तवृत्तिविशेषोऽमर्षः॥[१]

प्राग्वत्कारणानां कार्याणां च क्रमेण विभावानुभावत्वम्।

उदाहरणम्– "वक्षोजाग्रं पाणिनामृष्य दूरे यातस्य द्रागाननाब्जं प्रियस्य। शोणाग्राभ्यां भामिनीलोचनाभ्यां जोषं जोषं जोषमेवावतस्थे॥"

इह त्वाकस्मिकस्तनाग्रस्पर्शो विभावः। नयनारुण्यनिर्निमेषनिरीक्षणे अनुभावौ। ननु क्रोधामर्षयोः स्थायिसंचारिणोर्भावयोः किं भेदकमिति चेत्, विषयतावैलक्षण्यमेवेति गृहाण। तत्र तु गमकं झटिति परविनाशादौ परुषवचनवैमुख्यादिकंचेति कार्य वैलक्षण्यम्।

Trans.: The mental state caused by slience, harsh speeches etc., generated by various faults as insult given by others etc., is Resentment. Alike earlier (mood *i.e.,* awakening), the causes and effects are excitants and ensuants respectively.

Example: "When her lover, having touched with his hand, the end of her breast, went away, the young lady stood, silent, only gazing steadfastly at his lotus like face with her eyes, the corners of which had become red."

---

१. संपू, -प्रवृत्ति, in other editions प्रवृत्ति is missing.

Here, the touching of the top of the breast accidentaly is excitant. Redness of eyes-and looking silently are ensuants.

Objection: Well, It my be argued that what is the distingushing factor of the permanent mood Anger and transitory mood Resentment ?

Answer: It is to be understood as the distinctness in nature of mental states.

There (in the case of Anger) the desire of destroying other (rivals) in no time and (here in the case of indifference-ness and harsh expression etc.) oral arguments is the differen-ting factor of the effect.

RG. 110.

व्रीडादिभिर्निमित्तैर्हर्षाद्यनुभावानां गोपनाय जनितो भाव विशेषोऽवहित्थम्।

तदुक्तम्–'अनुभावपिधानार्थेऽवहित्थं भाव उच्यते।
तद्विभाव्यं भयव्रीडाधाार्ष्ट्य कौटिल्यगौरवैः॥'

यथा–"प्रसङ्ग गोपानां गुरुषु माहिमान यदुपते, रुपाकर्ण्य स्विद्यत्पुलकितकपोला कुलवधूः। विषज्वालाजालं झगिति वमतः पन्नगपतेः, फणायां साश्चर्यं कथयतितरां ताण्डवविधिम्॥"

अत्र व्रीडा विभावः। तादृशकालियकथाप्रसङ्गोऽनुभावः। एवं भयादिप्रयोज्यमप्युदाहार्यम्।

Trans.: The feeling generated by the cause as bashfulness etc., (and) ensuants (effects) as joy etc., for hiding (some secret) is Dissimulation (अवहित्थ).

As (it is) told: The transitory mood genereated by the excitants as fear, bashfulness (shyness), stupidness, cunning etc. for the realisation of ensuants, is called Dissimulation.

Example: "A high-born lady who had her cheeks prespring and horripilated byhearing the greantness of krisṇa in the midst of the cowherd elders at the time when **Kāliya**'s death by him was narrated, at once described with wonder the mode of the dancing (of कृष्ण)on the hood of the lord of serpents, emitting flames of poison."

Here, bashfulness (shyness) is excitant. The narration of the kaliya serpent in that manner is ensuant, Like this, the examples for the generation of fear etc., also can be illustrated.

RG. 111.

अधिक्षेपापमानादिप्रभवा किमस्य करोमीत्याद्याकारा चित्तवृत्तिरुग्रता।।

यदाहुः–

"नृपापराधोऽसदोषकीर्तनं चोरधारणम्।
विभावाः स्युरथो बन्धो वधस्ताडनभर्त्सने।।
एते यत्रानुभावस्तदौग्र्यं निर्दयतात्मकम्।।" इति।।

यथा–"अवाप्य भङ्गं खलु संगराङ्गणे नितान्तमङ्गाधिपतेरमङ्गलम्।
परप्रभावं मम गाण्डिवं धनुर्विनिन्दतस्ते हृदयं न कम्पते।।"

एषा कर्णेन पराभूतं गाण्डिवं निन्दन्तं युधिष्ठिरं प्रति धनंजयस्योक्तिः। युधिष्ठिरकर्तृका गाण्डिवनिन्दात्र विभावः। वधेच्छानु भावः। न चामर्षोग्रतयोर्नास्ति भेद इति वाच्यम्। प्रागुदाहृतेऽमर्षध्वनावुग्रताया अप्रतीतेः। नाप्यसौ क्रोधः। तस्य स्थायित्वेनास्याः संचारिणीत्वेनैव भेदात्।

Trans.: The mental state in the form of 'What can I do of him etc.' generated by blame and insult etc., is Ferocity (उग्रता). As (it is) told: The Ferocity in the form of cruetly, generated with the excitants as crime done against the king, propagating fault, which is false, catching the theif and with the ensuants as arresting, killing, beating, insulting etc.

Example: 'Is your heart not trembling, after being defeated by the king of अंग in the battle field, and by insulting my गांडिव bow ?"

This is the speech made by **Dhanañjaya** to **Yudhiṣṭhira**, who is insulting गांडिव bow, defeated by Karṇa.

Here, the insulting of गांडिव by **Yudhīṣṭhira,** is excitant. The desire of killing (to **Yudhīṣṭhira**) is ensuant.

Objection: It may be argued that there is difference between Indignation and Ferocity.

Answer: Not so. Because, the Ferocity in the suggestive indignation, in the earlier example is not realised.

Objection: It may be (accepted) as Anger here.

Answer: Not so. Because, the difference there in the form namely, that is (anger) a permanent mood and this (Ferocity) is a transitory mood.

RG. 112.

विप्रलम्भमहापत्तिपरमानन्दादिजन्यान्यस्मिन्नन्यावभास उन्मादः।।
शुक्तिरजतादिज्ञानव्यावृत्तये जन्मान्तम्।
उदाहरणम्–
"अकरुणहृदय प्रियतम मुश्चामि त्वामितः परं नाहम्।
इत्यालपति कराम्बुजमादायालीजनस्य विकला सा।।"

एषा प्रवासगतं स्वनायिकावृत्तान्तं पृच्छन्तं नायकं प्रति कस्याश्चित्संदेशहारिण्या उक्तिः। प्रियविरहोऽत्र विभावः। असंबद्धोक्तिरनुभावः। उन्मादस्य व्याधावन्तर्भावे संभवत्यपि पृथगुपादानं व्याध्यन्तरापेक्षयो वैचित्र्यविशेषस्फोरणाय।

Trans.: The realisation of one in other, generated by the separatioin, severe calamity, great pleasure etc., is Madness (उन्माद). The term 'generated by' is used to exclude the knowledge of silver in pearl etc.

Example: "Mad (on account of separation), holding the hand of a friend of hers, thus, she speaks to her (mistaking her to be lover): O cruel-hearted lover, I shall never, let you go hence forth."

This is the speech of some maid massenger to the lover, staying away (from house), who is asking about the welfare of his beloved. The separation from beloved is excitant. Incoherant speech is ensuant. Even it is possible to include with Sickness, still it is stated separately to show the extraordinary charmingness of madness than Sickness.

RG. 113.

रोगादिजन्या मूर्छारूपामरणप्रागवस्था मरणम्॥

न चात्र प्राणवियोगात्मकं मुख्यं मरणमुचितं ग्रहीतुम्।

चित्तवृत्त्यात्मकेषु भावेषु तस्याप्रसक्तेः। भावेषु च सर्वेषु कार्यसहवर्तितया शरीरप्राणसंयोगस्य हेतुत्वात्।

उदाहरणम्–"दयितस्य गुणाननुस्मरन्ती शयने संप्रति या विलोकितासीत्। अधुना खलु हन्त सा कृशाङ्गी गिरमङ्गीकुरुते न भाषितापि॥"

प्रियविरहोऽत्र विभावः। वचनविरामोऽनुभाव हन्तपदस्यात्रात्यन्तमुपकारकत्वाद्वाक्यव्यङ्ग्योऽप्ययं भावः पदव्यङ्ग्यतामावहति।

एतेन भावस्य पदव्यङ्ग्यतायां नात्यन्तं वैचित्र्यमिति परास्तम्।

दयितस्य गुणाननुस्मरन्तीत्यनेन व्यज्यमानं चरमावस्थायामपि तस्या दयितगुणविस्मरणं नाभूदिति वस्तु, विप्रलम्भस्य शोकस्य वा चरम मभिव्यक्तस्य पोषकम्। अयं च भावः स्वव्यञ्जकवाक्योत्तरवर्तिना वाक्यान्तरेण संदर्भघटकेन नायिकादेः प्रत्युज्जीवनवर्णने विप्रलम्भस्य, अन्यथा तु करुणस्य पोषक इति विवेकः। कवयः पुनरमुं प्राधान्येन न वर्णयन्ति। अमङ्गलप्रायत्वात्।

Trans.: The condition earlier to death in the form of senselessness, caused by desease etc., is Moriboundness (मरण). And it is not proper to understand the primary sense of Moribundness, in thr form of 'loss of life.' Because, it cannot be included in the transitory moods, in the form of mental states.

And because, the connection of body and soul is the cause due to the co-existance with the effects in case of all moods.

Example: "Alas ! the slender-bodied one, who was just seen to be recollecting the qualities of her lover even on her death bed, does not now utter a word, although questioned."

Here, the separation from beloved is excitant. The state of speechlessness is ensuant,

Even though the term 'हन्त' is a case of the suggestive sentence, yet, due to its excessive supportiveness, (it) holds the power to be named as the suggestive-word. By this, the statment namely 'there is the lack of excessive charmingness in the suggested-word is refuted hereby. And the suggested sense as: 'She has not forgotten the qualities of her lover even at the last moment of life (lit, moment of death)," by the expression namely' (she) has just seen to be recollecting (thinking) the qualities of (her) lover' etc. This later on, becomes favourable factor for the manifestation of suggestion of love-in-separation (विप्रलम्भ) or sorrow (शोक). This transitory mood becomes favourable towards love-in-separatioin by the narration of restoring to life (प्रत्युज्जीवन) of the lady by other describable sentences occuring, with having the suggestiveness of (this mood). Otherwise, it is favourable of sorrow and this is the distinct factor (among these two). Due to inauspicious (nature), the poets generally donot scribe to this (मरणभाव) with any importance.

RG. 114.

संदेहाद्यनन्तरं जायमान ऊहो वितर्कः॥
स च निश्चयानुकूलः।
"यदि सा मिथिलेन्द्रनन्दिनी नितरामेव न विद्यते भुवि।
अथ मे कथमस्ति जीवितं न विनालम्बनमाश्रितस्थितिः॥"

स्वात्मनि भगवतो रामस्यैषोक्तिः। भुवि सीतास्ति न वेतिसंदेहोऽत्र विभावः। भ्रूक्षेपशिरोङ्गुलिनर्तनमाक्षिप्तमनुभावः। न चासौ चिन्तेति शक्यं वदितुम्। चिन्ताया नियमेन निश्चयं प्रत्यप्रयोजकत्वात्। किं भविष्यति कथं भविष्यतीत्याद्याकारायाश्चिन्ताया, इदमित्थं भवितुमर्हति प्रायश इत्याकारस्य वितर्कस्य विषयवैलक्षण्योपलम्भाच्च। न विनेत्यादिनोक्तोऽर्थान्तरन्यासोऽप्यस्मिन्नेवानुकूलः।

Trans.: The alternate desires generated after doubt etc., is Deliberation.

And that is supportive of certainity.

Example: "How I am living if she, the daughter of the king of मिथीला, is surely not living on earth. as without sustantial support i.e. without, substractum the superitractum cannot exist."

This is a self speech of Lord Rāma (to himself). The doubt, as to, whether Sītā is alive or not (dead), in the earth is excitant here. The erection of eye-brows, moving of head, dancing like fingers etc., are ensuants.

Clarification: "It cannot be argued as (to be included in) Anxiety. Because, the anxiety is not the cause of dertionity invariably (as a rule). And because of the knowledge of the distinction of object of anxiety in the form of "what will happen," 'How it will happen' etc. from the Deliberation in the form of namely, 'mostly, this may be done like this.' And the figure of generalisation (अर्थान्तरन्यास) stated by the expression 'not without the substracturm' etc., (न विनालम्बन).

RG. 115.

इष्टासिद्धिराजगुर्वाद्यपराधादिजन्योऽनुतापो विषादः॥

उदाहरणम्–

"भास्करसूनावस्तं याते, जाते च पाण्डवोत्कर्षे।
दुर्योधनस्य जीवित कथमिव नाद्यापि निर्यासि॥"

अत्र स्वापकर्षपरोत्कर्षयोर्दर्शनं विभावः। जीवितनिर्याणाशंसा, तदाक्षिप्तं वदननमनादि चानुभावः। अस्मिन्नेव च विषादध्वनौ दुर्योधनस्येत्यर्थान्तसंक्रमितवाच्यध्वनिरनुग्राहकः। न चात्र त्रासभावध्वनित्वं शङ्क्यम्। परवीरस्य दुर्योधनस्य त्रासलेशस्याप्ययोगात्। नापि चिन्ताध्वनित्वम्। युद्ध्वा मरिष्यामीति तस्य व्यवसायात्। नापि दैन्यध्वनित्वम्। सकलसैन्यक्षयेऽपि विपदस्तेनागणनात्। न वा वीररसध्वनित्वम्। मरणस्य शरणीकरणे पराकर्ष जीवितस्योत्साहस्याभावात्। इदं पुनरत्र नोदाहार्यम्- "अयि पवनरयाणां निर्दयानां हयानां, श्लथय गतिमहं नो संगरं द्रष्टुमीहे। श्रुतिविवरममीमे दारयन्ति प्रकुप्यद्भुजगनिभभुजानां बाहुजानां निनादाः॥"

अत्र त्रासस्यैव प्रतीयमानत्वेन विषादस्याप्रतीतेः, लेशतया प्रतीतौ वा त्रास एव, आनुगुण औचित्येन ध्वनिव्यपदेशायोग्यत्वात्।

Trans.: The repentance caused by the non-availability of desired objects, crime done towards King, Teacher etc., is Despair (विषाद):

Example: "After the fall of son of the Sun-God (कर्ण) and after rising of the पांडव how, even now, the life of Duryodhana not going ?"

Here the seeing of one's own fall and rising of other's is excitant, seeking for the loss of life and facing downwards etc., caused by that, are ensuants.

And, the अर्थान्तरसंक्रमितवाच्यध्वनि is supportive of this suggestion of despair in the expression, namely, "the life of Duryodhana etc."

Clarification: There is no possibility of doubting the suggestion of the emotion of fright (त्रास) here, due to the absence of even little fright in the case of Duryodhana, great fighter. The suggestive mood of anxiety (चिन्ता) also cannot be doubted, because of his promise, namely, I would be killed after fighting.'

Even the suggested mood of Wretchedness (दैन्य) need not be doubted, becaused of the nonconsideration of the danger, even in the destruction of the entire army.

And finally the suggested heroic sentiment, also cannot be doubted, because of the lack of enthusiasm towards downfall of enemies life, resorting to death.

Further, the following cannot be an example: "O Charioteer ! slow down the speed of the cruel horses, moving like wind, I donot want to see the battle. The dreadful noise of the Kings, whose hands are like the angry serpents, is termenting my ears."

Due to the realisation of fright alone and due to the non-realisation of despair, or due to its negligible realisation, it is (a case of) fright alone. because, it is not fit to be treated as suggestion due to the propriety of supportive-ness (of that).

RG. 116.

अधुनैवास्य लाभो ममास्त्विवतीच्छा औत्सुक्यम्।।
इष्टविरहादिरत्र विभावः। त्वराचिन्तायोऽनुभावाः।
यदाहुः– 'संजातमिष्टविरहादुद्दीप्तं प्रियसंस्मृतेः।
निद्रया तन्द्रया गात्र गौरवेण च चिन्तया।।
अनुभावितमाख्यातमौत्सुक्यं भावकोविदैः।।' इति।
उदाहरणम्– "निपतद्बाष्पसंरोधमुक्तचाश्चल्यतारकम्।
कदानयननीलाब्जमालोकेय मृगीदृशः।।"

Trans.: The desire, namely, 'I sould get it right now,' is Longing (औत्सुक्य). The non-obtainment of desired objects, is excitant. Sudden anxiety etc., is ensuant. As (it is) told:

'Which is caused by the non-obtainment of desired objects, and developed by the rememberance of the desired (beloved), and by the ensuants like sleeping, unsteadiness, lazyness, anxiety etc., is called Longing by the knower of the theory of transitory moods."

Example: "When shall I see the blue-lotus-eyes of the dear eyed one, who had stopped her exciting looking by not shedding tears."

RG. 117.

अनर्थातिशयजनिता चित्तस्य संभ्रमाख्या वृत्तिरावेगः॥

उदाहरणम्–

"लीलया विहितसिन्धुबन्धनः सोऽयमेति रघुवंशनन्दनः।
दर्पदुर्विलसितो दशाननःकुत्र यामि निकटे कुलक्षयः॥"

एषा स्वात्मनिमन्दोदर्या उक्तिः। रघुनन्दनागमनमत्र विभावः। कुत्रयामीत्येतद्व्यङ्ग्यस्थैर्याभावोऽनुभावः। न चात्र चिन्ता प्राधान्येन व्यज्यत इति शक्यते वक्युम्। कुत्र यामीति स्फुटं प्रतीतेन स्थैर्याभावे- नोद्वैगस्येव चिन्ताया अप्रत्यायनात्। परं त्वावेगचर्वणायां तत्परिपोषक- तया गुणत्वेन चिन्तापि विषयीभवति।

Trans.: The mental state called, संभ्रम caused by great trouble, is Excitement (आवेग).

Example: "This son of Raghu (*i.e.* राम), built the bridge on the ocean without any strain, Ten headed (रावण) is over powered by pride. The destruction of the family is certain (nearer). Whre shall I go now?"

This is the speech of Mandodari to herself. The 'arrival of Raghunandana' is 'excitant' here. The suggestion in the form of the absence of steadiness, in the expression 'where shall I go' is 'ensuant'.

Objection: It may be argued that, there the 'anxiety' is primarily realised (suggested).

Answer: Because of the non-realisation of 'anxiety', like Excitement, by the absence of steadiness and by the clear realisation in the expression as 'where shall go', it is not correct. However, in case of the enjoyment of excitement, the 'anxiety', also realised subordinately, by becoming the object of that enjoyment as supportive (of that).

RG. 118.

चिन्तोत्कण्ठाभयविरहेष्टानिष्ठदर्शनश्रवणादिजन्यावश्य कर्तव्यार्थ-प्रतिसंधानविकला चित्तवृत्तिर्जडता।।

इयं मोहात्पूर्वतः परतश्च जायते।

यदाहुः–"कार्याविवेको जडता पश्यतः शृण्तोऽपि वा।
तद्विभावाः प्रियानिष्टदर्शनश्रवणे रुजा।
अनुभावास्त्वभो तूष्णींभावविस्मरणादयः।
सा पूर्व परतो वा स्यान्मोहादिति विदां मतम्।।"

उदाहरणम्–"यदवधि दयितो विलोचनाभ्यां सहचरि दैववशेन दूरतोऽभूत। तदवधि शिथिलीकृतो मदीयैरथ करणैः प्रणयो निजक्रियासु।।"

प्रियविरहोऽत्र विभावः। करणैश्चक्षुश्रवणादिभिः क्रियासु तत-प्रमितिषु प्रणयस्य शिथिलीकरणमनुभावः। मोहे चक्षुरादिभिश्चाक्षु-षादेरजननम्, इह तु प्रकारविशेषवैशिष्ट्येन बाहुल्येनाजननमिति तस्मादस्य विशेषः। अत एवोदाहरणे शिथिलीकृत इत्युक्तम्, न तु त्यक्त इति।

Trans.: The mental state devoid of knowledge of that 'What should be done', caused by 'anxiety', 'longing for', 'fear', 'separation','seeing the desired' and 'enjoying the desired' is Stuper and this generates (immideatelv) in the preceeding and succeeding movements of 'perplexity',

As (it is) told: The absence of 'judgement' of 'what ought to be done', 'seeing and also listening of injury' in case of a desired, by its 'excitants' as unfavourable of dear ones and 'silence', 'forgetfulness' etc. as its 'ensuants' is 'stuper', that is realised in the preceeding and succeeding of the realisation of 'perplexity' as is the view of some scholar.

Example: 'O friend ! My organs are made to realx, in the activites so long as the lover has gone faraway from my eyes by the fate.'

Here the separation from beloved is 'excitant'. The loseness of respective organs like eyes, ears etc., in the love-making activites are 'ensuants'. In the case of 'perplexity', the non-realisation of the konwledge regarding 'seeing' etc., by the 'eyes' etc., is there. However, here in the case of Stuper (जडता), there is the absence of clear knowledge to the peculiarity of things. This is different from that. Therefore, in the example, the term 'is made to relax' is employed and not 'discarded' (is employed).

RG. 119.

अतितृप्तिगर्भव्याधिश्रमादिजन्या चेतसः क्रियानुन्मुखतालस्यम्॥ अत्र च नासामर्थ्यम्। नापि कार्याकार्यविवेकशून्यत्वम्। तेन कार्याकरणरूपस्यानुभावस्य तुल्यत्वेऽपि ग्लानेर्जडतायाश्चास्य भेदः।

उदाहरणम्–

"निखिलां रजनीं प्रियेण दूरादुपयातेन विबोधिता कथाभिः।
अधिकंनहि पारयामि वक्तुं सखि मा जल्प तवायसी रसज्ञा॥"

एषा हि प्रियागमनद्वितीयदिवसे मुहुर्निशावृत्तान्तं पृच्छन्तीं सखीं प्रति रजनिजागरणजनितालस्यायाः कस्याश्चिदुक्तिः। अत्र रजनिजागरणं विभावः। अधिकसंभाषणाभावोऽनुभावः। जडतायां मोहात्पूर्व वर्तित्वमुत्तरवर्तित्वं वा नियतम्, न त्वत्रेत्यपरो विशेषः। गोपनीयविषत्वाद्यदि कथाभिरित्यविवक्षितवाच्यं तदा श्रमोस्तु परिपोषकः। श्रमजन्ये ह्यालस्ये श्रमस्य पोषकताया अवार्यत्वात्। अतितृप्त्यादिजनिते त्वालस्ये श्रमाद्विविक्तविषयमत्वं बोध्यम्।

Trans.: The non-inclinationness towards activites of mind caused by 'over-satisfication', 'preganancy', 'disease', 'labour' etc. is 'Indolence (आलस्य).

Here, the lack of strength is not the cause. Not also the lack of the konwledge of discrimination between prescriptions and prohibitions. Therefore, even the 'ensuants' in the form of not-performing "What should be done," is same (in case of Indolence, Weakness and Stuper).

Example: "I was awakened the whole night (by) lover's various stories, who has came from a long distance. O my friend ! I cannot speak more, is not your Iron-like tongue becoming tired ?"

This is the speech of some lady, feeling (lazy) due to not- sleeping during (last) night, to her friend, repeatedly asking the happenings of that night, in the following day (lit. second day) of the coming back of her lover. Here 'awakeing whole night' is 'excitant.' The 'absence of talking too much, is 'ensuant'. The Stuper invariably exists at the precceeding and succeeding moments in the case of 'perplexity' is definite. However, not here (in the case of Indolence) (*i.e.* not always true), thus is a further distiction (from perplexity).

If, due to the subject being confidential (private) the non expressed sense is realised by the expression कथाभिः etc., then let the 'fatigue' (श्रम) indeed be its supportive. Because, fatigue becomes supportive towards Indolence, if it generates from fatigue itself. (ie., the supportive of fatigue (for Indolence) cannot be avoided where indolence is caused by fatigue). Further, the objects are to be understood to be different from fatigue, where, Indolence is caused by 'over-satisfication.'

RG. 120.

परोत्कर्षदर्शनादिजन्यः परनिन्दादिकारणीभूत श्चित्तवृत्तिविशे-षोऽसूया॥

इमामेवासहनादिशब्दैर्व्यवहरन्ति।

यथा–

"कुत्र शैवं धनुरिदं, क्व चायं प्राकृतः शिशुः।
भङ्गस्तु सर्वसंहर्त्रा कालेनैव विनिर्मितः॥"

एषा भग्नहरकार्मुकस्य भगवतो रामस्य पराक्रममसहमानानां तत्रत्यानां राज्ञामुक्तिः। अत्रच श्रीमद्दाशरथिबलस्य सर्वोत्कृष्टताया दर्शनं विभावः। प्राकृतशिशुपदगम्या निन्दानुभावः।

Trans.: The mental state generated by 'seeing' etc., the prosperity of others and is the cause of sensuring others, is Envy असूया.

This is also expressed as non-tolerance.

Example: 'Where indeed is this bow of '**Śiva** and where is this small boy ! However, the breaking (of the bow) is accomplished by Almighty काल, the destroyer of all."

This is the speech of kings present there, envious thowards the strength of Lord **Rāma**, who has broken the bow of **Śiva**.' Noticing the most-superiority of strength of the son of **Raghu** (Lord **Rāma**), is 'excitant' here. The 'insulting', understood from the expression ordinary (प्राकृत) is 'ensuant'.

RG. 120.1

"तृष्णालोलविलोचने कलयति प्राचीं चकोरव्रजे/ मौनं मुञ्चति किं च कैरवमुले कामे धनुर्धन्वति/ माने मानवतीजनस्य सपदि प्रस्थातुकामेऽधुना/धातः किं तु विधो विधातुमुचितो धाराधराडम्बरः//"

अत्रापि यद्यपि तदीयोच्छृङ्खलतादिदर्शनजन्या अनुचित कारित्व-रूपनिन्दाप्रकाशानुभाविता कविगता विधात्रालम्बनासूया व्यज्यत इति शक्यते वक्तुम्, तथापि कार्यकारणयोस्तुल्यत्वादभिव्यक्तेनामर्षेण शबलितौवासौ न विविक्ततया प्रतीयते। नहि विधातुरपराध इव भगवतो रामस्यापराधोऽस्ति येन कवेरिव वीराणामप्यमर्षोऽभिव्यज्येत। स्वभावो हि महोन्नतक्रियानिष्पादनं वीराणाम्। अत्राप्रस्तुतचन्द्रवृत्तान्तेन प्रस्तुतराजकुमारादिवृत्तान्तस्य ध्वननान्नास्त्यसूयाधनित्वमिति तु न

वाच्यम्। एकध्वनेर्ध्वन्यन्तराविरोधित्वात्। अन्यथामहावाक्यध्वनेर-वान्तरवाकयध्वनिभि, तेषां च पदध्वनिभिः सह सामानाधिकरण्यं कुत्रापि न स्यात्।

Trans.: Or as (the example of Envy असूया) "When the female **chakora** birds, with their eyes unsteady on account of thirst, are looking towards the East; when the moon lotuses are giving up their silence (are blowing open), when cupid is twanging his bow and when the anger of proud women is on the point of giving way, is it., O creator, proper for you to spreed a cluster of clouds over the moon ?'

Eventhough, it is proper to hold that, the Envy, residing in poet for विधाता, is suggested having 'ensuants' like the expression of insults in the form of being the doer of, 'What is improper', caused by the sight of indisciplineness, still, it is a case of variegation (of moods *i.e.* शबलता) due to the similarity in causes and effects (of Envy), with the expression of resentment (अमर्ष). And this is not realised distinctly. Further, there is no fault of Lord **Rāma,** like the fault of विधाता by which the resentment of heroes (braves) is realised like the realisation of Envy, the emotion of poet (in the present verse), And it is indeed the nature of heores to perform great deeds.

Objection: It may be argued that due to the suggestion of the description of the प्रस्तुत, subject in question, as the prince etc., by the description of moon, the object of comparison *i.e.* अप्रस्तुत, the 'Envy' is not suggested here.

Answer: It cannot be argued so. The suggestion of one is not contradictory to (the realisation of) another suggestion. Otherwise, in no case, there would be co-existance (of expressions) of the suggestion of a महावाक्य with the suggestion of other sentences and of those (sentences) with the suggestion of words.

RG. 121.

वियोगशोकभयजुगुप्सादीनामतिशयाद्ग्रहावेशादेश्चोत्पन्नो व्याधि विशेषोऽपस्मारः॥

व्याधित्वेनास्य कथनेऽपि विशेषाकारेण पुनःकथनं बीभत्स-भयानकयोरस्यैव व्याधेरङ्गत्त्वं नान्यस्येति स्फोरणाय। विप्रलम्भे तु व्याध्यन्तरस्यापि च।

उदाहरणम्– "हरिमागतमाकर्ण्यमथुरामन्तकान्तकम्।
कम्पमानः श्वसन्कंसो निपपात महीतले॥"
अत्र भयं विभावः। कम्पनिःश्वासपतनादयोऽनुभावाः।

Trans.: The 'sickness', caused by 'long separation', excessive fear', 'sorrow', 'disgust' and due to force of inauspicious planets, is Epilepsy अपस्मार. Even though, this is expressed as 'sickness' earlier, still, it is narrated specifically to indicate its supportiveness of sentiments of 'disgustful' and 'Pathos', and in the case of other sentiments (not supportive). However, in the case of love-in-separation, the moods other than Epilepsy; can also be accepted as supportive.

Example: 'Listening the arrival of **Hari**, the destroyer of God of Death, to **Mathurā, Kaṁsa,** with shivering and long breath fell on the ground.'

'Fear' is 'excitant', here. 'Thrilling', 'breathing', 'falling' etc. are ensuants.'

RG. 122.

अमर्षादिजन्यवाक्पारुष्यादिकारणीभूता चित्तवृत्तिश्चपलता॥

यदाहुः–
"अमर्षप्रातिकूल्येर्ष्यारागद्वेषाश्च मत्सरः।
इति यत्र विभावाः स्युरनुभावस्तु भर्त्सनम्॥
वाक्पारुष्यं प्रहारश्च ताडनं वधबन्धने।
तच्चापलमनालोच्य कार्यकारित्वमिष्यते॥" इति।

उदाहरणम्–“अहितव्रत पापत्मन्वं मे दर्शयानमैनम्।
आत्मानंहन्तुमिच्छामि येन त्वमसि भावितः।”

एषा भगवदनुरक्तिविघटनोपायमपश्यतः प्रह्लादं प्रतिहिरण्यकशिपोरुक्तिः। भगवद्द्वेषोत्थापितः पुत्रद्वेषोऽत्र विभावः।

आत्मवधेच्छा परुषवचनं चानुभावः।

न चामर्ष एवात्र व्यज्यत इति वाच्यम्॥

सदैवभगवदनुरागिणि प्रल्हादे हिरण्यकशिपोरमर्षस्य चिरकालसंभृतत्वेनापत्मवधेच्छाया इदंप्रामितानुपपत्तेः।

इदंप्रथमकार्यस्यचेदंप्रथमकारणप्रयोज्यतया प्राचीनचित्तवृत्ति विलक्षणाया एव चपलताख्यचित्तवृत्तेः सिद्धेः। न चामर्षप्रकर्ष एवात्मवधेच्छादिकारणमभिव्यज्यतामिति वाच्यम्। प्रकर्षस्यापि स्वाभाविक विलक्षणलक्षणताया आवश्यकतया तस्यैव चपलता पदार्थत्वात्।

Trans.: The mental state generated by indignation etc., that is responsible for harsh speeches etc., is Inconstancy. As (it is) told: Where, the 'indignation', 'opposition', 'jealous', anger 'disliking' and 'selfishness', become the 'excitants' and 'abusing', 'harsh speech', 'caning', 'slapping', 'arresting', 'killing' etc., become the 'ensuants'. Unthoughtful action; that is called Inconstancy (चपलता).

Example: "O performer of inauspicious act ! Sinner!! donot show, your face to me. (I) want to kill myself because of giving birth the son like you."

This is the speech of हिरण्यकशिपु to प्रह्लाद after not finding a way to stop the affection (of his son) towards Lord विष्णु. Here, the disliking (द्वेष) (towards) his son, caused by the disliking towards Lord is 'excitant.' The 'desire to kill ownself', 'expression of harsh words' are 'ensuants.'

Objection: It may be argued that the mood 'indignation' is suggested here.

Answer : Not so. Because, due to the resentment of हिरण्यकशिपु for प्रह्लाद, the lover of Lord विष्णु, is always there from the beginning and the desire to kill himself cannot be justified to arisen for the first time.

The mental state called 'Inconstancy' is distinct from the earlier mental states, gets established, due to the rule that the first effect necessarily generated by the first cause.

Objection: It may be argued: The excessive Indignation is the cause of the desire of killing himself, is suggested here.

Answer: Not so. Because it is necessary that Inconstancy (चपलता), is to be distinct from the common (due to प्रकर्षता).

RG. 123.

नीचपुरुषेष्वाक्रोशनाधिक्षेपव्याधिताडनदारिद्रयेष्टविरहपरसंपद्दर्शनादिभिः, उतमेषु त्ववज्ञानादिभिर्जनिता विषयद्वेषाख्या रोदनदीर्घश्वासदीनमुखतादिकारिणी चित्तवृत्तिर्निर्वेदः॥

उदाहरणम्–

"यदि लक्ष्मण सा मृगेक्षणा न मदीक्षासरणिं समेष्यति।
अमुना जडजिवितेन मे जगता वा विफलेन किं फलम्॥"
नित्यानित्यवस्तुविवेकजन्यत्वाभावान्नासौ रसव्यपदेशहेतु।

Trans.: The mental state, in the form of aversion to worldy objects, generated by 'abuse', 'contempt', 'disease', 'beating', 'poverty', 'loss of desired objects', 'seeing the prosperity of others etc., in case of ordinary persons and 'disrespect' in case of noble presons, casuing the 'weeping', 'long breathing', 'pity-looking', etc., is despondency (निर्वेद).

Example: 'O **Lakṣman** ! If she, the deer eyes one (**Sītā**) will not come on the way of my eyes, then Alas ! what is the use of this life-less living and useless world."

It cannot be the cause to be called **rasa**, due to the

absence of the realisation of discrimination of real and false (unreal) objects.

RG. 124.

देवादि विषया रतिर्यथा–"भवद्द्वारि क्रुध्यज्जयविजय दण्डाहदिलत्किरीटाग्ते कीटा इव विधिमहेन्द्रप्रभृतयः। वितिष्ठन्तेयुष्मन्नयनपरिपातोत्कलिकया बराकाः के तत्र क्षपितमुर नाकाधिपतयः॥"

अत्रापमानसहनभगवद्द्वारनिषेवणभगवत्कटाक्षपाताभिला षादिभिर्ब्रह्मादिगता भगवदानलम्बना रतिर्नाभिव्यज्यते। अपि तु भगवदैश्वर्यमवाङ्मनसगोचर इति चेत्तथापि तादृशभगवदैश्वर्यवर्णनानुभावितया कविगतभगवदालम्बनरत्या ध्वनित्वमक्षतमेव।

इदं वोदाहरणम्–

"न धनं न च राज्यसंपदं नहि विद्यामिदमेकमर्थये।
मयि धेहि मनागपि प्रभो करुणाभङ्गितरङ्गितां दृशम्॥"

अत्र धनाद्यपेक्षाशून्यस्य भगवदृगन्तपाताभिलाषो[१] हि भगवत्यनुरक्तिं[२] व्यनक्ति।

एवं सक्षेपेण निरूपिता भावाः॥

Trans.: The example of pleasure (love) towards God etc: 'O Lord मुरारी, What of these poor Gods, where ब्रह्मा etc., are wating for your kindly sights, like insects, after loosing their किरीटs by the swords of angry जय and विजय, standing at your gate."

Objection: Here, the love residing in Lord, having 'tolerating the insult', 'waiting at the door of the Lord', 'desire to see Lord', etc. as sustaintial moods, is not suggested. But the prosperity of Lord, which is beyond the range of experience is suggested.

---

१. म,–अभिलाषा

२. मदु, म, –अत्यन्तानुरक्तिम्.

Answer : The suggestiveness of love is uninterrupted by the narration of such prosperity of Lord as अवाङ्मनसगोचर, and by love towards Lord, residing in the poet, as sustaintial moods.

Or it can be an example: "O my Lord ! I donot want wealth, not the kingdom and not the knowledge. I want only a little bit of your (favouring) sympathetic look on me."

Here, the 'desire' for the vaid look of God, devoid of the desires for wealth etc., indeed, suggested the love towards God. Like this, the (concept of) moods discussed here.

RG. 125.

अथ कथमस्य संख्यानियमः। मात्सर्योद्वेगदम्भेर्ष्याविवेकनिर्णय-क्लैब्यक्षमाकुतुकोत्कठाविनयसंशयाधार्ष्ट्यादीनामपि तत्र तत्र लक्ष्येषु दर्शनात् इति चेत, न। उक्तेष्वेवैषामन्तर्भावेण संख्यान्तरानुपपत्तेः।

असूयातो मात्सर्यस्य, त्रासादुव्देगस्य, अवहित्थाख्याद्भद्वेगवाद्भभस्य, अमर्षादीर्ष्यायाः, मतेर्विवेकनिर्णययोः, दैन्यात्क्लैब्यस्य, घृते क्षमाया, औत्सुकयात्कुतुकोत्कण्ठयो; लज्जाया विनयस्य, तर्कात्संशयस्य, चापलाद्धार्ष्ट्यस्य च वस्तुतः सुक्ष्मे भेदेऽपि नान्तरीयकतया तदनतिरिक्त-स्यैवाध्यवसायात्। मुनिवचनानुपालनस्य संभव उच्छृङ्खलताया अनौचित्यात्।

Trans.: Objection: How, the numbers of this (mood) is determined (as thirty-four). Because the jealousy (मात्सर्य), agitating (उद्वेग), hypocrisy (दम्भ), envious (ईर्ष्या). true knowledge of discretion (विवेकनिर्णय), weakness (क्लैब्य), patience (क्षमा), couriosity (कुतुक), eagerness (उत्कंठा), modesty (विनय), doubt (संशय), daring valour (धृष्टता) etc., realised in their respective places.

Answe: It cannot be argued so, Because, no other number (highter than thirty-four) can be postulated due to the inclusion of these in those, earlier stated. As a matter of fact, (in reality), even though there exist minor differences of jealousy from envey, agitating from fright, hypocrisy form dissimulation mood, envious from resentment, discretion from judgement, weakness from depression, patience from contentment, curiosity and eagerness from longing. modesty from bashfulness, doubt from deliberation, and the daring valour from inconstancy, due to their non distinctness, they are known as not different (from the accepted ones). And because, it is improper to disregard the view of the sages (ancient theorists) where it is possible to maintion.

RG. 126.

एषु च संचारिभावेषु मध्ये केचन केषांचन विभावा अनुभावाश्च भवन्ति। तथा हि-ईर्ष्याया निर्वेदं प्रति विभावत्वम्, असूयां प्रति चानुभावत्वम्। चिन्ताया निद्रां प्रति विभावत्वम्, औत्सुक्यं प्रति चानुभावतेत्यादि स्वयमूह्यम्।

Trans.: And amongst these transitory moods, some can become the excitants and ensuants for some (other moods). Accordingly, envious becomes excitant for despondency and ensuant for envy. (like this), anxiety becomes excitant for sleeping (drowsiness) and ensuant for longing. And (the rest) may be understood by scholars themselves.

Notes : PR narrates how out of these transitory moods, sometime become either excitants or ensuants for some. For example 'irṣyā' will become excitant for 'nirveda' and ensuant for other one. Similarly 'cintā' becomes excitant for 'nidrā' and ensuant for autsukya. This implies that the title excitant or ensuant or transitory depend on the situation and not absolute.

RG. 127.

अथ रसाभासः–

तत्र अनुचितविभावालम्बनत्वं रसाभासत्वम्।
विभावादावनौचित्यं पुनर्लोकानां व्यवहारतो विज्ञेयम्॥
यत्र तेषामयुक्तमिति धीरिति केचिदाहुः। तदपरे न क्षमन्ते।

मुनिपत्न्यादिविषकरत्यादेः संग्रहेऽपि वहुनायकविषयाया अनुभयनिष्ठायाश्च रतेरसंग्रहात्। तत्र विभावगतस्यानौचित्यस्याभावात्। तस्मादनौचित्येन रत्यादिर्विशेषणीयः। इत्थं चानुचितविभावालम्बनाया बहुनायकविषयाया अनुभयनिष्ठायाश्च संग्रह इति। अनौचित्यं च प्राग्वदेव।

Trans.: Now starts the discussion on रसाभास, the false attribution of sentiment (improper manifestation of sentiment). 'The improper manifastation of sentiment is, caused by the improper excitant etc.' The improperness of excitants etc., are to be known from the common behaviour. Some hold it to be the knowledge, namely, those are improper for those (sentiments). Others do no subscribe (lit. tolerate) to this view.

Because (if the improper manifestastion of sentiment is defined on the basis of improper excitants then) eventhough, the love (of a student) towards his teacher's wife etc., will be included, yet, in the case, where love of a lady having many lovers as the object, and love is not reciprocal (not based on both sides), cannot be included (in the improper manifestation of sentiment). Because, these causes donot lack the impropriety due to the improper excitants. Therefor, the improprietyness is to be the qualifier of 'love' (and not of the excitants). And like this, a) the 'love' based on improper excitant, b) 'love' based on more than one lovers, and c) 'love' not developed from both sides would be inculded. Improprietyness is to be explained as (explained) earlier.

Notes : After defining moods **PR** takes the concept of the sembalance of sentiment for discussion. He has made a detailed analysis on this. He also defines it and quotes the view of others. He writes the semblance of sentiment in terms of improper excitants and notes that impropritynes of excitants are to be determined from the common behaviour.

RG. 127.1.

तत्र रसाद्याभासत्वं रसत्वादिना न समानाधिकरणम्। निर्मलस्यैव रसादित्वात्। हेत्वाभासत्वमेव हेतुत्वेन इत्येके। नह्यनुचितत्वेनात्महानिः, अपि तु सदोषत्वादाभासव्यवहारः।

अश्वाभासादिव्यवहारवत्' इत्यपरे।

उदाहरणम्– "शतेनोपायानां कथमपि गतः सौधशिखरं सुधाफेन-स्वच्छे रहसि शयितां पुष्पशयने। विबोध्य क्षामाङ्गीं चकितनयनां स्मेरवदनां, सनिश्वासं श्लिष्यत्यहहसुकृती राजरमणीम्॥"

अत्रालम्बनमनुचितप्रणया राजरमणी। रहोरजन्याद्युद्दीपनम्। साहसेन राजान्तः पुरे गमनम्, प्राणेषूपेक्षा, निःश्वासाश्लेषादयश्चानुभावः। शङ्कादयः संचारिणः, निषिद्धालम्बनकत्वाच्चास्या रतेराभासत्वं रसस्य।

Trans.: According to one group (fo scholars), the state of being semblances of sentiment etc., is not similarly exists in the case of being sentiment etc., due to the fully recognised sentimentness etc., (of sentiments) like the cause and the false attribution of cause. According to other group (of scholars), there is no loss of one's own nature (आत्महानि) by the use in improper way, But however, due to the mixing of fault, it is used as semblance (of the real object), like the use of the defective horse etc., (in case of a horse).

Example: "Oh ! In secret having awakened the queen, sleeping on the bed of flowers like white foam of nectar, with surpassed eyes and with smiling face, the virtuous man who any how has reached the peak of palace by hundred of means, hugs with deep breaths."

Here, the queen with whom love making is improper is sustaintial mood. Secrecy. night etc., are enhancing moods.

Entering to the royal bed room bravely, neglectin won life, breathing, hugging etc., are ensuants, Misgiving (शंका) etc. are transitory moods. And, due to the prohibition of her love as sustaintial mood, it is a case of mere semblance of sentiment.

Notes : PR analysis about the status of the semblance of sentiments and semblance of moods and the relation between sentiments and moods, respectively. He records two distinct views. According to first view, semblance are to be vary from sentiment etc. As the **hetvābhāsa** pseudo are different from **hetu**. According to other view, they are called semblance of sentiments etc., due to lack of propriety or due to its association with the fault. Thus, it is not proper to completely discard it as not sentiments. He gives the example of a defective horse where the defect does not bar the horse to be called so.

RG. 127.2.

न चात्र चकितनयनामित्येन परपुरुषस्पर्शत्रास्त्राभिव्यक्त्या रतेरनुभयनिष्ठतेत्याभासताहेतुर्वाच्य। अस्याश्च चिराय तस्मिन्नासक्ताया अन्तःपुरे परपुरुषागमनस्यात्यन्तमसंभावनया क एष मां बोधयतीत्यादावुचित एव त्रासः।

अनन्तरं च परिचयाभिव्यक्त्या सोऽयं मत्प्रियो मदर्थं प्राणानपि तृणीकृत्यागत इति ज्ञानादुत्पन्नं हर्षमभिव्यञ्जयत्स्मेरवदनामिति विशेषणं रतिं तदीयामपि व्यनक्ति। परं तु प्राधान्यं नायकनिष्ठाया एव रतेः। सकलवाक्यार्थत्वात्।

Trans.: It cannot be argued that it is a cause of improper manifestation of 'sentiment' due to the love being not-reciprocal, by the suggestion of fear (त्रास) due to the touch of some one other than the lover by the expression चकितनयनाम् in the verse already mentioned. Because, due to utter non-probableness of the coming of anybody other than the lover in the inner chamber of her (the royal lady), attached to one lover for a long period, the fear namely, who is touching me, calling me, is natural, by knowing the identity. The word स्मेरवदनाम् which suggests the pleasure arising out of knowledge, namely, he is my that (old) lover, who has come to me putting his life at stake, reveals the love of the lady. However, (in this verse) the like of the hero is primarily suggested due to it being the sense of the entire expression.

RG. 127.3

यथा वा– "भवनं करुणावती विशन्ती गमनाज्ञालवलाभलालसेषु।
तरुणेषुविलोचनाब्जमालामथ बाला पथि पातयांवभूव॥"

अत्र कुतश्चिदागच्छन्त्याः पथि तदीयरूपयौवनगृहीतमानसैर्युवभिरनुगम्यमानायाः कस्याश्चिद्भवनप्रवेशसमयेनिजसेवासार्थक्यविज्ञानाय गमनाज्ञापनरुपलाभ लालसेषु तेषु परमपरिश्रमस्मरणसंजातकरुणाया गमनाज्ञादाननिवेदकस्य विलोचनाम्बुजमालापरिक्षेपस्यानुभावस्य वर्णनादभिव्यज्यमाना रतिर्बहुवचनेन बहुविषया गम्यत इति।

भवत्ययमपि रसाभासः।

यथा वा–"भुजपञ्जरे गृहीता नवपरिणीता वरेण वधूः।
तत्कालजालपतिताबालकुरङ्गीव वेपते नितराम्॥"

अत्र रतेर्नववध्वा मनागप्यस्पर्शादनुभयनिष्ठत्वेनाभासत्वम्।

तथा चोक्तम्–

"उपनायकसंस्थायां मुनिगुरुपत्निगतायां च। बहुनायक विषयायां रतौतथानुभयनिष्ठायाम्" इति।

अत्र मुनिगुरुशब्दयोरुपलक्षणपरतया राजादेरपि ग्रहणम्।

Trans.: Or the example: "The kind hearted lady, entering the house, moved her eyes like lotus garland on the young followers, greedy to get a bit of her permission to go back (return).

Here, the love realised with regard to many persons, in the experssion (namely तरुणेषु), is manifested by the narration of ensuant in the form of moving her sight like the lotus-garland with pity, as generated from the memory of that excessive labour as taken by them, with desire to get the benifit in the form of permission to go back. It reflects that the showing of their successful service at the time of entering in house of her, was, followed by young persons, accepting in mind the beauty and youth (of her) on the way of some lady. Thus, it is a case of रसाभास, the mere semblance of the sentiment.

Or the another example: "The newly married lady was hugged by cage like arms (of her) groom and now thrilling constantly like a young female deer as falling in the net all of sudden." Here this is a state of the mere semblance (of sentiment) due to the non-existance (of love) in both, Becuase the non-generation of love even a little in the case of newly married lady.

And as (it is) told: (The love) with regard to a paramour (by the lady); with the wife of sage or teacher (by the lover); with many lovers (by the lady) and where (the love) exists in either one of the two (it becomes रसाभास, the mere semblance). Here, in the expression namely, sage, teacher, the king etc., are also to be accepted by its indicative sense.

RG. 127.4.

अथात्र किं व्यङ्ग्यम्–

"व्यानम्राश्चलिताश्चैव स्फारिताः परमाकुलाः।
पाण्डुपुत्रेषु पाञ्चाल्याः पतन्ति प्रथमा दृशः॥"

अत्र व्यानम्रतया धर्मात्मताप्रयोज्यं युधिष्ठिरे सभक्तित्वम्, चलिततया स्थूलाकारताप्रयोज्यं भीमसेने सत्रासत्वम्, स्फारिततया

अलौकिकशौर्यश्रवणप्रयोज्यमर्जुने सहर्षत्वम्, परमाकुलतया परम-सौन्दर्यप्रयोज्यं नकुलसहदेवयोरौत्सुक्यं च व्यञ्जयन्तीभिर्दृग्भिः पाञ्चाल्या बहुविषयाया रतेरभिव्यञ्जनाद्रसाभास एवेति नव्याः। प्राञ्चत्वपरिणे-तृबहुनायकविषयत्वे रतेराभासतेत्याहुः। तत्र शृङ्गाररस इव शृङ्गारा-भासोऽपि द्विविधः। संयोगविप्रलम्भभेदात्। संयोगाभासस्त्वनुपदमेवो-दाहृतः।

Trans.: Now the suggestiveness in this verse is being discussed "पाञ्चालि"s eye sight (lit look) fall on the sons of **paṅdu** with being humble, being agitated, being widely diffused and being distressed in mind, respectively."

Here, the devotion (भक्ति) in **Yudhīṣṭhira,** due to his religious mind (suggested by) due to humbleness, the fright (त्रास) in Bhīmasena, due to his large-body (suggested by) due to agitation; the joy (हर्ष) in Arjuna, due to listing the extraordinary braveness (suggested by) diffusingness and the excitement in Nakula and Sahadeva caused by their most attractive (handsome) figures (suggested by) distressedness, are suggested in the eyes of पाञ्चालि.

Here due to the suggestion of love, regarding many objects (persons), it is a case of रसाभास *i.e.* the mere semblance of sentiments is the view of modern scholars. However, the ancient theorists hold thus: The love suggstive of one spinster regarding persons is semblance (of sentiment). Like the erotic sentiment, the semblance of erotic (sentiment) is also of two types-namely union and separation. The semblance of union erotic is shown just earlier (*i.e.* भुजपंजरे RG.127.3) etc.....

RG. 128.

विप्रलम्भाभासो यथा–

"व्यत्यतं लपति क्षणं क्षणमथो मौनं समालम्बते, सर्वस्मिन्विदधाति

किं च विषये दृष्टिं निरालम्बनाम्। श्वासं दीर्घमुरीकरोति न मनागंङ्गेषु धत्ते धृतिं वैदेहीकमनीयताकवलितो हा हन्त लङ्केश्वरः॥"

अत्रसीतालम्बनेयं लङ्केशगता विप्रलंभरतिरनुभयनिष्ठतया जगद्गुरु-पत्नीविषयकतयाचाभासतांगता, व्यत्यस्तं लपतीत्यादि भिरुक्तिभि-र्व्यज्यमानैरुन्मादश्रममोहचिन्ताव्याधिभिस्तथैवाभासतां गतैः प्राधान्येन परिपोष्यमाणा ध्वनिव्यपदेशहेतुः।

Trans.: The example for the false attribution of the (sentiment) love-in-separation as follows:

"Alas ! The Lord of **Laṅkā,** tormented with the pain of separation from **Vaidehī,** now talks incoherently and (now) assumes silence, (now) casts a vacant glance towards all things, fetches a long sigh and has not even the slighest strength in his limbs."

Here, (in this present example), love-in separation residing in **Rāvaṇa** (the king of **Laṅkā**) having Sitā as its sustantial mood, becomes a case of false attribution (of love), because of its non resistence in both, and because of it (love) having the wife of the revered teacher as its object. Suggested by the expression namely, 'talks incoherently etc.', and by the madness, fatigue, perplexity, anxiety, sickness etc., becoming false attribution (of the moods) like that (the love of Rāvaṇa), being developed and primarily becomes the cause of the expression (of the false attribution) of suggestion.

RG. 129.

एवं कलहशालकुपुत्राद्यालम्वनतया वीतरागादिनिष्ठतया च वर्ण्यमानःशोक, ब्रह्मविद्यानधिकारिचाण्डालादिगतत्वेन च निर्वेद, कदर्यकातरादिगतत्वेन पित्राद्यालम्बनत्वेन वा क्रौधोत्साहौ, ऐन्द्रजालि-काद्यालम्बनत्वेन च विस्मयः, गुर्वाद्यालंवनतयाच हासः, महावीरगतत्वेन भयम्, यज्ञीयपशुवसासृङ्मांसाद्यालम्वनतया वर्ण्यमाना जुगुप्सा च रसाभासाः। विस्तृतिभयाच्चामी नेहोदाहृताः, सुधीभिरुन्नेयाः।

Trans.: Like this the narration of sorrow of one without any attachment towards (his) quarrelsome (and hence) bad son; the detachment with regard to the चांडाल. etc., not fit for the study of scriputers; the anger and the heroism with regard to a bad and coward one and (one's own) father etc., the wonder with regard to a juggler etc., the laugh with regard to one's teacher etc., the fear with regard to brave; and the disgust with regard to blood, flesh, bone etc., of the sacrificial animal (for the respective sentiments). These are not illustrated separately, for, it would be too vast, which may be understood by scholars (themsleves).

RG. 130.

एवमेवानुचितविषया भावाभासः। यथा–

"सर्वेऽपि विस्मृतिपथं विषयाःप्रयाता, विद्यापि खेदकलिता विमुखीबभूव। सा केवलं हरिणशावकलोचना मे, नैवापयाति हृदया-दधिदेवतेव।।"

गुरुकुले विद्याभ्याससमये तदीयकन्यालावण्यगृहीतमान सस्यान्य-स्य वा कस्यचिदतिपतिषिद्धगमनां स्मरतो देशान्तरं गतस्येयमुक्तिः।

अत्र च स्वात्मत्यागात्यागाभ्यां स्रक्चन्दनादिषु विषयेषु, चिरसेविता विद्यायां च कृतघ्नत्वम्, अस्यां च लोकोत्तरत्वमभिव्यज्यमानं व्यतिरे-कवपुः स्मृतिमेव पुष्णातीति सैव प्रधानम्। एव च त्यागा भावगतं सार्वदिकत्वं व्यञ्जयन्त्यधिदेवतोपमापि। एषा चानुचितविषयकत्वा-दनुभयनिष्ठत्वाच्च भावाभासः। यदि पुनरियं तत्परिणेतुरेवोक्तिस्तदा भावध्यनिरेव।।

Trans.: Like this (sentiment), the improper objects are called the false attribution of moods.

Example: "Even all the objects of senses have been forgotten, and learning too, acquired by exertion, has turned away his face from me (has left me), only fawn-eyed lady, never disappears from my mind like a deity presiding over it."

This is the speech of some one, gone abroad, remembering a lady, prohibited (for enjoyment), or some one having in mind, the beauty of the daughter of his (teacher), at the time of learning at the house of Guru. And here, by forgetting the learning served for a long period, and not forgetting (the lady), the ungratefulness and gratefulness are suggested respectively; And since the suggestion of व्यतिरेक by suggesting the extraordinariness of the lady from learning, nourished the rememberance, (स्मृति) it is primary. And also the simple अधिदेवता, which is given to show the all time absence of the forgetting the lady. This rememberance is with regard to impropriate object and since not receprocal, is a case of false attribution of mood. And if it is the expression of one duly married person, then it would be a case of the suggestion of mood.

RG. 131.

अथ भावशान्ति–

भावस्य प्रागुक्तस्वरूपस्य शान्तिर्नाशः॥
स चोत्पत्त्यवच्छिन्न एव ग्राह्यः। तस्यैव सहृदयचमत्कारित्वात्।
उदाहरणम्–

"मुञ्चसि नाद्यापि रुषं भामिनि मुदिरालिरुदियाय।
इति तन्व्याः पतिवचनैरपायि नयनाब्जकोणशोणरुचिः॥"

इह तादृशप्रियवचनश्रवणं विभावः। नयनकोणगतशोणरुचेर्नाशः, तदभिव्यक्तः प्रसादो वानुभावः। उत्पत्तिकालावच्छिन्नो रोषनाशो व्यङ्ग्यः।

Trans.: Now, starts the discussion of the nature of the subsidence of mood:

The absence of the emotion as told earlier, is subsidence. And that (absence) should be understood as definited by the time of its generation. Because that is the cause of the charmingness of refined critics.

Example: The red hue of the corners of the lotus-like eyes of the beautiful eyed one was removed (lit. drunk up) by the words of her lover to this effect. **Bhāminī**, the line of clouds has arisen, and still you do not leave off your anger."

Here, the listening of the lover's speech as given is excitant. The removal of the reddish from the corners of the eyes, or the lucidity as manifested from that, is ensuant. The absence of anger, at the time of its rising is primarily suggested.

Notes : Here **PR** explains the subsidence of mood. He does not give a technical definition but explains through illustrations. In the subsequent texts, he discusses regarding other three aspects namely the co-existence, the rising and the variegations of moods also.

On the co-existence of mood **PR** talks about **sāmānā dhikaraṇaṁ** of moods which do not merge into one but are capable of doing so. On the co-existence of two moods, Nāgesha notes that, this co-existance is with regard to place and not to time (**ekadeśavṛtatvaṁ na tu ekakālavṛtitvam**).

RG. 132.

तथा–भावोदयो भावस्योत्पत्तिः॥

उदाहरणम्–"वीक्ष्य वक्षसि विपक्षकामिनीहारलक्ष्म दयितस्य भामिनी। अंसदेशवलयीकृतां क्षणादाचकर्ष निजबाहुबल्लरीम्॥" अत्रापि दयितवक्षोगतविपक्षकामिनीहारलक्ष्मदर्शनं विभावः। प्रियांसदेश वलयीकृतनिजबाहुलताकर्षणमनुभावः। रोषोदयोव्यङ्ग्यः। यद्यपि भावशान्तौ भावान्तरोदयस्य, भावोदये वा पूर्वं भावशान्तेरावश्यकत्वान्नानयोर्विविक्तो व्यवहारस्य विषयः, तथापि द्वयोरेकत्र चमत्कारविरहात्, चमत्काराधीनत्वाच्च व्यवहारस्य, (इति) अस्ति विषय विभागः।

Trans.: Like this, the generation of mood is called as the rising of mood (*i.e.* भावोदय).

Example: "Noticing on the bosom of her lover a mark of the necklace of a rival woman, the young lady at once withdrew her creeper-like arms that was placed round his shoulders."

Here also, noticing the mark, of the necklace of the rival woman on the chest of ones own lover, is 'excitant'. The withdrawal of ones own arms as circled on the shoulder of lover is ensuant. The emeragence of anger is suggested here. Even though, those two, are not the object of distinct usage, because of the necessity of 'rising of some other moods for the subsidence of one mood; or 'the subsidence of one mood for the rising of another mood; still, due to the absence of charmingness of these two together, and because of the principle, namely, the usage (of object) is dependant or (the expression) of charmingness, the distinction of objects is postutaled.

Notes : The subsidence of mood and the rising of mood, both are quite different. According to P. Srirmchandrudu, the subsidence of mood is invariably followed by the appearance of another mood, whereas the rising of mood is precceded by the subsidence of mood Their positions are to be determined according to the charmingness generated by those two.

RG. 133.

एवम्-भावसंधिरन्योन्यानभिभूतयोरन्योन्याभिभावनयोग्ययोः सामा-नाधिकरण्यम्॥

उदाहरणम्-"यौवनोद्गमनितान्तशङ्किताःशीलशौर्यबलकान्तिलोभिताः।
संकुचन्ति विकसन्तिराघवे जानकीनयननीरजश्रियः॥"

अत्र भगवददाशरथिगतस्य लोकोत्तरयौवनोद्गमस्य, तादृशस्यैव शीलशौर्यादेश्च दर्शनं विभावः। नयनगतसंकोचविकासावनुभावः।

व्रीडौत्सुक्ययोः संधिर्व्यङ्ग्यः।

Trans.: Like this, the moods, residing in one, fusing together, but fit to merge with each other is 'co-existance of mood.'

Example: "The beauties of the lotus-like eyes of Jānakī while falling on Rāma, contract on account of shyness, due to the advant of his youth, and expand on account of being tempted, by his good nature, valour, strength and charm."

Here, 'noticing the extra ordinary youthness', 'gentle nature', 'braveness in Rāma' (lit. Son of Daśaratha) is excitant' The shyness (contract) and expand in the eyes, is 'ensuant.' And the co-existance of bashfulness and eagerness are suggested.

Notes : PR defines the co-existence of moods here. The co-existence or as we can call it the confluence of two moods is the co-existence of moods. But it is further to be noted that these two moods should not be merged to one due to the lack of charmingness. Similarly, there will be no charm, from the co-existence of such moods which are not of opposite natures. He gives the example from his **sṛngāra vilāsa.**

RG. 134.

तथा–भावशबलत्वं भावानां बाध्यबाधकभावमापन्नानामुदासीनानां व्यामिश्रणम्॥

एकचमत्कृतिजनकज्ञानगोचरत्वमिति यावत्।

उदाहरणम्–"पापं हन्त मया हतेन विहितं, सीतापि यद्यापिता, सामामिन्दुमुखी विना बत वने किं जीवितं धास्यति।

आलोकेय कथं मुखानि कृतिनां, किं ते वदिष्यन्ति मां, राज्यं यातु रसातलं, पुनरिदं न प्राणितुं कामये ॥"

अत्र मत्ससूयाविषादस्मृतिवितर्कव्रीडाशङ्कानिर्वेदानां प्रागुक्त स्वस्वविभावजन्मनां शबलता।

Trans.: The mixing of moods, either being met with the conditions to make obstacles or being hesitants to each other, is the 'variegation of mood. ' And it is the object of knowlege, generated by an unitary (single) charmingness (from many).

Example: "Sin has been committed by me, the ill-fated one (lit.**Rāma**), that **Sītā** has been banished (exiled), what life can she, moon like faced, would live without me in the jungle? How can I face the saints? (lit. Look at the faces of), What will they speak off me? Let the Kingdom to hell, I donot want to live anymore."

Here, the variegation of moods is caused by respective excitants, as told earlier namely judgement, envy, despair, recollecton, deliberation, bashfulness, misgiving and despondency.

Notes : In the context of co-existence of moods there two moods exists, whereas in the case of **sabalatā** or the variegation of moods there may exist more than two moods at same time.

Many moods can be combined in a specific style with either antagonistic with each other or of neutral position. **PR** strongly refutes the view of Govinda Thakur (pradip commentator on KP) that, neither there is the suggestion of the oppression of the preceding mood nor there is any charmingness in such **upamarda.**

RG. 135.

यत्तु काव्यप्रकाशटीकाकारैः

"उत्तरोत्तरेण भावेन पूर्वपूर्वभावोपमर्दः शबलता" इत्यभ्यधीयत, तन्न। 'पश्येत्कश्चिच्चल चपल रे का त्वराहं कुमारी हस्तालम्बं वितर हहहा व्युत्क्रमः क्वासि यासि' इत्यत्र शङ्कासूयाधृतिस्मृतिश्रमदैन्य-मत्यौत्सुक्यानामुपमर्दलेशशून्यत्वेऽपि शबलताया राजस्तुतिगुणत्वेन पञ्चमोल्लासे मूलकृतैव निरूपणात्। स्वोत्तरविशेषगुणेन जायमानस्तु नाशो न व्यङ्ग्यः। न वोपमर्दपदवाच्यः। नापि चमत्कारी।

Trans.: Whatever is told by the commentators of **KP** namely, the destruction of procceeding moods by the generation of succeeding moods is the 'Variegation' is not true. Because, the original author (मम्मट) in the fifth chapter (of **KP**) has explained the 'Variegation of mood' as supportive (subordinated) to the 'praising of the king', eventhough, there is the absence of the destruction a little of the moods namely, anxiety, envy, contentment, recollection, fatigue, depression, judgement, longing in the illustration namely पश्येत् कश्चित चल चपल... etc. However, the destruction, caused by succeding (hence) specifical merits of those, is not suggestion. And that (destruction) is not expressive to the term उपमर्द (*i.e.* collapsing after destruction). And again, there is no charm at all.

RG. 135.1.

तस्मात्–"नारिकेलजलक्षीरसिताकदलमिश्रणे।
विलक्षणो यथा स्वादो भावानां संहतौ तथा॥"

अत्रेदं बोध्यम्–य एते भावशान्त्युदयसंधिशबलताध्वनय उदाहृतास्तेऽपि भावध्वनय एव, विद्यमानतया चर्व्यमाणेष्विवोत्पत्त्य वच्छिन्नत्वविनश्यदवस्थत्वसंधीयमानत्वपरस्परसमानाधिकरणत्वैः प्रकारैश्चर्व्यमाणेषु भावेष्वेव प्राधान्यस्यौचित्यात्, चमत्कृतेस्तत्रैव विश्रान्तेः। यद्यप्युत्पत्तिविनाशसंधिंशबलतानां तत्संबन्धिनां भावानां च समानायां चर्वणाविषयतायां न प्राधान्यं विनिगन्तुं शक्यते। तथापि स्थितौ भावेषु प्रधानतायाःक्लृप्तत्वात्, भावशान्त्यादिष्वपि तेष्वेव शान्तिप्रतियोगित्वादिभिर्व्यज्यमानेषु तस्याः कल्पयितुमौचित्यात्।

Trans.: Thus, it is said:

"As the unique taste (generates) by the mixture of the coconut water, milk, sugar candy, banana, (in the form of Liquid juice), so the realisation of co-existing moods are (generate).

Here, it should be understood that, those, suggestive

subsidence, rising, co-existance and variegation of moods illustrated, are also suggestive moods only. It is proper to hold the moods existing in the enjoyment of the moods delimited by the state of emergence, the state of subsidence, the state of co-existance and the state of variegation, is predominance. Because, the charmingness rests on that alone. Eventhough, the emergence, the subsidence, the co-existance and the variegation and the respective moods related to these, be equally become the object of enjoyment and, it is not possible to determine the predominance (of either) still in the existance, the dominance of the mood is certain. And in the case of subsidence of mood (*i.e.* भावशान्ति) etc., it is proper to accept the primary-ness of the moods (भाव) which is suggested as the counter positive of the subsidence of the mood.

RG. 135.2

किं च यदि भावशान्त्यादौ भावो न प्रधानम्, किं तु तदुपसर्जनकशान्त्यादिरेवेत्यभ्युपेयते, तदा व्यज्यमानभावेष्वभिहिततत्प्रशमादिषु काव्येषु भावप्रशमादिध्वनित्वं न स्यात्।

तथाहि–"उषसि प्रतिपक्षनायिकासदनादन्तिकमञ्चति प्रिये। सुदृशो नयनाब्जकोणयोरुदियाय त्वरयारुणद्युतिः॥"

अत्रोत्पूर्वकेणैतिना भावोदयस्य वाच्यतयैव प्रत्यायनात्, ननु उदयस्य वाच्यत्वेऽपि भावस्यावच्यत्वाद्ध्यनित्वं सुस्थमिति चेत्, प्रधानस्य व्यपदेशानौपयिकत्वेऽप्रधानकृतव्यपदेशानुपपत्तेः।

अस्मन्मते तूत्पत्तेर्वाच्यत्वेऽप्युत्पत्त्यवच्छिन्नस्यामर्षस्य प्रधानस्यावाच्यत्वाद्युक्त एव भावोदयध्वनिव्यपदेशः।

Trans.: And if it is accepted that, in the cases of 'the subsidence of mood' etc, the 'mood' (भाव) is not primary, but subordinated 'subsidence' etc., are primary, then there cannot be the suggestion of भावशान्ति etc., in a poetry, where the 'mood' becomes suggestive and 'the subsidence' etc., become expressive.

Accordingly, the mood (अमर्ष) is realised being expressive, by the usage of (उत्त+इत) उदय in the following verse.

"The raddish colour developed (उदय) at once in the corner of the lotus-eyed good looking lady, noticing the arrival of her beloved, from her rival lady's house at morning."

Objection: Well, it may be argued further that, even though the उदय is expressive, due to the non-expressiveness of the mood (by the expression of the term उदय), there is no difficulty in accepting its suggestiveness.

Answer: It cannot be so. because, there is no proof to name it as primary and it is improper to call it subordinate. Following our view, however, even though the rising of resentment is expressive, still due to the non-expressiveness of the resentment delimited by 'rising' (उत्पत्ति), which is primary, it is proper to call it as the suggestion of the भावोदय.

RG. 135.3

एवं व्यज्यमानभावप्रतियोगिकस्य प्रशमस्य वाच्यत्वे भावशान्तिध्वनित्वं न स्यात्।

यथा–"क्षमापणैकपदयोः पदयोः पतति प्रिये। शेमुः सरोजनयनानयनारुणकान्तयः॥"

ननु शब्दवाच्यानां प्रशमादीनामरुणकान्त्यैवान्वयात्, अरुणकान्तिप्रशमादेरेव वाच्यत्वं पर्यवसितम्। न तु तादृशप्रशमादिव्यङ्ग्यस्य रोषप्रशमादेः। व्यङ्ग्यव्यञ्जकभेदस्यावश्यकत्वात्। न चारुण्यव्यङ्ग्यरोषस्यैव वाच्यीभूतप्रशमाद्यन्वय इति वाच्यम्।

वाच्यव्यङ्ग्यप्रतीत्योरानुपूर्व्येण सिद्धतया वाच्यान्वयबोधवेलायां वाच्यैः सह व्यङ्ग्यान्वयानुपपत्तेः। अन्यथा 'सुदृशो नयनाब्जकोणयोः' इत्यस्यान्वयो न स्यात्।

Trans.: Like this, if the 'subsidence' is expressive, having the suggestion of the mood as its counter positive, the 'subsidence of mood' cannot be suggestion.

Example: "When the lover falls on the feet mainly responsible for forgiving (her beloved), the raddish colour in the eyes of the lotus-eyed one calms down.

Well, let the emergence of redness (anger in the face) and its passification (प्रशम) be expressive due to their relation with redness of face. The अमर्ष, revealed from these emergence of anger and its passification cannot be expressive but suggestive. Because, a distinction is to be maintained between the suggestions and the suggestives. It cannot be argued thus: it is improper to hold that, by this, the redness (in the face) arised, the अमर्ष' disappeared, which is suggested is being related to 'the rising' and 'disappearing', which are expressive. Because, there is the rule, of the definite in sequence occurrances of first and then second, between, 'what is expressive' and 'what is suggestive'. And at the time of understanding of, the expressed sense, the suggestive sense cannot be grasped (simultaneously). Otherwise, the expression सुदृशो नयनाब्ज etc., cannot be explaned properly.

RG. 135.4

मैवम्। एवमपि–

"निर्वासयन्तीं धृतिमङ्गनानां शोभां हरेरेणदृशो धयन्त्याः।
चिरापराधस्मृतिमांसलोऽपि रोषः क्षणप्राघुणिको बभूव॥

इत्यादावपि भावाप्रशमध्वनित्वापत्तेः। भावस्य वाच्यत्वेऽपि प्रधानस्य तत्प्रशमस्य व्यङ्ग्यत्वात्। उभयोरप्यवाच्यत्वमपेक्षितमिति चेत्, प्रागुक्तपद्यद्वये शमत्वोदयत्वाभ्यां शमोदयोर्वाच्यत्वादनुदाहरणत्वापत्तेः। इष्टापत्तिस्तु सहृदयानामनुचितैव। तस्माद्भावप्रशमादिष्वपि प्राधान्येन भावानामेव चमत्कारित्वम्, प्रशमादेस्तूपसर्जनत्वमतो न तस्य वाच्यता-दोषः।

Trans.: Not so. Because, there would arise the contingency of accepting the suggestiveness of 'subsidence of mood" in the following: "The anger of the ladies, looking at the beauty of Lord Hari, capable of destroying the mental steadiness of ladies, becomes short lived." Because, even though the mood (अमर्ष) is expressive here, yet the subsidence of that (mood) is primarily suggested. If it is argured that the both (mood and its subsidence) are intented to be non-expressive (suggestive), then there would arise the contingency of not accepting the two verses, stated earlier as illustrations (of भावोदय and भावशान्ति) due to the expressiveness of शम and उदय by शमत्व and उदयत्व respectively. And the desired contingency cannot be welcome by the connisseur (सहृदय). Therefore, in the cases of 'subsidence of mood' (भावशांति) etc., alike the suggestion of mood primarily, the charmingness lies in the moods and there is no problem for these, प्रशम subsidence etc., being expressive, due to their subordinateness.

RG. 135.5

इदं पुनर्भावध्वनिभ्यो भावशान्त्यादिध्वनीनां चमत्कारवैलक्षण्ये निदानम्-यदेकत्र चर्वणायां भावेषु स्थित्यवच्छिन्नामर्षादिकत्वम्, अमर्षादित्वमेव वा प्रकारः। अन्यत्र तु प्रथमावस्थत्वादिरपीति। रसस्य तु स्थायिमूलकत्वात्प्रशमादेरसंभवः। संभवे वा न चमत्कारः। इति न स विचार्यते।

Trans.: The cause of the distinction of the charmingness of the suggestion of 'subsidence of mood', from the suggestion of 'mood' etc., is that one cause of enjoyment, has the 'resentmentness;' or 'resentmentness' delimited by the presenceness as its qualifier, and the other (*i.e.* in the suggestion of) subsidenceness etc., However, the sentiments being based on permanent mood the risingness, the subsidenceness etc. of sentiments, are not possible (like the subsidenceness etc.

of moods). And if it is seen (possible), then that would not be charming, hence is not taken for discussion.

RG. 136.

सोऽयं निगदितः सर्वोऽपि रत्यादिलक्षणो व्यङ्ग्यप्रपञ्चः। स्फुटे प्रकरणे झगिति प्रतीतेषु विभावानुभावव्यभिचारिषु सहृदयतमेन प्रमात्रा सूक्ष्मेणैव समयेन प्रतीयत इति हेतुहेतुमतोः पौर्वापर्यक्रमस्या लक्षणा-दलक्ष्यक्रमो व्यपदिश्यते। यत्र तु विचारवेद्यं प्रकरणम्, उन्नेया वा विभावादयस्तत्र सामग्रीविलम्बाधीनं यमत्कृतेर्मान्थर्यमिति संलक्ष्यमोऽप्येष भवति। यथा–तल्पगतापि च सुतनुः इति प्रागुदाहृते पद्ये संप्रति इत्येतदर्थावगतिर्विलम्बेन।

न खलु धर्मिग्राहकमानसिद्धं रत्यादिध्वनेरलक्ष्यक्रमव्यङ्ग्यत्वम्।

Trans.: Like this, the nature of the entire suggested ideas in the form of love etc., are discussed. In the case, where the suggested context of marked sequentiality, the excitant, ensuant, and the transitory moods are grasped very quickly (and) (the suggested idea) is experienced very fast (lit. in little time), by the knower, the refined critic, and thus, due to the non-realisation of the sequence of precceding cause and succeding effect, it is called a case of suggested context of undiscovered sequentiality.

This becomes the case of suggested content of marked sequentiality, (संलक्ष्यक्रम) where the context is not clear (lit. to be understood after analysis), and the excitant etc., are to be (not so easily) grasped. Where, the realisation of the suggestation of charmingness is not instant, due to the realisation of the factors (विभाव etc.).

For example: in the verse तल्पगतापि च सुतनुः etc., stated earlier, the term namely 'now' is not instantly understoood.

RG. 136.1

अत एव लक्ष्यक्रमप्रसङ्गे–

"एवंवादिनि देवर्षौ पार्श्वे पितुरधोमुखी।
लीलाकमलपत्राणि गणयामास पार्वती॥"

इत्यत्र कुमारीस्वाभाव्यादप्यधोमुखत्वविशिष्टस्य लीलाकमल पत्रगणनस्योपपत्त्या मनाग्विलम्बेन नारदकृतविवाहादिप्रसङ्गविज्ञानोत्तरं व्रीडायाश्चमत्करणात्लक्ष्यक्रमोऽयं ध्वनिः" इति प्राहुरानन्दवर्धनाचार्याः। रसभावादिरर्थो ध्वन्यमान एव, न वाच्यः। तथापि न सर्वो लक्ष्यक्रमस्य विषयः इति चाभिनवगुप्तपादाचार्याः।

स्यादेतत्, यद्ययं रसादिः संलक्ष्यक्रमस्य विषयः स्यात्। अनुरणन-भेदगणन प्रस्तावे 'अर्थशक्तिमूलस्य द्वादशभेदाः' इत्यभिनवगुप्तोक्तिः, 'तेनायं द्वादशात्मकः' इति मम्मटोक्तिश्च न संगच्छेत। वस्त्वलंकारात्मना द्विविधेन वाच्येन स्वतः संभवित्वकविप्रौढोक्तिनिष्पन्नत्वकविनिबद्ध वक्तृप्रौढोक्तिनिष्पन्नत्वैस्त्रिभिरुपाधिभिस्त्रैविध्यमापन्नेन षडात्मना वस्त्वलंकारयोरिव रसादेरप्यभिव्यञ्जनादष्टादशत्वप्रसङ्गात्।

Trans.: Therefore in the context of संलक्ष्यक्रम, in the verse namely, "while the divine sage was speaking, thus **Pārvati,** who was by her fathers' side, counted the petals of her sportive lotuses, with a down-cast look." **Ānanda-vardhana,** told that, "this is suggestion of लक्षयक्रम, due to the presentation of charmingful 'bashfulness' after knowing the context of marriage, communicated by **Nārada,** due to the non realisation by **Pārvati**, who was counting petals, eventhough, the state of facing downwards is caused; by the childlike behaviour.

And according to respected **Abhinavagupta,** "the sentiments, the moods etc., are mostly suggested and not expressed, still all are not the cases of अलक्ष्यक्रम (*i.e.* the sequence of realisation cannot be grasped.)

Well, let it be like this: The sentiments etc., are the object of संलक्ष्यक्रम. Thus, there are twelve varieties of 'suggestion based on the literal sense' (अर्थशक्तिमूल ध्वनि), in the context of numbering the varieties', is the view of **Abhinavagupta.** And the statement made by **Mammaṭa** namely, 'therefore, this is of twelve types', does not stand valid. Because, there would arise the contingency of the suggestion of sentiment (based on sense) to be eighteen varieties, since the 'sentiment' etc., would be suggested by same suggestives alike the 'merefact' and 'figurative' poetries (अलंकार) along with the twelve varieties, based on mere fact (वस्तु) and figurative poetries which is again divided into three varieties based on that (i) which is naturally existing (inherent), (ii) which is created by the ornate expression of the poet and (iii) established by the speaker, introduced by the poet.

RG. 136.2

अत्रोच्यते–प्रकटैर्विभावानुभावव्यभिचारिभिरलक्ष्यक्रमतयैव व्यज्यमानो रत्यादिःस्थायिभावो रसीभवति।

न संलक्ष्यक्रमतया। रसीभावो हि नाम झगितिजाय मानालौकिक-चमत्कारविषयस्थायित्वम्। संलक्ष्यक्रमतया व्यज्यमानस्य रत्यादेस्तु वस्तुमात्रतैव, न रसादित्वमिति तेषामाशयस्य वर्णनेन न तदुक्तीनां विरोधः। उपपत्तिस्त्वर्थेऽस्मिन्विचारणीया।

रसभावादिरर्थ इत्यत्र रसादिशब्दो रत्यादिपरः। तदित्थंनिरूपित-स्यास्य रसादिध्वनिप्रपञ्चस्य पदवर्णरचनावाक्यप्रबन्धैः पदैकदेशैर-वर्णात्मकै रागादिभिश्चाभिव्यक्तिमामनन्ति। तत्र वाक्यगतानां पदानां सर्वेषामपि स्वार्थोपस्थितिद्वारावाक्यार्थज्ञानोपायत्वे समानेऽपि कुर्वद्रूपतया चमत्कारायोगव्यवच्छिन्नत्वेंनकस्यचिदेव ध्वनिव्यपदेशहे तुत्वम्। यथा 'मन्दमाक्षिपति' इत्यत्र मन्दमित्यस्य।

Trans.: Thus, it is said as: The permanent mood, namely, love etc., being suggested by अलक्ष्यक्रम indeed, (in the form of) by the excitant, ensuant and transitory moods, as defined earlier, attains the 'sentimentness' and not by the संलक्ष्यक्रम, (instantly).

The state of being sentiment is to be understood that, the state of permanent mood becomes the object of extra-ordinary charmingness which generates instantly (at very moment). However, the love etc., suggested by संलक्ष्यक्रम amounts to mere fact only and not generate (the state of) sentiment *i.e.* only love is manifested but not the sentiments. Thus, the statement given by opponents are not contradictory by narrating those statements. However, in this context. it should be realised that (the acceptance of sentiment in case of संलक्ष्यक्रम is not prohibited also), the word 'sentiment' here as explained namely 'sentiment', 'mood' etc.,are to be referred to love etc., (rasa means रत्यादि permanent moods and mood means transitory moods only).

So far, the entire concept of suggestion with sentiment etc., are discussed in the above manner, is manifested by 'word', 'syllable', 'composition', 'sentence', 'epics', 'some part of the word' and by the musical tune, which cannot be identified by 'syllables', is the view of some.

As a matter of fact, eventhough, all the 'words', in a sentence, are common as the cause of the sentence meaning by presenting their individual meanings, yet, only some become the cause to be called as suggestion, due to the charmingness delimitted by its invariably presence, as in the example namely, मन्दमाक्षिपति... etc. the suggestivness of मन्दम्.

RG. 137.

रचनावर्णानां तु पदवाक्यान्तर्गतत्वेन व्यञ्जकतावच्छेदक कोटि-प्रविष्टत्वमेव न तु व्यञ्जकत्वमिति यद्यपि सुवचम्, तथापि पदवाक्य-विशिष्टरचनात्वेन, रचनाविशिष्टपदवाक्यत्वेन वा व्यञ्ज कत्वमिति

विनिगमनाविरहेण घटादौ दण्डचक्रादेः कारणत्वस्येव प्रत्येकमेव व्यञ्जकतायाः सिद्धिरिति प्राञ्चः। वर्णरचनाविशेषाणां माधुर्यादि-गुणाभिव्यञ्जकत्वमेव न रसाभिव्यञ्जकत्वम्।

गौरवान्मानाभावाच्च। नहि गुण्यभिव्यञ्जनं विना गुणाभिव्यञ्जकत्वं नास्तीत्यस्ति नियमः। इन्द्रियत्रये व्यभिचारात्।

Trans.: However, eventhough, the fact that, the case of 'composition', and 'syllable', are included in the delimitor of the suggestiveness, due to their inclusion in 'words' and 'sentences' and are not suggestive; cannot be Justified. Still due to the lack of delimiting properly, namely, the suggestiveness as 'composition having word and sentence', or 'the word and sentence having composition', each is suggestive like the causes as staf and wheel etc., in the case of a pot., is the view of the ancient theorists. Because of the fault of logical heavyness and because of the absence of any valid means, the specific syllables and compositions suggest the merit of the sweetness etc., but does not suggest the sentiments, is the view of the modern school of thoughts. And there is no rule that in the absence of suggestion of sentiment, there cannot be the suggestion of the merits. Because, there would be deviation in case of the three sense organs (namely घ्राण, रसना and श्रोत्र).

RG. 137.1.

इत्थं च स्वस्वव्यञ्जकोपनीतानां गुणिनां गुणानामुदासीनानां च यथा परस्परोपश्लेषेणौदासीन्येन वा तत्तत्प्रमितिगोचरता तथा रसानां तदगुणानां चाभिव्यक्तिविषयतेति तु नव्याः। उदाहरणं तु 'तान्तमाल' इत्यादि प्रागुक्तमेव। वाक्यस्य व्यञ्जकतायामपि 'आविर्भूतायदवधि' इत्यादि च। प्रबन्धस्य तु योगवासिष्ठरामायणे शान्तकरुणयोः, रत्नावल्या-दीनिच शृङ्गारस्य व्यञ्जकत्वान्निदर्शनानि प्रसिद्धानि। मन्निर्मिताश्च पञ्च लहर्यो भावस्य।

Trans.: Like this, as the गुणी, presented by their respective suggestiveness and the different merits, become the object of knowledge, combindingly or distinctly. Similarly, the sentiments and merits etc., become the object of realisation is the view of the modern school of thoughts.

The example of the realisation of suggestion of 'syllable', and 'composition' namely, तां तमाल... etc., as already stated. The example of the realisation of the suggestion of sentence, namely, आविर्भूता यदवधि etc. is also quoted.

Due to the realisation of quietism, pathos and erotic in योगवासिष्ठ रामायण and रत्नावली respectively, these famous epics as given for illustrations. The 'five-waves', composed by me, are of the examples of (**bhāva**), transitory moods.

RG. 137.2

पदैकदेशस्य च 'निखिलमिदं जगदण्डकं वहामि' इति करूपतद्धितो वीररसस्य प्रागेवोदाहृतः। एवं रागादिभिरपि व्यङ्ग्यत्वे सहृदयहृदयमेव प्रमाणम्। एवमेषां रसादीनां प्राधान्येन निरूपिता-न्युदाहरणानि। गुणीभावे तु वक्ष्यन्ते, नामानि च। तत्र प्राधान्य एवैषां रसादित्वम्। अन्यथा तु रत्यादित्वमेव। नामनि रसपदं तु रत्यादि-परमित्येके। अस्त्येव रसादित्वं, किं तु न ध्वनिव्यपदेशहेतुत्वमित्यपरे॥

इति महोपाध्यायपदवाक्यप्रमाणपारावारपारीणश्रीपेरमभट्टस्य सूरेः सूनुना पण्डितराजजगन्नाथेन निर्मिते रसगङ्गाधरे रसनिरूपणात्मकं पूर्वमाननम्।

Trans.: And the example of suggestion of partial (पदैकदेश) word is quoted earlier in the context of heroic sentiment, viz, निखिलमिदं जगदंडकं वहामि due to the use of क and तद्धित. Like this, the experience of the refined critics is the proof for the suggestiveness of musical tunes. Thus, the examples of the primary sentiments are explained. The further examples for the subordinated sentiments are to be discussed with their proper names. When, they become dominent, they are called sentiments etc.; otherwise 'love' etc. In the expression **'rasavat'**, **rasa** refers to (रति) love, is the view of some. However, let sentiment etc., be there, but they cannot be cause for the expression of suggestion is the view of some others.

Thus ends the first ānana devoted to the explanation of setiment in Rasagaṅgādhara, composed by Paṇḍitarāja Jagannātha, the son of Sriperubhaṭṭa, who has mastered all sciences of पद, वाक्य and प्रमाण.

☆☆☆

PART II

RASAGAṄGĀDHARA : A CRITICAL STUDY

CHAPTER - I

INTRODUCTION

I.0 General Background

In the chronology of the text book writers of Sanskrit Poetics, the name of Paṇḍitarāja Jagannātha (=PR) comes last. He, being nourished and brought out in the midst of the unbroken tradition of Sanskrit literary criticism, is the last star in the galaxy of the great rhetoricians to have made significant contributions towards the enhancement of poetics studies.

Being the last, he enjoyed the privilege of recording, reviewing, refuting and reappraising the various theories on Sanskrit poetics in his magnum-opus Rasagangādhara, (=RG).

With his unique acumen of refined skill, he has chosen the right tool of Navyanyāya and has successfully employed too, the Navyanyāya technique to define his theories for unambiguous expression. Further, there are many a significant contribution of PR to Sanskrit poetics. In many occasions he differs from his predecessors substantially and fundamentally on some basic and important issues.

Thus, to bring out his contribution to Sanskrit poetics in general and to Sanskrit literary criticism in particular, is the aim and objectives of the present work. It may be worth, to record here, the fact that new-logic has influenced RG to a greater extent. This is precisely the reason why RG has left a permanent impression in the mind of the Sanskrit literary critics, due to the accuracy and preciseness in its presentation.

In spite of the fact that some researches are already done, still we do not have a particular work on RG that presents the specific contributions of Paṇḍitarāja. The doctrinal differences of RG from the earlier texts are also not presented in any work. Further, English Translation of RG is a long felt desideratum. There fore, the first Part of this book have its Translation only.

Coming to present situation there are several books on History of Sanskrit poetics and study works on poetics but they are not specific. We have indeed a few works, dealing with the present work, still they are neither exhaustive nor systematic nor accurate except that of Prof. P. Sriramachandradu and few more. Finally, it is noticed that even though these labourious works do not avoid the problems inside the pages of text, still they are lacking a proper analysis.

We have a few Commentaries and some critical studies on RG to choose and base our study in a perfect manner.

The concepts like the definition of the poetry, the porpose, the cause, the classifications of poetry, the nature of Rasa, the Guṇa, the Doṣa, the Bhāva etc., are discussed in this text. The RG is a vast work and is presented in two ānana's (parts) and our work is based on the first ānana only.

I.1 DATE, LIFE AND WORKS OF PR

As, it is already decided that PR belongs to last original writer in Sanskrit Poetics and some History books on Sanskrit poetics also declared his date without any doubt, therefore, we, are not giving a repetition of PR's time as well as his life history. In the work of V.A.R. Sastri, it is clearly observed by the author and he has given three groups of rhetoricians to choose the proper time of PR. PR's elder contemporaries, close contemporaries and younger contemporaries are given in detail.[1] Further, P.V. Kane is also very perfect to establish PR's time with great satisfaction in his History of Sanskrit poetics.[2]

On the basis of the earlier researches we can safely hold that PR flourished between 1590 A.D. to 1665 A.D.

Life of PR:

Alike his time, the life history also propounded by some critics without any hesitation. Starting from his childhood to youth, where he got a chair of Delhi emperor as a court poet and then at Assam state etc., is given in detail.[3]Though, Appayya Dikṣita, was a strong critics and a first rate rhetorician, yet PR refutes his work CM very sharply in his CMK. Basically, PR was a poet from southern part of India but spent his most of the life in Northern India.

Works of PR:

PR is more known as an ālaṁkārika. But at the same time, he was an able poet of his time. It may not be fair to compare him with poets like Kālidasa etc., but at the same time one must appreciate his skill in composing good poetry. As one can notice in the present work, he has utilised his own verses as illustrative examples. It is generally accepted that RG is his last work. However, P.V. Kane tells that PR wrote CMK after RG. He tells that, the work RG breaks off in the midst of the figure utara and the commentary of Nāgesh Bhaṭṭa, who flourished only about 50 years after PR, extends only upto the same figure. It is not to be supposed that PR passes away in the midst of the task of composing the RG, because from the second introductory verse to his CMK, it appears that he wrote the latter work after RG.[4] In the CMK, PR directs the readers to refer the RG for further details, specially for the udāharaṇa, a figure of speech.[5]

His verses are almost supported by alliteration and suggestive figures of speech and on his all works the verses are coming with very simple yet majestic and forcible style. "His mellifluous diction, his clear and pointed expressions, his weaving out poetry from Śāstric ideas and above all, his wide and deep erudition coupled with his poetic imagination have won for him the position of a great poet in Sanskrit literature".[6]

Really, he had a great fluentive power to produce such types of instance-verses as his RG carries all the examples, which are composed by himself. In his introductory verses to RG, PR declares that all the illustrative verses are his own and he has not borrowed a single verse from any others work.

nirmāyanutanamudāharaṇānurupaṁ
kāvyaṁ mayātra nihitaṁ na prasya kiñcit,
kiṁ sevyate sumanasāṁ manasāpi gaṇdhaḥ
kastūrikājanana saktibhṛtā mṛgeṇa.[7]

It means all the examples given in RG, for understanding the sense of the contexts, are composed by PR. It proves that he had a strong caliber to produce varieties of poetries as he wanted and put them in their proper places.

Beside RG, there are other works of PR, which are recorded here:

There are five waves (pañcalaharī) which carry the devotional verses mostly and in the view of poetic critics, these five waves are countable under the uttama or may be uttomottama poetry group, by their excellent senses and rhetoric sounds. Only by the author's imagination, there are such types of verses and we cannot tell them as ordinary like common works. PR himself calls these five small works as the main suggestion of bhāva.[8] These five waves are; Sudhā laharī, Amṛtalahari, Gaṅgā(piyūṣa) laharī, Laxmīlaharī and Karuṇālaharī.

1. Sudhālaharī (=SL) This is a small muktaka type of poem, of 30 verses composed in the praise of Sun-God in Sragdharā metre. Out of 30, two verses are given as examples in RG. As a matter of fact, only one verse is given as an example of madhyamakāvya group in RG.[9] Here, in this small work, "Sun-God is the protector of world"; is described in the 3rd, 4th, 11th, 16th 19th, 23rd and 27th verses. Again Sun is the devine tree (kalpataru) of his devotees, is given in the 3rd verse.[10]

He is the life-giver of all who suffer from physical and mental problems.[11] Further Sun is the father of two planets - Moon and Jupiter.[12]

We can compare it with Sūryaśataka of Mayūrakavi, that the former preserves the latters brightness.

2. Amṛtalaharī (=AL) Next to sūdhālaharī, it comes with full of devotional songs and some special poems of the holy river Yamunā. There are, in all, eleven verses and out of them, 10 verses are for main theme and last one is poets colophon. Yamunālaharī, the othe name of AL composed in śārḍūlavikriḍita metre. The first verse is a requisition verse to Goddess Yamunā.[13] The natural flows of Yamunā water and its purity, who can save any body from severe sin, is written in 7th verse.[14]

3. Gaṅgālaharī (= GL) It contains 52 verses, devoted to the prayer of Goddess river Gaṅgā and the last verse at the end contains a phalaśruti .This work also recorded as piyūṣ alaharī and there are some 15 verses, quoted in RG.[15] The style of this laharī is very simple.

4. Karuṇā- laharī (=KL) This is a poem of 65 verses in viyogini metre in praise of lord Viṣṇu. It is also named as viṣṇulaharī.In the introduction of Bhāminivilāsa[16], the author says that KL is of sixty verses. Till today, only 55 verses.are available.

5. Laxmilaharī (=LL) Goddess Laxmī is praised in this poem in 41 verses in Śikhariṇi. only one verse is quoted as an example verse in RG, from this laharī.[17]This is a laborious work that the narrations of each and every parts of Laxmī is given here as the eye-corner ,shining nails ,ankles, deep and round navel, instances etc.,

6. Āsafavilāsa (=Āvi) This is an ākhyāyikā and from its first passage and two verses, we know that PR was the patronage of king Āsafa in the time of Jahangir and shah jehan. This is a very small one of two paragraphs and two verses only, hardly have any liteary merits.

7. Prāṇābharaṇa (=PB) There are two works in different names; one is prāṇābharaṇa and the other is jagadābharaṇa carrying similarities in almost all places. P.V. Kane gives the number of verses of this work i.e. prāṇābharaṇa to be 51 but V.A.R.Sashtri has 53 verses in his edition,[18] which is supported by A. Sarma in his later edition too.

We present here some interesting verses from both the works to show the similarity between the two.

A] The fourth line of second verse as;

"jāgartu kṣitimaṇḍale ciramiha Srīkāmarūpeśwaraḥ,
"jāgartu kṣitimaṇḍalopari jagatsingho dharādhīswaraḥ".

B] The third and fourth lines of fourth verse as:

"māṇikyāvalīkāntidanturatarairbhūṣā sahasrotkarai,
"rvin dhyāraṇyaguhāgṛhāvaniruhāstatkāla mullāsitāḥ".

(PB)

"nānābhuṣaṇa ratnajālajaṭilāstatkālamevā bhavan;
vindhya kṣmādharagandhamādanaguhāsambandhino bhūruhāḥ."

(JB)

C] The last half of fourth line of fifth verse as:

"*. . . . srīprāṇanārāyaṇah*". (PB)

"*. . . . Srīkarṇanārāyaṇaḥ.*" (JB)

"*. . . . dīlīdharāvallabhaḥ*". (RG)

D] The last part of fifteenth verse as:

"*. . . . viditaḥ śrīkāmarūpeśwaraḥ*". (PB)

"*. . . . vidito dillīdharāvallabhaḥ*". (RG)

It is composed in different metres and is a eulogy of king Prāṇābharaṇa.

8. Jagadābharaṇa (= JB) As we have mentioned, this work has close similarities with Prāṇābharaṇa with only change of names.

Interestingly, the last verse of Prāṇābharaṇa (except first line only) is fully changed in JB[19]

Further, the MS, of this work, in BORI, Pune have missing two verses as their nos, are 15 and 16. The Commentary on 26th verse is not also available.

9. Bhāminīvilāsa (=BV) Probably it is not a single work but, we can call it samullāsa following P. V. Kane and there are four samullāsa's in BV in all. They are,

a. prāstavika having 122 verses.

b. śṛngāra having 180 verses.

c. karuṇa having 19 verses.

d. śānta having 44 verses.

In different editions the number of verses vary, we give below a table to show variations of these numbers in different editions.

Sr.	*"Editions"*	*Anyokti*	*Sṛngāra*	*Karuṇa*	*Śanta*	*Total*
1.	M. A. Bergaine's edn. Paris, 127 1872		182	19	46	374
2.	Prof. Tarantha's edn. Calcutta, 126 1872	102	18	46	293	
3.	L. R. Vaidya's	129	183	19	45	376
4.	S. M. Paranjpe's	101	102	19	33	255
5.	B. G. Bal's edn.,	101	101	19	33	254
6.	N.S.P. Bombay	101	102	19	32	254
7.	Dr. H. D. Sarma's	101	-	-	33	134
8.	Prof. Aryendra Sarma's edn. Hyderabad, 1985	122	180	19	44	365

(N. B. This table is given at the page No. 66 of JP, Only the last edition of Prof. Aryendra Sarma, 1958, is added]

Dr. P. Sriramchandradu thinks that perhaps PR proposed to make out a separate book naming it Bhāminivalāsa, in which two samullāsa's i.e. śṛṅgāra and Karuṇa can be included. But latter on he joined another two Samullāsa'a and now there is no connection or similarity to justify PR's idea. Also Prāstavika and śānta have nothing to fulfill the title Bhāminī *vilāsa in* a proper manner.[20]

10. Citramimāṁsā khaṇḍana (=CMK) : This, CMK, is not an original but a critical study work of CM, the poetic work of AD, a treatise dealing with figures of sense. We can get easily, the date of PR, that comes through this point as, this CMK, a criticism work was made after RG. In this work, PR strictly examined all the aspects regarding figures and timingly criticised those views, made by AD, thoroughly. In RG, PR refuted foremost instance like rasadhvani concept and other topics related to his own views. Alike this, in CMK, PR surpassed on so many cases as they mostly contains figures. PR emphasized the system of Neo-logic of his criticism of AD's views.

11. Manoramākucamardana (mardini))=(Mano) This is a work of Sanskrit Grammer where Prauḍha manoramā, the work of Bhaṭṭoji Dikṣita (BD) is refuted by PR. PR also refused to accept some views of BD in his second book Śabdakaustubha. In this book PR refuted the BD's explanation of the sūtras very shaprly along with some other views.

There was a strong rivalarity between PR and BD. The teacher of grammar of PR was Seṣa-śrīkṛṣṇa, whose name already mentioned by PR in his introductory verses to RG at the very beginning. BD was also a pupil of same teacher. Here PR took his chance to criticise BD and clarified the wrong views, given by BD in his grammar book. Again, PR followed his predecessors style to revamp BD's quotations and some texts from oldest time to gather much more sūtra's and vārtikas to establish his highly approved points.

12. Yamunāvarṇanacampū (=YVC) This is a prose work in praise of Goddess Yamunā alike PR's another work namely AL in poetry. But the prose examples for RG given in two places. Till today, there is no MS. of this Campū kāvya.

13. & 14. Aśvagati Kāvya and śabdakaustubha sāṇottejani

These two works, made by PR is available, still scholars remarks that the second one was written at Baranasi;[21]

Besides these, we come across many anyokti's attributed to PR. However, no specific work is extant now. These verses are collected by A. Sharma in his PKS.[22]

REFERENCE

1. JP. pp. 1-10
2. HSP, pp.
3. JP, pp. 11-18
4. *"Rasagangādhare citramīmāsāyāṁ mayoditāḥ, ye doṣāstetra saṁkṣipya kathyante viduṣāṁ mude."* . . . . cf. HSP, p. 322.
5. *"Viseṣastu udaharaṇālaṁkāra prakarṇe rasagangā dharādavaseyaḥ,"* CMK. p. 12
6. JP, p. 29.
7. RG (intro, verses No. 5) 12.
8. *"mat nirmitāśca pañcalaharyo bhāvasya"* RG, p....386.
9. RG. BHU, 1963 pp. 97-98, cf. JP, p. 30.
10. cf. PKS, p. 31, verse, 3.
11. *ibid.* p. 32 (verse 9) p. 33 (verse 23)
12. *ibid.* p. 32. (verse 10)
13. *ibid.* p. 13.
    "mātaḥ ! pātakapātakāriṇī...ramāvallabhaḥ."
14. *ibid.* p. 13.
    "svarṇa steyaparanapeyarasikān pāthaḥkaṇāste yadi brahmaghnān gurutalpagānapi paritrātuṁ gṛhitavratāḥ prayaścittakulairalaṁ tadadhunā mātaḥ paretā dhipa. praūhā haṁkṛtihārihuṁkṛtimucāmegre tava Srotasāṁ
15. JP, p. 52. The verses with their serial nos, and the page nos. of RG. NSP edn. are also give in this page.

16. The contri...Sriramachandradu, Vol. 1, 1983, p. 21.
17. PKS, 1958, p. 26. (verse 30)
18. HSP. p. 323, 1.9.
    cf. jp, p. 58, 1.2.
    cf.PKS. 1958, pp. 111-20.
19. PKS, p. 120 (verse, 53).
20. The Contribution...P. Sriramachandradu
    Vol. 1. p. 24, 11. 7-11.
21. PKS, Introduction, p. x.
22. PKS, 1958, pp. 123-90.

1.2 RESEARCHES ALREADY DONE

We now undertake here to make a critical survey of the research works already done on RG. Though the overall study of this Text was covered by some scholars still, we feel that some aspects are yet to be studied. We now record some important studies on RG, followed by a critical review and evaluation of these works.

1. Kane, P. V.: History of Sanskrit poetics, Delhi, 2nd Edn., 1923 pp. 321-24.
2. Shastri, Y.M.: "Appayya Diksita's Age". JORM, Vol. II, part III-IV, July-Oct. 1928. pp.
3. Shastri, Y.M.: More about the age and life of Appayya Diksita", JORM, Vol. III, Part III, April-June 1929, pp. 140-60.
4. Sastri, V.A.R.: Jagannath Pandit, Annamalainagar, 1942.
5. Jani, R.J.: "Jagannath's Classification of Kāvyaprakāsa's definition and classificaiton of poetry", BVM, Vol. XII, 1951, pp. 22-25.
6. Tyagi, J.: Rasagaṅgādharahṛdayam, Varanasi, 1960.
7. Gupta, G. S.: "Paṅditarāja Jagannāth", Trip., Vol. VIII, No. 10, July 1963, pp. 33-36.
8. Athavale, R. B.: "Paṅditarājas Commentry on Kāvya-prakāsa"; JOIB, Vol. XVII, No. 2, Dec.-1967.
9. Athavale, R.B.: "New lights on the life of Paṅditarāja": ABORI, XLIX, Golden Jublee, Vol, 1968, pp. 415-20.
10. Dvivedi, R. C.: Principles of literary criticism, Delhi, 1969, pp. 108, 109, 116-19, 190-94, 250-51.
11. Vijayawardhan, G. : Outlines of Sanskrit Poetics, Varanasi, 1970, pp. 3, 23, 109, 113-14, 122.
12. Patwardhan, M.V. & Massan, J.L.: "The Rasagaṅgā-

dhara on the definition and sources of poetry": JOIB, XIX, No. 4, 1970, pp. 416-27.

13. De, S.K.: History of Sanskrit Poetics, 4th edition, 1971.
14. Maheswari, C.: Rasagaṅgādhara, ek adhyayana (Hindi): Jaipur, 1974.
15. Walimbe, Y.S.: "Paṅditarāja Jagannāth: Mind and Personality" ABORI, Vol. LV, Part I-IV, 1975, pp. 93-106.
16. Goswami, Nipa; "Jagannāth's definition of Literature: A Critique", VIJH 15(2) 1977, pp. 211-15.
17. Walimbe, R.S.: "Paṅditrāja Jagannāth's equipment as a poeticism, JASB, 52-53, 1977, 78, pp. 337-41.
18. Sriramchandradu, P.: The Contribution of Paṅditarāja Jagannāth to Sanskrit Poetics, (Vol I & II) Delhi, 1983.
19. Gangopadhyaya, A.L.: Paṅditarāja Jagannāh on aesthetic Problems, Calcutta, lst edn. 1984.
20. Patwardhan, M.V.: "Jagannāth on a novel variety of aprastutaprasaṅsā": ABORI, Vol. LXVI. (Part I-IV) 1986. pp. 153-59.
21. Bhattacarya, S.P.: "Studies in Indian Poetics, Rasa gaṅgādhara and three lost master pieces of alankāra Literature", Indian Studies, Past & Present, Delhi, 1st edn. 1964.
22. Shriramchandradu, P.: Panditaraja Jagannatha, Tr. into Hindi by Mithilesh Chaturvedi, Sahitya Academy, Delhi, 1st edn. 1992.
23. Dubley, S.: "The Concept of Guṇas as presented by Paṅditarāja Jagannāth in his rasagaṅgādhara". Glimpses of ancient Indian poetics, ed. by Pandey. S.K., and Jha, V.N., Satguru Publication, Delhi, 1993, pp. 119-26.
24. Gode, P.K.: "Jagannāth Myth" Soc. - XXXIIII, i, pp. 1-9.

25. Choudhary, J.B.: "Muslim Patronage to Sanskrit Learnings" pp. 46-71.

26. Sastri, V.A.R.: "Works, life of Panditaraj Jagannatha," Journal of Annamalai University, Vol. II; pp. 201-208.

    Vol. III, pp. 106-16, pp. 229-244.

    Vol. IV, pp. 149-158, pp. 262-274.

Editions and Translations of RG:

There are so many editions of RG and three translations into some other languages as;

1. RG : Pt. Panduranga/Durgaprasad, with Nagesh Bhatta's Commentary, NSP, Bombay, 1st edn. 1888.
2. RG : Gangadhara Shastri with Nagesh Bhatta's Commentry, NSP, Bombay, 1st edn. 1888.
3. RG : Pandurang Parab with Nagesh Bhatta's commentry, NSP, Bombay 2nd edn. 1894.
4. RG: Pandurang/Durgaprasad, with Nagesh Bhaṭṭa's commentry, NSP, Bombay, 2nd edn. 1894.
5. RG : Durgaprasad with Nagesh Bhaṭṭa's commentry and Saralāṭikā by Mathurānath Shastri, NSP, Bombay, 5th edn. 1939.
6. RG : Mathuranath Shastri with Nagesh Bhaṭṭa's commentry and Saralā by Manjuntha, NSP. Bombay 6th edn. 1947
7. RG : (Tr. into Marathi): R. B. Athavale; TMV, Pune, 1st edn. 1953.
8. RG : Madhusudan Shastri with Nagesh Bhaṭṭas commentry and own commentry namely Madhusudhani, BHU, Banaras, 1st edn. 1963.
9. RG: Badarinath Jha with own commentary Chandrikā. Chaukhamba Vidyabhavan, Varanasi, 2nd edn. 1964.

10. RG : Kedarnath Ojha, with own commentary rasacandrikā, Sampurnanada Skt. University. Varanasi, 1st edn. 1977.
11. RG: (Tr. into Hindi): Purushottama Sarma Caturvedi, Kashi - nāgari Prasarini Sabha, Kashi, 2nd edn. Saṁvat. 2012.
12. RG (Tr. into Oriya): Suryamani Rath. OSA, BBSR, 1st edn. 1990.

Apart from all these works and articles, in the books of History of Sanskrit literature and Sanskrit poetics, we came across some minor discussions on PR and RG, which are not recorded, these not being very specific.

Infact, these various contributions by various scholars cover only a general background of PR and his work RG. The details study based on PR's outstanding masterly theories are not done properly. And again, unlike V.A.R. Shastri and Ramachandradu, the most intellectual themes are not introduced by further scholars.

Among these works, V.A.R. Sastri, J. Tyagi, C. Maheswari, P. Sriramchandradu and A.L. Gangopadhyaya are some major contributors. Their valuable remarks are accepted by modern scholars, with certain reservations. Most cases they base, not entered to interfere into the basic problems on RG, due to the laborious task. C. Maheswari's Hindi edition is a thesis but it does not fulfill our demands.

a) V.A.R. Shastri's work i.e., Jagannāth Paṅdit is a valuable work which contains nine chapters including conclusion. At the very first chapter Shastri brings out a brief history of the age of PR. 2nd chapter covers PR's life history. Then he proves this author as a poet in third chapter, by gathering all literary works of PR. Then the other three chapters discuss the main theme as RG including the figures of speech and here he has mentioned only 17 figures out of 70, given in the RG by PR. PR and other writers on literary criticism is a new discovery by Sastri in his 7th chapter, where he has given names of other rhetoricians, those are criticised by PR. Those rhetoricians are as; Appayya Diksitia, Mammaṭa, Rājānaka Ruyyaka, Jatyaratha, Ratnākara or Sobhākara (whose works name is Alaṁkara Ratnākara), Ānandavardhan, Abhinavagupta, and Vidyādhara. Apart from these authors, PR also criticised and cited the names of other predecessors namely Bhāmaha, Daṇḍin, Vāmana, Udbhaṭa, Srivatsalāñchana and some unknown Commentators.

In the 8th Chapter Shastri also gives a fresh study on PR and his knowledge on Sanskrit Grammar, that PR thoroughly criticised or refuted Prauḍhamanoramā of BD. And finally, Sastri finishes his work with a short conclusion to this work.

b) Another valuable work on RG is a concise one made by J. Tyagi, which is written in a very simple Sanskrit and there he explains some aspects of RG, after following some earlier texts and studies only.

c) C. Maheswari's Thesis-cum-book is written in Hindi and named as "RG: eka adhyayan" and it runs upto 2nd part of RG. Basically, no commandable or authentic views are found in it. Most probably, Maheswari avoids the critical concepts to elaborate in detail and further, she was interested only in the study of figures of speech and that is why she gives a detailed study of that. This book starts with the analysis of the definition of poetry.

d) P. Sriramachandradu's work is a worthy one and outstanding contribution towards the study of RG. It is presented in two volumes, in the first volume there are five chapters excluding Introduction. In this introduction the author has given a short history on Sanskrit Poetics, the life and works of PR, personality and nature of PR and finally a general study on RG. Among these five chapters the first one deals with the definition of poetry with a historical development of these concepts. Second chapter discusses the five types of dhvani and the concept of rasa. The dhvani concept again takes place in fourth chapter. The third chapter discuss the various definitions, discussions of guṇa. Like this the fifth chapter gives a detailed study on Abhidhā, Lakṣ anā. This was a Ph.D. Thesis at first stage. In this work the author adds some new views on some aspects and the first volume covers upto the end of first part of RG. Alike this, the second one adds only figures of speech.

e) Anantalal Gangopadyaya's handy work is remarkable for its flawless editing. Here Gangopadhya puts some valuable suggestions as well as accepts some views, made by other rhetoricians to bring out PR's views in a positive result. This work also contains so many references, made by other rhetoricians, before PR and systemetic arrangement of the themes and thoughts of various scholars.

In the research papers, R.B. Athavale, Y.S. Walimbe S.P. Bhattacharya, and P.K. Gode hold some credit for their outstanding labourious researches on various aspects of RG.

Further, P.V. Kane, and S.K. De's History of Sanskrit poetics add some brief stories regarding PR and RG. Frankly speaking, these two authors made it easy for others to study further on PR and RG as well.

To make a flawless edition of RG, the study of various previous editions and translations is most essential and further, the role of variants is also remarkable. We, hereby, try to point out some variants after the end of the texts, whereever they occur. There are three translations of RG in three regional languages, where some new opinions are made by respective translators. Among them, the Hindi translation of P. Chaturvedi is good one. The Marathi translation, made by Athavale is not actually a translated work but a study. Again Dr. S. Rath's Oriya translation does not fulfill our demands due to its incapale ideas on RG and so many faults.

CHAPTER - II

CONTENTS OF RG

II.1 THE DEFINITION OF POETRY

Like other rhetoricians, PR draws his very first topic as the definition of poetry. Before coming to this, PR also discusses the purposes of poetry that are described by him as being represented by attainment of fame, achievement of transcendental delight and acquisition of favour from the emperor and supreme God.[1]

PR defines poetry as comprised of expression presenting a charming content. The question as to "what is a poetry?" has kept engaged the attention of all the scholars since the very beginning of the emergence of Sanskrit poetics. In the text book tradition of Sanskrit poetics, we met with a definition of poetry in Bhāmaha first[2] and in subsequent period it attended a commandable position at the time of Vidyānātha. Even as late as the time of PR, the problem of defining poetry remained significant and that is why PR, the last major author of Sanskrit poetics, narrates his own definition giving importance on the aspect of sound only. The various definitions of poetry given by various scholars differ, according to their conception of the major element in poetry. It is interesting to note that in RG, the author has given a systematic analysis; first, he gives his own theory on a particular topic with clarifications and then records the view of earlier rhetorician, in their proper places, whereever is necessary. He attempts a critical examination and finally justifies his theory with arguments. In the context of defining poetry, the same logic of interpretation is followed. PR defines poetry as: "ramaṇīyārtha pratipādakaḥ śabdaḥ kāvyam"; As can be noticed, in this definition, importance is given on sound only unlike others who give equal importance on sound and sense. In this context it would not be out of place to discuss on the concept of poetry from the point of view of historical development. In the work of Sanskrit poetics, we have several definitions of poetry and we can classify these definitions into two main groups. The first group comprises of theorists who give more importance to word and are called śabdavādins.[3] The second group give emphasis on both (sound) word and sense. According to them sound and sense together are equally important in poetry and they are termed as ubhayavādins.[4] Our author PR belongs to the first group to define poetry in terms of sound alone. We have more theorists who belong to this group.

PR's definition is very precise and is similar to the definition as given by Dandin. A matter of fact, Dandin's definition is not a full phrased definition. Because Dandin's definition of poetry is the arrangement of words expressive of desired sense. Here, we cannot declare it as a simple definition of poetry but can say it as the body or sarīra of a poetry. So indirectly he indicates towards making of a poetry through making the sarīra of a poetry. As one can see PR himself has given three more definitions with a view to clarify and make the definition free from any type of technical faults.

Generally three faults, namely, avyāpti, ativyāpti and asaṁbhava may involve in a definition. To avoid these faults, PR qualified his definition with some qualifications. In his definition, there are two parts: i.e. the main or the definition proper and the qualification to the definition. "Ramaṇīya" and "arthapratipādaka" are two given qualifications for 'Sabdaḥ kāvyam', which is the main definition. PR further adds three definitions. The first one runs as follows:

'Camatkārajanakabhāvanāviṣayārthapratipadakaḥ' Sabdatvam.'

Interestingly, there is no difference between the main and the first amplified definitions as it is shown in this diagram given below.

Definition	**1st modified definition**
1. ramaṇīya =	1. camatkārajanaka bhāvanāviṣaya
2. arthapratipādakaḥ =	2. arthapratipādakaḥ
3. Śabdaḥ =	3. sabdatvaṁ
4. Kāvyam =	4. Kāvyatvam

The critical view falls in the first sentence of both sides as ramanīya is interpreted as camatkārajanakabhāvanāviṣaya, where ramanīya is similar to these objects having pure aesthetic pleasure i.e., charm. Further, bhavanā, which comes after recollection of previous knowledge, gives the idea to the refined critic (reader) to choose a proper poetry and not an improper one like 'putraḥ te jātaḥ' etc.

The second amplified definition is nothing but the same as the first amplified definition.

After establishing his own view in general way, PR shows some unique ways to prove his own view. Before PR's definition, there were a large number of definitions of poetry by various rhetoricians. Therefore, PR has all those definitions before him, and he tries to incorporate the best, in or underlying all these definitions. PR's definition is applicable to all the poetries, including modern works and according to the text of the rhetoricians of any school.

As P.V. Kane rightly remarks: 'On the whole, Jagannātha's definition is preferable as it avoids all reference to debatable points.[5]

We have already noted that, to clarify one definition, PR adds three more definitions as they are modifications of the main definitions as they are modifications of the main definition. This is the general practice adopted by PR, throughout this text, to give a general definition and to come to a definite conclusion after examining the pros and cons of the subject with the help of the views of other rhetoricians. As PR promised to give his own views without taking others help,[6] now he gives this definition of poetry in its technical sense, carefully avoiding the three common defects of the definition. If the meaning of the word ramaṇīya in the qualification part of the definition is to be understood in the general way, the defect ativyāpti arises; for, statements like 'you are blessed with a son', 'A big fortune is awaiting you' etc., are sources of pleasure, yet they cannot come under the purview of a poetry. To avoid this, PR explains the ramaṇīyatā, as synonymous with 'lokottarāhlādajanakajñāna gocaratā'.

The pleasure that is derived from the above statement is only laukika or worldly pleasure.[7] Again PR makes the lokottaratā a synonym to camatkāratā, and accepts it to be a universal, to avoid the lack of comprehension.

As is seen above, PR is inclined to give prominance to sound only as the major aspect for a proper poetry. Therefore he finds out faults with his opponents views. In this context PR finds two definitions to declare them as defective definitions, the definitions from KP and SD are given here.

The defintion of KP as follows:

'tadadoṣau śabdārthau saguṇāvanalaṁkṛtī pūnaḥ kvāpi'.[8]

Here PR discusses the demerits in this definition of his predecessor, which is based on both sound and sense.

'Śabdārthau kāvyam' is the main part of the definition. If both sound and sense together comprises a poetry, then the logic behind composition of Veda etc., will face problems. So to avoid this type of fault, PR tells that the sound only plays a major role to compose poetry.

Defining poetry, in true term, is one of the greatest problem faced by literary critics and PR. the last original author criticises the theories of Mammaṭa here. According to PR, if poetry is accepted as of both word (sound) and sense, it is to be answered whether poetryness rests with sound and sense together (vyāsakta) or separately (paryāpta). Either of the alternatives, is untenable because in the first case i.e., in vyāsakta, such expressions like "the sentence of the verse is not a poetry" would have come into vogue, on the basis of the general rule that "one is not two". Alike this, the second alternative that two poetries will have to be accepted in one verse, therefore, PR concludes, the definition of a poetry to be defined technically in term of sound only.

Further, PR finds some other faults with the components of the definition. Those are: merits, figures of speech and free from the blemishes. PR tells that, there are some poetries like 'Uditaṁ maṇḍalaṁ vidhoḥ', 'gatostamarkaḥ' etc., which are devoid of any merit or figures of speech, but they are giving good ideas and hence falling under the purview of poetry. Here, the logical fault avyāpti takes place. The guṇatva and alaṁkāratva being non-comprehensive, they cannot be counted as proper poetries. Following Mammaṭa's own view; Merits are considered as the qualities of sentiment and figures of speech as its emblishments, then it is impossible to make association of these factors with the main body. The term adoṣau i.e., literary absence of faults, is also not proper in the definition. On this topic PR's discussion is remarkable.

To get support for his own definition, PR hopefully adds other definitions like "āsvādodbodhakaṁ kāvyam" etc. PR is of the view that any expression which is capable of producing aesthetic pleasure is poetry, be it suggestive of rasa, bhāva, vastu or alaṅkāra.

Now PR takes Viśvanātha's definition of poetry from SD for analysis. The definition recorded as follows: "Vākyaṁ rasātmakaṁ kāvyam".

This definition consists of sentiment only excluding vastu and alaṁkāra. PR, refutes this type of view given in SD, pointing out that it does not fulfill the necessary qualities. Further, this definition gives prominance to both sound and sense. But PR tells that fault of avyāptī cannot be avoided here; Because, this cannot include among poetries, such works which do not give predominance to the sentiment. PR says that such works should not be ignored as not being poetries, because many of the poetries of even great poets will have to be discarded as not being poetries, against the established convention. Like this PR concludes the refutation of his predecssors.

Interestingly, Mammaṭa's definition was refuted by Viśvanatha, earlier to PR in his SD.[9]

In the words of Dr. Raghavan "It is again on the basis of this camatkṛta, that Jagannatha gives his most comprehensive definition of poetry in his RG. Camatkāra, he says, is the super mundane, artistic delight brought about by the contemplation of beauty and poetry is such verbal expression as is the embodiment of an idea conveying such beauty.[10]

It may be observed that a poet has to have a perfect knowledge of the choice of words or the alaṁkāras, that he is using in his poetry. The presence of literary merits and the absence of poetic blemishes are the good qualities of a poetry. But too mch abundance of poetic embellishments is a mark of a poor characteristic of a poetry as excess of embellishment kills the original charm of a poetry.

The poet has to be very careful while beautifying his poetry with high poetic words and figures of speech like 'rāghvavirahajwālā samtāpita. etc. PR cites illustrations such as 'uditaṁ maṇḍalaṁ vidhoḥ', 'gatostamarkaḥ' etc., which are genuine poetries. Therefore before composition of a poetry by a certain poet, he should make his ideas very clear regarding his knowledge on poetic factors.

Before concluding it may be worth to remark that PR's definition of poetry is criticised and refuted by Négesh and by some modern scholars on sanskrit poetics namely Gangādharasashtri and Madhusudan Shastri. According to them PR does not hesitate to follow the group of ubhayavādin (i.e., sound and sense together) in his definition. Though PR's definition 'ramaṇīyārthapratipādakaḥ śabdaḥ kāvyam' is based on sound, ultimately it amounts to the same view of ubhayavādin's where the term śabda is qualified by ramanīyārthapratipādaka; due to the power of sense, the sound becomes the main object for poetry. The definition of PR is very original. Whatever is told by Daṇḍin as īṣṭārtha, by Vāmana as saundarya, by Kuntaka as lokottarālhāda etc., are same to ramaṇīyārtha of PR. Therefore, PR himself declares that ramaṇīyārtha is lokottarāthādajanaka. . etc. By repetition of knowledge or repeated reading of a poetry gives charm to a refined reader.

REFERENCES

1. tatra kīrtīparamālhādagururājadevatāprasadādyaneka prayojanakasya..., etc., RG. pp. 12-13.

2. śabdārthau sahitau kāvyam, kāvyā, 1.16.
3. Sabdavādi: Daṇḍin, Bhoja, Réjasekhara, Visvanāth, Jaydeva, Jagannath etc.
4. Ubhayavādi: Bhāmaha, Udbhaṭa, Rudraṭa, Vāmana, Mammaṭa, Vāgbhatta (I & II)
5. HSP, p. 353.
6. nirmāya nutanamudāharaṇa... etc., cf. RG, PP-10-11
7. p. Sriramchandradu, op cit., pp. 43-44.
8. KP, p. 14.
9. Vide SD, pp.18
10. Some concepts of alaṁkāra śāstra, p. 271.

II.2. THE CAUSE OF POETRY

After establishing his definition of poetry, PR takes the next major topic for discussion i.e. the cause of the poetry or the source of poetry.

According to PR, pratibhā is the unseen merit on one side and erudition (vyutpatti) and practice (abhyāsa) together on the other side which together lead for the strengthening of the poetic-talent. The predecessors of PR accepted that there are three causes behind poetic-talent. The three causes are:

a) intuition i.e., pratibhā,

b) erudition i.e., vyutpatti and

c) practice i.e., abhyāsa

All these three together help a poet to compose poetry. But PR strongly refutes this view saying that only intuition is the main cause, because the erudition and the practice only help to better the status of intuition or make the poet more powerful and more confident. But the intuition is there in him. No poet can compose poitry in the presence of only the erudition and the practice, if the poet lacks poetic talent. In order to prove this point, PR cites the example of those children who have acquired very little education have read very few books but have turned out to be great poets in their lives. Erudition and practice are totally absent in these but only due to intuition, they are able to compose good poetries. PR here tells that this is possible because of the main cause i.e., intuition (pratibhā) of their ancestors which has been transferred in those children. Who have got poetic talent with the help of constant practice and high erudition, are capable of composing good poetries. Thus, he proves his view by telling that one can become a great poet if he is having intuition only. But mere erudition and practice in the absence of the intuition can make no poet a great poet. Practice and erudition only help to strengthen the talent.

This concept i.e., kāvyahetu has been the major topic of discussion for almost all the rhetoricians. Therefore one has to admit that our rhetoricians are well-aware of this problem.

Among these rhetoricians, some are unanimous in constructing the case as three aspects and some others holding the intuition only as the cause. The difference lies only in accepting the relative superiority of pratibhā over the other two, or in ascribing equal importance to all the three qualities or in accepting the last two qualities as auxiliaries to the former. Thus we can divide the rhetoricians into three groups:

a) Those who give equal importance to all the three, each one being the cause of poetry separately,

b) Those accepting superiority of pratibhā over others which are helpful to it, and

c) Those who accept that pratibhā, vyutpatti and abhyāsa, all these three put together, are the source of poetry.[1]

Now, the forecoming discussions are notable to examine the natures of these three aspects. Pratibhā or poetic talent is otherwise known as śakti, which is well explained by various authors in similar terms. Bhaṭṭatauta, Abhinavgupta, both give long difinitions and others like Mammaṭa, Vāgbhaṭ a, Rudraṭa, Rājaśekhara etc. give verses to examine its nature. Bhaṭṭatauta writes as;

"Prajñānavanavonmeṣa śālinī pratibhā matā,
Tadanuprāṇanājivavarṇanānipuṇaḥ kaviḥ,
Tasya karmaṁ smṛtaṁ kāvyam,"

Abhinavagupta tells:

Pratibhā apūrvavastunirmāṇakṣamā prajñā.

On the nature or śakti or power of composing poetry, he further tells:

'śaktiḥ pratibhānaṁ varnanīyavastu viṣayanūtano llekha-śālitvam'.[2]

According to Mammata:

śaktiḥ kavitvavījarūpaḥ saṅkāraviśeṣaḥ.[3]

Vāgbhaṭṭa gives a new definition and tells that:

Pratibhā is sarvatomukhī.[4] Rudraṭa writes that *manasi sadā susamādhini visphuraṇamanekadhābhidyā, akliṣṭani ca padāni vibhānti yasyāmasau śaktiḥ, pratibhetya parairūktaḥ.*[5]

In *Kāvyamīmāmsā, Rājaśekhara says that 'yā śabda grāmamartha ... sā pratibhā.*[6]

According to some others pratibhā is the instinct, in not only men but also in animals and birds which alone is responsible for their peculiar capacities like building of their nests etc.

P. Sriramchandradu very neatly reproduces the views of several rhetoricians alongwith Mahimabhaṭṭa. Mahimabhaṭ ṭa explains. Pratibhā as the (Prajñā) stirred by a momentary contact with his own self of a poet whose mind is calmly concentrated on the 'śabda's' and 'arthas' appropriate for the rasa.

Rasānuguṇaśabdārthacintā stimitacetasaḥ,
Kṣaṇaṁ svarūpasapārśotthā prajñaiva
Pratibhā kaveḥ.
Sā hi cakṣurbhagavataḥ tṛtīyamiti gīyate
Yena sākṣāt karotyeṣa bhavānstraikālyavartinaḥ.[7]

Kuntaka narrates this poetic talent as the result of the development of Saṁskāras accumulated in the present and the previous births:- Prāktanādyatanasaṁskārapraudḥā pratibhā kācideva kavi śaktiḥ.[8]

Coming to the conclusion on poetic talent, all are accepting that śakti and pratibhā, both are identical except

Rājasekhara, who tells that the śakti is the root-cause of pratibhā. It is root cause of erudition also.

> *Viprasṛtiśca sā (śaktiḥ) pratibhavyutpattibhyāṁ,*
> *śaktikartṛkai hi prtibhā vyutpatti karmaṇī.*[9]

He writes :

a) Pratibhā is the natural instinct of a man, mainly inherited from his previous births,

b) It unfolds itself in the ever-new regions of understanding and imagination,

c) It is the genious of the poet culminating into the creation of things not familiar previously,

d) it gives the poet the capacity to give a form and local habitation to the things of mental creation and

e) It also presents the poet with words and senses and alaṁkāra's etc., suitable and helpful for the creation of fine poetry.[10]

Alike prathibhā, the second cause is vyutpatti or erudition. Rudraṭa, for the first time recognized its definition and to him, the eruditon is nothing else but the proper knowledge which arrives from the śāstras of various branches with the help of proper understanding.[11] Again Abhinavgupta in his locana, finds a place to say that vyutpatti helps the pratibhā by supporting discriminatory power in arranging the materials.[12]

Abhyāsa is the third and final factor for composition of a proper poetry. The practice of perfect knowledge to bring out a highly authentic poetry is very essential. Vāmana and Rudraṭa mainly lay out some good definitions on abhyāsa.[13]

From Bhāmaha to PR, all are accepting this (cause) concept with great interest and giving defintions for the cause behind the composition of poetry.

I) Daṇḍin makes it clear that there are three causes, which are pure poetic-talent, pure knowledge of Śāstras and high practice.[14]

II) 'Rudraṭa and Kuntaka follow the numbers given by Daṇḍin as śakti, erudition and practice.[15] For śakti, Rudraṭa further adds one verse containing the nature of this cause in his work.[16]

III) Vāmana, also admits these three numbers with different terms as loka, vidyā and prakīrṇa[17]

IV) Mammaṭa highly utilised these above statements later on and put three as the cause.[18]

V) Rājaśekhara makes it two types after giving a definition and tells that pratibha stays in two hearts i.e., the talent for poet is kārayitrī and for a refined critic is bhāvayitri[19]

VI) In the vṛtti of KP, there is an instance to know what is śakti i.e., poetic talent.[20] Rājasekhara again finds that Maṅgala[21] was the first ever person to recognise practices as the only cause. Later on this view is refuted automatically due to the authorship of Vālmikī whose first work Rāmāyaṇa became so popular, without any practice by the author. So, above all PR's findings are as best, as the natural and poetic talent is supported by deep erudition and high practice only.

We conclude our discussion by quoting the remarks on pratibhā by P. Sriramchandradu: At the very outset, PR says that only pratibhā is the root-cause of poetry. He defines pratibhā as the quick presence of words and senses useful for the composition of kāvya.[22] Further the pratibha is the result of either some adṛṣṭa, an unknown cause, the grace of Gods or great men (which may be of the previous birth or present one) or of peculiar vyutpatti and abhyāsa. Thus, though being a pratibhāvādin, PR gives a relatively more important place to Vyutpatti and abhyāsa.[23] Interestingly, Nāgesh makes this erudition etc., only as sahakārikāraṇas.[24]

REFERENCES

1. CPRSP. I. p. 57.
2. locana. p. 12, p. 317.
3. KP. p. 8.
4. Vāg. p. 4.
5. Ru. Kāv. p. 6.
6. KM. P. 26-27.
7. *ibid*. p. 452-53
8. CPRSP, p. 59, cf. VJ (kuntaka) p. 107.
9. Kāvyamimāmsa p.26.
10. CPRSP. p. 59.
11. Ru. Kāv. p. 6
12. Locana - p. 317.
13. KSV, p. 10-11, cf. Ru. Kāv. p. 20.
14. KA. 1-103.
15. Ru. Kāv. 1.14; cf. VJ 1-24
16. *ibid*. 1.15
17. KSV. 1.3.1. & 1.3.11.
18. KP. 1.3.
19. KP. (4th Chapter)
20. KP (Vṛtti). 1.3.
21. Abhyāsaḥ iti mangalaḥ, KM.
22. CPRSP. p. 64, cf. RG p. 9.
23. *ibid*. p. 64.
24. Marmaprakāśa Comm.

II. 3 THE DIVISION (CLASSIFICATION) OF POETRY

After describing the cause of poetry, now PR describes the issue of the proper divisions of the poetry. It is clear that from Bhāmaha, this issue was stressed seriously and later on other rhetoricians also added some important aspects to re-place it in a proper manner. Among these rhetoricians, some like Ānandavardhana, Mammaṭa Visvanātha and PR etc., were important for their contributions.

The hisotry of classification of the poetry is started from Bhāmaha and he further gave a new light on this concept as, we can divide the poetry into many groups on different counts. A poetry can be separated on so many ground. Therefore, his (Bhāmaha's) classification of the poetry is not only for rhetoricians in particular but for any writer on Sanskrit in general.

Bhāmaha's classification was basically two types; according to composition of poetry ie.e., gadyakāvya and padyakāvya. Secondly, according to languages, there are three types of poetry i.e., saṁskṛta, prākṛta and apabhraṁsa. Again, based on the theme, four types are mentioned by Bhāmaha as devādicaritaniṣṭha, utpādyaniṣṭha, kālāśrayī and śāstrāśrayī. Another division based on its construction is also available like sargabandha, abhineyārtha, ākhyāyīkā, kathā and anibaddha.

Sargabandha type poetry, having so many chapters or sargas like RV etc., and abhineyārtha is alike drama. Both kathā and ākhyāyīkā are prose works like Kādambarī etc. Anibaddha type poetry is free from each other, written in verse style like nitiśataka etc.

Bhamaha's calssification is only based on the external aspects and from the time of Ānandvardhana, the remaining rhetoricians turned towards internal aspects to find out some proper divisions.

Ānandavardhana and Mammaṭa divided poetry into three groups namely uttama, madhyama and adhama, where Dhvani, sub-ordinate dhvani and citra poetries are revealed in these groups. Further Mammaṭa's Citra group i.e., third variety of the poetry faced another division with two names as śabdacitra and arthacitra. This style was fully supported by others excluding Viśvanātha and PR.

Viśvanātha firmly rejected third type of poetry, made by Mammaṭa with the proper arguments and claimed only two types of poetry.

A newly combined varieties was laid down by PR and uttomottama group was propounded there in. For establishing this group, PR showed so many positive grounds and further he refused to accept one "fifth" group as adhamādhama. He claimed that adhama is the lowest grade of the poetry and adhamādhama alike uttamottama is not required.

After mentioning four types of poetry, PR rules out one by one on his way and refuted AD's view two times. To establish his own view, PR, took help of Dhvanyāloka and Vyaktiviveka and very shaprly, told that the examples given by AD is far away from the main issues and not proper to count them in this context.

PR's idea on refutation of fifth variety is also remarkable. He further added that if in any case, the poetry, lacking any charm or beauty, can be included in fourth variety instead of creation of a fifth variety as adhamādhama.

According to madhusudana Shastri, if fifth varieity is needed, then another two varieties i.e., sixth and seventh even an eighth variety also necessary following the importance of word. The sixth variety is for, where the charm of sense is fully visualised through charm of word and the seventh variety is for, where charm of sense is lacking the charm of word.[1]

Now, we have to re-examine, the success of PR's interpretation of varieties in a new style. Visvanatha rejected citra variety as a separate poetry. This stand of Visvanatha is justified to some extant in view of his definition of poetry. Inspite of all that is written by him, Visanatha's classification does not seem to be in conformity with his definition, for, once he accepts guṇibhūtavyaṅgya as a variety of poetry, which cannot be rasapradhāna and thus "rasātmaka" is not contracting his own definition. That is why only Mammaṭa's classification, which can claim the general support of Dhvanikāra has been popular with later rhetoricians, except our present author PR.[2] Among these four varieties, uttamottama is frist one. According to PR, all varieties deserve their proper interpretation and that is why, following the tradition, he narrates all these in a systematic way. In this process the views of some predecessors are strongly refuted. Mammaṭa, AD, Visvanāha, were three, those are strongly criticised for their previous definitions and illustrative verses in their respective works.

The first one i.e., uttamottama, is almost similar to the definition of Ānandavardhana and Mammaṭa. But PR additionally holds as a major factor. For that, he gives importance to camatkāra at every places. Prof. P. Srīrama-chandradu remarks: this camatkāra was recognized by Ānandavardhan and this credit goes to him. PR only follows later on to this term.[3] PR says camatkāra as the source of poetry for the term as Kāmapi. Here due to kāmapi, the atigūḍhavyaṅgya and sphuṭavyaṅgya which are out of any beauty, are devoid from this first variety.

Further, the fault of ativyāpti is avoided by using the

phrase gunibhāvitātmānau. Therefore all the Dhavanis of sentiment, rasābhāsa and basic moods etc., come under this variety. For this variety, PR cites one beautiful example as "sayitā savidheapya . . ."[4] Here PR brings some objections, which would be raised by his successors, and clearly puts them in such a way that, no further questions should be asked.

In this context, the example verse given by AD is strongly criticised with a detail discussion and PR claims that the verse given by AD is not only full of faults but is unnecessary to count as a poetry of uttamottama variety.

In uttama i.e., second variety of poetry, PR dras a line of distinction between these first and second varieties by telling that the camatkāra, caused by the uttamottama is greater than the one caused by the uttama, for, the vyaṅgya is pradhāna in the one and is not pradhāna in the other. Thus the prādhānya or otherwise of the vyṅgya and the ādhikya or the alpatā of camatkāra seem to be inter related, but ultimately camatkāra alone has to decide the status (position) of the vyaṅgyārtha and vācyārtha, i.e. anayorbhedayoranap. . . etc.[5]

Further, it should be understood that what is given as prādhyānyāprādhānyābhyām is of camatkāra but not of vyaṅgya. This, however, to be realised by experienced readers (i.e. refined critics).

Some modern scholars find it difficult to co-operate with the vews of PR. Badarīnath Jhā's view in this context goes little ahead after saying that 'there is some kind of difference like pradhānibhūtavyāṅgya and guṇibhūtavyaṅgya between the uttamottama and uttama and feels that PR's writing goes against the opinion of Ānandavardhana. By Ānanadavardhana, it is said that "cārūtvo (camatkāra) tkarṣa nibandhanā hi *vācyavyaṅgyagoḥ* prādhānyavivakṣa" Moreover, the concept camatkāra is getting a wider scope because it can be associated with vācya and śabda etc.[6] Further, Badarināth Jha, finds another fault with PR's findings in the cases of Kāvyas of sandigdha and tulya-prādhānya.

Alike above two varieites, the third one i.e., madhyama is also well narrated by PR. Under this variety the poetics having the figures of speech like utprekṣā comes.

In the context of examples for these four poetries, PR strongly finds faults with AD in the famous verse," niśeṣ acyuta. . . etc."[7]

Here, PR tells in two grounds that it is not a proper poetry to give an example for uttama poetry.

He finds two faults namely,

a) it is against the accepted theories of ancient rhetoricians like Ānandavardhana and Mammaṭa, and

b) it is also beyond proper justification.

PR concludes his discussion by making the remakrs that whatever he has said on this point is based on the view of the ancient rhetorician;

Ityālaṁkārikasiddhānta niṣkarṣaḥ.[8]

REFERENCES

1. RG (comm. Madhusudanī) p. 96.
2. CPRSP. pp. 68-69.
3. *ibid.*, p. 70.
4. RG. p. 64.
5. CPRSP. p. 71, cf. RG. 89
6. *ibid.*, pp. 71-72.
7. CM. P. 2. Cf. R.G. 72.
8. RG. p. 84.

II. 4 THE CONCEPT OF RASA

The most interesting and important concept in entire Sanskrit Poetics is the concept of rasa, which PR takes off for analysis after the discussion of the definition of poetry. His treatment of rasa is more significant in the sense that his work flourished in a time when the theory of rasa was well developed. Thus, he had before him a stupendous task of analysing the theory. PR has quoted the views of other eleven rhetoricians beginning with Bharata.[1] Nandikeśwara was the first ever writer on rasa, who is known to us by a mere reference made by Rajaśekhara in his KM, for no work of Nandikeswara is available and nothing specific is known on his view of rasa theory. The next rhetorician to have written on rasa theory was Bharata. In the sixth chapter of NŚ, the theory of rasa explained. After NŚ, Bhāmaha, Daṇḍin, Udbhaṭṭ, Vāmana, Rudraṭa etc., accept this theory of Bharata. Vāmana had nothing to add to this theory of rasa of Bharata and therefore may be he includes rasa with guṇa. However, Rudr-aṭa, for the first time has given an independent position to rasa amongst the text book writers, in his work. Bharata accepted eight rasa and later on its number increased upto ten. Rudraṭa remarks that Sānta and Preyān both are to be counted as rasas. Further the Nirveda etc, which are transitory moods, can be counted as separate rasa according to him.

Then after defining the rasa, now PR quotes many views including four views, that of Abhinavagupta[2] (and Mammaṭa), Bhaṭṭanāyaka[3], Bhaṭṭalolaṭa[4] and Śrī śaṅkuka.[5] Overall there are eleven views. Some say that rasa is produced when the permanent mood is associated with other moods. Bharata explains that rasa is a laukikavastu which is like a pākarasa. By the help of some condiments of different tastes, the extraordinary taste comes out. Like this, the nātyarasa comes by the mixture of moods with permanent mood. Here the permanent mood transferred to rasa when it is associated with other moods.[6]

PR further declares at the very beginning that Rasadhvani is most powerful than other dhvanis and that is why he takes up this concept with great interest excluding other four varieties namely vastudhvani, alaṁkāradhvani, arthāntarasaṃkramitavāchya and atyantatiraskṛtavācya.[7] For this, the definition looks like unending and with the help of many a logical terms the rasa is defined.

PR records eleven different interpretations of rasa attributed the opponents including the four we have already quoted.[8] To elaborate this:

1. According to Abhinava and Mammaṭa, rasa is that permanent mood, which is associated with other moods at the time of pure knowledge, which is free from all types of ignorances i.e. ajñānarūpa.[9]
2. Bhaṭṭanāyaka indirectly follows the previous view but a little about changed, as especially a bhāvanā should be included, to get rasa.
3. Some modern scholars are accepting as; the actor in a drama etc., (dṛśyakāvya) or poet in a poetry (Śravyakāvya) are creating sentimental conditions for audiences or readers respectively. To these conditions, if we rearrange with the help of some moods like vibhāva etc. then rasa will take place.[10]
4. Others are viewing that rasa is not at all suggestive or out of speech. We can manage to reach to rasa through the illusion, as thinking that the actress acting in the role of Śakuntalā is real Śakuntalā. Here, the imaginary knowledge is rasa only.[11]

5. Whatever is staying in the actors like Duśyanta etc, that mental condition is called as rasa.
6. When by the help of anumāna one feels that the real one is the same as the actor, then rasa produces.[12]
7. Vibhāva, anubhāva and vyabhicāribhāvas jointly called as rasa.[13]
8. Which one is most charming among these three bhāvas is called as rasa and again, if this charm does not stay with any of these three moods then all are disqualified to be named as rasa.
9. Rethinking of vibhāva is rasa.
10. Rethinking of anubhāva is rasa and
11. Rethinking of vyabhicāribhāva is rasa.

Mostly these possible interpretations of rasa as presented by PR are imagined by him, do not belong to any rhetoricians as such.

Now the most intelligent theory for rasa, developed by Bharata is applied with these all new theories for comparison. After a brief study on this issue PR tries to bring out the originality of these rasas in special manner. He quotes the verse of his predecessor as;

> *"Śṛṅgāraḥ karuṇaḥ śānto raudro vīrodbhutastathā,*
> *hāsyo bhayānakaścaiva bībhatsaśceti te nava".*

and pionts out the fixed number of rasas as nine. To accept śanta as separate rasa, he further gives some possetive clues to make his views more convincing.[14] For these nine rasas, nine permanent moods are there.[15] The positions and conditions of these permanent moods are well discussed in the concept of bhāva. The details about these nine rasas are also well narrated in their proper places during the study of the text. However, these nine rasas need a secondary study and threfore we are discussing them in brief.

Śṛṅgārarasa is of two types namely saṁbhoga and vipralaṁbha. The former one is due to the presence of rati or love and the latter one is due to the sepration of the couple. PR has defined and explained it by suitable illustration as : 'śayitā savidhepyanīśvarā etc.' Here PR has quoted the view of AD from his CM on śṛṅgāra and has refuted it.

The second one in order is karuṇa having śoka as its permanent mood, is described. Then he takes śāntarasa, raudrarasa etc. for discussion in brief.

The vīrarasa is given some prominence in RG. First PR devides it into four types, namely, dāna, dayā, yuddha and dharma. He explains these by suitable illustrations. Following to this type of divisions of vīrarasa as made by PR, one can claim to count some more varieties as satyavīra, pāṇḍityavīra, kṣamāvīra, balavīra etc. But PR strongly refutes those objections raised by opponents showing their impossibility of rasatva in those verses.[16]

In adbhutarasa, PR quotes the example verse of Mammaṭa and has refuted it as an example of this rasa,[17] after giving his own view on this.[18] For hāsyarasa, it seems that PR has adopted the view of his predecessor on the nature and division of this rasa.[19] The six separate groups of laughing according to the qualities of various people is given in detail. For uttama, madhyama and adhama people, these six groups of laughing is well mentioned.

The bhayānakarasa and bibhatsarasa are explained briefly in RG.

Before concluding PR makes the following point; rasadhvani and rasālaṁkāra both are quite different; where rasa is prominent it is rasadhvani and when rasa becomes subordinate it is rasālaṁkara.[20] Some objections on this account are quoted and refuted as well.[21]

The number of rasas, as we have already stated earlier, is fixed. Bhakti is described as a rasa which is not true. Because, it is a transitory mood or bhāva. Bhakti arises due to the proper devotion to God. It is not quite same with Śāntarasa.

He also talks about the supporting and conflicting rasas for each other. Among them, vīra and śṛṅgāra. śṛṅgāra and hāsya, vīra and adbhuta, vīra and raudra, śṛṅgāra and adbhuta are supportive of each other. Those, conflicting rasas are; śṛṅgāra and bibhatsa, śṛṅgāra and karuṇa, vīra and bhayānaka, śānta and raudra, and śānta and śṛṅgāra.

On the virodha i.e., confliction between two or more than two sentiments, PR rightly marks that this is of two types as sthitivirodha and jñānavirodha[22].

Further, the poetic blemishes related to rasas as well as to poetry are not fully explained by PR in this work. Only a brief note on rasadoṣa is given. To avoid these blemishes, some prose styled examples are also mentioned.

In this way, this large chapter on rasa comes to an end. It may be stated here that the style of adopting rasa and doṣa by PR is followed and accepted, to be sound and logical, by various modern scholars on Sanskrit poetics.

REFERENCES

1. RG, pp. 68-69.
2. 'Tathā cāhuḥ—vyaktaḥ sa tairvibhāvādaiḥ. . . ' *ibid*, pp. 70-76.
3. *ibid*, 'Tāṭasthyena rasapratītāvanāsvādyatvaṁ . . .'pp. 76-81.

4. *ibid.*, 'kāvye nāṭye ca . . .' pp. 83-86.
5. *ibid.*, 'vyañyjanavyāpāra . . . pp. 86-86.
6. NŚ, VI. 7.
7. evaṁ pancātmake dhvanau. . . etc., RG, p. 99.
8. See f.n. 2,3,4 and 5.
9. RG, pp. 107/121.
10. *ibid.*, pp. 131-140.
11. *ibid.*, pp. 140-146.
12. *ibid.*, pp. 148-149.
13. *ibid.*, p. 149.
14. *ibid.*, p. 153.
15. *ibid.*, p. 156.
16. vastutastu bahavo vīrarasasya . . . etc. *ibid.*, 188-191.
17. Citraṁ Mahāneṣa etc.' *ibid*, p. 193.
18. *ibid.*, p. 191-192.
19. *ibid.*, p. 194.
20. *ibid.*, p. 199.
21. *ibid.*, pp. 199-201.
22. *ibid.*, p. 204.

II. 5 THE POETIC-MERIT (GUṆA) AND BLEMISH (DOṢA)

The next important topic in RG is the concept of Guṇa i.e., poetic merit. PR lays down certain broad principles to avoid the improperness in sentiments and in their combination etc. In poetic studies, this concept is as old as that of the alaṅkāra sāstra itself and is studied in the context of merits. The guṇa, having two groups in general, come across a very long way with new interpretations by different writers. That is why the concept of guṇa has undergone considerable changes. In NŚ, this kāvyaguṇa occurs and perhaps this is the first extended work of mention, with ten varieties.[1] Later on, this guṇa was divided into three categories i.e., śabdaguṇa, arthaguṇa and ubhayaguna.

Bhāmaha accepted only three guṇas – mādhurya, prasāda and ojas. Some rhetoricians like Bharata, Daṇḍin, Vāmana[2] accepted ten guṇas for artha. Ānandavardhana, Mammaṭa and some others have accepted Bhāmaha's theory.[3]

Vāmana increased this number to twenty by accepting ten śabda guṇas and ten artha guṇas. According to him, guṇas produce beauty in poetry whereas the alaṅkaras help in increasing it. Further he says that even without alaṅkāras, the guṇas are capable of producing beauty in a poetry. But the alaṅkāras cannot have independent existence and threfore he calls the guṇas as nityas.[4] Vāmana, the first systematic writer on Indian poetics draws hugely in elaborating the guṇa doctrine in his KSV. Further in KA, Daṇḍin's view points on guṇa doctrine are very much clear from his definitions and illustrations. Any way, we will present the clear picture of this concept after giving the views of PR.

In RG, a detailed study on merit is given by PR where the importance of guṇas for sentiments is well narrated.

According to PR, merits are conductive through the combination of selected letter, words and phrases to the development of sentiments. This combination depends on the poetic merits both of word and sense. This is duly propounded by Ānandavardhan about guṇa and combination in the poetry as: guṇānāṁ. . . vācyayoḥ."[5]

Abhinavagupta, in his locana, comments that the three merits, namely, mādhurya, ojas and prasāda are nothing else but the cittavṛttis i.e., druti, dīpti and vikāsa. Against this view, PR holds that guṇas rest in sentiments and produce cittavṛttis; hence cannot be identical with it.

Following the statement given by Abhinava, mādhurya and dīpti are opposed to each other and as such, mādhurya exists in karuṇa, vipralaṁbhaśṛṅgāra and saṁbhogaśṛṇgāra, while dīpti exists in raudra, vīra and adbhuta. These existences of madhūrya is in an increasing order. In the case of hāsya, both mādhurya and dīpti exist equally. In śāntarasa, varying with conditions, both are found. And prasāda is the vitally important guṇa in the nine sentiments.[6]

But here in RG, Panditarāja clearly gives ten merits for word and sense separately, which was expounded by Daṇḍin and other predecessors.[7]

These ten merits for word and sense are : ślesa, prasāda, samatā, mādhurya, sukumāratā, arthavyakti, udāratā, oja, kānti and samādhi. For each one, the definitions according to word and sense are fully different.

At the very first definition of ślesa in word section, PR supports his predecessor's view on this context after reproducing the former's definition.[8] Interestingly, PR records the view of some commentators of KP and has refuted those, particularly on the merit namely udārata.[9]

He tells that vikaṭatā, which is only the movement of

words is not correct. Here, no 'oja, at all is there. Further, having 'oja' there is no charm at all. The refined readers should not realise this type of movement of words. Instead of 'oja', there is a chance to call it mādhurya. Like this type of argument, the total chapter of poetic merit comes to an end. Before this, some more suggestions are laid by PR. Bhoja, in his work SKB has enumerated as many as 48 guṇas; 24 ṣabdaguṇas and 24 arthaguṇas. Bhoja also accepts, for the first time, that besides these two varieties, one special kind of merit called as vaiśeṣika guṇas.[10] Interestingly Vidyānāth, a follower of Bhoja, mentions only 24 guṇas instead of 48. In Pratāparudrīya, he says that guṇas sould not be accepted as pertaining to artha also, because they are mainly considered to be dharma of Sanghaṭana.[11]

Further, an interesting point to note is that Vāmana accepts doṣas as guṇābhāvarupā in the sense that the opposite of doṣas are guṇas.[12] According to PR, foolishness is a doṣa and vidyā or knowledge may be negation of such doṣa. Here vidyā is not guṇa.[13] Thus guṇas are not necessarily the absence of doṣas.

Whatever may be, rhetoricians like Daṇḍin, Bhāmaha etc., think that these poetic merits are a kind of figures of speech and especially Daṇḍin goes a little ahead to declare that poetic merits are same as to alaṅkāras. Vāmana, is the only such author who has tried his best to make a clear distinction among these poetic merits and alaṅkāras.

In this context, it is notable that PR first states the views of Mammaṭa, regarding guṇa and its three varieties in his RG namely mādhurya, oja and prasāda. After giving a brief analysis on this, PR proceeds to examine this view. Are guṇas the real dharma of the sentiment? This question is raised by PR only to keep the tradition of his ancient authors and strongly replies that due to lack of proper evidence, this view cannot be accepted. Further, these guṇas are also not the dharmas of the upādhis of the sentiments.[14]

Whatever is told in rasacandrikā, the commentary on RG that 'kāvyaprayojya camatkṛtiprayojakatātvaṁ guṇatvaṁ' is very clear to note that, the poetic merit is only the source for a poetry with addition to its proper beautification.[15]

In RG, after giving all the theories of his predecessors, now PR puts his own remarks telling that there are 20 merits and subject to equal names for both śabda and artha groups, which is same as mentioned by Mammaṭa. PR 'explains all the ten 'sabda guṇas with proper definitions with their necessary examples, followed by the artha guṅas.

Again PR clearly points out that out of these given numbers of merit, some can be included with the famous three guṇas. For example, śleṣa, prasāda, udāratā and samādhi can be included with oja guṇa.[16]

A detailed comparison of merits of Vāmana, Siddhacandragaṇī and PR is given in the book of Prof. P. Sriramchandradu.[17] Further this author finds that nothing new is invented by PR for this concept. Only the amplification of his predicessors theories are reproduced with a new extant by PR. On this, the remarks of P.C. Lahari is worth quoting.

The blemishes (Doṣa)

After establishing the need of merits in a poetry, PR discusses the poetic blemishes. Unlike others, PR has not discussed the concept of doṣa in detail. Also he has not attempted a historical analysis of this concept. He makes a passing remark on this and says that the faults should be rejected from the poetry.[18] Then follows a short discussion on Rasa doṣas.

For example, kakubhasurabhi, vitatayātra etc. Here, ka, ta are coming twice each and this is one type of aśravya.

Further adhikadoṣa, where the example is: 'vitatatarastarureṣa bhāti bhumau'. Like these instances, there are many a type of blemishes to be avoided.

REFERENCES

1. NS. XVII. 69.
2. cf. KA. cf. KSV.
3. DA. cf. KP.
4. KSC
5. DA III. 6,
6. RG, p. 137.
7. KA. I. 43. cf. RG. p. 235.
8. 'sliṣṭamaspaṣṭa. . .' RG, p. 235.
9. *ibid.*, 'padānāṁ nṛtyatprāyat . . .' p. 240-241.
10. ŚKB.
11. Pratāp.
12. KSV.
13. RG.
14. RG. Text.
15. RG. p. 251.
16. CPRSP. pp. 176-182.
17. Concept . . ., p. 265-268.
18. RG. pp. 214-22.

II. 6 THE MOOD (BHĀVA)

The treatment of bhāva is one of the most important chapter of RG, where the views and the theories of the predecessors of PR are referred to, by reproducing those. PR has made a critical analysis as used and after refuting the views opposed his theory and gave his own opinion on bhāva. The discussion of bhāva starts with the discussion on rasa, where PR analysed nine sthāyibhāvas corresponding to nine rasas. Again after a gap of two chapters i.e., after discussing guṇa and doṣa, he resumes the discussion of bhāvas. Here, he discusses vibhāvas, anubhāvas and vyabhicāribhavaṣ etc. We have already stated that invariably his discussions have followed the method of recording the views of his predecessors. Sometimes some theories which are mostly imagined by himself in the form of doubt, he quotes by mentioning 'ityapare', 'ityanye' etc., and refutes those leading to the establishment of his own view.

If we present the contents of bhāva in the line of PR we see that he defines sthāyibhāvas first.[1] Then he enumerates nine sthāyi (bhāvas) and discusses various theories with regard to the relation between sthāyibhāvas and rasas. Here also, the views of his predecessors are quoted and analysed followed by the presentation of his own few points.

Sthāyibhāvas:

This is a vast topic and PR has devoted so many pages for discussing this. The themes of the bhāvas need a critical study to bring out its originality and significance in the enjoyment of rasa. According to PR, first of all, the bhāva is called as sthāyibhāva or permanent mood and equal in number with the rasa. That is why nine permanent moods are reserved separately for nine rasas.

The nine sthāyibhāvas are: rati, śoka, nirveda, krodha,

utsāha, vismaya, hāsa, bhaya and jugupsā correspond to the nine rasas namely; śṛṅgāra, karuṇa, śānta, raudra, vīra, adbhuta, hāsya, bhayānaka and bībhatsa.

The position of the sthāyibhāvas with the rasas are well narrated by the predecessors of PR.[2] Normally this type of narration or detailed treament on bhāvas is not found in any other poetic works till the time of PR, though Mammaṭa has discussed it in some detail.

The permanent mood exists till the existence of the sentiment i.e. rasa forever, permanently and the other moods coexist with this also. PR refutes the views of those who hold that rasa is diferent from sthāyibhāva.[3]

A good example is quoted by PR to show the difference between sthāyibhāva and vyabhicāribhāva in RG from the work namely SR.[4] PR further adds that, in a poetry having heroism as main sentiment, the sthāyibhāva namely anger (Krodha) is not a permanent mood but a transitory mood. Same are the cases with raudra rasa and utsāha mood and with sṛngāra rasa and laughing (hāsya) mood. Now in RG, the author has given nine sthāyibhāvas starting with the topic of rati. Here, for the love sentiment, the rati or pleasure is a permanent mood. That is the love, where the mental condition of a person or a state of mind is always laying with some objects like thinking of the relation of a couple etc. If this is holding rati as his sthāyibhāva, then in other positions also rati can be counted as a permanent mood. To avoid such problems, PR writes that this mood namely rati becomes a transitory mood when it contains to the Teacher, God or Son etc. When it becomes a cause for production of the rasa it is called as vibhāva, where the cause is the affection for Teacher, God, Son etc., then rati cannot be a sthāyibhāva but a vyabhicāri-bhāva.

For the third sentiment i.e. śānta, the nirveda is a sthāyibhāva. It takes place when the state of mind renounces the worldly objects, having a proper knowledge on good and bad themes and having a taste of mental power to judge the eternal and non-eternal objects. But this nirveda or detachment becomes a transitory mood when it comes from the quarrellings of a house matter.

Alike these two sthāyibhāvas the remainings are well narrated stating that this permanent mood have some assistants and by the help of these other assistants, the permanent mood spreads all over.

Now PR comes to the discussion of vibhāva and anubhāva excluding vyabhicāribhāva. A very short definition is given here for the concept of vibhāva.[6] In Madhusudani, it is commented as . . . yā ratiniṣṭā kāryatā, tādṛśakāryatānirūpitā yā tādātmya saṁbandhāvacchinnā kāraṇatā, tādṛśakārṇatāvatvaṁ vibhāvatvaṁ iti.[7] Further, for the cases of anubhāva and vyabhicāribhāva, both PR's and Madhusudani's definitions are pointed out.[8]

These vibhāvas, anubhāvas and vyabhicāribhāvas are fully noticed in these several instances, quoted for the rasas in this text. The definition of vyabhicā ribhāva is referred to all thiry four varieties, which are described after the narration of rasabheda, rasadoṣa, guṇa and its varieties.

Vyabhicāribhāva: PR's definition of bhāva is as follows: "vibhāvādivyajyamānaharṣādyanyatamatvaṁ tattvaṁ" i.e. the transitory mood is an object suggested by vibhāva etc, being like harṣa etc. To clarify his own definition, PR quotes the definition from KP; vyabhicāryanjito bhāvah.[9]

Then PR quotes three more different definitions of bhāva. It seems that the first one is more preferred by PR.[10] They are:

a) Harṣādināṁ ca sāmājikagatānāmeva sthāyibhāva-nyāyenā bhivyaktiḥ,

b) Sāpi rasanyayeneti kecit and

c) Vyaṅgyāntaranyāyenetyapare manyante.

It may be observed that the real exponants of these, are yet to be idnetified. After listing the 34 vyabhicāribhāvas PR proceeds to define and explain each.

According to PR, harṣa, the first variety of bhāvas, is that, where the special type of pleasure produces due to accidental receiving of most desired things etc. Here also he quotes from his predecessors.[11] For this variety the example runs as: "avadhau divasāvasānakāle bhavanadvāri vilocane dadhāna, avalókya samāgataṁ tadā māmatha rāmā vikasanmukhi vabhuva.".

Here the coming of the beloved in proper time is the excitant mood or vibhāva and the smiling face is anubhāva (or ensuant). To see the long standing lover in time and at proper place is something great for the smiling lady, so automatically the transitory mood harṣa arises here.

For smṛti, the second variety of bhāva, PR gives a definition as: Smṛti is the knowledge which arrives from a man's good deeds in his previous birth, Here the example states that the cause is the anxiety etc., and anubhāva i.e. kārya is the position of bodily actions etc.

According to PR, thinking of future which is not known yet, is a mood called śaṅkā. For the following bhāvas PR has given his own definitions, after refuting the views of his predecessors: Śaṅkā, moha, glāni, dainya, cintā, mada, śrama, garva, mati, supta, vibodha, amarṣa, vitarka, viṣāda, ālasya, asūyā, capalatā etc., are facing strong objections from PR. To these moods, some predecessors views are refuted. After rati, the discussion of vyabhicāribhāvas comes to an end.[12]

Number of bhāvas fixed

The number of bhāvas are accepted to bc more than 34 by others.[13] For them, PR declares that we can include those new varieties, counted by others, in the given varieties. The extra bhāvas other than the 34 accepted by PR as well as others are:

Mātsarya, udvega, daṁbha, īrṣyā, vivekanirṇaya, klaivya, kṣamā, kutuka, utkaṅthā, vinaya, saṁsaya, dhārṣṭya etc.[14] But PR feels that mātsarya in asūyā, udvega in trāsa, daṁbha in avahittha, īrṣyā in amarṣa, viveka nirṇaya in mati, klaivya in dainya, kṣamā in dhṛti, kutuka and utkaṇṭhā in autsukya, vinaya in lajjā, saṁsaya in tarka, dhārṣṭya in capalatā can be included.

After this, six minor topics namely, rasābhāsa, bhāvābhāśa, bhāvaśanti, bhāvodaya, bhāvasaṁdhi and bhāvaśabalatā, are taken for discussion.

Rasābhāsa:

Rasābhāsa is there where the reflection of a sentiment occurs and slightly the rest of the sentiments become subordinate to the main sentiment. PR defines: 'anucitavibhāvālaṁbanatvaṁ rasābhā satvaṁ',[15] i.e. the narration of the improper vibhāva is rasābhāsa. The divisions are quoted in the texts. So, vibhāva have two divisions namely, ālaṁbana and uddipana. Here, if the ālaṁbana comes improperly then rasābhāsa exists. The following example is given for rasā bhāsa;

'satenopāyānāṁ kathamapi . . . ' etc.

Bhāvābhāsa:

Alike rasābhāsa, the bhāvābhāsa also uccurs in the poetry where the reflection of bhāva is more visible. For example, 'sarvepi vismṛtipathaṁ viṣayāḥ. . . etc.

What is difference between rasadhvani and *rasābhāsa* and also between bhāvadhvani and bhāvābhāsa, it is properly stated by PR.[16]

Bhāvaśānti

Accidental generation of a mood like harṣa etc, which are defined earlier, is bound to disappear and this disppearance of a particular mood is its end or śānti. This is to be realised that after its utpatti (generation) it should be colapsed and there a reader should recognise the charm. It is a state of self-realization but not for others. To this definition, a fine verse is illustrated by PR.[17] To get a mood, the other moods should disappear.

Bhāvodaya:

Hopefully, there is no much difference between bhāvaśānti and bhāvodaya. For bhāvodaya, the rising of a mood is enough. For bhāvaśāti this happens with addition of other moods collapsing at a time. The example for bhāvodaya is separate one, though the technical sense for both bhāvaśānti and bhāvodaya is likely same.

Bhāvasaṁdhi :

It is co-existance of two moods of different groups: by their original natures. This is a new style innovated by PR for first time in poetics.

Bhāvaśabalatā:

P. Sriramchandradu remarks: unlike in bhāvasaṁdhi, many bhāvas either antagonistic with each other or of neutral nature can be combined in a beautiful way in bhāvaśabalatā.[18]

Govindathakura, a commentator on KP[19] and others have presented a new definition regarding bhāvaśabalatā, which is refuted by PR. According to PR, the given example by opponents is wrong to hold this bhāvaśabalatā following this view that, neither there is the suggestion of the oppression of the preceeding bhāva nor there is any beauty. The extraordinary beauty comes due to the proper mixture of many a bhāvas as coconut water, milk, sugar etc., jointly becomes a super juice with plenty of taste. This is for bhāvaśabalatā that these objects give the own tasks, but at the time of addition of the objects, the new taste takes place. Like this the realisation of charm in poetry is laying in moods, should be understood by refined readers. In this way the concept of bhāvas comes to an end.

REFERENCES

1. "ratiḥ śokaśca nirvedakrodhotsāhaśca vismaya."
   hāso bhayaṁ jugupsā ca sthāyibhāvaḥ kramādamī".
   RG., p. 156.
2. Rg, pp. 158-159.
3. *ibid.*, ratyādyanyatamatvaṁ sthāyitvam; RG. p. 159.
4. *ibid.*, p. 160,
5. *ibid.*, p. 160.
6. *ibid.*, vibhāvayantiti vyutpatteḥ; RG, p. 164.
7. *ibid.*, Madhusudani on RG, p. 164.
8. *ibid.*, pp. 164-167.
9. *ibid.*, p. 283,
10. *ibid.*, p. 283-284.
11. *ibid.*, p. 287.
12. *ibid.*, p. 343.
13. *ibid.*, p. 343.
14. *ibid.*, pp. 343-344.
15. *ibid.*, p. 346.
16. *ibid.*, p. 358.
17. *ibid.*, p. 359.
18. Contribution of PR to SKt. Poetics, p. 50.
19. Vide. 'uttarottareṇa bhāvena . . . etc. RG. p. 363.

11. 7 THE CONCEPT OF DHVANI

Now the last major topic in this part of the book is Dhvani. Though, the entire issue is given in second part, which is not considered here, still a general discussion of the nature of dhvani, its varieites etc, are briefly discussed here.

Ānandavardhana has given the definition of dhvani. Abhinavagupta in his locana explains it thus:

Dhvani is of two types a) Avivakṣitavācya and b) vivakṣ itānyapara vācya. The former is of two kinds i.e. atyantatira-skṛtavācya and arthāntarasaṁkramitavācya. The latter one is of two kinds namely alakṣya-kramarūpa and anuraṇanarūpa. Here, besides these various varieties of dhvani, the alakṣ yakrama is accepted as only one kind.

Technically, alakṣyakramadhvani is said to be having mainly five varieties on account of the difference of its vyanjakas namely varṇa, pada, vākya, saṅghatanā and prabandha and other varieties namely part of Pada and the tune of music etc.[1] But our present discussion lies on PR's views only and that is why we are confining our study on RG and excluding other's views. At the very beginning of the concept of the sentiment PR himself quotes that only major varieites of dhvanis are to be discussed here; Tatra dhvaneḥ uttamottamasya asaṁkhyabhedasyāpi sāmānyataḥ kepi bhedāḥ nirūpyante, dvividho dhvaniḥ abhidā mulo, lakṣanāmulaśceti; tatrādyastrividhaḥ rasavastvalaṁkā radhvanibhedāt. Rasadhva-nirityalakṣyakramopalakṣaṇāt rasabhāva tadābhāsabhāva-śāntibhāvodayabhāvasaṁdhibhā vaśābalatvānāṁ grahaṇam. Dvitiyaśca dvividhaḥ; arthā-ntara-saṁkramita vācyotyantatir-askṛtavācyaśca.[2]

Alike Ānandavardhana, Abhinavagupta in the pre-dhvani or may be dhvani period, and Mammaṭa and Viśhvanātha in post- dhvani period, PR, also is a great exponent of dhvani theory. He has mentioned this concept in brief but its up to date classifications and proper illustrations are yet majestic.

PR classifies this dhvani theory on two basis. On the basis of suggested sense, he says that rasadhvani, vastudhvani and alaṅkāradhvani are three in number. But, technically the rasadhvani is only important to compose a poetry, having much pleasure. Rightly V.A.R. Shastri remarks that the other two dhvanis do not stand on par with the former, in that they are not themselves viśrāṅtidhāmans, but are described as anyaśābdavailakṣaṇyakārins.[3] The second basis of classification of dhvani is on vyanjakas i.e. abhidhā and lakṣaṇā.

REFERENCES

1. RG, pp. 376-377.
2. *ibid.*, p. 99.
3. JP., p. 121.

III. 1 PREDECESSORS CRITICISED BY PR

Indian Śāstric tradition follows the norm and principles of refinement by making omissions, additions and refutations as and when necessary on the view of the predecessors. Following this tradition, our present author, theorist in his work RG, has tried to examine and critically evaluate all the past work on Sanskrit Poetics, with the objectives of giving the traditional work with some new theories. In this process, he had adopted the view of his predecessors after criticising where he does find it suitable. Therefore, in RG we found so many contexts, that PR overwhelmingly criticised now and then the view of the earlier authority on poetics.

Here follows a brief account of the criticism of the predecessors by PR.

(a) Appayya Dikṣit

PR's main literary rival was Appayya Dikṣita who was a senior contemporary of PR. Out of several works, his best poetic work was CM, where he has given a detailed study of figures of speech (12 figures only). Till today, this work is not fully available. PR took this work with great interest and criticised systematically in the right places, in his separate work called CMK. In CM, the 12 figures are upamā, upameyopamā, ananvaya, smaraṇa, rūpaka, pariṇāma, saṅdeha, bhrāntimān, ullekha, apahnuti, utprekṣā and atisayokti.

These 12 figures are important figures among others also. Alike CMK, PR also took the charge of criticism of AD in his RG. The very first instance comes at the context of rasadhvani, where AD's verse i.e., 'niśśeṣacyutacandana-stanataṭa. . . ' etc., fully refuted with two prime objections.[1] One is 'prācinagranthvirodha' and the other is 'upapatti-virodha'. Secondly, PR criticised at the place of second variety of the poetry with the views related to guṇibhutavyaṅgya poetry. The verse comes like this:

praharaviratau madhye. . . . . .
. . . . . . sabāṣpagalajjalaiḥ.[2]

According to AD, the example, the expressed sense is fully supported by the suggested sense which is an instance of second variety of poetry with the term guṇī bhutavyaṅgya-vācyasiddhyaṅga.[3]

But according to PR, this verse is a very good example of rasadhvani type. V.A.R. Sashtri observed that PR's final remark was that although one accepts the support of vācyārtha by the suggested sense, yet one cannot deny in this verse the realisation of the beautiful sentiment-love in separation by all sahṛdayas, a fact which indubitably secures to the position of first grade poetry i.e. uttamottamakāvya.[4]

Further, on the issue of the division of the poetry, AD divides his poetry into three categories as dhvani, gunībhūtavyaṅgya and citra in his work CM. But PR tries to refute some aspects on this case and points out the faults.

Kalidasa's famous verse which is the first one in RV runs as follows:

"Vāgarthāviva saṁpṛktau vāgarthapratipattaye,
Jagataḥ pitarau vande pārvatīparameśvarau."

This verse, AD accepts as a case of rasadhvani and later on PR marks it as only a verse of rasavadālaṁkara instead of rasadhvani. Because, the rati of Parvati and Śiva, is in this example, subordinate to the main sense of the sentence, i.e. Kalidasa's full devotion *to God. Here the idea behind this verse is only a prayer.*

Further, AD was criticised on so many occassions in the cases like the definition of abhidhā, definition of upamā, luptopamā, example for vācakaluptopamā, divisions of upamā, example for vācakaluptopamā, divisions of upamā, luptopamā, definition of upameyopamā example for ananvayadhvani, definition of smaraṇa, rūpaka, example for rūpaka, comment on pariṇāma figure with example and view on apahnuti with detailed explanation. Further, PR took the subjects like the example of apahnuti, the two new varieties on atisayokti (made by AD), with their examples, view on vyatireka with AD's third group of this figure and then the samāsokti figure and so on. Near about twentyfive instances are available for our present disucssion. Among them the refutation as well as criticism of five definitions, ten illustrative verses, one case of classification, four views on particular concepts, three varieties and so on are discussed here.

The definition of abhidhā in Vṛttivārtika is as follows:

'Śaktyā pratipādakatvamabhidhā'[5] i.e., which is too significant by the power or Śakti is called as abhidā. But PR strongly criticises this by telling that due to absence of upapatti it cannot be called so.[6]

Upamā, and alaṁkāra of sense is studied in detail by PR as well as by AD. According to AD, the two types of upamā is given in CM.[7] PR criticised this strongly. Here PR tells that the word in AD's definition for upamā as stated namely varṇana is not true. Because this word may arise the charm for this particular alaṁkāra. So the word varṇana and charm both are different and therefore these definitions are wrongly interpreted by AD.[8]

In the case of upameyopamā, another alaṁkāra, PR again holds the objection for refutation of AD's definition. In CM, this alaṁkāra runs as follows:

'anyonyopamā bodhyā vyaktyā vṛttyantareṇa vā,
ekadharmāśrayā yā syāt sopameyopamā matā.[9]

i.e., it consists in the narration of similarity between upamāna and upameya which is understood by suggestion or by any other source of word, on the basis of one same attribute. PR refuses this giving this verse in his RG:

'ahaṁ latāyāssadṛssītya kharvaṁ
gaurāṅgi garvaṁ na kadāpi yāyāḥ
gaveṣaṇenālamihāpareṣā
meṣāpi tulyā tava tāvadasti'.[10]

Here, the tanutva is the common atttribute between the upamāna and upameya, due to parasparopamā by one abhidhā. But this verse is not correct to be declared as an example of upameyopamā, because, it does not negate the third similar object.

In Smaraṇa alaṁkāra, AD's definition is also rejected by PR. The total concept of this alaṁkāra is reproduced in RG for a wider discussion.[11] The definition and its all the illustrations are firmly discussed by PR telling that these all given statements are not suitable.

'tadetatsarvamaramaṇīyaṁ. . . etc.'.[12] To this, the statement of Ruyyaka also is quoted for its refutation.[13]

For rūpakālaṁkāra, AD gives the following definition:

"biṁbāviśiṣṭe nirdiṣṭe viṣaye yadyanihnute,

uparañjakatāmeti viṣyaī rūpakaṁ tadā tadā."[14]

Here the definition aims at the propriety of each part of its body that bimbaviśiṣṭe distinguishes rūpaka from nidarśanā. Again the word nirdiṣṭe differs rūpaka from atisayokti alaṁkāra. Here the former one is invariably biṁbapratibiṁbabhāva and the latter is associated with suppression of viṣaya or object. To this PR strongly criticises telling that the relation of biṁbapratibiṁba is also associated with rūpaka; so bimbaviśiṣṭe word cannot differentiate rūpaka from nidarśanā.[15]

After discussing the definitions, now we may take other aspects of refutation by PR. PR takes ten instances to refute AD's given various examples in various contexts. Since the examples for rasadhvani and guṇibhūta vyaṅgya are already discussed, the remaining may be discussed.

In ubhayacitra, one variety of Citrakāvya, AD gives the following verse for an example.

Varāhaḥ kalyāṇaṁ vitaratu sa vaḥ kapavirame
vinirdhunvannaudanvatamudakamurvī mudavahat,
khurāghātatruṭyatkulaśikharikūṭapraviluṭha
cchilākoṭisphoṭaspuṭaghaṭitamaṅgalyapaṭahaḥ."[16]

PR declares this verse as defective, due to samāptapunarāttatvadoṣa it cannot be called even as citra poetry. Again PR points out that, in this verse, no poetic charm is laying for a reader.

The example for vācakaluptopamā is taken by PR for refutation. The verse runs as follows:

"rupayauvanalāvaṇyaspṛhantiyatrākṛtiḥ,
purato hariṇāksīṇāmeṣa puṣpāyudhiyati."[17]

According to PR, this verse suffers from apaśabda doṣa and therefore the incapability of the poet of this verse is coming out.[18]

The following verse is quoted as an example of ananvaya by AD:

"adya yā mama govinda jātā tvayi gṛhāgate
Kālenaiṣā bhavetprītistavaivāgamanātpunaḥ"[19]

Here, Vidura reveals his hearty pleasure to see Kṛṣṇa, entering to home and this pleasure is a special type of that. But PR says that here, there are two pleasures i.e., one is already told by Vidura and next is the hoping of another home coming of Kṛṣṇa. So here, in both pleasure, there is no much difference at all. Therefore, the verse given above is not proper.[20]

In rūpakālaṁkāra AD cites the following example even in vaiyadhikaraṇya-

> *"tārānāyakaśekharāya jagadādhārāya dhārāhara-*
> *cchāyā dhārakakandharāya girijāsaṅgaikaśṛṅgāriṇe,*
> *nadyā śekhariṇe dṛśā tilakine nārāy aṇe nā striṇe,*
> *nāgaiḥ kaṅkaṇine nāgena gṛhiṇe nāthāya seyaṁ natiḥ."*[21]

While PR quotes this verse, wrongly in his RG for Pariṇāmālaṁkāra. According to AD this verse mainly explains highness of Śiva and with that purpose Śiva is qualified with the adjuncts namely, "nadyā śikhariṇe". PR became successful in refuting this verse, but was himself refuted by Nageśa.

Again AD started criticising Vidyādhara for the example of pariṇāma in his Ekāvalī. The verse is as follows:

> "narasiṁgha dharānātha ke vayaṁ tava varṇane,
>
> api rājānamākramya yaśo yasya vijṛṁbdhate."[22]

On this, PR gives his own view and further Nāgeśa also gives his own statement in his commentary following PR's view.[23]

In apahnuti one verse is quoted by AD for this alaṁkāra as "tvadālekhye kautūhalataralalanvī... etc.[24] , where sādharṃyamulā is discussed. Further in atisayoktialaṁkara this type of refutation also occurs in RG.

Alike the refutation on definitions and examples, PR also tries to refute some views in some contexts given by AD in his work.

The first view falls on the statement of upamā where the verse from Kumārasaṁbhava of Kalidasa is quoted by AD. According to AD, the verse is one variety of upamā. But PR refuses to follow this view and further claims that the same verse is suitable for udāharaṇālaṁkara instead of upamā.[25]

AD counts two varieties of upamā namely, pūrṇā and luptā where seven kinds are taken under pūrṇā on the basis of different aspects of common-ness. Further he says that, these seven kinds are not suitable to add under luptā. PR, however says that even without the anugāmidharma, kinds of luptā are found as in the Pūrṇā on the basis of biṁbapratibiṁbabhāva.[26]

The third view arises at the time of narration of apahnuti. AD describes this alaṁkāra with a variety namely paryastāpahnuti in Kuvalayānanda with adding one example.[27] To this PR comments that apahnuti consists in the negation of upameya on which upamāna is superimposed. But in the above example there is no negation of the upameya instead of having only the superimposition of upamāna on upameya. Therefore, one can count this verse for rūpaka instead of apahnuti. The commentator in his vimarsini also follows the statement of PR.[28]

The other views on atiśayokti and samāsokti also refuted by PR. The discussions on varieties are also accepted and later on refuted by PR in their proper places.

(b) Mammaṭa

Mammaṭabhaṭṭa flourished in the last half of the eleventh century. Alike AD, this author was also refuted and criticised by PR in so many occasions. Some Kārikās and Vṛttis of KP are disqualified and rejected by PR. Interestingly in many cases the view of KP is taken to refute some other opponents and establishes his positions by PR. It may be noted that the rivalry between PR and his predecessors was only on śāstric content and not on personal count as thought by some. As one can notice the style of quoting Mammaṭa by PR where he was quoted with due regard and care. In all some eleven cases PR has quoted Mammta. In five cases his view is quoted by name and rest without name: Prannñcaḥ,[29] Kāvyaprakāsa kṛtam,[30] Kecit,[31] Tathācāhuḥ,[32] Mammatabhṭṭa,[33] Kāvyaprakāśagata,[34] Sahṛdaya-śiromaṇih,[35] Jaratarāḥ,[36] apre,[37] Kāvyaprakāśaṭikākārāḥ,[38] and Mammaṭoktiḥ,[39]

I. To begin with: PR, while giving his definition of poetry, refutes this definition of poetry as given by Mammaṭa. The poetry is defined by Mammaṭa as follows:

"adoṣau saguṇau sālaṁkārau śabdārthau kāvyam."[40] PR first objects to this very notion of "śabda and artha to form the part of poetry, as defined by Mammaṭa. To him only sound is enough to form the part of poetry, as defined by Mammaṭa. To him only sound is enough to compose poetry. The three qualifications to the main part of the definition namly, 'adoṣau','saguṇau' and 'sālaṁkārau' are also defective and irrelevant. PR comments that in this definition, the qualifications are not proper also. Ironically, Madusudanasarswati, the commentator on RG comments that at the time of adoption of RG, Paṇḍitaraja whole heartly promised to make poetry definition having the guṇa, alaṁkāra etc. and now at the time of refutation of his predecessors view, the same author refuses to accept these qualifications in poetry. The summary is like this: this pleasures excluding worldly or common pleasure some thing else like reading of poetry is the most charming. The moods are major attributed aspects for poetic charm. This is called as alaukika or extraordinary pleasure. This pleasure, further Nāgesa continues as only the proper experience of śāstric knowledge.[41] Further, guṇa is the ātmadharma and not similar to alaṁkāra which is beautifier to that ātmadharma. So both guṇa and alaṁkāra are very different from each other.[42]For doṣa, PR declares that if the word consisting extraordinary charm, is called as good poetry and if not so, then called as faulty poetry. So no necessary to put the qualification adoṣau following this old tradition, for them, "the poetry having blemishes is not poetry, should be accepted.

II. Some commentators on KP, are also refuted by PR on the issue of second variety of poetry. The commentators like śrīvatsalāñcchana and others give a separate definition for this variety of poetry. The definition runs as follows:— "Citrānyatvam. . . etc. This is also in the definition Haimavati commentary. According to Haimavati a detailed statement is given and this commentary was written after RG.[43] Further the definition of KP is not fully suitable. PR rejects this definition of the critics by pointing out that this would amount to the fault of avyāpti in the cases of paryāyokta, samāsokti etc.

III. In this context of classification of poetry PR tried to criticise Mammaṭa directly. For the first time PR introduced this fourfold classification, which remains steady for later rhetoricians till the date. Mammaṭa followed the traditional style to count three varieties of poetry as uttama, madhyama and adhama. The uttamottama is the invented one by PR. In RG, both the uttama and madhyama varieties are somehow excluded for criticism. But following the statement of Mammaṭa on adhama variety where both śabdacitra and arthacitra came under one variety, PR tries to make a well distinction in his RG. That's why PR tells that one refined reader can have the realisation of both citras and therefore, it is quite difficult to add both citras under one variety. Her we reproduce the same statement of Mammaṭa's views on arthacitra poetry:

"vinirgataṁ mānadamātmamandirāt bhavatyupaśrutya yaddṛcchyāpi yaṁ sasaṁbhramendradrutapātitārgalā nimītākṣīva bhiyāmarāvatī.[44]

The other illustrative verse as:

"sa cchinnamūlaḥ kṣatajena reṇustasyopariṣṭātpavanā-vadhūtaḥ,

aṅgāraśeṣasya hutaśanasya pūrvotthito dhūma ivāva-dhāsate."[45]

These types of examples, PR strongly, disagrees to count them under one variety. It needs to be discussed as separate poetries. To prove its difference from above verses PR quotes the following verse from KP.

"Svacchandocchatadacchakacchakuhar acchātetarāṃ-bhaśchṭā-

mūrcchanmohamaharṣiharṣavihitasnānāhnikāhnāya vaḥ,

bhindyādudyadudāradarduradarīdairdhyadaridradruma-

drohordekamayormimeduramadā mandākinī manda-tām"[46]

Before this context, earlier, PR takes a view from KP to show the inability of AD's views on first variety of poetry.

IV The next most important topic comes again to be refuted by PR is the definition of permanent mood of KP. According to Mammaṭa, the permanent mood is something else than the transitory moods like rati or love etc. This view is strongly held by PR. He says that due to rati and other moods, the permanent mood occurs. How can one omit these transitory moods to get the permanent mood. Mammaṭa writes: "ratyā dyanyatamatvaṁ sthāyitvam."[47]

V. In the rasa section, the verse from KP comes for raudrarasa as:

"kṛtamanumataṁ dṛṣṭaṁ vā yairidaṁ gurupātakaṁ." etc.[48] Here, according to PR, the sentimental suggestion is fully lacking its charm to be as a raudrarasa. The style of writing this verse is fully wrong. Only the non-capability of the poet is revealed. Therefore the verse given by PR is proper to be raudrarasa.[49]

VI. Alike raudrarasa, in the context of adbhutarasa, Mammaṭa is again refuted by PR. In this verse, the word citra, is itself expressive, which is lacking the pure suggestiveness.[50] Secondly, this verse aims towards devotion and this devotion is a major factor than suggestiveness of adbhutarasa. Therefore, according to PR, it is a verse of rasālaṁkāra instead of rasadhvani.

VII. Some commentators on KP have declared that vikaṭ atā is a separate poetic merit. This topic is taken for wider discussion in the udāratā guṇa. The commentators are also giving examples.[51] But these definitions and examples are criticised by PR.[52]

VIII. On rasavirodha, PR giveds a detailed study and further tells that some sentiments are supporter to other sentiments and some are dissimilar to others. Here, KP describes this topic and give the following example:

bhureṇudigdhān nava-pārijāta. . . etc.[53]

Here first the narration of bivatsarasa and then vīrarasa and finally the śṛngārarasa are presented in one instance. PR narrates this virodha of two types.[54]

IX. Regarding transitory moods, PR has presented so many contexts rather than refutation. This is the only concept where PR shows some positive attitude towards his predecessors. Moreover, he does not find any such type of rejection. But anyhow, PR tries to refute and on his way, gets some clues for the formation of his own theories. Therefore, Mammaṭa's views regarding bhāva is not included in refutation. Secondly, all the views regarding bhāva are quoted after giving the predecessors statement in his own language. Like vibodha, supta etc., some bhāvas are facing objections from PR.

X. For śabda śaktimulādhvani in second part of RG, Mammaṭa is criticised by PR in detail.[55]

XI. The concept of upamā alamkāra, PR finds out fault in KP's statement. The definition of upamā in KP is as:

"sādharmyamupamā bhede.[56] Mammaṭa explains this as the similarity is based on upamāna and upameya, but not based on kārya and kāraṇa. PR declares that this definition is not so charming. To refute this statement, PR takes some other definitions of other predecessors likely Ruyyaka and Śobhākara (Ratnākara)[57]

Mammaṭa's view are quoted also as: yadāhuḥ, ... tathoktam etc, by which the statements of Mammaṭa is taken for refutation. PR, at each context, holds those statements quite properly and declares them as not suitable.[58]

(c) Viśvanātha

Now PR holds another predecessor for refutation of his theory on the definition of poetry. Viśvanātha in his SD, discussed this definition of poetry starting with a short statement as "vākyaṁ rasātmakaṁ kāvyam."[59] To explain this, Viśvanātha says that the sentiment is only the sole of a poetry and without interpretation of the sentiment the poetry lacks its charm.[60]

To this explanation, PR strongly criticises. According to him the dhvani rests on rasa, vastu and alaṁkāra. But to this obstacle, the remaining two dhvanis are omitted to be counted as good poetries. Here, the first grade poets like Kālidasa and so on are composing poetry having these three aspects of dhvani, but not only rasa. Some are narrating poetry with the various subjects like flowing of water, fall of water, the merry making of children, monkeys etc. Here one cannot hesitate to acept that in these above instances of poetry, the rasa does not take place. If so, then poetry like the 'cow is walking', 'the dear is running' will also contain the rasa.

The same author of SD strongly refutes the definition of KP and PR refutes both these predecessors.

Finally we can conclude with the following statement that refutation of predecessors by their successors in poetics is becoming a tradition and style of adoption. Since PR is the last original text book writer on Sanskrit Poetics, so a large scope of refutation was well available before him. Therefore PR had a chance of adopting the criticism on various issues while he composed RG. the name of Viśvanātha occurs once in this context which is discussed by PR.

(d) Rājānaka Ruyyaka

As we have mentioned that so many cases of refutations by PR has taken place in both part of RG, but our research work limits to the first part only where the number of refutaions are less rather than second part. For the readers interest, we are reproducing a few cases of refutations from second part as well.

Rājānaka Ruyyaka, the author of Alaṁkāra Sarvasva, Sāhitya mīmāmsā, Vyaktivivekavicāra etc., was the teacher of Maṅkhaka, is cleraly notified as a poetics author of twelveth C.A.D. He defines upameyopamā thus: "dvayoḥ paryāyeṇa tesminnupameyopamā."[61]

But according to PR, the word dvayoḥ does not make any significant support for the said definition. Rightly V.A.R. Sastri tells that, if the word dvayoh has any prupose, it would differentiate the upameyopamā from ananvaya in that the upamānopameyabhāva in the former is mutually between two objects while in the latter it rests on one single object. But the word paryāyeṇa in the body of the definition explains that the mutual upamānopameyabhāva is not simultaneous i.e., when one is considered the upamāna, it is not the upameya; this indicates well that the upamānopameyabhāva in upameyopamā is mutually between two objects and that this can be effected only in two separate vākyas. This mutual similarity in cases where there is vākyabheda cannot be explained in ananvaya. So the utility of the word dvayoḥ i.e., to differentiate the scope of upameyopamā from that of ananvaya cannot be established.[62]

Like this alaṁkāra, Ruyyaka's next definition faces criticism of PR is smaraṇa alaṁkāra. In Alaṁkārasarvasva, he has defined smaraṇa as:

"Sadṛśānubha vādvastrantarasmṛtih smaraṇa.[63]

This is the figure of sense that in which the recollection of one fact, comes from the earlier experience of another fact or object. But according to PR it is defective and therefore he refutes it in the following sentences; the example for this alaṁkāra as: 'the thinking of lord Viṣṇu from the recollection of cloud and cātaka bird etc., is, not proper. Here the experience or realisation of similar facts converts into similar knowledge. It is smaraṇa but not smṛti there by. [64]

Ruyyaka adopts pariṇāma as:

"āropyamāṇasya prakṛtopayogitve."

To this, he further explains in detail after giving this short definition.[66] What is the proper sense of 'āropyamāṇasya prakṛtopayoga' is well discussed by PR and in detail PR counting this with the citation of both example verses of Ruyyaka and refutes them.[67]

In the example verse of vyatireka, another alaṁkāra, Ruyyaka quotes the following verse.

"Kṣiṇaḥ kṣiṇopi śaśī bhuyo bhuyobhivardhate nityaṁ,
Virama prasīda sundari youvanamanivarti yātaṁ tu".[68]

Here Ruyyaka as well as Jayaratha, the commentator on formers text, both take this verse telling the inferiority of upameya and upamāna in the case of vyatireka. But PR says that this verse as an example for vyatireka is the superiority of upameya to upamāna in stead of inferiority.[69]

(e) Jayaratha

The commentator of alamkārasarvasva of Ruyyaka in his work namely vimarsini gives views on upameyopamā in the following verse

"rajobhiḥ syandanoddhūtairgajaiśca ghanasaṁni bhaiḥ,
bhuvastalamiva voma kurvanvyomeva bhūtalam."[70]

as an example of this fugures of speech. But PR refuses to agree with this view. It is well discussed in RG.[71]

(f) Śobhākaramitra

Most probably, Śobhākaramitra was the author of Alaṁkāraratnākara which is referred as ratnākara by PR very often. This work contains several alaṁkāras. PR takes up this work for refutation of some alaṁkāras. The definitions of upamā, asama, the example of upameyopamā and the classificaiton of ananvaya alaṁkāras are important in this context.

"Prasiddhagunenopamānenaprasiddhagunasyopameyasya sādruśyamupamā." But PR declares it as improper definition. This definition cannot be applied in cases of sliṣṭopamā which is the poet's invention and is devoid of upamāna.

According to Śobhākara, the ananvaya is of three types : the first containing the upameya itself fancied as the upamāna, the second with one part of the upameya as upamāna and the last containing the upameya as upamāna. PR tells that as the term ananvaya implies the negation of a second similar object is considered to be the chief feature of this alaṁkāra. A similar object cannot be taken as a particular, since the same can be explaiend as the example of kalpitopamā.

Śobhākara gives the following example for upameyopama:

"savitā vidhavati vidhurapi savitarati dinanti yāminyaḥ yāminayanti dināni ca sukhaduḥkhavasīkṛte manasi."

To this verse, PR declares as an unsuitable verse. Further, PR criticises the definition of asama given in alaṅkāraratnākara.[72]

(g) Vidyānātha

Vidyānātha, the author of pratāparudrīya, is also criticised by PR. His definition of upamā is called defective and alike in the case of Mammaṭa, PR applied this definition of upamā to vyatireka alaṁkāra involving the negation of Sādṛśya.

(h) Ānandavardhana

PR got only one place to criticise Ānandavardhana in the context of rūpakadhvani. The example verse for rūpakadhvani as given by him while PR accepts the same verse for bhrāntimad dhvani. Otherwise this author and his work are quoted by PR in RG, mostly in support of his discussions. The above said criticised verse is as follows:

"prāptaśrīreṣa kasmātpunarapi mayi taṁ manthakhedaṁ

vidadhyannidrāmaphayasya pūrvāmanalasamanasaho naiva saṁbhāvayāmi, setuṁ badhnāti bhūyaḥ kimiti ca sakaladvī panāthānuyātastvayyāyāte, vikalpāniti dadhata ivābhāti kampaḥ payodheḥ."[73]

REFERENCES

1. CM, p. 17.
2. *ibid.*, p. 26.
3. "Atra Sakalamahaḥ. . . guṇibhūtavyaṅgyaṁ etc."
4. JP, p. 234.
5. Vṛttivārtika, p. 1.
6. RG, II, pp. 129-30
7. CM, p. 78.

8. RG, II, p. 247.
9. CM, p. 164.
10. RG II. p. 401.
11. *ibid.*, pp. 467-70. cf; CM, pp. 189-92.
12. RG, II, p. 470.
13. *ibid.*, pp. 472-73. cf; Alaṁkāra Sar., p. 41.
14. CM, p. 211.
15. RG, II, pp. 486-87.
16. CM, p. 29.
17. *ibid.*, p. 108.
18. idaṁ ca padyamapaśabdaduṣṭamavaiyākaraṇatāṁ kartuḥ prakāśayati. RG, II, p. 292.
19. CM, p. 185.
20. RG, II, p. 432.
21. CM, p. 247.
    cf; RG, II, p. 550.
22. RG, II, p. 561.
23. Marmaprakāśa on RG, II, pp. 461-62.
24. *ibid*, pp. 638-39.
    cf; CM, p. 308.
25. RG, II, pp. 324, 458.
    cf. CM, p. 48.
26. RG, II, pp. 325-27.
27. Kuvalayānanda.
28. RG, II, p. 632. cf; Vimarsinī, on Alaṁkāra sar.
29. RG, pp. 22, 202.
30. *ibid.*, p. 74.
31. *ibid.*, pp. 95-199.
32. *ibid*, pp. 107, 130, 235, 247, 273, 283, 300, 302.
33. *ibid.*, pp. 117, 156, 254.
34. *ibid.*, pp. 176, 208.
35. *ibid.*, p. 193.
36. *ibid.*, p. 235.
37. *ibid.*, p. 251
38. *ibid.*, pp. 56, 240, 363
39. *ibid.*, p. 375.

40. *ibid.*, p. 22.
    The original definition in KP is "tadadoṣau śabdārthau saguṇāvanalaṁkṛtīḥ punaḥkvāpi"
    cf. KP. I-4.
41. Madhusudani on RG, pp. 33-34.
42. RG, p. 43.
43. Comm. K.P. I.5.
44. RG, p. 96. cf; KP, I-5.
45. RG, p. 96. cf; CM. p. 29.
46. RG, p. 96, cf; KP, I-4.
47. RG, p. 159.
48. *ibid.*, p. 179, cf; KP, IV. 39.
49. . . . raudrarasavyañjanākṣamā nāsti vṛttiḥ, atastatkare raśaktireva'; RG, p. 179.
50. *ibid.*, p. 193. cf; KP, I-43, p. 93.
51. 'Svacaraṇa viniviṣṭairnūparairnartakināṁ. . . etc; RG, p. 240.
52. *ibid.*, pp. 240-41.
53. *ibid.*, p. 208. cf; KP. VII-63.
54. RG, pp. 204-205.
55. RG, II, pp. 15-19.
56. KP, X-126.
57. RG, II, p. 252.
58. See in detail of text part of this work.
59. RG, p. 44.
60. "rasa evātmā sārarūpatayā. . . etc." SD, p. 19.
61. Alaṁkara Sar., 13, p. 39.
62. JP, p. 280, cf. RG, II, pp. 406-407.
63. Alaṁkāra Sar., 14, p. 40.
64. RG, II, p. 465, pp. 472-73.
65. Alaṁkāra Sar., 16, p. 51.
66. *ibid.*, pp. 50-52.
67. RG, II, pp. 553-57.
68. Alaṁkāra Sar. p. 102.
69. RG, II.
70. Vimarsini on Alaṁkāra Sar. p. 39.
71. RG, pp. 410-11.
72. *ibid.*, p. 441.
73. *ibid.*, p. 543.

III.2 PR CRITICISED BY HIS SUCCESSORS

We have already discussed in the foregoing pages how PR has criticised and refuted the views of some of his predecessors, in detail. And now, we present a brief analysis on criticism of PR at the hands of his successors. In spite of the fact that PR is glorified by his successors, for his outstanding contributions in his RG still at places, some of his views are criticised and refuted. We have a number of text book writers who have criticised PR on some points:

A) Viśveśwara Paṇḍita (1760 C.A.D.),

B) Viśveśwara Pandeya (1850 C.A.D.),

C) śriśivadata śarmā (1900 C.A.D.),

It is to be noted that, excluding these writers, there may be some others, who have criticised the views of PR but, to give a short idea and to point out the opposite aspects of PR's views, we have selected a few prominent works. These three authors have not accepted the theories, propounded by PR. Here folllows a categorical analysis of their refutations. Though the present work does not deal with figures of speech, which occur in second ānana of RG, yet, to make this chapter more interesting, for readers, we have included all the refutations under this discussions.

A) Viśveśvara Paṇḍita in his Alaṁkārakaustubha (=AK):

Viśveśvara Paṇḍita's work, as suggesting the title, discusses only about figures of speech, as his work is confined only to alaṁkara varieties. It does not discuss the other concepts of poetry like rasa, doṣa, guṇa etc. While discussing the different alaṁkāras, the author has quoted the views of many a predecessor like Daṇḍin, Kaiyaṭa, Viśvanātha, Bhojarāja, Jayadeva, Vidyādhara, AD, along with PR at several occasions. Some times the views of predecessors has been taken to establish his own view with more authentic way. RG has been quoted and disapproved nearly at thrity places on many contexts.

Viśveśvara Paṇḍita's style of interpretation is very concise and unique and some times it matches to PR's style of interpretation. To this vast text, the author's own glossary (commentary) is very helpful for further studies. Without naming this gloss, the author has tried to explain some of the difficult contexts in detail and there fore, alike his book AK, the 'glossary' also needs to be studied with great care. It seems that the author, while refuting the view of PR, does not always record his name or the name of the text i.e. RG. Most of the times, though he quotes the views of PR, in order to criticise or refute, he records it as the view of 'some' or 'of those' or 'as it is told' etc. Somehow, we find at some places he quotes as 'rasagangādharakāraḥ' as in other cases like 'iti kecit', 'apare' etc. The very same style is accepted by the other authors also.

At the very beginning, Viśveśvara draws the attention of the readers to find out some faults with PR's views at the time of discussing 'upamā', the simile. The entire concept of 'upamā', having so many articles, with the predecessors statements, is a major alaṁkāra where PR has been criticised atleast in seven occasions. I quote here these according to the order of their occurrences;

1) "*........'śvābhāvaprayojakābhāvapratiyogikoṭyapraviṣṭatve sati' iti viśeṣaṇāt. Svapadaṁ sāddṛśyaparam. sadṛśi-lābhaniṣedhasya ca na sādṛsyābhāvaprayojakatvameveti na vyabhicāraḥ, etena dīkṣ itānu-yāyino rasagaṇgādharakṛtopi nirastāḥ,*"[1]

2) *Rasagaṇgādharakṛtastu-'varṇanasya vilakṣaṇaśabdā tmakasya vilakṣaṇajñānātmakasya vā śabda*

vācyatāvirahеṇa arthālaṁkāratābādhaḥ, varṇanasya sarvathaivāvyaṅgyatvāt svaniṣedhāparyavasāyi duṣṭa vyaṅgyasādṛśya varṅanaṁ upamā, iti taduktaphalitalakṣaṇe avyaṇgyatva viśeṣaṇaṁ vyarthaṁ it arthaḥ yadi tu . . . ca ativyāptiḥ.[2]

3) *Kecittu-evaṁsati. . . gajaiva yaḥ puruṣah . . . ajananāt. . . vanāderananvayāpatteḥ ca . . . uktakāryakāraṇa bhāvaśca na angikāryaḥ* (and also) *kecittu . . . vācakadharma . . . . ityāhuḥ, tat na.*[3]

4) *yattu rasagaṇgādhare - maharṣeh vyāsa. . . iti udāhṛtaṁ, tat cintyaṁ, atra upamitasamāsa eva, bādhakābhāvāt sāmānyadharmaprayogābhāvāt.*[4]

5) *yadyapi rasagaṇgādhare ṣ ahinacandrālasatānanena. . . atra keṣāṁ toṣāya na syāt ityuktyā virahiṇām api toṣājankatvapratīteḥ. śuklapakṣ arātreśca tat toṣa janakatvābhāvāt nāyikāyāḥ tādātmyāpattyāt upapatiḥ uktaṁ tadapi asat. yoṣādoṣāyoḥsamāsābhāvepi kṣativiraheṇāsūklapakṣ arātryabhinnāyoṣeti raopakenaiva tat saṁbhavāt.*[5]

6) . . . . *ivārthaśaktimūlapariṇāmadhvaniprakaraṇe-*

"pānthaḥ madamatekiṁ vā . . . śāntimavāpsyasi iti udāharaṇa rasagaṇgādharaḥ api parāstaḥ, abhedaviśaya sambhavāt dhvanitvānaucityat, yadapi cirādvisahate . . . iti citramīmāṁsāyām udāhṛtaṁ praiṇāṁdhvanitvaṁ rasagangādhare dūṣ tam.[6]

Not only the basic alaṁkāra as 'upamā', is criticised but the varieites like 'mālopamā' etc., also taken for discussion and refutation by the author.

In the case of 'ananvaya', Viśveśvara quotes PR's definition of 'asama' with an example to point out its errors. Here the author clearly refers PR as 'yattu' instead of quoting the particular names of the author.

In 'upameyopamā', the author has quoted the views of PR and AD jointly for analysis and later on refuted it. He quotes; 'yattu atra citramīmāmsā rasagaṅgādharādayoḥ . . . iti . . . tat tuccham etc."[7]

Like these alaṁkaras, mentioned above, Viśveśvara also has criticised some other alaṁkāras. We quote a few more here.

a) *Sasaṁdeha alaṁkāra: rasagaṅgādhare tu - surya kiraṇadharmikaśaṁśayasya guṇībhūtasya vyaṅjanāgamya tvād viṣayaviṣayiṇorāropānukūlavibhaktyanapekṣatvāt tat vinaivāropa saṁbhavāt na adhyavasānaṁ ityuktam tat cintya, mānasasaṁśayepi dharmiṇa idaṁtvena evopasthiteḥ . . . saṁdehasya asaṁbhavāt.*[8]

b) *Rupakālaṁkāra; atra kecit - karmadhāraye hi abhedaḥ viśeṣaṇasya saṁsargaḥ 'mukhaṁ candraḥ', iti vākye 'candrapratiyogikābhedavat mukham, iti pratiyogitva mukhaḥ mukhacandraḥ, ityādisamāse tat mukhānuyogikābhedapratiyogī candra iti anuyogitvamukhaḥ tadubhayatrāpi candrābheda eva saṁsargaḥ . . . viśeṣaṇapratiyogike evābhedaḥsaṁsarge na tu tadanu yogika iti tu durāgrhaḥ, nirbijatvāditi.*[9]

c) *Apahnutiralaṁkāra; rasagaṇgādharastu - upameyaniṣedha upamānāropasścetyapanuteḥ bhāgadvayam.. . . mukhaṁ candraḥ ityādau api . . . vācyam. puṇḍari-kākṣasya varṇyatvābhāvena. . . . . . . vyākhyānāt. . . . yuktamevāpatinutitvaṁ ityāhuḥ iti.*[10]

d) *Śleṣālaṁkāra:. . . . . sādharmyārthakalpanamityupamāṇga mayaṁ śleṣaḥ iti. atra rasagaṇgādharakṛtaḥ - yat tāvat uktam "aprakṛtārthasya vyangyatvaṁ na prācām abhimataṁ kintu upamādereva." iti, tadayuktam. "anekārthasya śabdasya vācakatve niyaṅtrite, saṁyogādaiḥ avācyārthādhikṛdvyāvṛttiranjanam" iti tad granthavirodhāt.*[11]

e) *Nidarśanālaṁkāra: . . . evam ca bhede rūpātisśayokti-apahnutyorapi rūpaka, evāntarbhāvaḥ ityatra kṣatyabhāvādiṣṭāpattirityatiśayokteḥ api rūpakāntarbhāvasvīkartṛṇāṁ mate tu lalitasyālaṁkārāntaratva saṅkā api na saṁbhavati iti rasagaṅgādharakṛtaḥ.*[12]

f) *Aprastutaprasaṁsālaṁkāra: tatra rasagaṅgādharakṛtaḥ - atrāpyaprastuta pasaṁsaiva bhavati iti na alaṁkārānta rakalpanaṁ. kiṅcit ukti vaicitryeṇa tat kalpane alaṁkārānantyaprasaṁgāt. na ca tat lakṣaṇānākrānta tvāt kathametaditi vācyam. na hi aprastutaṁ sarvathā prastāvarāhityaṁ vivaksitam. kintumukhyatātparyaviṣayībhutārthātiriktatvaṁ, ... tat lakṣaṇākrāntatvaṁ spaṣṭam eva ityāhuḥ.*[13]

g) *Atiśayoktiralaṁkāra: rasagaṇgādharakṛtaḥ tu - veśyāmityādeḥ nidarśanāyām eva antarbhāvaḥ. na ca atra nidarśanā mithyādhyavasityoḥ saṅkaraḥ iti vācyaṁ. mithyādhyavasitau mānābhāvāt. anyathā - hariścandreṇa saṁtaptāḥ pragītya. . . namostu te, iti. . . āpatteḥ ityāhuḥ.*[14]

h) *Prativastūpamālaṁkāra:*

vaidharmyeṇa yathā rasagaṇgādhare -

gīrbhirgurūnāṁ paruṣākṣarābhi. . .

. . . maṇayo vasanti atra. . . .

ākṣipyate . . . (And also) rasagaṅgādharakṛtastu.

. . . nedaṁ vaidharmyodāharaṇaṁ yuktam.[15]

i) *Dṛṣṭāntālaṁkāra; atra rasagangādhara kṛtaḥ-prativastūpamāyāṁ prakṛtāprakṛtayoḥ sādṛśya-pratiteḥ na tu dṛṣṭānte iti ājñāmātraṁ. . . . sādṛśyapratīti mātreṇaikyābhyupagame sarva viplavāpatteḥ it dik.*[16]

j) *Vyatirekālaṁkāra: yadyapi upameyāpakarṣodāharaṇaṁ rasagaṅgadhare kṛtaṁ - "jagatrayatrāṇa-dhṛtavratasya. . . tulāṁ dvinetraḥ", atra. . . pratīteḥ alaṁkāratā it, tadapi cintyam. dharmāntarapra-yuktasādṛsyaiva kṣā-garbhadharma viśeṣaprayukta-sādṛśya niṣedhaḥ saiva vyatirekasarīratvena sar-vābhyupagatatvāt.*[17]

k) *Ākṣepālaṁkāra: yattu rasagaṇgādhare - tapanidheḥ kauśika. . . . . api jīvabhājaḥ, tatra, dasarathasya viśvāmitraṁ prati uktau mānaiṣīriti niṣedho vyaṅgya iti saṁkṣepaḥ.*[18]

l) *Vibhāvanālaṁkāra: kāraṇābhāvepi kāryotpattiḥ it atra kāraṇatāvacchedakasambandhena kāraṇatā vacchedakā vacchinnapratiyogitā kābhāvasya viviksṣ anīyatvāt iti rasagangādharakṛtaḥ, tat cintyam. tikṣ natvādeḥ kāraṇatāvacchedakatva svīkāre ukti daṁbhavepi kāraṇatvābhiprāye ṇaivādīkṣitaiḥ bhe-dāntara varṇanāt.*[19]

m) *Kāvyaliṅgālaṁkaraḥ: (I) yattu rasagangādhare - anumitikaraṇatvena sāmānyaviśeṣa bhāvābhyāṁ ca anālingtaḥ . . . ityuktvā - vinindyānyunmattairapi ca. . . sarveṣāmaghamathanadarpaṁ dalayasi . . ityudāhṛtaṁ, tat parasparavirudham iti spaṣṭam eva. (II) atra rasagaṅgādhara kṛtaḥ-satyamatrā numitirūpevopapattiḥ, tathāpi nedaṁ anumānālaṁkāraḥ. (III) yadapi [rasagaṅgādhare] samarthanādṛḍhatara pratyayo nā numitiḥ-sahi na prātyakṣikaḥ . . . na śābdo mānaso vā, anumitisāmagryābalavatvāt. iti, tadapi asat satyāṁ. vyabhicārasphūrtā vanumitisāmagrya eva abhāvāt.*[20]

n) *Paryāyoktālaṁkāra: atra rasagngādhara kṛtaḥ - sarva kārasya tāvbadyathā śrutatyāgabījamuktameva. . . yogārthaḥ tathā ca - dasavadananidhanakāri dāsarathi puṇḍarikākṣah, . . . ityuktam, yat, tadasat. . . anyathā namo rāhuśiraśchedakārīṇe duḥkhahārīṇe ityatrāpi paryāyoktaprasamgāt.*[21]

o) *Anumānālaṁkāra: tatra rasagangādhara kṛtaḥ anumānālaṁkāreṇaivagatārthatvādanayoratiriktatvānupapattiḥ. . . . pāribhāṣikāpi na atra anumitiriti parāstam.*[22]

p) *Anyonyālaṁkāra: rasagaṅgādharakṛtastu -*

svavyadhikaraṇavyāpārasādhyasaiva paropakārasya camatkārādhāya katvaṁ na tu. . . svavyāpārasādhyasyopakārasya acamatkārakatvādato nedaṁ anyonyāt antaraṁ ityāhuḥ.[23]

q) *Viṣamālaṁkāra: yattu (rasagaṇgādhare) - "kva suktayaḥ kva muktā vā kva paṁkaḥ vā ca pankajaṁ kva mṛgaḥ, kva ca kastūrī dhigvidhāturvidagdhatāhi" ityādrunāyaṁdaṁkāraḥ. vastustastu, lokasiddhatvena alaṁkāra ayogāt. Kavipratibhāmātra kalpitānām arthānām alaṁkāratvāt.*[24]

B) Viśveśvara Pandeya in his Alaṁkāra muktāvalī (=AM):

Another major work on poetics, containing only figures of speech called 'AM' is taken for analysis. In the context of 'samāsokti' alaṁkāra the author has quoted the definition of RG and has criticised it. Here PR's view is refuted along with the view of Ruyaka.[25]

Here, we observe that in this work, there is one case where Pandeya objects to the view of PR.

C) Śriśivadata Sarma in his Kāvyarasāyana (=KR):

In Kāvyarasāyana, the rhetoric work of Sarmā, some major concepts of RG alongwith other remarkable rhetoricians, are cricitised. This text is composed in three main chapters with many a sub-chapter, starting with the definition of poetry and goes upto the analysis of some important alaṁkāras. This work is also remarkable for its logical interpretation of various concepts. However, we have taken this text to point out the cases, where Sarma has criticised the views of PR which are quoted below:

a) *yat ca tadvyākhyātṛbhiḥ vāmanācāryaiḥ: "yattu rasagaṇgādharakāraiḥ - "ramaṇīyārthapratipādakaḥ śabdaḥ kāvyaṁ" iti kāvyalakṣaṇaṁ kṛtvā uktaṁ: yattu prāñcaḥ (Kāvyaprakāśakārādayaḥ) śabdārthau kāvyamityāhuḥ tatra vicāryate, api ca kāvyapadap-ravṛttinimittaṁ..... tattu āgrahamūlaṁ eva, ata eva tat ṭikāyāṁ marmaprakāśākhyām 'ucitā' iti pratikam upādāya nāgojibhaṭṭaprāhuh āsvādavyanjaka tvasya ubhayatrāpyaviśeṣāt . . . tena anupahasanīyakāvya lakṣaṇaṁ . . . tat bhitimūlakam.*[26]

(Here, accordingly PR first cricitised his predecessors views along with Viśvanātha. Viśvanāth also criticised Mammaṭa earlier, and Sarma, the last rhetorician, again criticised PR's view.)

b) *Yattu gangādhare. . . sayitāsavidhe api anīsvarā. . . "ityudāhṛtaṁ, tatra, 'aho pūrṇaṁ saro yatra iti ivarthāntaraparyyavasāyitvaṁ kutona syāt iti cintyam.*[27] *(Here the verse given as an example for the first type of poetry viz. 'uttamottama', is strongly critisized. A passage is also given the prose discussions of PR as: 'tatra hi tatparaṁ prāṇān dhārayituṁ na śaknomi iti asya vyaṇgyasya 'harati gamanaṁ vālā, iti vācyasiddhyaṅgatvena prātipatsitatvat. anyathā samayākūlī.*[28]

Even the next example of RG, also is criticised. *"yattu gaṇgādhare. . . 'praharaviratau. . . ' etc., tat upekṣyam."*[29]

c) yattu gangādhare. . . sakya. . . doṣah darśita, tadā grahamūlaṁ, dhānyena dhanavān ityādāviva tṛtīyāyā abhedakārthatvāt.[30]

d) yattu gaṇgādhare 'śakya saṁbandha lakṣaṇa' ityabhihitaṁ, anyatra tadasphurtteḥ. . . tat nirūpaṇe abhidhāyā lakṣaṇātvaṁ tāddṛśa lakṣaṇāyāścābhidhātvaṁ kathaṁ na prabhavati . . . . anyathā tu samayanirodhaḥ; tathā sati śabdaniṣṭhatvasvīkāre pūrvamudāhṛtāpattiḥ, anyathā tu ayuktam..

"yattu gaṇgādhare . . . . sakya . . . tatredam abhidheyāni. . . etc.[31]

e) yacca. . . carācarajagat jālaṁ vadanaṁ sadanaṁ tava. . ., iti Jagannātha. . . udāhṛtaṁ, tadapi na manoramaṁ,. . . vikṣyetyādipaḍānām evoddipanādeḥvācyatvāt. . .

bālaprabhāva varṇanāparāyāṁ ca yaṣodoktau guṇībhāvāt ca. . hṛtcetanā iti vācyasiddhyangatvāt ca vyaṅgyasya.[32]

(Here, the example for wonderful sentiment in RG, is refuted, because there is no charm at all according to Sarma in this example).

D) Criticism of RG found in its Commentary literatures:

Unlike other texts on Poetics, RG does not have many commentaries, as already recorded. The well known grammarian Nāgesa, is the first person, to write a Commentary on RG, namely 'Gurumarmaprakāsikā' or 'Gurumarmaprakāsa'. This commentary is very brief and most concepts (contexts) of RG are not explained. It hardly fulfills the need of a Commentary. The other commentaries are 'Saralā, 'Candrikā', 'Rasacandrikā', 'Visamapadī', 'Madhusudani', 'Tattvakathānamu' (Telugu). Among these Commentaries, the one Madhusudani is written by Madhusudan Sashtri, a modern scholar. It is only Nagesa and Madhusudani, at times find some faults in RG.

Madhusudani starts on with the criticism of the first, second and fourth introductory verses.[33] The definition of the poetry, the 'bhāvanā, and some topics related to the cause of the poetry, the views of Mammaṭa, including some aspects as 'guṇa' 'alaṁkāra', 'doṣa' etc., are criticised by the Commentator in his Madhusudani. On the way of refutation, this commentator supports the definition of poetry as given by Mammaṭa and even Viśvanātha. For a detail study of this commentary, we, are quoting the views on 'Pratibhā', the cause of the poetry, 'Pratibhā', the poetic talent or intuition, as prescribed the only cause for composition of poetry by PR, is strongly refuted. Here the views of the author goes ahead to interpret sixteen more possible statements on pratibhā and finally concludes that, what ever is given by Mammaṭa for this cause is better than the PR's view.[34] The sixteen types of causes for the poetry are:

1) 'Samādhi' is the vyāpāra or the cause.

2) Practice, knowledge on śāstras, talent, together become the cause.
3) Erudition is only cause.
4) 'Sakti' is only cause. This 'śakti' is generated by 'samādhi', and practice. Then, developed by talent and erudition.
5) 'śakti is only cause from which talent and erudition generated.
6) Talent and erudition together become cause.
7) Erudition, practice and talent in sequence, become cause.
8) Talent is only cause. (This talent has two varieties namely 'sahajā' and 'utpādyā').
9) Talent is only cause (this talent has three varieties namely 'sahaja", 'āharyā' and 'aupadesikī').
10) 'śakti' or talent in the form of 'vāsanā' or 'saṁskāra' residing in poet is only cause.
11) 'śakti', 'nipuṇatā' (erudition) and 'abhyāsa' (practice) jointly become poetry.
12) 'śakti' is only cause.
13) 'Svāsthya', 'pratibhā abhyāsa (practice), 'sakti' (power), 'bahusṛtatā' (well versed), 'vidvānsangati' (company of learned people). *dṛḍhasmṛti* (strong memory) and 'utsāha' (interest); these eight together generate cause.
14) *'lokavṛtta', 'sakalavidyā', 'upavidyā(kalā)' 'kāvya-jñāna', 'abhyāsa', 'vṛddhasevā', 'avekṣaṇa', 'pratibhā', and 'avadhāna';* these nine together genrate cause.
15) *'śṛti', 'smṛti,' 'itihāsa', 'purāṇa', 'pada', 'vākya',*

'pramāṇa', 'upavidyā (kalā),' 'samayavidyā, 'rājasiddhāntatrayī', 'lokavṛtta', 'viracanā', 'yukti' and *'koṣa';* these fourteen together generate cause.

Here *'pada', 'vākya', and 'pramāna'* should be understood as *vidyā whereas 'viracanā* is referring to epics.

16) These four namely *'ucitasaṁyoga', 'yoktṛsaṁyoga' 'utpādyasaṁyoga'* and *'saṁyoga vikāra'*, with addition to above fourteen varieites together became the cause of the poetry.

After this detail treatment of cause, now the commentator criticises the first variety of poetry i.e., uttamottama, as given by PR, including its illustrative verses.

"sayitāsavidhe. . . etc. 'gurumadhyagatā. . etc., and 'talpagatāpi. . . etc.' Alike the case of first variety, the second and third varieties are also taken for discussion and refutaiton.[35]

In the context of various rasa theories, the theory of new logicians and other one theory (group) is also criticised in 'Madhusudani'. The same process is followed here at the context of 'guṇa'. A detailed study on this by the Commentator is given beside the running Commentary in the introduction of RG.[36]

In conclusion, it may be stated that, in the subjective analysis of various concepts of poetics, it is very difficult to hold some view on as absolutely correct and flawless.

As one can notice, PR has criticised so many views of his predecessors and has given his own views and interpretaions, still, he has been criticised by Visvesvara Pandita, Pandeya, Sarma, Madhusudan Sastri etc.

Inspite of the fact that PR has been criticised in some

cases, like the definition of poetry, the cause of poetry, the two varieties of the poetry, etc., still, one is not certain as to the exact position with regard to its accuracy and the correctness of these theories. Thus, it is no gain to say, whether PR is right or his predecessors or his successors on some issues.

REFERENCES

1. AK. p. 21.
2. *ibid.*, p. 24.
3. *ibid.*, p. 91, 106.
4. *ibid.*, p. 161 cf. RG II, p. 548.
5. *ibid.*, p. 163 cf. RG II, p. 549.
6. *ibid.*, p. 164 cf. RG II, p. 564.
7. *ibid.*, p. 178.
8. *ibid.*, p. 201 cf. RG II pp. 573-74.
9. *ibid.*, p. 223 cf. RG II, p. 525.
10. *ibid.*, p. 238 cf. RG II, p. 639.
11. *ibid.*, p. 250.
12. *ibid.*, p. 268.
13. *ibid.*, p. 276.
14. *ibid.*, p. 283.
15. *ibid.*, p. 283-87.
16. *ibid.*, p. 290.
17. *ibid.*, p. 298.
18. *ibid.*, p. 310.
19. *ibid.*, p. 313.
20. *ibid.*, p. 338-40.
21. *ibid.*, p. 343.
22. *ibid.*, p. 354.
23. *ibid.*, p. 361.
24. *ibid.*, p. 374.
25. AM. pp. 22-23.
26. KR. pp. 6-7. cf. RG p. 13.

27. *ibid*., p. 10 cf. RG p. 64, 80
28. *ibid*., p. 10 cf. RG p. 86
29. *ibid*., p. 11 cf. RG. p. 86.
30. *ibid*., p. 13.
31. *ibid*., p. 18.
32. *ibid*., p. 53 cf. RG. 191.
33. Madhusudani. RG. pp. 1-2, pp. 6-7 (Sanskrit Comm.)
34. *ibid*., p. 36.
35. *ibid*., pp. 41-43.
36. *ibid*., pp. 52-53.

IV.1. SOME TEXTUAL PROBLEMS IN RG

While going through the text of RG, one meets with some readings which do not go properly with the text. Again in different editions of this text, we have cases of different readings, out of which a few are very significant. Since RG was composed in the latter half of seventeenth C.A.D., the reading do not pose much problem. Further, as the text is written in a style, which is not very much common, we have less scope of omissions and commissions in the hands of the scribes. We have consulted all the available editions of this text, to compare the readings and our preference to a particular reading is based on the exactness and appropriateness of the reading to the context. We do not intend to discuss all the readings having some scope of confusion. All the available variants including the minor words like 'ca', 'tu', 'vā'. 'atra', etc., are presented in the appendix at the end. We have also recorded the variant readings in each texts wherever they occur, just after the texts. In the present chapter we will be discussing a few selected readings as examples.

Nāgeśa in his commentary (i.e. marmaprakāśa) on RG, has suggested some improvements on the texts and has given his preference on the reading. In most cases, his comments points out to the fact that the readings are of the author himself and not ascribed to any later scribe or kind. For example:

1. *"akhaṇḍam" iti pāṭhastu cintya eva.* (p. 49)
2. *"itaḥ prāk yathā vā ityapapāṭhaḥ".* (p. 217)
3. *"smṛtāpi iti kvācit kaḥ apāpaṭhaḥ".* (p. 255)
4. *"cintotkarṣa" iti pāṭhāntaraṁ.* (p. 330).

In his commentary to RG, Madhusudana Sastri, (i.e. Madhusudani), also has suggested and pointed out some problems with regard to the construction of the text and reading as well. To quote a few examples:

1. *tasmāt anākalanāditi granthāntaralipikartṛṇāṁ, pūrva rūpapāṭhakānāṁ vā pramādādāgato lekhaḥ bhrāmakaḥ. ".*(p. 84)
2. *"...ata eva iti pāṭhotrāśuddhaḥ pratibhāti* (p. 106)
3. *"tathā ca viṣayitāśatī bodha iti ucitaḥ pāṭhaḥ kāvyārtha bhāvanājanya iti pāṭhopi adhikaḥ"* (p. 240)
4. *"atra madhuratvamadhurataratvādi gunānāṁ iti duṣ pāṭhaḥ* (p. 231)
5. *"atyantapāketi pāthaḥ vicāraṇīyaḥ"* (p. 252)

Let us now take some texts of RG, for discussion and analysis. In the context of the division of poetry, PR quotes the view of AP, who has given the verse. The verse runs as follows:

"niḥśśeṣacyutacandanaṁ stanataṭaṁ nirmṛṣṭarāgodharo
netre dūramanañjane pulakitā tanvī taveyaṁ tanuḥ,
mithyāvādini ! dūti! bāndhavajanasyā jñātapīḍāgame
vāpīṁ snātumito gatāsi na punaḥ tasyādhamasyānti-kam."[1]

This may be translated as: "Oh messenger! Your breasts are free from sandal paste; your lower lip is devoid of red colour; your eyes are destitute of black pigment; your tender body is all in horripilation. Oh liar! You have not realised the anguish of your dear friend. From here you have gone only to the tank for a bath and not to that accursed (wretched) person."

Here this above quoted verse is given as an illustration of suggestive poetry or suggestion. To him only "saṁbhoga-sṛṅgāra i.e., love-in-union is suggested from the description. He also gives the reason as to why that is the only possibility or only cause which can explain the situation properly.

Against this view of Appayyadikṣita, PR proposes the theory of 'Kāraṇasādhāraṇavāda' that is, more than one possibility namely a) bathing b) love making etc., as the causes of such a situation and hence, one can not accept the suggestion of 'love-in-union' from the expression. "niḥśśeṣa cyuta. . . etc." To criticise Appayyadikṣita, PR writes by explaining the verse -

"ayi bāndhvajanasyājñātapīḍāgme.! svārthaparāyaṇe, snānakālātikramabhayavaśena nadīmadīyapriyayorantika magatvaiva vāpīṁ snātumito mamāntikad gatāsi na punaḥ tasya paravedanānabhijṅatayā duḥkha dātṛtvenādhamasya antikam.[2]

In these expressions, the use of two negatives namely "madīyapriyayoḥ antikam agatvā eva" and "tasyā dhamasya antikaṁ na gatāsi" are absurd and meaning less. There is no way by which this text can be better constructed. The text may be translated like this - 'O selfish one! On the pretext that you will be late for bathe, instead of going to the river and my lover, you have gone from here to the nearby tank and not to that 'adhama' (my lover).[3]

All the editions we have consulted have this text. It is

only Madhusudana Shastri who has noted this in the following lines:

"tataśca lekhoyaṁ paṇḍitarājasya cintya eva."[4]

Thus, he suggests that the fault has its origin in the author himself, which is difficult to accept. A writer of the calibre of PR, a poet by himself, who even compose all his illustrative verses of his own, cannot have committed such a mistake. But nothing can be said for certain. If we drop the words 'madīyapriyayoḥ antikaṁ' then the text would be proper. Thus, it is possible that this clause might have been added later by some scribes, as is common practice in cases of Sanskrit writers.

Now let us take a further reading for analysis. Commentary on the same verse 'niḥśśeṣacyuta etc., PR answers to some one who proposes to resort to 'lakṣanā' instead of 'vyanjanā' like Appayyadikṣita. He writes "evaṁ sādhāraṇeṣ u eṣu vākyeṣu mukhyārthabādhābhāvāt, tātparyārthasya jhaṭ iti anākalanāt, kutotra lakṣaṇā vakāśaḥ."[5]

This is the reading available in all the editions. This expression says that there is no "mukhyārthabādha" namely, 'the maid had gone to take a bath', which goes well with the description and hence no need to resort to lakṣaṇā for this knowledge. But how to understand the second line "tātparyārthasya jhaṭiti anākalanāt iti". Since, the intended meaning is not obtained instantly, which is not true in the present case, there may be the necessity to adopt to lakṣaṇā, Hence, the expression, "Kutotra lakṣaṇāvakāśa" is superfluous. As a matter of fact, for lakṣaṇā, no reason has to be presented. Here the main reason, mukhyārthavādha is not there. And the other reason may be the difficulty in understanding the fact instantly. Thus, the text may be reconstructed as atra lakṣaṇāvakāśaḥ and not "kutotra lakṣaṇāvakāśaḥ".

But PR do not want lakṣaṇā to be postulated here. Hence, the reading may be (accepted as) mukhyārthasya jhaṭiti ākalanāt and not anākalanāt.

Following Abhinavagupta, PR gives an alternative theory of the enjoyment of sentiment. He writes vibhāvādicarvaṇāmahimnā sahṛdayasya nijasahṛdayatāvaśonmiṣitena vibhāvādisaṁsṛḍṭa tat tat sthāyi upahitasvasvarūpānandākārā samādhau iva yoginaḥ cittavṛttiḥ upajāyate.[6] Here for this text, we have another reading bhāvanāviśeṣa mahimnā for vibhāvā dicarvaṇā mahimnā etc.

Out of these two, the reading vibhāvādicarvaṇā mahimnā does not go properly with the text. Let us elaborate: In the second line also, vibhāvādi etc., is repeated. And in the enjoyment of sentiment, the excitant, ensuant etc., are mere media which helps the enjoyment. They cannot be taken as the prime-factor. Thus, the expression vibhāvādi carvaṇāmahimnā; i.e. due to the power of the knowledge of excitant etc., cittavṛttiḥ upajāyate, is not proper. Rather it is the power of extraordinary bhāvanā, i.e. repeated thinking, which is responsible for the enjoyment of the respectively sentiment based on respective permanent moods (sthāyis), developed by the respective excitants etc.

Further, the expression "nijasahṛdayatāvaśonmiṣitena" goes very well with bhāvanā (pūrvavāsanārūpā) and not with "vibhāvādi carvaṇā" etc. Again PR has referred to this type of expression namely "bhāvanā viśeṣamahimnā" else where as well. For example, while quoting the view of modern rhetoricians, he writes: "navyāstu kāvye nāṭye ca kavinā naṭena ca prakāśiteṣu vibhāvādiṣu. . . . bhāvanāviśeṣa rūpasya doṣasya mahimnā . . . śakuntalādi viṣayaka ratyādireva rasaḥ."[7]

In his definition of poetry, in way of classification, he writes - "ittham ca camatkārajanaka bhāvanāviṣayārthapratipādakaḥ śabdatvaṁ (kāvyatvaṁ)."[8] Even in his main definition of sentiment, PR uses this expression.

". . . . tadīyasahṛdayatāsahakṛtena bhāvanā viśeṣa mahimnā vigalita duṣyantaramanītvādibhiḥ alaukika vibhāvānubhāva . . . prāk viniviṣṭa vāsanā rūpo ratyādireva rasaḥ.'[9] Thus, we can say that the reading here would be "bhāvanā viśeṣa mahimnā" and not "vibāvādicarvaṇā mahimnā".

REFERENCES

1. Supra, RG Text No. 14.
2. RG, pp. 81-82.
3. Comm. on RG. p. 82.
4. *ibid.*, p. 82.
5. RG, p. 83.
6. *ibid.*, p. 114.
7. *ibid.*, pp. 131-133.
8. *ibid.*, pp. 16-18.
9. *ibid.*, pp. 101-106.

IV.2 INFLUENCE OF NEO-LOGIC ON PR

The science of logic was rightly acclaimed by the scholars of ancient India as the light of all the branches of learning - "pradipaḥ sarvavidyānāṁ sarvaśāstrānām." This perhaps can more appropriately be said in regard to the Navya Nyāya system of logic which gradually flourished in India after Udayanācarya (1000 A.D.) and particularly at the time of Gangeśopadhyāya, the illustrious author of 'Tattvacintāmaṇi'.[1] In later period, this branch of learning was made so perfect and useful for unambiguous expression of subtle ideas that it became absoluteley unavoidable to compose any thing on any branch of Sanskrit studies which were written after the development of Navyanyāya. This technique of Navyanyāya is so thorough and subtle that it is almost impossible to conceive a more perfect and unambiguous method of expression in Sanskrit, if not in any other language. The super excellence of the technique of Navyanyāya is clearly borne out by the fact that the whole of the India spontaneously accepted this technique as the instrument par excellence to give expression to any subtle idea that might have occurred in the minds of the scholars in any branch of Sanskrit studies.[2]

On the style of Navyanyāya writings, D.C. Guha writes: "The language of Navyanyāya has got a peculiar ring of music of its own for the appreciation which the mind and the ear have got to be systematically trained. . . and I think it should be repeated a thousand and one times in the traditional method of study as is still in vogue in our coutnry in the Sanskrit Tols and Pāthaśālās.[3]

As we have mentioned above the entire community of traditional writers were so much influenced by the style of Navyanyāya expression that in each and every branch of Sanskrit learning, we have texts, written in this style. PR, a great admirer of Navyanyāya style of writings, composed his RG by making use of Navyanyāya tools of exressions which made his work perfect and precise. One comes across in his text the usage of many technical devices in his writings. With a view to make his definition flawless, unambiguous and precise, he preferred the right tool of Navyanyāya techniques. Almost each and every definitions are framed on the lime of Navyanyāya expression. It is not possible to present here all the instances where PR has utilised this technique of Navyanyāya, which we have mostly pointed out in our explanations of the text. We present here, a few cases to show and justify how the Navyanyāya technique of expression has helped PR in framing his definitions. We have repeatedly mentioned that RG is the outstanding contribution of PR towards the study of Sanskrit Poetics and this is because of his employment of Navyanyāya style. Very frequently, we come across the technical terms like akhaṇḍopādhi pp. 49, 283, anugamaka p. 37, anuvādyatāvacchedaka p. 67, anvayavyatireka p. 39, avacchedakatva pp. 10, 11, 35, 215, avacchedakatvasaṁbhaṁdha pp. 17-18, vyāpti p. 35, avyāpyavṛtti pp. 23, 42, upādhi p. 49, kāraṇatāvacchedakatva pp. 48-49, 228, jāti pp. 15, 49, paryāptisambandha p. 25, vinigamana pp. 23, 379, viśeṣya p. 118, viśeṣyatāvacchedaka pp. 13, 135, viśeṣyatā saṁbandha p. 14, vyāsajya vṛtti p. 25, vyāsajyavṛttidharma p. 20, śakyatāvacchedaka saṁbandha pp. 290-291, and so on, in RG. It is not possible to explain these terms here which, one can get from any good work on Navyanyāya like materials for the study of Navyanyāya of D.H.H. Ingalls or 'Navyanyāya' doctrine of negation of B.K. Matilal and Navyanyāya system of logic of D.C. guha.

We cite here a few cases where these techniques are utilised in RG. We will also try to justify how PR has attained perfectness and preciseness in framing his definitions by employing these techniques.

The definition of poetry as given by PR is as follows: "ramaṇīyārthapratipādakaḥ śabddaḥ kāvyam." In this definition, PR has tried to avoid all types of faults like avyāpti (under-application), and ativyāpti (over-application) etc.[4] The definition is short and sweet at the same time which suggest the preciseness and accuracy of his definition. By defining poetry in terms of 'word', he has overcome the objections which were raised against the definitions of these defining poetry in term of 'word and sense' together, like Bhāmaha, Vāmana, Udbhaṭa Rudraṭa, Anandavardhana, Kuntaka, Mammaṭa etc. Further, by excluding the qualifications like adoṣau (free from faults), saguṇau (with merits) and sālaṁkārau (with figures of speech) etc. in the body of the definition as found in case of Mammaṭa etc.,[5] and other qualifications as well PR has avoided the possible objections raised in case of those definitions. Again he defines ramaṇīyatā as 'lokottarāhlādajanakajñānagocaratā and lokottaratva is defined further in terms of a unversal (jāti) as 'camatkāratva' residing in the 'āhlāda', which is determined by one's experience (i.e. anubhavasākṣika jāti viśeṣaḥ). By defining this extraordinaryness (lokottaratva) in term of 'jāti ' a great preciseness is attained, because, all case of camatkāras are included in this. He has given three further modified definitions which are clear, precise and accurate. They are: "itthaṁ ca camatkāra janakabhāvanā viṣayārthapratipādakaḥ-śabdatvam" etc.[6] In this definition, he has employed the term 'bhāvanā' namely 'camatkārajanakabhāvanā viṣayaka' etc., 'yat pratipā. . . bhāvanātva' etc., instead of 'jñāna' by which the definition of poetry will not be erroneously applicable to the expressions that generates worldly pleasures like 'A son is born to you' or 'I shall give you wealth' etc. Further, he has made this 'bhavanātva i.e., bhāvanā-ness as the delimitor of the generatingness of cāmatkāra or charmingness, by which all cases of expression that generates extraordinary pleasure are included in poetry.

In the same context while examining and criticisng the view of theorists, who define poetry in terms of 'word and sense together', he asks:-"Whether, the condition of referring poetry resides in both 'word' and 'sense' together (śabdārthau vyāsaktam) or individually in each word and sense (pratyekaṁ prayaptaṁ). And by the help of device of 'vyāsajyavṛtti saṁbandha' and 'samavāyasaṁbandha' he has rejected the theory that word and sense together forms poetry.

While discussing on the cause of the poetry i.e. kāvyahetu, PR says, 'tasya ca kāraṇaṁ kavigatā kevalā pratibhā' and he defines this kāraṇa of poetry in terms of a universal. To him, the causality of poetry is to be delimited by the universal called 'pratibhātva'. It is either a 'jāti' or 'akhaṇḍopādhi' "tadgataṁ ca pratibhātvaṁ kāvyakāraṇatā vacchedakatayā siddho jātiviśeṣaḥ upādhirūpaṁ vākhaṇḍam."[7]

In order to justify the case where, even in the presence of erudition (vyutpatti) and practice (abhyāsa), the poetic-talent or intuition (pratibhā) is not seen, he notes that there is the absence of the delimitor of causality - "kāraṇatāvacchedakānavacchinnatvāt,[8] and he qualifies the kāraṇatā (causality) with the absence of any obstructing factor. Like this, through out in his text, PR has tried to define the poetic theories by the help of Navyanyāya techniques. He has also tried to avoid logical heaviness (gaurava), throughout his writings, and has shown his preference for economy in expressions (lāghava). There is no need to quote any instance, where, he has not adhered to this principle of gaurava and lāghava. I quote here a few instances:

1. na ca tatra pratibhāyāḥ. . .
   pratibhāhetutvakalpane lāghavāt. (pp. 37-38).
2. . . . prāstāvikarūpeṅaiva rasānāṁ kāraṇatopapattau guṅakalpane gauravāt (p. 226. II. 1-2)
3. . . . mādhuryavattvena kāraṇatāyā gurubhūtatvāt. itthaṁ ca prātisvikarūpeṇaiva kāraṇatve lāghavam (pp. 231-32, I.1)
4. na tatra tayoḥ janmāntarīyayoḥ kalpanam vācyam. gaurvāt. . . . (p. 53, II. 2-3).

While quoting some views of his predecessors, which he wants to criticise his style of expression is:

a) yathā citramīmāṁsā kṛtoktaṃ. . . praharaviratau madhye etc. . . tan na. (p. 89, II. 5-11)
b) yattu prāñcaḥ adosau. . .
   ityāhuḥ tatra vicāryate (p. 22, I. 1)
c) yattu āsvādodbodhaka. . . tan na. (pp. 24-25, I. 4.)
d) yattu rasvadeva. . . tan na (p. 44, I. 2)
e) yadāhuḥ : "padārthe . . . ca iti" (p. 247, I.24)

Sometimes he hesitatingly accepts some views and ultimately rejects it:

a) astu vā tataḥ paraṁ. . . ko nivārayet (pp. 90-91, I.6)
b) vastustastu. . . ca siddham. (pp. 118-19, I. 2.)
c) astu vā prādhānyena. . . tathāpi. . . (pp-280-81, I.4)
d) vastutas tu. . . na kṣatiḥ. (p. 285, II. 2-5)

While introducing the views of some opponents, actual or imaginary, he invariably introduces in the following expression.

a) nanu evam api rateḥ astu nāma. . . iti cet, satyam, (pp. 136-37, I.6)

b) nanu cvam prāguktaṁ . . . cen na (p. 88, II. 4-5)

c) nanu krodhāmarṣayoḥ. . . ceti, kāryavailakṣaṇyam. (p. 319, II. 4-6)

d) nanu ca uttarārdhe. . . iti cet, abhivyakteḥ (p. 297, II. 2-4)

For supporting and clarifying his position, he starts with the expression namely:

a) tathā cāhuḥ. . . iti (p. 221, II. 6-8)

b) tathā hi - śleṣodāratā. . iti vācyam. (p. 251, II. 6-9)

c) taduktaṁ . . . devabhartṛ. . . tām ādiśet iti. (p. 287, II, 6-11)

d) tathā hi virarasa. . . pratīyamānaḥ (p. 309, 11. 6-10)

e) teṣāṁ mate . . . udāharyam (p. 316, II, 8-11)

f) tathā coktaṁ . . . iti (p. 353, II. 5-7)

g) ata eva caramādhyāye. . vyavasthāpitam. (pp. 155-58, I. 6)

In some cases, he gives more than one interpretaions, for which he uses the expression yadvā etc.

a) yadvā bhāvanā. . . upajāyate (p. 114, II. 2-4)

b) na vā upamarda vācyaḥ. . . nāpi camatkārī (p. 363, I. 9)

Thus, we can conclude that PR has attained great success of preciseness and accuracy by adopting the Navyanyāya style of expression. His theories, definitions have become sharp and forceful only because of his employment of Navyanyāya technique which we have amply elaborated above through examples.

REFERENCES

1. D.C. Guha. Navyanyāya system of logic, p. 1.
2. *ibid.*
3. *ibid.*
4. RG, pp. 14-19.
5. KP, I.1.
6. For other two definitions, Vide RG, pp. 17-19.
7. RG, pp. 48-49. I. 1.
8. *ibid.*, p. 60, I. 1.

IV. 3 INFLUENCE OF PREDECESSORS ON PR

PR flourished in a time when poetics or rather the various theories were well developed. We have already stated elsewhere that PR is as 'if last gloomy luminary in the galaxy of Sanskrit poetics.[1] We have also stated that it is quite natural that PR's RG is a more work of compilation than an original one. Thus, it is quite natural that one can notice profound influences of predecessors on PR. This does not suggest that PR has nothing original to his credit. Infact, he has contributed a lot in the form of new interpretations and advanced theories etc., in Sanskrit poetics with regard to various concepts which are described on different occasions. The detail analysis of each and every concept with regard to the influence of predecessors on RG is shown in the respective place while dealing with the text.

Here follows a brief discussion on RG to show the influence of predecessors on PR. We will be showing here only the concepts and theories which PR has accepted in his text and not the disputes which PR has rejected.

Overall 56 instances are available in this work where PR has accepted the theories of his predecessors. Interestingly the refutation of the views of his predecessors are most advanced. The acceptance of views rather than the refutations, comes latter on.

Whereas the first instance of refutations occurs in the concept of definition of poetry, the accepted theory of his predecessors occurs in the concept of classificaiton of poetry.[2]

I. At the very outset on the issue of the classification of poetry, the views given by AD is criticised in detail. The example verse namely, "niśṣesacyuta . . . etc." is not proper in this first variety of poetry is the sole statement of PR. To get support for his own statement and to overcome on AD, Panditarāja directly hints the same discussions as given by Mammaṭa in his KP. Mammta explains that without any remnant of sandal paste does not mean that the fall of sandalpaste is only due to love making. While taking bath, also the sandalpaste can fall. So here for one effect there are so many causes and that is why the description given by AD is not so logical. In this context, we observe the influence of Mammṭa on PR on refuting AD.[3]

Further KP's example namely, "O pious one, you may now walk about freely. . . etc."[4] is quoted by PR and thus the views of AD are strongly criticised. Also there are two rejoinders quoted from VV and DA in this context.[5]

II. The second instance comes in the rasa concept. PR quotes the definition of rasa from KP after giving his own definition. According to Mammata the rasa or the sentiment is as: With the proper amplification by vibhāva etc., the permanent mood is called as sentiment. Here, the amplification made by vibhāva etc. is nothing else but the reflection of suggestive sense.[6] Abhinavagupta also narrates the definition of rasa in detail and his statement is well adjusted by PR.[7]

"Raso vai saḥ", "rasaṁ hi evāyaṁ labdhvānandī bhavati" etc., are also quoted from Veda.[8]

III. After Abhinavagupta's rasa theory now PR rewrites the theories made by Bhaṭṭanāyaka and so many others. At present, Bhaṭṭanāyaka's views runs as "tāṭasthyena rasapratitāvanāsādyatvaṁ" etc. as the definition of rasa.

IV. Now, besides these above statements regarding rasa, another seven minor statements are quoted here by PR. Though these forecoming remarks are not well mentioned and the exponents of these theories are not known, therefore it is imagined that PR himself has raised these objections.[9] The text, the commentators are silent on the issue of the exponents of these theories till today.

V. In this entire rasa theory, according to PR, the famous rasasūtra of Bharata is now discussed in RG.[10] Further there are eight types of separate and elaborate explanations given by PR himself, following the rasasūtra of Bharata. These eight types of explanations are given in detail in the text.

VI. After narrating the rasa theory, now PR shows the number of rasa and refuting the views of those counting eight rasas only, after addition of Śānta as ninth rasa. For this, PR takes help of Vyāsamunī and the author of SR.[11]

VII. Now, for these nine rasas nine permanent moods are quoted which is similar with the text of Mammata[12] and the permanent mood is also narated.[13] The difference between the permanent mood and the othermoods like the transitory mood etc., is quoted from SR.[14]

VIII. The difference between a rasadhvani and a rasālaṁkāra is briefly written by PR. Where the importance of rasa with the help of suggestive sense occurs there the rasadhvani takes place. Unlike this if the position of rasa becomes subordinate, then rasālaṁkāra takes place. For this PR follows the ancient tradition.[15]

IX. Now PR gives the detailed study of nine rasas. On the process of this study on hāsya or the laughing, after giving the proper example for this PR elaborates his predecessors views regarding the nature and classification of the said rasa. In all six types of hāsya namely smita, hasita, vihasita, upahasita, apahasita and atihasita are given there. Further, these six types of hāsya are grouped into three, according to three types of people namely uttama, madhyama and adhama.[16]

X. Regarding transitory mood, the traditional theory, basically from Bharata, is reapproached in the context of rasa theory.

"ratirdevādiviṣayā vyabhicārī tathāñjitaḥ bhāvaḥ proktahstadābhāsānyanaucityapravartitāḥ."[17]

XI. Regarding sentimental theories on poetic blemishes, specially for rasadoṣa, the famous quotation of DA is given here.

XII. This is the only cause to make disturbance in rasa and therefore, poet should be very careful when composing poetry.[18] Further, for this topic one illustrative verse is taken from Mahanāṭaka.

XIII. The position of guṇas in rasas is given here in a systematic way. The praticular guṇa takes place in various rasas but its position increases from one to another rasas, according to their demands. On this, three separate statements are quoted by PR.[19] According to mammaṭa and others, there are three states or mental conditions for three guṇas. Druti, dīpti and vikāsa are those three conditions. These are called as cittavṛttis.[20]

The tradition accepts ten different guṇas having the same names for both śabda and arthaguṇas. Here PR, declares that these terms as given by old theorists as ten in number, are different and they each vary from śabda to artha.[21] For example, in the very first śabdaguṇa i.e., sleṣa, the original definition of PR is given and then his predecessors statement is quoted,[22]

In arthguṇa section, the ojaguṇa also gets the proper support from the view of PR's predecessor. The predecessor's view is as follows: "padārthe vākya racanā . . . . etc."[23]

Here, both PR and his predecessors views are same as there are five types of oja. Finally, PR concludes the guṇa concept accepting three major guṇas and further, he includes all the ten guṇas in these three guṇas. This is almost similar to the view or explaination of Mammata and PR has clearly stated so.[24]

XIV. For special type of guṇa and ritī concepts, PR tells that even after having the sense of composing of a good poetry, yet the poet should be more careful for adoption of sentiments. Here, some old views are quoted.[25] For rīti, the verse for example is taken from Amaruśataka.

"śūnyaṁ vāsagruhaṁ vilokya śayanādutthāya kiṅciccha-naiḥ . . . .
lajjānamramukhī priyeṇa hasatā bālā ciraṁ cuṁbitā."[26]

XV. The transitory moods plays a vital role in RG and the full study of all the varieites of the transitory moods are given in order. The definition of bhāva of KP, is taken here to get support to his own definition by PR.[27] Interestingly, three more definitions for bhāva are reproduced here. Among these three, the first one is supposed to be a modified definition of PR. that runs as follows:

"harṣādināṁ ca sāmājikagatānāmeva. . . etc."[28]

Now PR prescribes thrity four moods, including the last two as nirveda and rati. In the first type of these bhāvas, the harṣa gets support from ancients. Here both PR and his predecessors statements are equally same and the nature of both the definitions are also include on one theme. For both of these definitions, suitable examples are given by PR.29

Like this, the another bhāva called as moha is given in RG. For this, PR gives a new definition, made by logicians; 'avasthāntaraśabalitā sātathā. . . etc.'[30]

Further, for the bhavas like mada,[31] śrama,[32] trāsa,[33] avahittha,[34] ugratā,[35] autsukya,[36] jaḍatā,[37] and capalatā,[38] PR has drawn upon his predecessors.

XVI. For rasābhāsa, the predecessors views are quoted by PR. After clarifying all the theories on this brief topic, which is like an example verse, is quoted which shows the influence.[39]

XVII. For dhvani section, the only one variety, alakṣ yakrama rūpa, is discussed in this part of the RG. And for this both DA and locana, are taking the verse from KS.[40]

This above written study is only a short listed document to show the influence of the predecessors on PR.

REFERENCES

1. See introduction of RG, cf. CM. p. 2.
2. 'yattu prāñcaḥ "adoṣau saguṇau sālaṁkārau. . . etc.," *ibid.*, p. 22.
   'prācīnasakalagranthaviruddhatvādupapatti

virodhācca. . . etc.' *ibid*, p. 74.
3. 'niśśeṣityādi gamakatayā yāni. . . etc.' *ibid.*, p. 74.
4. "bhama dhammia vīsattho so sunao ajjamālido teṇa, golāṇaīkacchakuḍaṅgavāsiṇā dariasīheṇa" *ibid.*, pp. 75-77.
5. for VV & DA. Vide RG, p. 77.
6. 'vyaktaḥ sa tairvibhāvādaiḥ. . . etc.' ibid, p.I.7.
7. ". . . ityāhuḥ Abhinavaguptā. . . etc." ibid, p.121.
8. Vide Upanishad.
9. *ibid.*, pp. 147.50.
10. "Vibhāvānubhāvavyabhicāri saṁyogādrasaniṣpattiḥ" *ibid.*, p. 150.
11. "aṣṭāveva rasaḥ nātyeṣviti kecidacūcudan tadacāru yataḥ kaṁcinna rasaṁ svadate naṭaḥ." *ibid.*, p. 156.
12. "ratiḥ śokaśca nirvedakrodhotsāhaśca visayaḥ, hāso bhayaṁ jugupsā ca sthāyibhāvāḥ kramādami". *ibid.*, p. 156.
13. *ibid.*, pp. 158-59.
14. *ibid.*, p. 160.
15. *ibid.*, p. 199.
16. *ibid.*, pp. 194-97.
17. *ibid.*, p. 202.
18. *ibid.*, p. 221.
19. raseṣu cāiteśu nigaditeṣu mādhuryaujaḥprasādākhyāṁ-srīnguṇānāhuḥ, tatra 'śṛṅgāre. . . etc. . .
20. *ibid.*, pp. 223-24.
21. "nāmāni puna stāneva lakṣaṇaṁ tu bhinnaṁ" ibid, p.235.
22. śliṣṭamaspaṣṭaśaithilyaṁ śleṣam. . ." *ibid.*, p. 235.
23. *ibid.*, p. 247.
24. *ibid.*, p. 254.
25. *ibid.*, p. 273.
26. *ibid.*, p. 275.
27. "vyabhicāryañjito bhāvaḥ". *ibid.*, p. 283.

28. *ibid.*, p. 283.
29. *ibid.*, p. 287.
30. *ibid.*, p. 295.
31. 'saṁmohānandasaṁbhedo mado madyopayogajaḥ.' *ibid.*, p. 303.
32. "ekaikaśo davanda śo vā trayānāṁ vā prakopataḥ" etc.,
33. "autpātikairamanaḥ kṣepastrāsaḥ kaṁpādikārakaḥ" *ibid.*, p. 312.
34. *ibid.*, p. 320.
35. *ibid.*, p. 321.
36. *ibid.*, p. 328.
37. *ibid.*, pp. 330-31.
38. *ibid.*, p. 338.
39. "upanāyakasaṁsthāyāṁ munigurupatnīgatāyāṁ ca, bahunāyakaviṣayāyām ratau tathānubhayaniṣṭhāyāṁ." *ibid.*, p. 353.
40. "evaṁvādini devarṣau pārśve pituradhomukhī līlāyamala-patrāṇi gaṇayāmāsa pārvatī." *ibid.*, p. 374.

IV.4 IMPORTANCE OF RG IN SANSKRIT POETICS

This chapter aims at discussing the various aspects of RG and also the position that it holds in the entire Sanskrit poetics. It is often seen in the works of Sanskrit Poetics that the auther shifts his attention from the main topic following the title of his work. For example, NS, KP,SD and CA are some ancient texts where the author has failed to concentrate his work according to the title. At several places a lot of digressions are found which are made purposefully and are quite irrelevant to the main theme of the work. For e.g. in NS. the author should have devoted his work wholly to explain Nāṭya Sāstra i.e. science of dramaturgy very much in detail. But instead of doing this, he explains elements such as the nature and classification of hero and heroine, rasa, bhāva (mood) and figuers of speech. These topics are no doubt essential but not so that the author should shift his study from explanation of NS to the explanation of these elements. Not only NS, even in KP, SD and CA same process of study has been repeated.

But PR has been very careful not to repeat this mistake and he has been very much successful in confining his field of work to the main topic i.e. Rasa. His title and his text both are very well intertwined together. At few places we come across few digressions, but those digressaions are made simply to enable the reader to understand his text thoroughly. In short the digressions are made only as much as required and it is done deliberately. Unlike the authors of NS, KP and CA etc. he does not shift from the main study work of his text.

Adopting style of various concepts in particular:

The various concepts namely ramaṇīya, camatkāra, bhāvanā, upādhi, jāti, uttamottama, sahṛdaya, etc. are widely discussed in RG, where as such type of discussions are not found in any of his predecessors texts. To bring out a clear picture of these topics, PR was so interested that the entire relevant factors are narrated by him in their proper places.

Among these, much importance has been given to the treatment of ramaṇīyatā, the charmingness. At the very beginning of the work, this term has been discussed to make easy the understanding of the definition of poetry. The charmingness of word and sense has fully ruled over the RG. May be, some suggestive senses are hiding in this term (ramaṇīyatā). But in our study, the ramaṇīyatā is only giving extraordinary pleasure or lokottaracamatkāra, which is well narrated in the text and the translation part of this thesis. Rightly, Gangopadhyaya remarks on the second term as Camatkāra, "Of the other post dhvani writers, PR deserves mention: his RG being the last remarkable work on poetics. Though, mainly a follower of the dhvani school of Indian doctrines, as also to leave the beaten track carved by the ancients. He defines poetry as a linguistic composition, which brings a charming idea into expression, and gives a beautiful analysis of charmingness which is said to belong to an idea, causing unwordly or disinterested pleasure. This quality of disinterestedness, which is a fact of internal experience is an attribute of pleasure, being synonymous with camatkāra or strikingness. Thus, PR gives an analysis of the charmingness and thereby connects the concept camatkāra with that of rasa in the domain of literary activity".[1] Further following PR's statement, Madhusudan Sastri says that Camatkāra is nothing else, but only synonymous with ramaṇīya, ślāghya, viśeṣa or spṛhaṇiya, etc.[2]

Bhāvanā, the qualitative imagination is the main factor in this sense that without imagination, the understanding of the main definition becomes difficult. To this point,

Gangopadhyaya quotes seven types of imagination in detail.[3] Like this, some other terms, as we say concepts in particular, are highly placed by PR in his RG, which is unique in entire poetics. Uttamottama, a newly invented variety of poetry, created sensation among the scholars. Having such logical points to prove, PR managed to clarify his status on this newly made variety and till today, it remains popular. At the very beginning, PR's own introduction promises that without taking help from any others works, all the needed illustrations are taken from his remaining works, as PR declares: "nirmāya nūtanamudāharaṇānurūpaṁ, Kāvyaṁ mayātra nihitaṁ na parasya kiṅcit, kiṁ sevyate sumanaśaṁ manasāpi gandhaḥ, kastūrikā jananaśaktibhṛtāmṛgeṇa."[4] Very frankly, PR's Bhāminīvilāsa, a collective poetry, gets this credit from where, maximum quotable verses are taken. The matured and soft verses are proving PR's capacity regarding his poetic-talent. It is right that the rhetoricians often quote their illustrative verses from the writings of different poets.

The examples taken in his RG are basically used for more than a single purpose. Firstly, to explain and illustrate his own sūtras and, secondly, to refute or show the right track to his predecessors views. The third group of poetries are used, as they are well known verses from classical works as 'Bhramadhārmika. . . .,' 'Niśśeṣacyuta. . . ', 'Asyāsarga. . .', 'Purāyatra. . . .,' etc. PR has refuted AD and from the work of the same opponent, that is CM, he has quoted a few verses in his RG against his own view.

Prof. Sivaprasad Bhattacharya says that PR's definition of poetry has been regarded as a crowning achievement of the author. Thus he remarks, "the student of alaṁkāra śāstra is struck by its affinity to the description of the śarīra of kāvya by Daṇḍin at the outset this is not as it should be in a śāstra the thing defined must be expressed in terms of the entities, covered by it."[5]

Alike this type of understandable topics in RG, there are many topics like the cause of the poetry, the classification of poetry, the nature of rasa etc, which are narrated in a manner, where a scholar can study the magic words of RG without taking help of any other source.

In fact, the presence of commentaries and sub-commentaries play a vital role in the case of critical Sanskrit texts in any branch. Without taking help of these commentaries in some Nyāya and Vyākaraṇa texts in particular, it seems difficult to understand the subjects. Keeping this point in mind, the latter rhetoricians tried to compose some commentaries through their suggested thinking on the very original texts. Even though, these commentaries are named as secondary texts, yet, in modern time, the position of commentaries are becoming more significant like the original works. To add to this point, some texts like KP, SD and so on, have a record numbers of commentaries. Till today, KP, SD etc., are more difficult, as seems to scholars, than RG, which is written with the addition of full of logical words.

The basic clue to this is the self satisfied themes with proper language is charged or fixed by PR himself, where an additional commentary is not needed at all. On RG, only a few countable commentaries are written since its composition.

Further, PR's text does not contain any Kārikā or Vṛtti like the kārikās and vṛttis of KP, SD, etc. Even 'Bharatamuni' in his NŚ, was incompetent to bring out all factors in detail as it is general to say due to the non availability of theories at large. Again, at the hands of Ānandavardhana, this type of lacking process continued yet having all aspects or factors in front of his text. But, overall PR makes it clear that the entire faculties are roped in one text which is a worth record for coming rhetoricians. All the traditional themes are, therefore, rearranged by him.

Another factor, to make RG a great text is, without having many commentaries, the text is well understandable by readers. Because, whatever problem lies in text is already discussed by PR himself in his original work. Coming back to Commentaries on RG, Nāgeśa Bhaṭṭ was the first person to comment throughout the text in very few aspects, named as Marmaprakāśa or Gurumarmaprakāśikā. According to latter Commentators this Commentary does not deserve its place, due to its open criticism of RG. Further, Saralā, Rasachandrikā, Candrikā, Madhusudani (modern), Tattvakathanamu (Telugu script) are a few, those are discussing some major problems of RG. (for detail vide our Introduction). Madhusudana Sastri fully supported to the views given by Nāgeśa Bhaṭṭa in his commentary, and sharply criticised PR's views at so many places.[6]

Knowledge on Neo-logic method:

The rhetoricians have power of poetics sense. But our author was much superior to others as he quotes his examples from his own works, but to mark it, in each sentence, there he used the logical language. According to Prof. Bhaṭṭ acharya, PR is very clear and precise and as a matter of course, elaborate in his presentation. His expression does not suffer from the terse and laconic manner met with in Mammaṭa, whether in his Kārikā or in his Vṛtti or in Jayadeva because of his aphoristic text, where sūtravṛtti and illustrations are compressed or condensed into one whole. XXX His versatility and familiarity with the nyāya method of argument are enough safeguards against both forms of omission and commission.[7] At the very first text avacchedakatā is discussed by PR. Jati narrated in the next sentence. To amplify his main definition of poetry, three sub-ordinate or clarified definitions are drawn having full support from logical background.

Avyāpti, ativyāpti asaṁbhava, these faults are very often utilised in RG. For example, uditaṁ mandalaṁ vidhoḥ-. . . etc., PR draws the help of nyāya and Madhusudani, the commentary also gives a wide scope to discuss this sentence with full of nyāya techniques. Further, anupapatti, iṣṭāpatti, vyabhicāra, anvayavyatireka etc., are fully quoted in RG, where the need of logical interepretation is necessary. Overall, the knowledge of PR on neo-logic is already quoted by himself in the introductory verses, in reality, he had utilised this system in this work. We have discussed the influence of Neo-logic in RG in a separate chapter, hence need not be elaborated here.

REFERENCES

1. Contribution of AD. . . ., p. 11.
2. RG, Intro. by Madhusudana Sashtri, p. 44.
3. Contribution of AD. . . ., p. 167.
4. RG, Intro. Verse no. 6.
5. Studies in Indian Poetics, p. 11.
6. RG, Intro. of Madhusudana Sastri, pp. 1-58.
7. op. cit. fn. 5.

IV. 5 OBSERVATIONS AND CONCLUSION

In our introductory chapters, we have discussed in detail the contents of RG and the contribution in the form of introduction of new theories, presentations etc., PR has made, towards the development of Sanskrit Poetics in particular and Indian Poetics in general. We reproduce here in a nutshell the essence of what has been discussed and elaborated in so many pages in the form of observations which forms our conclusion. PR's definition of poetry in terms of 'ramaṇīyatā' is original, superb and leaves no scope for any type of objections which are common and invariably associated with the definition of poetry of others. Whatever is intended as 'iṣṭ ārtha' by Daṇḍin, whatever is imagined as 'saundarya' by Vāmana and whatever is fancied as 'lokottarāhlāda' by Kuntaka are same to 'ramaṇīyata of PR. This is the novelty of PR in defining poetry. Amongst the other significant contributions, in the form of new introductions, which are worth quoting is his classification of poetry into four heads namely 'uttamottama', 'uttama', 'madhyama' and 'adhama'. In many cases, he has presented the tradition with a new style of approach. His treatment of rasa theory is very significant. He has presented as many as eleven interpretations of the rasasūtra including those prominent four of *Abhinavagupta, Bhaṭṭanāyaka, Bhaṭṭlollaṭa and Śrīsaṅkuka.* He has accpeted the interpretation of *rasa* following *Abhinavagupta* which we have discussed in detail in the introduction. He has nothing special to add on his treatment of 'Kāvyahetu' and the poetic merits. Unlike other concepts, PR has not discussed the concept of doṣa i.e. the poetic blemishes in detail and not attempted a historical analysis of it. Only a passing remark on this is given. The nature of permanent moods, excitant, ensuant and transitory moods are discussed throughout where the views and the theories of his predecessors are referred to.

At some places, the illustrative verses from his predecessors works has been quoted and refuted. Here it is remarkable to note that, PR did not borrow any verse for the illustrations. In RG, we find that the entire illustrative verses are either composed by him suitable to the requirement or taken from his other creative works. Another significant contribution of PR has been to critically examine the theories as propounded by his predecessors.

A glance at the works of poetics would reveal the fact that the text book writers of Indian poetics, were very much interested in developing the thoughts and thus, the systems, by mutual dialogues. That is why, in each and every text, we find that a particular view of the predecessors are invariably quoted, analysed, examined and ultimately adopted or rejected with suitable grounds, in favour of the adoption or against the rejetion, as the case may be. We have already made elaborated discussion on the refutation of some of the views of the predecessors of PR like Mammaṭa, Viśvanātha, Appayyadikṣita etc., in the respective places. We have noted that PR was very clear and in case of difference of opinions, he has put it in very clear and unambiguous terms. He is very confident about his conviction and understanding of a particular theory, which he supports or rejects, which is evident from his expression. Our aim is not to propagate and argue in favour of the doctrine as proposed by PR. We are also not for to agree on all points of disagreement of PR with his predecessors. Our only aim is to show how a seventeenth century rhetorician has criticised and refuted the views of some of the acclaimed authorities of system and has made a permanent place for himself in the system.

In one of our chapters, we have given a fair account of those rhetoricians who have not accepted the views of PR and also have tried to find faults with some of his theories. In this context it may be mentioned that in the case of theories dealing with the subtle concepts of fine arts like poetry, one cannot be sure of the exactness of the doctrines. We have only tried to show the issues, the line of arguments, the specific cases and the particular rhetoricians, who have criticised PR or to whom PR has criticised.

In the chapter of textual problems in RG, we have given an elaborate list of available readings in the various editions of RG. The readings found in its Commentaries like 'Marmaprakāśa', 'Madhusudanī' etc., are also included. It is interesting to note that some of the readings found in most of the editions do not go with the text concerned. We observe, that, since we do not have any evidence for rejecting those readings, though, contextually unacceptable, we have no other go than accepting those, as original and it is possible that PR himself intends those readings. Only Madhusudana Shastri, who finds faults with many of the readings and tries to suggest emandations.

PR's knowledge on Navyanyāya is unquestionable and his understanding of it is beyond any doubt. Not a line of RG can be studied and understood without the aid of Navyanyāya. PR has employed the tool of New logic to compose his RG. It is this style of New-logic that makes RG the most monumental work to have come at the fag end of the declination of the development of Indian Poetical thoughts. It is not necessary to quote how by the employment of Neological techniques, he was succeeded in presenting various doctrines of poetics in a precise, unique and flawless manner. Like a true logician, he has always tried to see that his definitions do not suffer from any type of theoretical faults which are normal in case of definitions.

BIBLIOGRAPHY

Primary Sources

Appayya Dikṣita : **Citramīṁaṁsā.** Ed. by J. C. Mishra, CSS. Varanasi, Ist edn. 1991.

Anandavardhana : **Dhvanyāloka.** Ed. by J. Pathak, C.V.B. Varanasi. Ist edn. 1965.

Bhāmaha : **Kāvyālaṁkāra.** Ed. by D. N. Sarma, Bihar Rashtrabhasa Parisada, Patna, Ist edn. 1962

Bharata : **Natyaśātra.** (Hindi) Ed. by R. S. Nagar, Primala Publishers, Delhi, 1st edn. 1981.

Daṇḍin : **Kāvyādarsā.** Ed. By D. K. Gupta, Meharchand Laxamandas, Delhi, Ist edn. 1973.

Jagannātha : **Bhāminivilāsa.** Ed by H. D. Sharma, OBA, Pune, 1st edn. 1935.

Jagannātha : **Rasagangādhara.** Ed. by Dugā-prasada and Pandurang Parab **NSPB** 1st edn. 1888.

Jagannātha : **Rasagangādhara:** Ed. by Gangā dhara Sashtri, Varanasi. 1888.

Jagannātha : **Rasagangādhara:** Ed. by Pandurang Parab, **NSPB,** 2nd edn. 1894.

Jagannātha : **Rasagangādhara:** Ed. by Panduranga Parab and Durgaprasad **NSPB,** 2nd edn. 1894.

Jagannātha : **Rasagangādhara :** Ed. by Durgāprasad, with Saralā Comm. by Mathuranath Sastri, **NSPB,** 5th edn. 1939.

Jagannātha : **Rasagangādhara :** Ed. by Mathuranath Sastri, Saralā Comm. by Manjunāth. **NSPB,** 6th edn. 1947.

Jagannātha : **Rasagangādhara :** Ed. by Mathuranath Shastri with own comm. 'Madhusudani' & own Hindi glossary 'Bālakriḍā', **BHU,** Varanasi, 1st edn. 1963.

Jagannātha : **Rasagangādhara:** Ed. by Badarinath Jha, with own Comm. 'Candrika' , **CVB,** Varanasi, 2nd edn. 1964.

Jagannātha : **Rasagangādhara:** Ed. by Kedarnath Ojha, with a comm. Rasachandrika' SSU, Varanasi, 1st edn. 1977.

Jagannātha : **Rasagangādhara:** (Into Hindi) Tr. by Purusottama Sarma Chaturvedi, Kashinagari Prasārini Sabhā, Kashi, 2nd edn. Saṁvat-2012.

Jagannātha : **Rasagangādhara :** (Into Oriya) Tr. by Suryamani Ratha, OSA Bhubaneshwar, 1st edn. 1990.

Kuntaka : **Vakroktijivita,** Ed. by R. S. Mishra, CSS, Varanasi, 1967.

Mammaṭa : **Kāvyaprakāsa:** Ed. by R. D. Karmākar, BORI, 7th edn. 1965.

Mammaṭa : **Kavyaprakāsh** (English) Tr. by R. C. Dvivedi, MLBD, Delhi, 1966.

Prabhākarasastri : **Bālālamkāra:** Laxmi Venkatswami Press, Kalyan, Mumbai, 1st edn. 1902.

Rājaśekhara : **Kāvyamīmāṁsā:** Ed. by. G. S. Roy, CVB. Varanasi, 2nd edn. 1977.

Rudraṭa : **Kāvyālaṁkāra :** Ed. by S. D. Choudhury, Vasudeva Prakasana, Delhi, 1st edn, 1965.

Sivadata Sarma : **Kāvyarasāyana,** Calcutta, 1st edn. 1903.

Udbhaṭa : **Kāvyālaṁkara :** Ed. by N. D. Banhatti, BORI, Pune, 1st edn. 1925.

Vāmana : **Kāvyālaṁkārasūtravṛtti:** Ed. by. N. N. Kulkarni, **OBA**, Pune, 1st edn. 1927.

Viśvanātha : **Sāhityadarpaṇa :** Ed. by Durgāprasad, **NSPB,** 1st edn. 1931.

Viśvanātha : **Shityadeepa:** (only Introduction Part) Ed. by Sesarāja Śarma 'Regmi' Krisnadass Academy, Varanasi, 1st edn. 1981.

Viśveśvara Pandit : **Alaṁkāra kaustubha:** Ed. by. Pandurang Parab and Pt. Sivadatta, NSPB, 1st edn. 1968.

Viśverśvara Pandey : Alaṁkāramuktāvalī, NSPB, 2nd edn. 1998

Secondary Sources

Athavale, R.B. "PR's Commentary on KP" JOIB, vol. XVII-No.2, Dec. 1967.

Athavale, R.B. "New lights on the life of PR", ABORI, Golden Joblee Vol.- XLX, 1968.

Bhattācarya, S.P. Studies in Indian Poetics, Indian Studies Past &Present, Delhi, 1st edn.- 1969.

Chaitanya, K. History of Sanskrit Literature.

Chaudhury, B.M. Rasasidhānta ke analocitapakṣa (Hindi) janta Publication, Delhi, 1st edn. 1978.

Chaudhury, S.D. rasasidhānta ke pramukha Samasyāen (Hindi); Alaṁkāra Prakasana, Delhi, 1st edn. 1973.

Chaudhury, S.D. Bharātiya Kāvyasāstra, Alaṁkara Prakasana, Delhi, 1st edn. 1974.

Dasgupta. S.N. & De, S.K. History of Sanskrit Literature, Calcutta University. 2nd edn. 1977

De, S.K. History of Sanskrit Poetics. 4th edn. 1971.

De, S.K. Some problems of Sanskrit, Firma, K.L. Mukhopadhyaya puhlishers, Calcutta -1959.

Dubley, S. "The concept of guṇas as presented by PRJ in his **RG**" in Glimpeses of ancient Indian Poetics. Ed. by Pandey,

S. K. and Jha, V. N., Satguru Publication, Delhi- 1993.

Dvivedi, R. C. Poetic Lights, Vol. I & II, MLBD. Delhi. 1966.

Dvivedi, R. C. principles of Literary criticism, MLBD, Delhi, 1969.

Gangopādhyaya, A. L. Contribution of AD to Indian Poetics. 1st edn. 1971.

Gangopādhyaya, A. L. PRJ's aesthetic Problems, SPB, Calcutta, 1st edn. 1984.

Gode, P. K. "Jagannath Myth", 'Soc. XXXIII,'

Goswami, N. "Jagannath Pandita's definition of literature. A criticque", VIJH 15 (2), 1977.

Gupta, G. S. "PRJ", Trip. Vol. III, No. 10, July, 1963.

Jani, R. J. "Jagannatha's Classification of Kāvyaprakāsa's definition and Classification of poetry," BVB, Vol. XII, 1951.

Kale, M. R. Kumārasaṁbhava, MLBD, Delhi, 7th edn. 1981.

Kane, P.V. History of Sanskrit Poetics, MLBD, Delhi, 4th edn. 1971.

Krisnamacri, M. History of Sanskrit Literature. MLBD, Delhi, 1st edn. 1937.

Kaur, A. Samskruta Kāvyaśāstra Para Bharatiya darsana kā prabhāva (Hindi), BVB. 1st edn. 1979.

Kulkarni, V. M. Studies in Sanskrit Sahityasāstra, BLIT, Patan, 1st edn. 1983.

Kulkarni, V. M. Some aspects of the rasa theory, BLIT, Patan 1st edn. 1986.

Lavaniya, R. C. Kāvyaśakti (Hindi), Niraja Book centre, Delhi, 1st edn. 1985.

Lahiri, P. C. Concept of riti and guṇa in sanskrit Poetics, Oriental Book reprint Co. Delhi, 1st edn. 1974.

Maheswari, C. Rasagangādhara: ek adhyayan (Hindi), Rajsthan Hindi Granth Academy, Jaipur, 1st edn. 1974.

Nagendra, Dr. Rasasiddhānta (Hindi) National Publishing House, Delhi, 2nd edn. 1969.

Patwardhan, M. V. "Jagannath on a novel variety of aprastutaprasaṁsā" ABORI, Vol. LXVI, (part I- IV), 1986.

Patwardhan, M. V. "The **RG** on the definition and Source of Poetry," JOIB, Vol. XIX, No. 4, 1970.

Patwardhn, M. V. & Masson, J. L. Aesthetic Rapture (Vol. I &II), Deccan College, Pune, 1st edn. 1970.

Saran, R. Saṁcāribhāvon Kā śāstriya adhyayan (Hindi), L. B. S. Sanskrit Vidyapeetham, Delhi, 1st edn. 1973.

Sarma, R. K. — Kāvyaprakasarasaganādharayoḥ tulanā. (Sanskrit). Nag Publishers. 1st edn. 1997.

Sastri, Carudatta — Laukika Samskrita Sahitya (Hindi), CVB, Varanasi, 1st edn. 1967.

Sastri, V. A. R. — Jagannath Paṇḍita, Anamalainagar, 1st edn. 1942.

Sastri, V. A. R. — "Works, Life of PRJ. " JAU, Vol II, III, IV.

Shastri, G. N. — A concise history of classical skt. Literature, MLBD, Delhi, 2nd edn. 1960.

Shastri, Y. M. — "AD's Age", JORM, Vol. II, Part III-IV, July-Oct. 1928.

Shastri, Y. M. — "More about the age and life of AD", ORM, Vol III, Part III, April-June 1929.

Sriramachandradu, P. — The contribution of PRJ to Sanskrit Poetics, Vol I & II, Nīrājanā Publishers, Delhi, 1st edn. 1983.

Srivastav, S. N. — Adbhuta rasa aur Bharatiya kāvyāsāstra (Hindi), Bihar Grantha Kutir, patna, 1st edn. 1978.

Tyagi, J. — Rasagangādḥarahṛdayaṁ (Sanskrit), CBV, Varanasi, 2nd edn. 1960.

Varadacari, V. — History of Sasnkrit Literature, Allahabad. 2nd edn. 1960.

Vajayawardhan, G. — Outlines of Sanskrit Poetics, CSS, Varanasi, 1st edn. 1970.

Walimbe, Y. S. "PRJ : Mind and Personality", ABORI, Vol. IV, Part I-IV, 1975.

Walimbe, Y. S. "PRJ's equipment as a poeticism" JASB, 52-53, 1977-78.

INDICES

(A) INDEX TO TECHNICAL TERMS

(B) INDEX TO WORKS

(C) INDEX TO AUTHORS

(D) INDEX TO DEFINITIONS

1. "ramaṇīyārthapratipādakaḥ śabdaḥ kāvyam"; Text. 2
   cf. RG. p. 13
2. ramaṇīyatā ca lokottarāhladajanaka janagocaratā lokottaratvaṁ ca ālhādagatascamatkāratvāparaparyāyaḥ aunbhavasākṣīkaḥ jātiviseṣaḥ; Text. 2. 1.
   cf. RG. pp. 14.15.
   āsvādodbodhakatvameva kāvyatvam; Text. 4.
   cf. RG. p. 24.
3. "itthaṁ camatkārajanakabhāvanāviṣayārthapratipādaka-śabdatvam;" Text. 2.3.
   cf. Rg. pp. 16-17.
4. "Yat pratipāditārthaviṣayakabhāvanātvaṁ camatkārā vacchedakaṁ tattvam"; Text. 2.3.
   cf. RG, pp. 17-18.
5. "svaviśiṣṭajanakatāvacchedakārthapratipādakatāsaṁ-sargeṇa camatkāratvavattvameva vā kāvyatvam";
   Text. 2.3
   cf. RG. pp. 18-19.
6. "tasya ca kāraṇaṁ kavigatā kevalā pratibhā"; Text. 8
   cf. RG. p. 46.
7. "śabdārthau yatra guṇībhāvitātmānau kamapyarthamabhi-vyaṅktastadādyam"; Text. 11.
   cf. RG. p. 61.
8. "yatra vyaṅgyamapradhānameva saca camatkārakāranaṁ tad dvitīyam"; Text. 17.
   cf. RG. p. 85.
9. "yatra vyaṅgyacamatkārāsamānādhikaraṇo vācyacamat-kāraḥ tat tṛtīyaṃ"; Text. 18
   cf. RG. p. 92.
10. "yatrārthacamatkṛtyupaskṛtā śabdacamatkṛtiḥ pradhānaṁ, tadadhamaṁ caturtham"; Text. 19.
   cf. RG. p. 94.

11. "yadyapi yatrārthacamatkṛtisāmānyaśūnyā, śabda camatkṛtistat pañcamamadhamādhamam"; Text. 19.1.
cf. RG. p. 95.
12. "vyaktaḥ vyaktiviṣayīkṛtaḥ"; Text. 24
cf. RG. p. 107.
13. "vyaktiḥ ca bhagnāvaraṇā cit" Text. 25.
cf. RG. p. 107.
14. "vakṣyamāṇa śrutisvārasynea ratyādyavacchinnā bhagnāvaraṇā cit eva rashḥ"; Text. 27.
cf. RG. p. 118.
15. "janyatvaṁ ca svajanyabhāvanājanyaratyādi viṣayakatvam"; Text. 38.
cf. RG. p.139.
16. "ratyādyanyatamatvaṁ sthāyitvam"; Text. 48.
cf. RG. p.
17. "strīpuṅsayoranyonyālambanaḥ premākhyascittavṛtti viśeṣ aḥ ratiḥ sthāyibhāvaḥ;" Text. 49.
cf. RG. p. 161.
18. "putrādiviyoga-maraṇādi janmā vaiklavyākhya ścitavṛttiviseṣaḥ śokaḥ"; Text. 49.1.
cf. RG. p. 161.
19. "nityānityavastu vicārajanmā viṣayavirāgākhyaḥ nirvedaḥ", Text. 49.2
cf. RG. p. 162.
20. "gurubandhu vadhādiparamāparādhajanmā prajwalanākhyaḥ krodaḥ"; Text. 49.3
cf. RG. p. 162.
21. "paraparākramadānādismṛtijanmāaunnatyāḥ utsāhaḥ"; Text. 49.4
cf. RG. p. 163
22. "alaukikavastudarśanādijanmā vikāsākhyaḥ vismayaḥ"; Text 49.5
cf. RG. p. 163.

23. "Vāgaṅgādivikāradarśanajanmā vikāsākhyaḥ hāsaḥ";
Text. 49.6
cf. RG, p. 163.
24. "Vyāghradarśanādijanmā paramānarthaviṣaykaḥ vaikla-vyā-khyaḥ sa bhayam"; Text. 49.7
cf. RG. p. 163.
25. "kadaryavastuvilokanajanmā vicikitsākhyaḥ cittavṛtti viseṣ aḥ jugupsā"; Text 49.8
cf. RG. p. 164.
26. "rateḥ saṁyogakālāvacchinnatve pratamaḥ (saṁyogaḥ)";
Text. 52
cf. RG. pp. 169-70.
27. "viyogakālāvacchinnatve dvitīyaḥ" (vipralaṁbhaḥ);
Text. 52
cf. RG. p. 170
28. "ādyaḥ tadadhikaraṇāvṛttitārūpaḥ" (sthitivirodhaḥ);
Text. 65.
cf. RG. p. 204.
29. "Dvitīyaḥ tatjñānaprativaddhajñānakatva lakṣaṇah";
Text. 65
cf. RG. p. 205.
30. "antarniveśaśca tadubhayacarvaṇākālāntarvartikālagata carvaṇākatvam"; Text. 65.1
cf. RG. pp. 207-08.
31. "vādhyatvaṁ ca rasasya pravalaiḥ virodhino rasasyā ṅgaiḥ vidyamāneṣvapi svāṅgeṣu niṣpatteḥ pratibandhaḥ";
Text. 67.1.
cf. RG. p. 212.
32. "śabdānāṁ bhinnānāmapaikatvapratibhāna prayojakaḥ saṁhitayaikajātīyavarṇavinyāsaviseṣaḥ gāḍhatvāpara paryāyaḥ śleṣaḥ"; Text. 72.1
cf. RG. p. 235.

33. "gāḍhatvaśaithilyābhyāṁ vyutkrameṇa miśraṇaṁ bandhasya prasādaḥ"; Text. 72.2
cf. RG. p. 236.

34. "upakramādāsamāpterītyabhedaḥ samatā"; Text. 72.3
cf. RG. p. 237.

35. "samyogaparahrasvātirikta varṇaghaṭitatve sati pṛthakpadatvaṁ mādhuryam"; Text. 72.4
cf. RG. p. 238.

36. "aparuṣavarṇaghaṭitatvaṁ sukumāratā"; Text. 72.5.
cf. RG. p. 238.

37. "jhagiti pratīyamānārthānvayakatvamarthavyaktiḥ; Text. 72.6.
cf. RG. p. 239.

38. "kaṭhina varṇaghatanārūpavikatatva lakṣaṇā udāratā"; Text. 72.7.
cf. RG. p. 239.

39. "saṁyogaparahrasvaprācuryarūpaṁ gāḍhatvaṁ ojaḥ"; Text. 72.8.
cf. RG. p. 241.

40. "avidagdha vaidikādiprayogayogyānāṁ padānāṁ parihāreṇa prayujyamāneṣu padeṣu lokottarasobhā rūpaṁ aujjalyaṃ kāntiḥ"; Text. 72.9.
cf. RG. p. 242.

41. "bandhagāḍhatva-śithilatvayoḥ krameṇāvasthāpanaṁ samādhiḥ" Text. 72.10.
cf. RG. p. 242.

42. "evaṁ keiyāparamparāyā vidagdhaceṣṭitasya tadasphuṭ atvasya tadupapādakayukteḥ ca sāmānādhikaraṇyarūpaḥ saṁsargaḥ śleṣaḥ"; Text - 73
cf. RG. p. 243.

43. "yāvadarthakapadatvarūpamarthavaimalyaṁ prasādah;" Text 73.1.
cf. RG. p. 243.

44. "Prakramābhangenārthaghaṭanātmakamavaiṣamyaṁ samatā;" Text. 73.2.
cf. RG. p. 244.

45. "ekasyā evokteḥ bhaṇgyantareṇa punaḥ kathanā tmakamukti vaicitryaṁ mādhuryam," Text 73.3
cf. RG. p. 244.

46. "akāṇḍe śokadāyitvābhāvarūpamapārūṣyaṁ sukumāratā;" Text 73.4
cf. RG. p. 245.

47. "vastuno varṇanīyasyāsādhāraṇakriyāṁ arthavyaktiḥ"; Text. 73.5.
cf. RG. 246.

48. "grāmyārthaparihāra udāratā"; Text. 73.6
cf. RG. p. 246.

49. "ekasya padārthasya bahubhiḥ padairbhidhānaṁ, bahunāṁ caikena, tathaikasya vākyārthasya bahubhirvākaih, bahu vākyārthasyaikavākyenaābhidhānaṁ, viśeṣaṇānāṁ sābhi-prāyatvaṁ ceti pañcavidhamojaḥ; Text. 73.7.
cf. RG. p. 246.

50. "prauḍhiḥ pratipādanavaicitryam"; Text. 73.7.1.
cf. RG p. 247.

51. "sābhiprāyatvaṁ ca prakṛtārthapoṣakatā,"Text. 73. 7.5.
cf . RG. p. 249.

52. "dīptarasatvaṁ kāntiḥ" Text. 73.8.
cf. RG. p. 250.

53. "avarṇitapūrvoyamarthaḥ, purvavarṇitacchāyo veti kaveḥ ālocanaṁ samādhiḥ"; Text. 73.9.
cf. RG. p. 250.

54. "anadhikapadatvātmā prasādaḥ"; Text. 75.
cf. RG. p. 253.

55. "uktivaicitrya vapuḥ mādhuryam"; Text. 75.
cf. RG. p. 253.

56. "apāruṣyaśarīraṁ saukumāryam"; Text. 75.
cf. RG. p. 253.

57. "agrāmyatvarūpaḥ udāratā"; Text. 75.
cf. RG. p. 253.

58. "vaiṣamyābhāvalakṣaṇā samatā"; Text. 75.
cf. RG. p. 253.

59. "svabhāvasphuṭatvātmikārthavyaktiḥ"; Text. 75.
cf. RG. p. 253.

60. "suhṭarasatvarūpā kāntiḥ"; Text. 75.
cf. RG. pp. 253-54.

61. "ebhiḥ viśeṣvaiṣayaiḥ sāmānyair api ca dūṣanairahitā, mādhuryabhārahaṅgurasundarapada varṇa vinyāsā, vyupattim udgirantī nirmātuḥ yā prasādayutā, tāṁ vibudhā vaidarbhiṁ vadanti vṛtiṁ gruhītaparipākāṁ"; Text. 86.
cf. RG. p. 274.

62. "vibhāvānubhāvabhinnatve sati rasavyañjakatvaṁ bhāvatvam"; Text. 87.
cf. RG. p. 277.

63. "vibhāvādivyajyamānaharṣādyanyatamatvaṁ tattvam"; Text. 88.
cf. RG. p. 283.

64. "iṣṭaprāptyādijanmā sukhaviśeṣo harṣaḥ"; Text. 91.
cf. RG. p. 287.

65. "saṁskārajanyaṁ jñānaṁ smṛtiḥ"; Text. 92.
cf. RG. p. 188

66. "Strīnāṁ puruṣamukhāvalokanādeḥ pusāṁ ca pratijñābhangaparābhavāderutpannovaivarṇyādho mukhatvādikāraṇībhūtascittavṛttiviseṣo vrīḍā"; Text. 93.
cf. RG. p. 293.

67. "bhayaviyogādiprayohyā vastutattvānavadhāriṇī cittavṛttiḥ mohaḥ"; Text. 94.
cf. RG. p. 295.

68. "lobhaśokabhayādijanitopaplavanivāraṇa kāraṇībhūtaḥ cittavṛtti viśeṣaḥ dhṛtiḥ"; Text. 95.
cf. RG. p. 296.
69. "kimaniṣṭaṁ mama bhaviṣyatītyākāraścittavṛttiviseṣaḥ śaṁkā"; Text. 96.
cf. RG. p. 297.
70. "ādhivyādhijanyabalahāniprbhavo vaivarṇyaśithilā ḍṛgbhṛmaṇādihetuḥ duḥkhaviseṣo glāniḥ"; Text. 97.
cf. RG. p. 297.
71. "duḥkhadāridryāparādhādijanitaḥ svāpakarṣabhāṣaṇādi hetuścittavṛttiviseṣo dainyaṁ"; Text.98.
cf. RG. p. 299.
72. "iṣṭāprāptyaniṣṭaprāptyādijanitā dhyānāparaparyāyā vaivarṇyabhulekhanādhomukhatvādihetuscittavṛtti viśeṣaḥ cintā"; Text. 99.
cf. RG. p. 301.
73. "madyāyupayogajanmā ullāsākhyaḥ śayanahasitādihetuḥ cittavṛttiviseṣaḥ madaḥ"; Text. 100.
cf. RG. p. 303.
74. "bahutaraśārīravyāpārajanmā niḥśvāsāṅgasaṁmardanidrādikāraṇībhūtaḥ khedaḥ viśeṣaḥ śramaḥ"; Text.101.
cf. RG. p. 306.
75. "rūpadhanavidyādipratyuktātmotkarṣajñānādhībaoarāvahelanaṁ garvaḥ"; Text. 102.
cf. RG. p. 308.
76. "śramādiprayojyaṁ cetaḥsaṁmīlanaṁ nidra"; Text. 103
cf. RG.p. 310.
77. "śāstrādivicārajanyamarthanirdhāraṇaṁ matiḥ";
Text.104
cf. RG. p. 310.
78. "rogavirahādiprabhavo manastapo vyādhiḥ"; Text. 105
cf. RG. p. 311.

79. "bhīroḥ ghorasatvadarśananasphūr jathuśravaṇādijanmā cittavṛttiviseṣaḥ trāsaḥ"; Text. 106.
cf. RG. p. 312.

80. "nidrāvi(nā)bhāvotthajñānaṁ suptaṁ"; Text. 107.
cf, RG. p. 313.

81. "nidrānaśottaraṁ jāyamāno bhodhaḥ vibhodhaḥ";
Text. 108
cf. RG. p. 315.

82. "parakṛtāvajñādinānāparādhajanyo mauna vākpāruṣ yādikāraṇībhūtaḥ cittavṛttiviseṣaḥ amarṣaḥ"; Text. 109.
cf. RG. p. 318.

83. "vrīḍādibhiḥ nimittaiḥ harṣādyanubhāvānāṁgopanāya janito bhāvaviśeṣaḥ avahitthaṁ"; Text. 110.
cf. RG. p. 319.

84. "adhikṣepāpamānādiprabhavā kimasya karomītyākārā cittavṛttiḥ ugratā"; Text. 111.
cf. RG. p. 321.

85. "vipralaṁbha mahāpattiparamānandādijanyānyasmin-nanyāvabhāsa unmādaḥ"; Text. 112.
cf. RG. p. 322.

86. "rogādijanyā mūrchārūpā maraṇaprāgavasthā maraṇam";
Text. 113.
cf. RG. p. 323.

87. "saṁdehādyanantaraṁ jāyamāna ūhaḥ vitarkaḥ";
Text. 114.
cf. RG p. 324.

88. "iṣṭāsiddirājagurvādyaparādhādijanyonutāpa viṣādaḥ";
Text. 115.
cf. RG. p. 326.

89. "adhunaivāsya lābho mamāstu iti icchā autsukyam";
Text. 116.
cf. RG. p. 328.

90. "anarthātisayajanitā cittasya saṁbhramākhyā vṛttiḥ āvegaḥ";
Text. 117.
cf. RG. p. 329.

91. "ciñtā utkaṇṭhābhayavirahaiṣṭāniṣṭadarśanaśravaṇādijanyāvaśyakartavyārthapratisaṁdhānavikalā cittavṛttiḥ jdatā";
Text. 118.
cf. RG. p. 330.

92. "atitṛptigarbha vyādhiśramādijanyā cetasaḥ kriyānunmukhatā ālasyaṁ"; Text. 119.
cf. RG. p. 332.

93. "parotkarṣadarśanādijanyaḥ paraniṅdādikādikāraṇī bhūta cittavṛttiviseṣaḥ asūyā"; Text. 120.
cf. RG. p. 333.

94. "viyogaśokabhayajugupsādīnāmatisayāt grahāveśādeḥ ca utparnno vyādhiviśeṣaḥ apasmāraḥ"; Text. 121.
cf. RG. p. 337.

95. "amarṣādijanyavākpāruṣyādikāraṇībhūtā cittavṛttiḥ capalatā"; Text. 122.
cf. RG. p. 337.

96. "nicapuruṣeṣu ākrośanādhikṣepavyādhitāḍanadāridrya, iṣṭavirahaparasaṁpaddarśanādibhiḥ, uttameṣu tu avajñādibhirjanitā viṣsyadveṣākhyā rodanadīrgha śvāsadīnamukhatādi kāiṇī cittavṛttiḥ nirvedaḥ"; Text. 123.
cf. RG. p. 340.

97. "anucitavibhāvālaṁbanatvaṁ rasābhāsatvam"; Text. 127.
cf. RG. p. 346.

98. "evaṁ anucitaviṣayā bhāvābhāsāḥ"; Text. 130.
cf. RG. p. 357.

99. "bhāvasya prāguktasvarūpasya śntiḥ nāśaḥ"; Text. 131.
cf. RG. p. 359.

100. "bhāvodayo bhāvasyotpattiḥ"; Text. 132.
cf. RG. p. 360.
101. "bhāvasaṁdhiranyonyānabhibhūtayoranyonyābhibhavana yogyayoḥ samānādhikaraṇyam"; Text. 133.
cf. RG. p. 361.
102. "bhāvaśabalatvaṁ bhāvānāṁ bādhyabādhakabhāvamāpannānāmudāsīnānāṁ vā vyāmisraṇam"; Text. 134.
cf. RG. p. 362.
103. "ekacamatkṛtijanakajñānagocaratvaṁ (śabalatā)"; Text. 134.
cf. RG. p. 362.

(E) CITATIONS IN RG FROM OTHER WORKS (PROSE)

(The numbers in the parenthesis refers to the page numbers if the thesis)

1.	atādṛśiguṇibhūta	RG. pp. 86-87 ( )
2.	adoṣau saguṇau	RG. p. 22, 1.2
3.	adhamatvamaprakṛṣṭatam	RG. p. 80, 11. 8-9.
4.	aparinetṛvahu	RG. p.
5.	ayaṁ dhvaniḥ	RG. p. 73, 1.8.
6.	arthaśaktimūlasya	RG. p. 374, 1. 11.
7.	ale le ! sadḥ samu	RG. p. 223, 11. 2-3.
8.	avasthāntarabhāva	RG . p. 295, 1.8.
9.	Avidyā dhyaṃsakalyaṃ (Vibodhaḥ)	RG. p. 316, 1.8.
10.	aśvābhāsādivyava	RG. p. 349, 1, 4.
11.	asyānubhāvāḥ	RG. p. 314, 11, 3-4.
12.	ahopūrṇasaro	RG. p. 80, 1.5.
13.	āsvādodbodhaka	RG. p. 24, 1.4.
14.	evaṁ vādini	RG. p. 374. 11. 4-5.
15.	annidryadaurbalya	RG. p. 78, 11. 7-8.
16.	autpattikairmana	RG. p. 312, 1. 9.
17.	kāryāviveko	RG. pp. 330-31, 1. 8.
18.	kṛtamanumataṁ	RG. p. 179, 1. 8.
19.	gatostamarkaḥ	RG. p. 35, 1 .2.
20.	citramahāneṣaḥ	RG. p. 193, 11. 3-4.
21.	cintautsukyānmana	RG. p. 300, 11, 305.
22.	tyāaḥ sapta	RG. p. 184, 1. 2.
23.	tvarayā yāti	RG. p. 245, 1. 10.
24.	devabhartṛguru	RG. p. 287, 11. 7-11.
25.	daurgatyādera	RG. p. 300, 1. 6.
26.	dhvanyātmabhūte	RG. p. 273, 11, 5-6.
27.	dhyānaṁ cintā	RG. p. 302, 1. 8.
28.	naṛṭo mohaḥ	RG. p. 316, 11. 9-10.

29.	nārīkelajala	RG. pp. 363, 1. 11.
30.	niḥśvāsaiṛ	RG. p.
31.	niḥśśeṣacyuta	RG. p. 72, 1. 5.
32.	nṛpāparādho	RG. p. 321, 11. 4-5.
33.	padārthe vākya	RG. p. 247, 11. 3- 4.
34.	pasyāmi devāṁ	RG. p. 193, 11. 8-9.
35.	paśyetkāścit	RG. p.
36.	praharaviratau	RG. p. 89, 11. 6-9.
37.	brahmannadhya	RG. p. 222, 11. 2-5.
38.	bhūreṇudig	RG. p. 208, 11. 3-4.
39.	bhramadhārmi	RG. pp. 75-76, 1. 2.
40.	mākurukaśāṁ	RG. p. 313, 11. 5-6.
41.	ratiḥ devādi	RG. p. 202, 1. 4-5.
42.	ratiḥ śokasca	RG. p. 156, 11. 10-11.
43.	ratyādyanya	RG. p.
44.	ratyādayaḥ sthāyī	RG. p. 106, 11. 5-6.
45.	vāgarthāviva	RG. p. 170,. 1. 8.
46.	vinirviṣṭai	RG. p. 204, 1. 2.
47.	vinirgatamāna	RG. p. 96, 11, 2-3.
48.	vibhāvā	RG. p. 302, 11. 3-7.
49.	viruddhiraviruddhi	RG. pp. 158-59. 3-7.
50.	vyktaḥ sa tai..	RG. p. 107, 1. 2.
51.	Śātasya śama..	RG. p. 103, 11. 6-7.
52.	śūnyaṁ vāsagṛha	RG. p. 275, 11. 10.13.
53.	śleṣaḥprasada	RG. p. 235, 11. 3-4.
54.	śramaḥ khedodhvara	RG. p. 306, 1. 10.
55.	saṁjātamiṣṭa	RG. p. 328, 11. 9-11.
56.	Sacchinna mūla.	RG. p. 96, 1. 3.
57.	sajātīyavijā	RG. p. 159, 11. 6-7.
58.	sukhamātyantika	RG. pp. 120-21 1. 5.
59.	Svacchandocchalad.	RG. p. 96, 11. 3-4.

TABLE - 1

रस	रसगंगाधरस्थश्लोक	आलम्बन	उद्दीपन	अनुभाव	व्यभिचारीभाव	स्थायिभाव
१. क) संभोग शृंगार	शायितासविधे	नायक	रहस्थानादय	मुखनीरीक्षण	त्रपा, औत्सुक्य	रति
ख) विप्रलंभ शृंगार	वाचो मांगलिकी	नायक	प्रवासप्रस्थान	निश्वास	विषाद, चिन्ता, आवेग	रति
२. करुण	अपहाय सकलबान्धव	बन्धुनाश	बन्धुवृत्तांत्त श्रवण	अश्रुपात गात्रक्षेप	ग्लानि, क्षय, मोह, विषाद चिन्ता, औत्सुक्य	शोक
३. शान्त	मलयानिल कालकूटयो	अनित्यसंसार	वेदान्त श्रवण तपस्वीदर्शन	विषयारुचि	हर्ष, उन्माद, स्मरण, मति	निर्वेद
४. रौद्र	नवोच्छलितयौवन	अपराधकर्ता	तदपराध	अस्तग्रहण परुषभाषण	अमर्ष आवेग उग्रता	क्रोध
५. क) दानवीर	कियदिदमिधकं मे...	याचक	स्तुति	कवचादिदान	गर्व, स्मृति	उत्साह

रस	रसगंगाधरस्थश्लोक	आलम्बन	उद्दीपन	अनुभाव	व्यभिचारीभाव	स्थायिभाव
५. ख) दयावीर	न कपोत भवन्तम...	कपोत	तदगतव्याकुल	स्वकलेवरार्पण	धैर्य	उत्साह
ग) युध्दवीर	रणे दीनान् देवान्...	भव	रणदर्शन	रावणावज्ञा	गर्व	उत्साह
घ) धर्मवीर	सपदि विलयमेतु...	धर्मविषय	धर्मरक्षा	शीरच्छेदांगीकार	धृति	उत्साह
६. अद्‌भूत	चराचर जगज्जाल...	वदन	विश्वरूपदर्शन	रोमांच	त्रास,	विस्मय
७. हास्य	श्रीतातपादैः...	तार्किकपुत्र	तदीयानिश्शंकोक्ति	रुदनप्रकाश	उद्वेग	हास
८. भयानक	श्येनमम्बरतला...	श्येन	सवेगापतन	शुष्कानन	दैन्य	भय
९. बीभत्स	नखैर्विदारिता...	शव	आन्त्रविदारण	नेत्रनिमीलन	आवेग	जुगुप्सा

TABLE - 2

RG.	BHU.	मदु.	वादु.	गंगा.	संपु.	चौ.	म.	ओ.
७१	अग्राम्यत्व प्रक्रमत्व अधिकपदत्व	अग्राम्य	अग्राम्य प्रक्रम ...	... ...	अग्राम्य प्रक्रम अधिकपद	अग्राम्य प्रक्रम ...	अग्राम्य प्रक्रम ...	अग्राम्य प्रक्रम अधिकपद
६४.	अत्र	...	...	...	तत्र	...	तत्र	तत
१५.२	अन्यलभ्यस्य	...	...	...	...	अनन्यलभ्यस्य	...	अनन्यलभ्यस्य
१५.३	अन्यच्च	...	...	...	...	अपिच	...	...
१२८.१	अनुरक्तिं अभिलापो	अत्यंतमनुरक्ति अभिलाषा	... अभिलाषा	... अभिलाषा	... अभिलाषा	अत्यंतअनुरक्तिं अभिलाषो	अत्यंतानुरक्तिम अभिलाषा	अत्यंतमनुरक्तिम अभिलाषः
९३.	अभिव्यक्तस्य	...	...	...	...	total changed	अभिव्यक्तस्यैव (भावस्य)गुणी– भूतव्यंग्यव्यप देशहेतुत्वात	...
५९.६	अवज्ञानुभावः अवगतये	... ...	... ...	... ...	... ...	अवज्ञानुभवः अवगतयो	... ...	 अवगततया

RG.	BHU.	मदु.	वादु.	गंगा.	संपु.	चौ.	म.	ओ.
१५.४	आमर्षात आवहति	आमर्शात ...	आमर्शात	आमर्शात	आमर्शात	आमर्शात	आमर्शात आहवति	आमर्शनात
११.२	आननाम्बुजम					आननम		आननम
२५.	इव साक्षी						इव वा साक्षी	
७९.	इति ऩ	न	न	न	न	न	न	
७९.	उक्तिवैचित्र्य	वैचित्र्य	वैचित्र्य	वैचित्र्य	बैचित्र्य			
१७.३	उत्तमता	उत्तमोत्तमता	उत्तमोत्तमता	उत्तमोत्तमता	उत्तमोत्तमता	उत्तमोत्तमता	उत्तमोत्तमता	
६१	एवमसंलक्ष्य-कमतायामेव				एवमसंलक्ष्यक्रम व्यंगतायामेव			
५८.१	गालगतम	(नागेश कायगतम नतु कालगतम)						
१४	कतैव						कतैवा	
२४	केवलसाक्षि-भास्यत्व	साक्षिभास्यत्व	साक्षिभास्यत्व	साक्षिभास्यत्व	साक्षिभास्यत्व	साक्षिभास्यत्व	साक्षिभास्यत्व	साक्षिभास्यत्व
७१.२	गुरुभूतत्वात					गडूभूतत्वात	गडूभूतत्वात	गडूभूतत्वात

RG.	BHU.	मदु.	वादु.	गंगा.	संपु.	चौ.	म.	ओ.
११.३	चुम्वामि		चुम्वयामि			चुम्वेयम		चुम्वेयम
११८	चिन्तोत्कंठा	चिन्तोत्कर्ष	चिन्तोत्कर्ष					
६७	चोभयो	वोभयो		वोभयो	वोभयो	वोभयो	वोभयो	वा उभय
७०	च रसानु	च प्रतीत्यारसातु	च प्रतीत्यारसानु	च प्रतीत्यारसानु	च प्रतीत्यारसानु	च प्रतीत्यारसानु	च प्रतीत्यारसानु	च प्रतीत्यारसानु
७३	चेत					चेत न		
११२	जन्य	जन्म	जन्म		जन्म	जन्म		
१५	जाताया	ज्ञाताया	ज्ञाताया	ज्ञाताया	ज्ञाताया	ज्ञाताया	ज्ञाताया	ज्ञाताया
८८.८	झयव्दय	सवर्णझयव्दय	सवर्णझयव्दय	सवर्णझयव्दय	सवर्णझयव्दय	सवर्णझयव्दय	सवर्णझयव्दय	सवर्णझयव्दय
१६	झटित्या(ना) कलनात	झटित्यानाकलनात	is in all other	editions.				
६७	तत्र						अत्र	अत्र
६७.४	तत्रांगमस्तु				तदंगमस्तु			तदंगमस्तु
७३.१	द्रुतत्वद्रुततर	द्रुततर	द्रुततर	द्रुततर	द्रुततर	द्रुततर	द्रुततर	द्रुततर
६१	न वा कथं					कथं न वा		कथं न वा

RG.	BHU.	मदु.	वादु.	गंगा.	संपु.	चौ.	म.	ओ.
७२	निरतिशयितम	अतिशयितम	अतिशयितम	अतिशयितम	अतिशयितम	अतिशयितम	अतिशयितम	अतिशयान्वितम
८०	नानुप्रास	अनुप्रास	अनुप्रास		अनुप्रास	अनुप्रास	अनुप्रास	अनुप्रास
७६	परम्पराया	परम्परया				परम्परया	परम्परया	परम्परया
४५.१	प्रधानतया	प्रधानताया	प्रधानताया			प्रधानताया	प्रधानताया	
९१.३	प्रकारक ज्ञाने	प्रकार ज्ञाने	प्रकार ज्ञान				प्रकार ज्ञान	
९६.१	पदव्यंगत्वे	पदव्यंग्यत्वे	पदव्यंग्यत्वे	पदव्यंग्यत्वे			पदव्यंग्यत्वे	
१०३.१	प्राघान्येनानव-बोधनात	प्राघान्येनाव-वोधनात	प्राघान्येना-वोधनात	प्राघान्येनाव-वोधनात		प्राघान्येना-वोधनात	प्राघान्येना-वोधनात	प्राघान्येना-वोधनात
११३.१	परुषवचन		वचन	वचन	प्रवतित्तवचन	वचन	वचन	प्रवत्तिवचन
१७.५.१	बाष्पगलत	सबाष्पगलत	सबाष्पगलत	सबाष्पगलत	सबाष्पगलत	सबाष्पगलत		
१५.२	भवतैवतस्या-पिअर्थापत्ति			भवतैवार्था-न्निवेद्यताया		भवतैवार्थापति	भवतैवार्थापति	
२५	भावनाविशेष-महिम्ना				विभावादिचवर्णा-महिम्ना			

RG.	BHU.	मदु.	वादु.	गंगा.	संपु.	चौ.	म.	ओ.
७३.१	मधुरत्व	मधुर	मधुर	मधुर	मधुर	मधुर	मधुर	
१५.४	ममान्तिका-दगतासि					मदन्तिकात गतासि		मदन्तिकाद
२६	मम्मट				अभिनवगुप्त-मम्मट	अभिनवगुप्त-मम्मट	अभिनवगुप्त-मम्मट	
४४	मानम					प्रमाणम्		प्रमाणम
५९.११	राज्ञामा(राजा) ज्ञामात्रम			राजाज्ञामात्रम		राजाज्ञामात्रम		राजामात्रम
७३.१	रसधर्मत्वे					रसमात्रधर्मत्वे		
६०	विद्यमानापि-पुत्रगता				पुत्रगता			
८८.२	विसर्गादेश-सकारप्राचुर्यम	विसर्गप्राचुर्ययथा	विसर्गप्रा-चुर्ययथा	विसर्गसकार-प्राचुर्ययथा		विसर्गप्राचुर्यंयथा	विसर्गप्राचुर्यं	विसर्गप्राचुर्यं
१५.२	वक्ति					वदति		

RG.	BHU.	मदु.	वादु.	गंगा.	संपु.	चौ.	म.	ओ.
८४	वलन	चलन	चलन					
२६	विभावादि				तत्तत विभावादि	तत्तत विभावादि	तत्तत विभावादि	तत्तत विभावादि
३१	विलक्षण...	काव्यार्थभावना जन्माविलक्षण	काव्यार्थभावना जन्माविलक्षण	काव्यार्थभावना जन्माविलक्षण	काव्यार्थभावना जन्माविलक्षण	काव्यार्थभावना जन्मविलक्षण	काव्यार्थभावना जन्माविलक्षण	काव्यार्थभावना जन्माविलक्षण
४९.२	विरागाख्यो						विरामाख्यो	
६५	विरोधाभावाच्च					विरोधासंभवात		
४८	स्तोकम	स्तोकै	स्तोकै	स्तोकै	स्तोकै	स्तोकै	स्तोकै	
६६	स्वातंत्र्यायोगात	स्वातंत्र्ययोगात	स्वातंत्र्ययोगात		स्वातंत्र्ययोगात	स्वातंत्र्यायोगात		स्वातंत्र्यायोगात
९७	स्वकुच	तत्कुच	तत्कुच	तत्कुच	तत्कुच	तत्कुच	तत्कुच	तत्कुच
१६.१	हिनकर्म					This term is missing		
६४	अत्र	तत्र	तत्र		तत्र	तत्र		
९	प्रति इति			प्रतीति		प्रतीति	प्रतीति	

N.B.—RG. 79 & 93 are fully changed.

DIAGRAM - 1

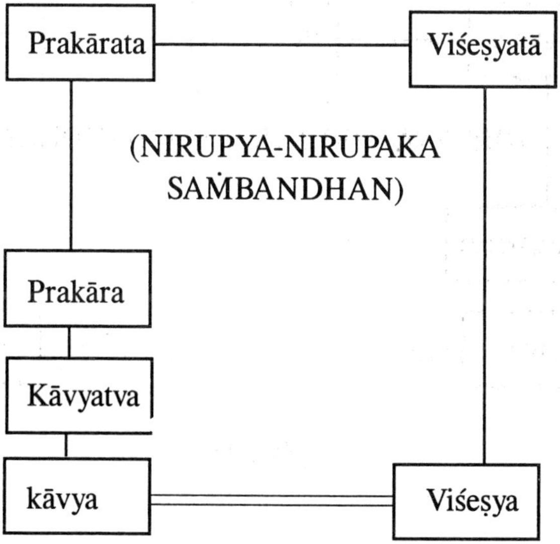

(RG: 1)

DIAGRAM - 2

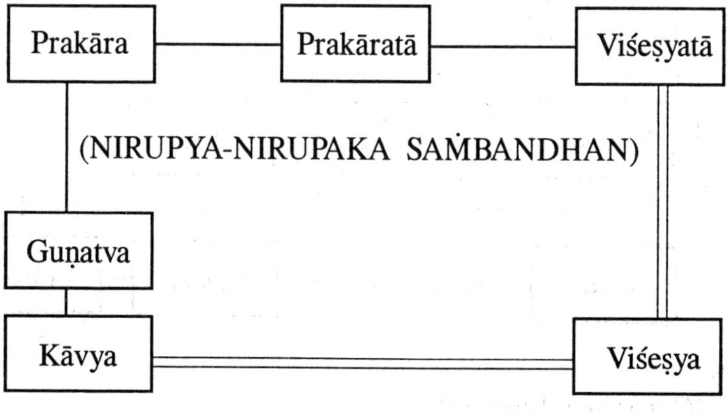

(RG.:1)

DIAGRAM - 3

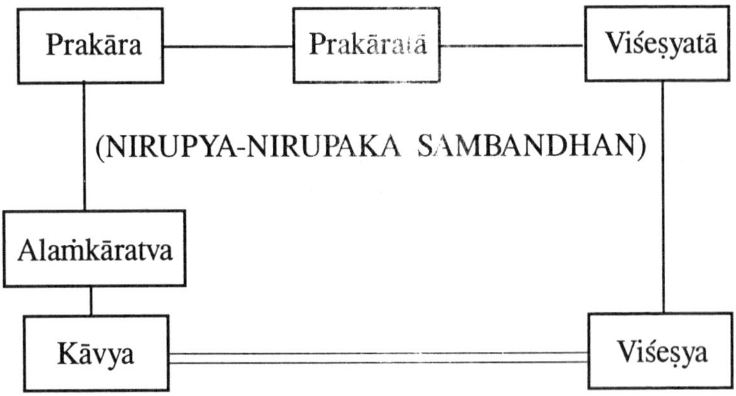

(RG.:1)

DIAGRAM - 4

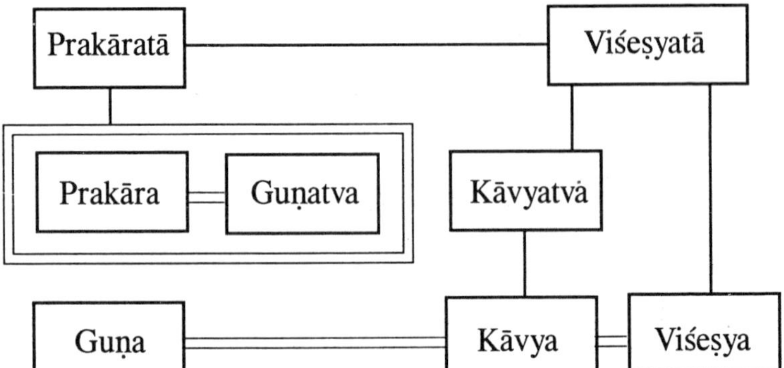

(Guṇādimat Kāvyam)

(RG.:1)

DIAGRAM - 5

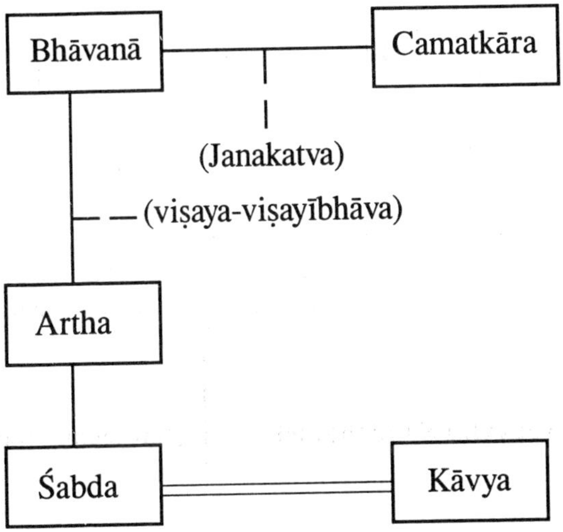

(RG.: 2.3)

DIAGRAM - 6 (A)

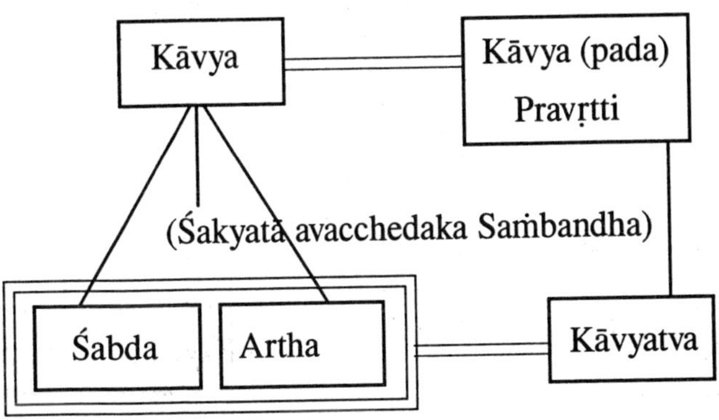

(RG: 5)

DIAGRAM - 6 (B)

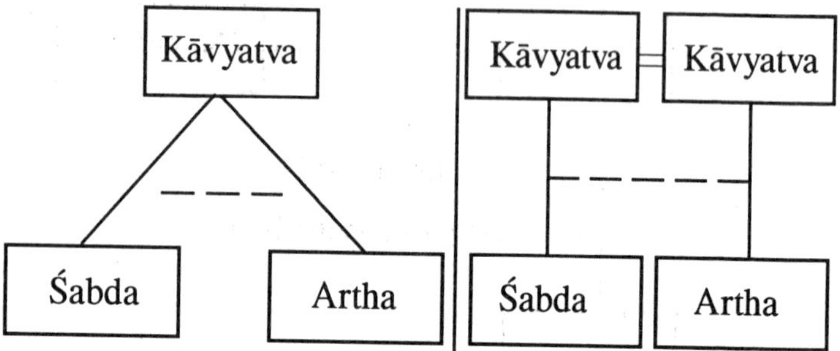

(Paryāpti Saṁbandhaḥ) (Samavāya Saṁbandhaḥ)

(RG.: 5)

DIAGRAM - 7

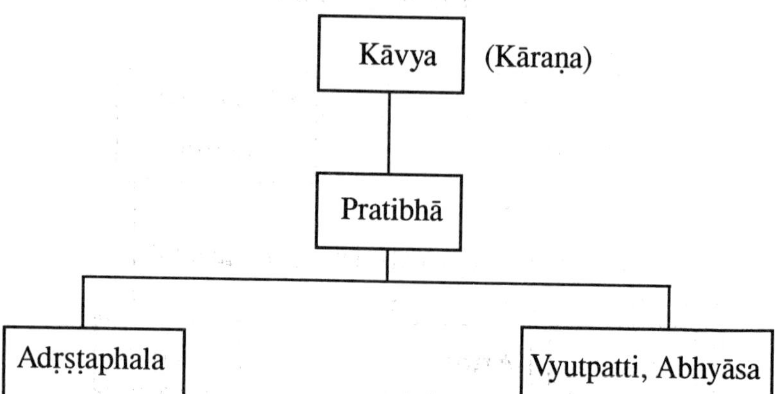

(RG.: 8)

DIAGRAM-8

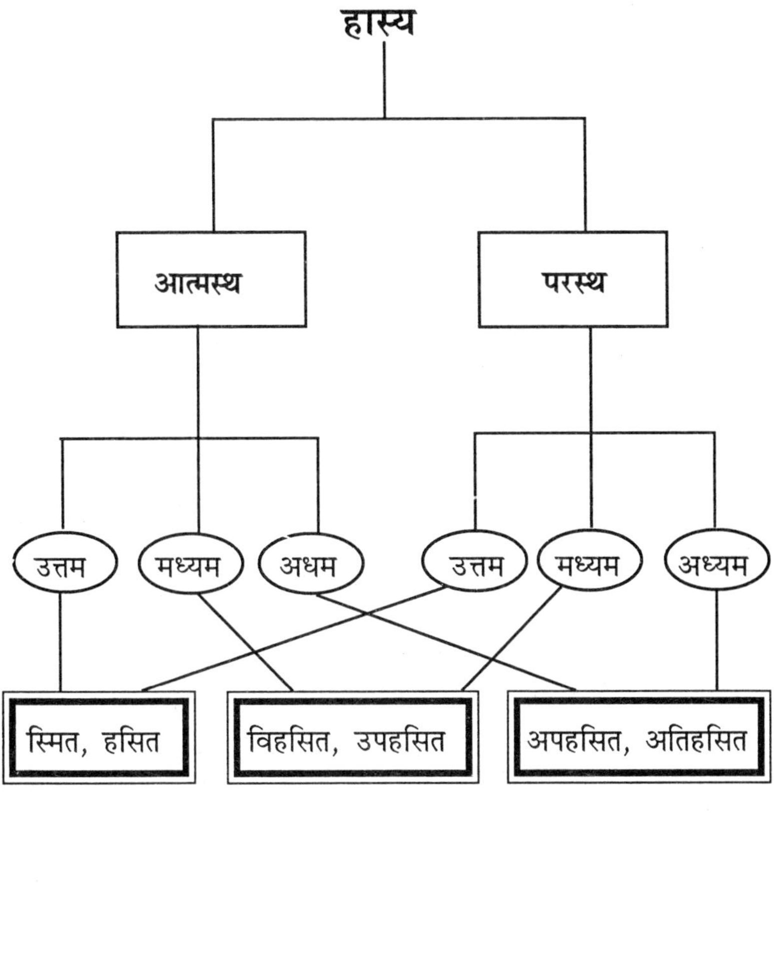
हास्य
आत्मस्थ
परस्थ
उत्तम
मध्यम
अधम
उत्तम
मध्यम
अध्यम
स्मित, हसित
विहसित, उपहसित
अपहसित, अतिहसित